For Nancy, whose love and playfulness have inspired this book.

INTERACTIONS IN THE CLASSROOM

Facilitating Play in the Early Years

Jeffrey Trawick-Smith

Eastern Connecticut State University

Merrill, an imprint of
Macmillan College Publishing Company
New York

Maxwell Macmillan Canada
Toronto

Maxwell Macmillan International
New York   Oxford   Singapore   Sydney

Cover photo: Comstock
Editor: Linda A. Sullivan
Production Editor: Louise N. Sette
Art Coordinators: Lorraine Woost, Vincent A. Smith
Photo Editor: Anne Vega
Cover Designer: Russ Maselli
Production Buyer: Pamela D. Bennett
Electronic Text Management: Ben Ko, Marilyn Wilson Phelps

This book was set in Century Schoolbook by Macmillan College Publishing Company
and was printed and bound by R. R. Donnelley & Sons Company. The cover was printed
by Phoenix Color Corp.

Macmillan College Publishing Company
866 Third Avenue
New York, New York 10022

Macmillan College Publishing Company is part of the
Maxwell Communication Group of Companies.

Maxwell Macmillan Canada, Inc.
1200 Eglinton Avenue East, Suite 200
Don Mills, Ontario M3C 3N1

Library of Congress Cataloging-in-Publication Data
Trawick-Smith, Jeffrey W.
    Interactions in the classroom : facilitating play in the early
years / Jeffrey Trawick-Smith.
        p.   cm.
    Includes bibliographical references and index.
    ISBN 0-02-412511-3
    1. Play.   2. Early childhood education—Curricula.   I. Title.
LB1137.T73   1994
372.5—dc20   93—15194
                                                                         CIP

Printing: 1 2 3 4 5 6 7 8 9   Year: 4 5 6 7 8

Photo credits: Barbara Schwartz/Macmillan, pp. 1, 9, 10, 17, 34, 42, 58, 67, 78, 83, 94, 105,
114, 117, 143, 147, 159, 178, 183, 192, 199, 205, 209, 218, 228, 241, 250, 260, 269, 273, 286,
298, 313, 325, 338, 351; Anne Vega/Macmillan, pp. 5, 25, 47, 126, 135, 171, 237, 309.

PREFACE

Interactions in the Classroom: Facilitating Play in the Early Years is a practical guide on facilitating play across the curriculum in preschool, kindergarten, and primary grade classrooms. It was written with several purposes in mind.

It could serve as the primary text for an undergraduate or graduate course in either early childhood curriculum or play.

Since its focus is on teacher-child interactions, it would be a useful handbook for an early childhood education practicum, internship, or student-teaching experience.

The book would help seasoned, in-service teachers to look at curriculum and play in new ways.

There are three underlying philosophical perspectives woven through these chapters that make the book unique. First, every idea presented in this volume is based on the assumption that children learn best when they are playing. Play is defined here in broad terms—any activity which is self-chosen, open-ended, spontaneous, and enjoyable is considered play. Even conducting scientific experiments, writing stories, or solving math problems are viewed as instances of play if these are freely chosen, pleasurable, and process-oriented. In contrast, seemingly playful activities such as block building or make-believe are not considered play if these have been assigned or directed by an adult. From this perspective, play can occur across the curriculum in early childhood education.

A second philosophical perspective reflected in these chapters is that the early childhood curriculum is as much a way of interacting with children as it is a collection of lessons or carefully constructed learning materials. The ways that teachers ask questions, give warmth and encouragement, provide assistance, and challenge students' thinking determine whether materials and methods will hold personal meaning and ultimately lead to learning. This book provides guidelines for interacting with children across the curriculum. It suggests strategies for promoting learning in such areas as literacy, mathematics, science, the arts, and motor development. Several chapters focus on enhancing symbolic and social play skills and on nurturing positive views of self and others.

A final premise of the book that sets it apart from other curriculum texts is that knowledge in early childhood education comes from both research and the wisdom of practice. In this text, research is regularly translated into practical suggestions for teaching. At the same time, numerous vignettes drawn from this author's personal experience as a teacher are included to bring the book's content to life. This blending of research with real-life stories makes the book both practical and empirically based.

In summary, this book advocates a play-based curriculum in which children guide their own learning with informal assistance from skilled play facilitators. When teachers intervene in unobtrusive ways in children's play activities, they foster learning across the curriculum.

Acknowledgments

I am grateful to many individuals for their support and encouragement. I wish to thank my wife and children for their caring and patience during the writing of this book. I also wish to acknowledge the support of Kelvie Comer, Dean of Professional Studies at Eastern Connecticut State University, who provided time and resources to complete this project. To other colleagues at my university—particularly Sharon Griffin, Ann Gruenberg, and June Wright, who shared insights and criticisms—I am deeply indebted.

The late Annie Butler, my advisor and professor at Indiana University, was the first to show me the value of play and to convince me that adults could be trusted to play with children. I am thankful for her guidance and teaching.

I wish to thank Linda Sullivan at Merrill for her counsel and good humor as we worked through the many machinations of this text. The suggestions and comments of reviewers of the book were invaluable: Beth C. Anderson, Moorhead State University; Jane H. Bugnand, Pace University; Tena Carr, San Joaquin Delta College; Phyllis Cuevas, McNeese State University; Doris Fromberg, Hofstra University; Connie Green, Appalachian State University; Peg Ketron, Indiana Vocational Technical College; Linda Reiten, University of Mary, Bismarck, ND; and Kevin Swick, University of South Carolina. I am also appreciative of Anne Vega's creative efforts in obtaining photographs—particularly her success in capturing developmentally appropriate practice in elementary classrooms.

I would like to acknowledge the unique contributions of two friends—Dick Thompson, who kept me laughing during this project, and Jim Devoe, who provided round-the-clock technical assistance whenever my computer misbehaved.

Finally, I would like to thank the children whose learning and behavior are described in the stories and vignettes of the book: Benjamin, Joseph, Matthew, Meggie, and Brenna; and the students of the Windham Willimantic Child and Family Development Center in Willimantic, Connecticut; the Temple Early Childhood Education Center and the former John Marshall Elementary School in Louisville, Kentucky; the Christian Center Child Care Center in Bloomington, Indiana; the University of Minnesota Child Care Center in Minneapolis, Minnesota; and the Oak Grove Montessori School in Mansfield, Connecticut.

BRIEF CONTENTS

CONTENTS

3
Facilitating Sociodramatic Play   **47**

4
Promoting Social Competence 83

5
Promoting Language and Literacy 117

6
Promoting Logico-Mathematical Reasoning 147

7
Sciencing With Young Children   183

8
Enhancing Artistic and Musical Expression   209

9
Fostering Motor Development   241

1

FACILITATING PLAY
ACROSS THE CURRICULUM

A four-year-old sits on a large hollow block clutching a saucer in both hands. For many minutes she pretends to drive an imaginary truck, turning her make-believe steering wheel left and right, and producing engine noises.

A teacher moves over to her and asks, "May I have a ride?"

"Sure!" the child responds, "Here is your place!" She quickly fashions a passenger seat next to her own with another block and invites the teacher to sit down. Then she continues her journey.

At one point the teacher exclaims, "Oh, no! Is there something wrong with our front tire? I hear a terrible noise coming from there!"

"Let's get it to the gas station! It could blow up!" the child responds in a worried tone. She drives a minute longer, then emits a tire's screeching sound to indicate that they have arrived at the station.

She climbs from her block and approaches another child who is playing alone. "Let's say you're the mechanic guy and help us, okay? So our car won't blow up, okay?" she entreats.

At first this second child seems reluctant.

"Can you help us repair our car?" the teacher asks.

"All right. But these are the tools." He holds up two long blocks.

"Okay," says the first child. "Come on and fix it."

Together they make "fixing" noises and gestures with the make-believe tools. The teacher quietly leaves the play area.   ❖

In a separate area of the classroom three four-year-old children have just completed a traditional card game, "Concentration."

"I won!" one young player announces.

A teacher approaches and asks, "How did you figure out that you won the most cards?"

"Well, because!" exclaims the child, holding a mass of cards in one hand and then placing them next to a playmate's pile in comparison. "See? I've got more!"

"Wait a minute!" another child protests. "Let me look at something." He spreads his cards end-to-end in a line on the floor. This line contains so many cards that it extends from the math area out into the center of the classroom. He makes similar lines next to his own with each of his playmate's cards.

The teacher, observing this, asks, "Well, what do you think?"

"Look. See?" he answers. "My line is longer. I won!"

"Does everyone agree?" the teacher asks the group. "Are there other ways to figure out who won?"

With the teacher's encouragement the group continues to try solutions to the problem until snack time.   ❖

In another area, a child is dropping various items into a "float and sink" tub. Soon the bottom of the tub and the surface of the water are crowded with the objects of her experimentation.

A teacher moves to this area and says, "I know a fun way to check on which objects float and which ones sink. Let me show you." Together he and the child remove the objects from the tub. The teacher suggests, "Just before you drop an object into the water, I want you to make a guess: Do you think it will float or do you think it will sink?"

The child picks up a small cork, examines it carefully, then predicts, "It'll sink." She tests her hypothesis, then laughs with surprise at her discovery. "Ah! It floats!"

She continues her experimentation even after the teacher has left the play area.   ❖

Later, some children are chasing one another around the playground. One five-year-old boy stands alone watching. He smiles now and then, indicating amusement and interest in his playmates' game.

A teacher approaches. "Let's chase after the wolf too. He's getting away! Come on!" She takes the child's hand and together they race after the other children.

"We'll catch that wolf!" the teacher exclaims in a funny voice. This results in screams from the group.

"Yes, we will!" responds the five-year-old, now running along with the others.

Eventually the teacher drops out of the game and watches as the child who was standing alone is now included in the group.   ❖

These examples illustrate ways that skillful teachers intervene in children's play to promote social and cognitive development. In the first episode, make-believe enactments and social interaction are encouraged. In the second, a clash of opinion over the outcome of a card game is guided into a mathematics lesson. Scientific thought processes are promoted by the teacher in the third episode. The isolated child of the final example is shown successful peer group entry strategies.

In each case the intervention is brief and unobtrusive. The teacher accomplishes a specific purpose and then withdraws from the play. Children continue their own self-chosen activities after this departure, though now their play is more social, organized, imaginative, or thoughtful. Such skillfully delivered interventions allow the teacher to play a direct role in guiding learning, while at the same time assuring self-direction, autonomous thought, and playful spontaneity.

The purpose of this book is to provide teachers and future teachers with guidelines for intervening in the play of preschool, kindergarten, and primary-grade classrooms. Developmentally appropriate ways to guide children in their spontaneous classroom activities in all curriculum areas will be presented.

❖ ❖ ❖

What Is Play and Why Is It Valuable?

Play has been defined in various ways. In this book any activity which is self-chosen, spontaneous, open-ended, and enjoyable will be considered play (Rubin, Fein, & Vandenberg, 1983). Even conducting scientific experiments, writing stories, or solving math problems will be viewed as instances of play if these are freely chosen, pleasurable, and process-oriented. In contrast, seemingly playful activities such as block-building or make-believe will not be considered play if these have been assigned or directed by an adult. From this perspective, play can be seen to occur across the curriculum in early-childhood education (Johnson, Christie, & Yawkey, 1987).

Play serves many important functions in human development. For centuries, play has been recognized as a fundamental form of stress reduction and a means of coping with anxiety (Axeline, 1969; Freud, 1961; Spencer, 1954). Research has demonstrated that through play children can reduce tensions associated with modern, "hurried" life (Barnett & Storm, 1981; Elkind, 1981). Experienced teachers have regularly witnessed the stress-reduction value of play as they accompany children onto the playground after a long morning of achievement testing in an elementary school or after many hours of indoor time in a child-care center. As children run and scream, assume fantastic make-believe themes, or test their muscles through climbing or swinging, they are both discharging energy and regaining a sense of control and power over their lives. They demonstrate sheer joy in their play; these activities may be considered the most exciting and happy endeavors of childhood (Trawick-Smith, 1989).

Psychologists have long suggested that play is the ideal context for acquiring social skills and forming friendships (Connolly & Doyle, 1984). Many spontaneous childhood games are inherently social. In make-believe, children must negotiate roles and pretend situations (e.g., "I'll be the firefighter, you be a lady who almost gets burned up, okay?"). In group games they must adopt and modify rules (e.g., "Let's say if you land on this space you have to go all the way back to start and lose your turn and you have to give everyone some of your bonus chips."). In outdoor motor play children engage in "besting contests" (e.g., "I can go higher. Look. See how high up I'm going.") or cooperate to solve problems (e.g., "Help me up on the tire. I can't get on 'cause it's swinging too fast.").

Young children learn most in self-directed play.

Although most parents and teachers have appreciated for a long time the positive social and emotional aspects of play, its contributions to intellectual growth have been recognized only recently. New research has shown that as children play they exercise fundamental cognitive processes—they use language (Pellegrini, 1980), practice creative thinking and problem solving (Dansky, 1980; Peppler & Ross, 1981), and consider the perspectives of others (Rubin, Fein, & Vandenberg, 1983). In spite of powerful evidence that play enhances cognitive development, it is still undervalued as a learning medium by some parents, teachers, and researchers (Bergen, 1988). An underlying assumption of this book is that children learn best when they are playing.

Programs in which children are able to pursue their own play interests throughout the school day have been found to have positive and long-lasting effects on development. One research study found that young children enrolled in "nondidactic" preschools—those in which all learning was self-directed—scored higher on eighth-grade achievement tests than those attending direct-instructional programs (Miller & Bizzell, 1983). In a similar longitudinal investigation, Schweinhart, Weikart, and Larner (1986) discovered that students who attended child-centered programs committed fewer acts of delinquency and violence at age fifteen than peers enrolled in teacher-directed preschools.

The benefits of such play-based programs have been explained in various ways. Learning is more exciting and fun when one can choose which activities to pursue. An early love of learning and a positive attitude toward school are nurtured, then, in the child-centered classrooms. Self-directed programs allow individualized education, since students can choose those tasks ideally suited to their particular developmental level.

In active, play-based classrooms children develop important learning processes—they learn how to learn. Since they are responsible for their own activity, they become less dependent on adults, come to trust their own thinking, and are more willing to solve problems independently.

One explanation for the success of child-directed programs is that the playful activities that children choose (as opposed to the academically oriented tasks that adults often select for them) are developmentally useful. Common childhood play activities are related to general intellectual ability (Salz & Brodie, 1982), language development (McCune-Nicholich & Fenson, 1984), social and emotional development (Bretherton, 1984; Trawick-Smith, 1992) and creativity (Pellegrini, 1984). Table 1-1 summarizes these developmental benefits of play.

In a position statement on developmentally appropriate practice, the National Association for the Education of Young Children (1986) summarizes the importance of child-directed, play-based programs:

> Knowledge is not something that is given to children as though they were empty vessels to be filled. Children acquire knowledge about the physical and social world in which they live through playful interaction with objects and people. Children do not need to be forced to learn; they are motivated by their own desire to make sense of their world. (p. 21)

Play and the Curriculum

Play can occur at any time of the day and in any area of the classroom. As children play they acquire knowledge and skills in all curriculum areas. Children can learn mathematics concepts while building with blocks, playing lotto, or filling containers at the water table. They can learn to read and write by printing make-believe shopping lists in the dramatic play area, pretending to read books to dolls, or making road signs for an imaginary block city. When children alter the direction or speed with which they roll a ball in a game of bowling they learn simple physics. They come to understand the world as they attempt to represent people, places, or objects in their drawings and paintings.

Classrooms can be structured so that virtually all curricular goals are met within playful contexts. The following descriptions of one child's activities on a single day within a play-based kindergarten classroom show how this may be accomplished.

Table 1-1
Developmental Benefits of Play

Benefits	Examples
Cognitive development	A child pretends to be a father dressing his child (a doll) for school. As he does so he practices general cognitive abilities such as perspective-taking and symbolizing.
Problem solving	A child building in the block area has used all the long blocks and yet needs one more to finish her building. She solves the problem by combining two smaller blocks to equal the length of one long one.
Language development	A child is pretending to be a doctor discussing his diagnosis with a patient. "I am afraid we will have to perform a surgery," he says in a grown-up tone of voice. He is practicing adult forms of language.
Creativity	A child on the playground pretends to be a fairy who can with a touch turn other children into chocolate pudding. The play becomes increasingly imaginative and elaborate as other students join in.
Healthy personality formation	A child who is anxious about going to the dentist pretends to extract a tooth from a stuffed animal in the dramatic play area. In doing so he is bringing his fears to the surface and gaining mastery over them.
Reading	Three children play school in the book area. One pretends to be the teacher and reads a story to her two "students."
Social development	Two children argue over whether to pretend to be fire fighters or mothers. "Let's be mothers who put out fires," one child compromises, settling the dispute.

Ding Fang begins her morning in the dramatic play area which has on this day been arranged into a make-believe airport. She pretends to buy a ticket to Taiwan from a peer who stands behind the ticket counter. "Taiwan!" her peer states in mock disbelief. "Is that a state or something?" A teacher's aide who overhears the conversation intervenes to explain to the child where Ding Fang was born. Satisfied with this explanation, the "ticket agent" now "writes" a ticket in large scribbles. "What are you writing there?" Ding Fang asks. The child runs his fingers along his "writing" and says: "It says: 'Ticket to Taiwan.' Go get on the plane now." Ding Fang continues to buy tickets and later writes tickets for other children until group time.

After the group meeting, Ding Fang chooses to play at the water table. On this day straws and various floating objects are available. She joins her peers in a game—by blowing with the straws they attempt to move ping-pong balls across the water or to sink floating jar tops and other objects. She alters the strength of her blows and varies her aim in order to accomplish these objectives. A teacher joins them and asks: "How could you make your ball travel faster?" or "What do you think would happen if you used two straws?" Ding Fang is absorbed in this activity for much of the morning.

Later she joins peers in a board game. Players roll dice and move markers the indicated number of squares along the board. If they land on certain squares they draw cards and follow instructions printed on them. They help one another read the cards; one experienced peer has the messages memorized. A conflict erupts as one child insists that Ding Fang has moved too many squares on her turn. They count and recount the spaces she has moved. They reach a settlement and play resumes.

After snack and a story, Ding Fang moves into the art center. She makes an elaborate drawing with markers and writes several lines of scribbles across the top. She "reads" her story to a teacher who asks questions and gives a friendly hug. She begins a second drawing; an end-of-the-morning group meeting is called before she can finish. She places the drawing in her art file so that she might resume her work the next day.   ❖

In one morning this child has had opportunities to construct concepts in language and literacy ("writing" airline tickets or words on her drawings), mathematics (counting spaces on a board game), science (experimenting at the water table), social studies (discussing airports and other countries in the world), and art (drawing at the art center). Could she have learned as much from teacher-directed, whole-group lessons?

There are several unique features of the classroom described above that distinguish it from "traditional" kindergarten programs. Most of the classroom space is organized into play centers equipped with a broad selection of enticing materials. These materials relate to children's interests and developmental levels; many are open-ended and do not require correct answers or specific uses (e.g., sculpting dough or water play). All materials allow independent play; adult direction is not required. In such classrooms the environment facilitates much of the learning. Important teaching functions are performed before children even arrive at school; teachers of such classrooms spend many out-of-school hours setting the stage for positive play experiences. Ideas for arranging play space and developing materials and activities can be found in a variety of excellent curriculum textbooks. (Please see the list at the end of this chapter.)

Developmentally useful play occurs at any time of day in any area of the classroom.

Why Should Teachers Play with Children?

If self-directed activity is so important, why should teachers play with children? Does adult intervention interfere with natural play processes?

Sometimes teachers should not participate in children's activities. Domineering, directive strategies that alter the course of children's self-chosen play themes are inappropriate and a misapplication of play intervention research. What is valuable about play is that it is planned and regulated by children. If adults are too forceful in their guidance these qualities may be lost. When children do not wish to play with adults, teachers should not intervene. Some children want to play only with adults and become dependent on teacher guidance in their play. In these instances teacher-child interaction should be minimized.

Unobtrusive, carefully crafted adult interventions can, at the right times, enrich children's play activity. Research findings reveal that children's play becomes more complex and developmentally useful when they are playing with adults and continues to be so even after their adult playmates have withdrawn from these interventions (Christie, 1983; Smilansky & Shefatya, 1990).

In spite of overwhelming evidence that adult play intervention is beneficial, teachers spend only two to six percent of their classroom time playing with children (Johnson, Christie, & Yawkey, 1987). A purpose of this book is to

Adults can enrich children's play in unobtrusive ways.

encourage teachers of young children to spend more time entering the play worlds of their students. Such sojourns will prove useful for children, who will reap these cognitive and social benefits, and for teachers, who will discover a great deal about the lives of their students.

When To Play with Children

There are times when it is especially important for teachers to intervene in play. When children do not become involved at all with peers or play materials, or need support in maintaining complex play themes, adults can facilitate or enrich their activity. When a "teachable moment" arises, a purposeful intervention can lead to the learning of a new concept. Sometimes children invite teachers to play with them. At these times adults might play along to make warm and enjoyable contacts with their students.

These reasons for play intervention are discussed below. In Table 1-2, examples of appropriate adult-child interactions are provided.

Table 1-2
Purposes of Play Intervention

Purpose	Example
1. To increase play involvement and social participation	**Teacher** (playing restaurant with a group of children, addressing an isolate child, Dana): "Dana, why don't you come order lunch with me. The potato salad is excellent here!" **Dana:** "Okay." (Joins the group.)
2. To enhance play skills	**Teacher** (to a child who is sitting by himself producing fire truck noises): "Jeremy, can you help me fight this fire? Here is the fire hose." (Makes gestures to indicate an imaginary hose.) "Can you hold this end of the hose?" **Jeremy:** "Okay, I'll squirt it!" (Performs a make-believe enactment.)
3. To capitalize on a "teachable moment"	**Teacher** (to a child who is placing a large block on top of an already-teetering block structure): "What do you think will happen when you put that big block on?" **Child:** "Will it fall?" (Places the block on; the building collapses.) **Teacher:** "Oops! What happened?" **Child:** "It was too biggish, I think."
4. To make personal contact with a student	**Child** (to a teacher who has entered the dramatic-play area): "Now, we're playing divorce. You be the dad who doesn't live with us. You come over to see your little girl." (As the teacher enacts this role, he listens carefully to the anxieties and concerns expressed in this child's play.)

When Children Don't Play at All

Children often play alone; isolate play is very important in development (Rubin, 1982). Some young children never interact with materials or peers, however. Teacher intervention has been found to facilitate greater social participation among these "isolates" (Mize & Ladd, 1990; Trawick-Smith, 1988). By playing with or around such children and offering gentle invitations to participate, adults can increase social contact, promote friendships, and enhance social skills. Some children will remain more involved and social even when adults have withdrawn from the play setting after these interventions.

Specific guidelines for working with isolate children are presented in later chapters. Example 1 of Table 1-2 illustrates this type of intervention.

When Children Need Support in Their Play

All play is valuable; teachers should respect unique play styles and not tamper too vigorously with them. Some children do need support, however, in various aspects of their play. They may not interact cooperatively with others, for example. Through play intervention adults can promote more pro-social behavior and positive peer interaction (Smilansky & Shefatya, 1990). Some children do not persist at play activities; they quickly shift from one action to another and are easily distracted. Several studies have shown that when an adult plays with children they are likely to engage in longer-lasting, more elaborate play experiences (Sylva, Roy, & Painter, 1980; Dunn & Wooding, 1977). Increased play persistence resulting from these interactions might lead to greater attention in school-related tasks later in life.

Other studies indicate that many children engage in simple, repetitive play actions that are less likely to lead to social and cognitive development. Johnson, Christie, and Yawkey (1987) conclude the following from these studies:

> There does appear to be a need to enhance the level of play that occurs in classrooms. If children are to reap the full benefits of play, it is necessary for them to engage in high-quality sociodramatic and constructive play, the types of play that have the biggest roles in intellectual and social development. (p. 25)

There is research to support their contention (Bruner, 1980; Christie, 1983). In a classic study conducted in Israel, for example, Smilansky (1968) demonstrated that a special form of play intervention could increase the sociodramatic play abilities of less playful children. She found that it was not enough simply to provide these children with more opportunities and materials to engage in this form of social pretend play. Only when adults played with children, enhancing certain play abilities, were gains achieved in play and language development.

In Chapter 3 and elsewhere in this volume Smilansky's strategies will be described in detail. Example 2 of Table 1-2 presents an illustration of her general approach.

When a "Teachable Moment" Arises

Many children engage in high-quality play and gain much from these experiences without adult involvement. However, an opportunity may arise now and then for learning a new concept or thinking about a problem in a new way. Such moments might come and go without significance unless carefully phrased questions, suggestions, or warm encouragements are provided by an adult. At such times teachers can intervene to take advantage of these "teachable moments."

Teachers might add new information to an exploration, give a hint to help solve a problem, or ask a question to guide thinking. Information delivered in this way is likely to be retained longer than when provided in more formal, large group activities (Stallings, 1975).

In later chapters specific strategies for promoting thinking and learning are detailed. In Example 3 of Table 1-2 a question-asking technique during a "teachable moment" is illustrated.

When Children Invite Adults To Play

Sometimes children invite teachers to play along because adults can be interesting and enjoyable playmates. Teachers should take advantage of such invitations; they can learn a great deal about their students while playing with them. Children will sometimes reveal their anxieties or concerns in their play (Curry & Bergen, 1988). They demonstrate their social competence (or lack of it), exercising abilities such as peer persuasion or group entry strategies as they play (Mize & Ladd, 1990). In play children show what they know and how they think (Kamii, 1982). Play situations, then, provide a window through which adults may view children's development and mental health.

Play intervention allows a warm personal contact with children. There is much affection, laughter, and reverie in such interactions. Simply stated, playing with children is great fun.

Teachers sometimes intervene in children's play, then, to invigorate themselves and enhance their relationships with students. Guidelines for these warm and playful interchanges are provided throughout this book. An illustration of one such interaction is included in Table 1-2, Example 4.

How To Use This Book

This book presents guidelines for playing with children. Reading these chapters will familiarize the reader with techniques and provide a rationale for informal, child-centered interventions in children's play activities. Reading this volume is not enough, however, to become an effective facilitator of play. Hands-on experience is required to become truly good at play intervention. It is recommended that readers practice suggested strategies with real children as they read these chapters. Those preparing to teach might practice intervention behaviors as they complete field experiences or student teaching in early childhood classrooms. Experienced teachers might try out techniques with their own students. To assist in this practice, suggested activities are included at the end of each chapter.

Summary

Programs in which young children direct their own activity and learning are most effective in promoting positive development. This does not mean that teachers have no role in the learning process. Rather than adopting direct-instructional, traditional teacher roles, however, adults can use informal play-intervention techniques in their classrooms.

Sometimes intervening in children's play is not appropriate. Times when teachers should play with their students include:

1. when children don't play at all
2. when children need support in their play
3. when a "teachable moment" arises
4. when children invite teachers to play

It is not easy to learn how to play with children in unobtrusive and developmentally beneficial ways. This book provides guidelines for engaging in such intervention. Readers should also practice techniques described here in real-life classrooms in order to become truly proficient players.

Suggested Activities

1. Observe teachers and children interacting in an early-childhood classroom (or view a videotape of such interactions in your own classroom). Write an analysis of children's play experiences, guided by the following questions:
   a. For what portion of the day do children engage in open-ended, self-directed play? What recommendations would you make for scheduling adequate play time?
   b. What play activities or materials are available to children?
   c. How would you characterize this teacher's play interventions?
      1. To what degree does the teacher intervene in children's activities?
      2. In what ways, if any, does the teacher dominate children's activities? In which instances does unobtrusive intervention take place?
      3. What techniques does the teacher use for withdrawing from the play setting? What happens to the play after these departures? To what degree does the play theme continue? How does the play change?

4. In which areas does the most play intervention occur? In which areas is there less intervention? Why is there a difference in teacher involvement across these areas?

5. What recommendations, if any, would you make about toys, equipment, and the arrangement of play space?

2. Observe a teacher intervening in young children's play activity (or view a videotape of your own play intervention in your classroom). Write an analysis of the purposes and effects of these interventions, guided by the following questions:

a. What appears to be the purpose of each intervention you observed? In what ways does the teacher attempt to enrich play? to teach concepts? to make warm, personal contacts with students? to settle conflicts or quiet the group?

b. How do children react to these interventions? In what ways do they communicate that the teacher is welcome or unwelcome? What changes do you observe in the organization of their play, language, or interactions with one another as a result of the intervention?

c. What happens when the teacher withdraws from the setting? In what ways, if any, is the play more organized or complex? less organized or complex?

d. What recommendations would you give about the teacher's play-intervention techniques?

Further Reading

Axline, V. M. (1969). *Play therapy*. New York: Ballantine Books.

Bergen, D. (Ed.). (1988). *Play as a medium for learning and development*. Portsmouth, NH: Heinemann.

Elkind, D. (1981). *The hurried child*. Reading, MA: Addison-Wesley.

Fein, G., & Rivkin, M. (1986). *The young child at play. Reviews of research* (Vol. 4). Washington, DC: National Association for the Education of Young Children.

Johnson, J. E., Christie, J. F., & Yawkey, T. D. (1987). *Play and early childhood development*. Glenview, IL: Scott, Foresman and Company.

National Association for the Education of Young Children. (1986). Position statement on developmentally appropriate practice in programs for 4- and 5-year-olds. *Young Children, 41*, 20–29.

Rogers, C. S., & Sawyers, J. K. (1988). *Play in the lives of children*. Washington, DC: National Association for the Education of Young Children.

Rubin, K. N., Fein, G. G., & Vandenberg, B. (1983). Play. In E. M. Hetherington (Ed.) & P. H. Mussen (Series Ed.), *Handbook of child psychology: Vol. 4. Socialization, personality, and social development* (pp. 698–774). New York: Wiley.

Trawick-Smith, J. W. (1985). Developing the dramatic play enrichment program. *Dimensions, 13*(4), 7–11.

Textbooks in Early Childhood Education Curriculum

Brewer, J. A. (1992). *Early childhood education: Preschool through primary grades*. Needham Heights, MA: Allyn and Bacon.

Feeney, S., Christensen, D., & Moravcik, E. (1991). *Who am I in the lives of children?* (4th ed.). New York: Merrill/Macmillan.

Hendrick, J. (1992). *The whole child* (5th ed.). New York: Merrill/Macmillan.

Hildebrand, V. (1990). *Guiding young children* (4th ed.). New York: Merrill/Macmillan.

Morrison, G. S. (1991). *Early childhood education today* (5th ed.). New York: Merrill/Macmillan.

Seefeldt, C. (1987). *The early childhood curriculum: A review of current research*. New York: Teachers College Press.

2

FACILITATING PLAY: GUIDELINES AND TECHNIQUES

Teachers differ in their approaches to play intervention. Some are more directive when playing with children; others encourage their students to maintain control over play activities. The two vignettes below provide sharply contrasting styles.

❖ ❖

Vignette 1 (A directive teacher)

Three five-year-olds are playing in the dramatic-play area. Two are pretending to be snakes and the third is their "trainer." As the "snakes" hiss and wiggle on the floor, the "trainer" calls out tricks for them to perform. As the play gets rather loud a teacher intervenes.

Child A: (The "trainer") Okay. Now roll over! (The "snakes" respond.) Sit up! (Again they perform as directed.) Now clap!

Child B: (A "snake") Wait a minute! Snakes can't clap!

Before they can discuss this controversy further, the teacher enters the play area.

Teacher: Did you see that we have the dramatic play area set up like a restaurant?

Child A: (Looking at the teacher) Hmm . . . (looking back at his playmates). Let's say you can clap 'cause you're special snakes, okay?

Teacher: (Persisting, in a playful tone) Who'd like to order some lunch? I'll be the waitress. I need a helper. Jeremy, you can be a waiter too. Sean and Michael will be our customers.

The children move over to the teacher and begin to assume the roles they have been assigned.

Vignette 2 (A skilled play facilitator)

Three children ride "big-wheel" tricycles around a circular sidewalk. As they whirl around, they make loud engine noises, pretending to be race-car drivers. A fourth child stands alone watching. She complains to a teacher that there are not enough riding toys for her to play. One of the riders suggests that she can be a "watcher" (i.e., a spectator) but this does not appease her.

Teacher: Why don't you and I be the pit crew? They give the race cars gas when they run out and fix the engines when they break.

Child A: (Tentatively) Okay.

Teacher: (To the "race car drivers") We're your pit crew. Please come over if you need more gas.

Child B immediately rides his tricycle over to Child A and the Teacher.

Child B: Okay! Put some gas in!

Teacher: (To Child A) Can you pump the gas? I'll check the tires.

Child A: (After making "pumping" sounds and gestures) That will be forty-nine dollars, please!

Child B makes gestures of handing money to Child A, then drives off. Children C and D have already lined up to get gas.

Teacher: (Examining Child C's tricycle) Oh, oh! I hear a noise in this car. What could that be?

Child A: That's the engine, I think. We need to fix this thing. Get off, Melissa, we need to fix up your engine a little.

Child C gets off the toy. Both children turn it upside down so it is resting on its handlebars. Together they work on the "car" with imaginary tools. The teacher backs away from the play setting and watches from a distance. ❖

How do these two teachers differ in their interactions with children? The first teacher is highly directive. Although she is warm and friendly, she dominates children's play, assigning a new play theme and roles to each participant. Generally this teacher interrupts children's activities rather than enriching them.

In contrast the second teacher demonstrates many play-intervention skills. He gives just the right amount of guidance to help a child join a play group. He intervenes in an unobtrusive manner so that the child-selected play theme is preserved. He offers suggestions for enhancing make-believe and asks open-ended questions that enrich the play. Most important, he withdraws from the setting after a brief time, allowing children to continue playing undisturbed. In general, his interactions illustrate several important guidelines for play intervention. In this chapter these general guidelines are introduced. In later chapters techniques and principles described here will be discussed in depth in relation to specific curriculum areas.

Key Decisions in Play Intervention

Unlike planned whole-class activities, play-intervention strategies must be administered spontaneously within the unpredictable world of children's play. Teachers do not have time to formulate carefully phrased questions or discussion topics. They cannot select ahead of time which concepts to introduce or which skills to enhance. Teachers must be able to analyze a particular play situation and make judgments on the spot about which methods of intervention, if any, to employ. Careful observation is a critical component, then, of play intervention. Before entering a play situation a teacher must assess what children are doing, what they are thinking about, and what they need at that moment for optimal development to occur. Experience in observing and interpreting children's play activities is the best preparation for becoming a skilled play facilitator. This section will provide a discussion of key decisions teachers must make when playing with children.

When To Play with Children and When Not To

One of the most difficult decisions to make in play intervention is when to play with young children. In Chapter 1 several specific circumstances in which intervention would be appropriate were identified—when children do not play at all or need support in their playing, when a teachable moment arises, or when teachers or children desire a friendly, warm contact. Teachers will need to study each play episode carefully to determine if one of these conditions exists. If children are observed wandering, day-dreaming, or engaging in much onlooking without involvement in materials or peers, for example, the decision might be made to intervene. If highly repetitive motoric activity is observed (e.g., continually stacking and knocking down blocks, endlessly rocking a doll in a rocking chair, or mindlessly turning the pages of a book while staring at another part of the classroom), a teacher might also choose to intervene (Johnson, Christie, & Yawkey, 1987).

Identifying and effectively responding to teachable moments requires particular skill. Much learning should occur through self-guided discovery; too much of this sort of intervention can be harmful (Garvey, 1977; Pellegrini, 1984). Judicious use of concept teaching, however, can promote learning. Teachers can watch for situations in children's play where a carefully phrased question, a suggestion, or the offer of new materials might lead to an insight that would not otherwise occur. As children play a card game, for example, a simple question such as "Who's won the most cards?" could change the game into a significant mathematics lesson.

Teachers must also decide when it is appropriate to play with children to make interpersonal contact. When a teacher notes that particular children have not recently received much one-to-one adult interaction, they might choose to play with them for periods of time. A child undergoing a stressful life event, such as a parental divorce or a recent hospitalization, might receive extra adult play sessions. At times when both teachers and children are in need of emotional release or re-energizing (e.g., after a morning of administering and taking state-mandated achievement tests in a primary-grade classroom) playful encounters on the playground are appropriate. Often teachers enter children's play worlds for pure enjoyment. Play is the ideal context for enjoying warm and pleasant contacts with students.

Johnson, Christie, and Yawkey (1987) have warned, however, that "too much and the wrong kind of intervention" (p. 26) can be harmful. Teachers must come to recognize situations when it is not appropriate to play. Sometimes children are playing in such an organized, productive fashion that intervention could serve only to interfere. When children are engaging in cooperative activity with peers, using much language, thinking and solving problems, and showing interest and enthusiasm, teachers might choose to stay away. Researchers have found, however, that children in preschools engage in play of this high quality only 16% of the time (Sylva, Roy, & Painter, 1980; Tizard, 1977).

In some instances, children do not want teachers to play. They give signs that they are weary of their adult playmates, showing annoyance or lack of interest in teacher initiatives. Sometimes they are less than subtle in expressing these feelings, as the example below reveals:

❖ ❖

Four five-year-olds are pretending to work at a restaurant in the dramatic-play area. A teacher sits down at a table to order a make-believe meal.

Teacher: M-m-m-m! Something smells delicious. I'm really hungry. What can I order at your restaurant?

Child: (Curtly) I'm sorry, but there's not any food left for you!

Teachers should always honor children's wishes to be left alone. Play intervention is not effective if it is imposed upon children.   ❖

How To Enter and Exit the Play Setting

Once a decision has been made to intervene, the teacher must formulate a strategy for entering the play setting. The skillful teacher can enter a play situation, briefly enrich children's activity, then exit the area without causing major disruption to the play in progress. Such unobtrusive, respectful entrances and exits assure that children's self-chosen play themes will be maintained while adults are present and after they have left the area.

Entrances

Manning and Sharp (1977) have provided general guidelines for entering play situations. First, adults should observe the situation to determine what sort of intervention, if any, is needed. One important purpose of this observation is to ascertain what children are currently playing. The teacher can then make an entry that supports and enriches current play themes rather than disrupting them. According to Manning and Sharp, adults should join in activities that are already in progress. Only in rare instances is it appropriate to suggest a new play theme. They should enter quietly, assuming the status of respectful and enlightened playmates rather than all-powerful and authoritarian directors of play.

An adult who is too imposing can destroy a play episode. The directive teacher in Vignette 1 described at the beginning of this chapter, for example, fails to observe and understand the nature of children's current play activities and engages in interventions that disrupt rather than build on what children are already doing. In contrast, the skilled facilitator of Vignette 2 understands children's activities and smoothly joins in to enrich them.

The timing of an entry is extremely important. As previously discussed, there are times when play intervention should not occur at all (Johnson, Christie, & Yawkey, 1987). In other play situations, intervention is important but teachers should wait until the ideal moment to join in. They might briefly hold back, for example, when they observe children deeply absorbed in thought or actively performing a make-believe enactment. At these times adult involvement might lead to distraction (Garvey, 1977; Pellegrini, 1984). Transition points in the play (when children step out of their make-believe roles, take a break from in-depth problem solving, or stop for a discussion with peers about what to do next) are better times for adult entry.

Exits

The goal of play intervention is not to provide continuous adult-guided activity, but to enrich children's self-directed play. Thus, exiting play situations so that children can interact on their own is an extremely important step in playing with children. Johnson, Christie, and Yawkey (1989) have argued that, "stepping back returns control of the play to children and helps promote independence and self confidence" (p. 37). These authors cite evidence that carefully planned "phase-out" procedures enhance the effectiveness of play intervention.

The key to exiting is to withdraw in an inconspicuous manner, so that play will continue uninterrupted. This is not always easy to accomplish. Sometimes a teacher's departure from an activity leads quickly to its dissolution. Several steps can be taken to avoid this. A gradual exit can be planned. Well before departing, a teacher might encourage children to interact more intensively with one another and at the same time gradually disengage from the play. Once an adult has become a less integral part of the activity, the departure is less likely to jeopardize the play theme.

Several specific exiting behaviors are common. Simply leaving without comment works well when children are especially absorbed in their own activities. It may be many minutes before children even notice that the teacher is gone.

Indirect strategies are useful, particularly in sociodramatic play or other make-believe situations. For example, excusing oneself after eating a lunch at a make-believe restaurant and announcing, "Oh, look at the time! I need to go back to work now!" allows the teacher to exit without threatening the make-believe world children have created. "Waiters" and "customers" can stay in their roles and continue their play while sending the teacher off.

It is not unusual for children to protest a teacher's departure. In these circumstances more direct explanations and discussions are required. Teachers can directly state that they need to move to other areas of the classroom or to help other children. If protests are great, a gradual withdrawal strategy might be implemented: "I'm going to check on the art table for a moment. You keep working on our building; I'll be right back." The teacher might return and then depart again several times, on each occasion extending the time away. With this approach, children slowly become reaccustomed to playing on their own.

In the following vignette a teacher reflects these exiting guidelines when gradually disengaging from a science experience:

❖ ❖

A teacher sits at the science center with two six-year-old children who are placing objects onto a balance. The teacher has been asking, "Which of these will weigh more?" Now she is assuming a less active role in the game. She has stopped posing the question; children are doing this themselves. She just observes, making brief comments.

Teacher:	(Quietly getting up from the table) I need to get Rachel some more paint.
Child A:	(In a whiny tone) No. You need to stay here.
Teacher:	(In an enthused voice) Why don't you do these two objects together? I'll help Rachel and come back in a few minutes.
Child B:	(Emulating the teacher's enthusiasm) Yeah! Let's do these two!

The children place the objects on the balance and discuss their observations on their own. The teacher pours paint for one child, converses with another about a painting, then returns, remaining in a standing position.

Child A:	Look! The corn weighs more!
Teacher:	(Quietly, still standing) Yes.
Child B:	C'mon. Let's do more!

Once the children are actively involved in the next experiment, the teacher backs away from the table a few steps. She watches another minute, then leaves the area. The children take no notice of her final departure. ❖

What Type of Intervention To Use

According to Smilansky (1968), teachers must decide between two fundamental types of intervention at the moment of entry into the play setting. They can intervene from *outside* the play episode, asking questions and commenting as an external observer; or they can participate from *inside*, actually joining children's play themes. When teachers ask about the outcome of a game without playing themselves, present several new chairs to be used in a make-believe emergency room without taking on the role of a patient or doctor, or comment on a block building without helping to build it, they are engaging in outside intervention. In inside intervention teachers play a game with children, take a role in a make-believe enactment, or build a block structure alongside their students.

The type of intervention selected depends on the particular play situation and the needs of individual children. Outside intervention may be most useful if only brief interaction is needed. For example, the teacher can ask a question of children (e.g., "Why is your baby crying?" or "Are there more objects that float or more that sink?") without taking the time to join the activity itself.

Outside intervention is also appropriate in situations where teachers wish to keep a distance from the problem-solving or play decisions. If, for example, a child is quite dependent on adults for learning, external interventions (e.g., "Can you figure out which ones float and which ones sink?") rather than internal ones (e.g., "Let's sit together and figure out which ones float and sink") might nurture more independent behavior and thinking.

Some activities require external intervention. Di Leo (1982) has argued that adults should never draw with children, since this inhibits creativity. Children will wish to copy adult forms rather than create their own. So, inside intervention (e.g., "I'll draw rabbits with you") may never be appropriate in such artistic activities as painting or drawing.

Inside intervention, on the other hand, allows the teacher to enter the child's play world and to gain a child's perspective on the pleasures and purposes of play activities (Forman & Kuschner, 1984). In inside intervention there is less risk of dominating, directive behavior because the teacher assumes the role of a player rather than an external adult authority. When adults play inside children's activities they give the message that play is important, and that even grown-ups engage in it now and then. At the same time they show children how to play. Such modeling is critical for those who are of limited play ability (Smilansky, 1968).

There are several forms of inside intervention that a teacher can use (Johnson, Christie, & Yawkey, 1987)—parallel playing, co-playing, and play tutoring.

In "inside intervention" the teacher takes the role of a make-believe character and plays with children.

Parallel Playing

Teachers can enrich play simply by sitting near children and playing parallel to them in interesting and elaborate ways. If a child sits alone in the dramatic play center rocking a doll, for example, the teacher might move into the area and model a more elaborate make-believe theme, setting the table, cooking dinner, and eating. A teacher might play parallel to students at the water table to model the use of new measuring containers, announcing to no one in particular, "I wonder how many cups of water it takes to fill up this bucket."

The very presence of a teacher in these situations may lead to greater social participation and persistence (Sylva, Roy, & Painter, 1980). Children may choose to copy the more elaborate play of the teacher or even to play along. This modeling effect is the primary benefit of parallel playing.

This kind of play intervention is least obtrusive since the adult makes no attempt to approach children directly; they choose whether or not to interact with the teacher. Forman and Kuschner (1984) offer the following example of parallel play interaction:

The teacher observes Erik engaged in his cycle of building and leveling mounds of sand and recognizes the situation as an opportunity to enter the child's world. She is cautious not to interfere with the child's self-set goal. She approaches the sand table, careful not to violate the child's personal space. She begins to make sand mounds near enough to Erik for him to see, but not so close that he feels he is about to be pressured into an interaction with the adult. The teacher begins to build mounds without comment. Periodically Erik glances over to see what the teacher is doing. After all, teachers often have interesting ideas and this teacher is gentle and unobtrusive. (pp. 137-139)

Co-Playing

Teachers can also choose to be more active co-players, joining the play in progress as characters or participants and interacting directly with children. In co-playing the teacher just plays along, allowing children to control the direction of the play (Johnson, Christie, & Yawkey, 1987). When doing so, teachers can watch for teachable moments, when a question or comment will stimulate curiosity, contribute to play organization, raise the level of make believe, or lead to the learning of a new concept. When playing with children, teachers frequently use much language, including question-asking and enthusiastic responding (Gowen, 1987; Johnson, Christie, & Yawkey, 1987). These verbal behaviors promote language acquisition.

Generally this form of play intervention is quite informal, open-ended, and spontaneous. The following is an example of co-playing in a second-grade classroom:

❖ ❖

A teacher is playing a board game with two seven-year-olds. They are using a die to move game pieces across the board; his marker is ahead of the other players.

Child: (In silly, mocking voice) Heh! Heh! I'm going to win!

Teacher: (Playfully) Why do you think so? I'm ahead!

Child: Yeah, but you just had your turn. Then it's Chris's turn, then it's mine again. So then I'll go ahead.

Teacher: You think you'll go ahead on the next move, huh?

Child: (In a silly voice) I will! You don't stand a chance!

Teacher: What would you need to roll to go ahead of me?

Child: Let's see . . . (counts spaces) Seven.

Teacher: Okay. We'll see what happens.

On his next turn the child rolls a six and moves his piece accordingly.

Child: Ah! I couldn't catch you! (A thoughtful expression crosses his face. He laughs.) Oh! There's the problem! You can't get a seven on this stupid dice!   ❖

Many opportunities for conversation and learning arise when children play in open-ended ways with enlightened and interesting adult playmates. In the spontaneous interchanges described above, the teacher has created a quantification problem for a child. Through open-ended questioning he sets the stage for self-discovery.

Play Tutoring

At times a teacher may choose to influence children's play behaviors more directly. If a particular child needs support in specific aspects of play, the teacher might decide to intervene to enhance these areas. A teacher might enter a play setting and directly facilitate social interaction, for example, between an isolate who rarely plays with peers and more pro-social playmates. If a child does not persist at play tasks, the sole focus of play intervention might be to keep the child involved for longer periods.

One of the most common forms of this focused intervention—often called "play training" or "play tutoring" (Johnson, Christie, & Yawkey, 1987)—is the enhancement of sociodramatic play skills. Approaches to sociodramatic play tutoring are discussed in detail in the next chapter; the following is an example of this type of interaction:

A four-year-old has been found to perform very little make-believe in his play. A teacher intervenes in his "firefighter" theme, targeting this specific play deficit.

Child:	(Wearing a firefighter's hat and running in circles and making siren noises) A fire! A fire!
Teacher:	I'll help you fight the fire.
Child:	(Loudly) Okay! C'mon! (Continues with siren noises.)
Teacher:	Where is your fire truck?
Child:	(Pauses, puzzled) It'll be this. (Pulls two chairs together.)
Teacher:	Great! Since you're behind the steering wheel (gestures in the air to identify an imaginary steering wheel), you can drive.
Child:	(Turning the make-believe wheel) Let's go.
Teacher:	(After riding for a period of time without event) Let's say this is the building that's on fire. (Points to a corner of the play area.) Oh, no! Are there people inside the burning building, do you think?
Child:	We need to save them! (Leaves his chair and pretends to fight the fire.) ❖

Here the teacher regularly models or encourages two fundamental make-believe acts—make-believe in regard to objects (creating an imaginary steering wheel) and make-believe in regard to situations ("Oh, no! Are there people inside?") (Smilansky, 1968). The adult's play with the child is clearly much more focused, directive, and purposeful than in parallel playing or co-playing interactions. It is important to note, however, that the child still maintains most control of the play, is able to pursue his own play interests, and may terminate the theme altogether if he chooses. In spite of the rather imposing name for this type of intervention, play tutoring is still very much child-directed interaction.

How Much Help To Give

One critical decision to be made in play intervention is how much help to give. In some situations much support and guidance are needed. In others, prompts or suggestions are in order. Sometimes the teacher should give the child full responsibility for solving a problem or making a play decision.

The work of psychologist Lev Vygotsky (1962, 1978) is helpful in deciding how much help to give. He has suggested that if children are to become competent they must develop self-regulation—the ability to control and guide their own attention and thinking, to monitor their own successes and failures, to formulate their own solutions to problems, and generally to learn independently. Children can't always regulate themselves in the early years; adults often assist in this regulation. Parents of infants and toddlers, for example, may be observed directing their children's attention, reminding them of the task to be completed, or evaluating their successes. As children get older, however, it is important that adults gradually give up this regulatory role and encourage children to perform these functions independently.

Vygotsky specifies that adults can transfer this regulation to children by performing three kinds of actions while playing with them:

1. **Adults should take responsibility for those tasks which are clearly beyond the child's capabilities.**

Sometimes children are faced with insurmountable obstacles in their play. According to Vygotsky it is appropriate at these times for adults to directly regulate activity. The following examples illustrate this:

❖ ❖
Vignette 1

A five-year-old child from a multi-grade classroom has taken a complex jigsaw puzzle from the shelf and is struggling with the pieces.

Child: I can't do this!

Teacher: Let me help you. I'll make the edges of the puzzle to get you started. Then you can fill in the middle pieces. (She completes the boundary of the puzzle for the child.)

Vignette 2

A three-year-old is building with blocks. Her structure continually topples over because she is placing smaller pieces and triangular blocks at the base. She shows signs of frustration.

Teacher: Here, let me show you something. If you put these long blocks down first, your building might stay up. (He moves the small and triangular blocks away from the play space and lays several of the longest blocks down.) There, try that. ❖

In these vignettes the teachers have made a determination that major obstacles interfere with play and that these children need direct assistance in overcoming these. Rather than guide them toward other less-taxing activities, these teachers help them stick with these tasks by completing some steps for them.

2. **Adults should guide children with hints, questions, or encouragements during tasks that are within the child's "Zone of Proximal Development," that is, which are just beyond the child's mastery level.**

Teachers must watch for periods in an activity when the child is challenged just the right amount, is confronted with a problem requiring a slightly more advanced form of thinking or a new skill. Through careful intervention at these points, adults can promote acquisition of concepts or abilities and teach children how to learn independently. These interventions are very different from direct instruction; teachers in such actions guide children to perform on their own, as the following examples reveal:

❖ ❖
Vignette 3

After the teacher of Vignette 1 has created the boundary of the jigsaw puzzle for the child she guides him in filling in more pieces.

Teacher: Look. These pieces look like Mickey's feet. Where do you think his feet should go?

Child: (Studying the puzzle for a minute) Oh! Down here, I think! (Places the pieces appropriately.)

Vignette 4

After the teacher of Vignette 2 lays the long blocks down, he assists the child in proceeding with the task.

Teacher: We put the very longest blocks down first. Which blocks do you think should go down next?

Child: Um . . . These? (Holds up medium-length blocks.)

Teacher: What do you think?

Child: Yep! (Places the blocks on the structure.)   ❖

Both teachers above now give hints; the children are encouraged to take most responsibility for these tasks.

3. **Adults should give full responsibility to the child for tasks that can easily be completed.**

It is important that teachers not nurture dependence on adults to help with problems. Once an activity reaches a point when children can perform on their own, teachers should withhold all helping behaviors. The following examples demonstrate how teachers can continue to encourage children without directly assisting them:

❖ ❖

Vignette 5

With the teacher's guidance the child of Vignettes 1 and 3 has placed a few more pieces on the puzzle. The remaining pieces will be easier to place.

Child: (Holding up a piece) Where do you think this goes?

Teacher: (In an enthused tone) I think you can find that one.

Child: (Studies the puzzle, then places the piece) There!

Teacher: Look. Now you can see Goofy's head.

Vignette 6

With the teacher's assistance the child of Vignettes 2 and 4 has come to discover the secret to successful block-building—larger ones on the bottom, smaller ones on the top. There are now several blocks remaining.

Child: Which one next?

Teacher: You know, I think.

Child: (Laughing) This one? (Holds up an extremely small block.)

Teacher: (Laughing) What do you think?

Child: No! This one! (Holds up more appropriate choice and places it successfully.) This is my office building.

Teacher: Tell me about it. Who works there?

In Vignettes 5 and 6 the teachers refrain from giving assistance. It is important to note that they do not even encourage the children to keep working or to finish the projects. According to Vygotsky, children must learn to attend to and persist at tasks on their own. Although the teachers do not help the children, they convey continued interest in the projects and make interesting comments to encourage them.   ❖

Freund (1990) conducted a study to test the effectiveness of Vygotsky's approach. Adults who were taught to adapt their helping behaviors to the degree of difficulty of tasks, as Vygotsky has suggested, were more effective in teaching children to solve a problem than those who tried to instruct them directly.

Adults can give too much help when playing with children. Overly active, directive adult playmates might stifle productive play. Generally, teachers should be careful not to make all play decisions or give away answers to problems.

It is important to note that children often give one another the kind of help and guidance described above. When a child needs support in a play task, a teacher might not always give direct assistance, but encourage a peer to do so (Johnson, Skon, & Johnson, 1980). Vygotsky has observed that in such "cooperative learning situations," one child will often challenge another to think within the zone of proximal development.

Play Intervention Behaviors

In any type of playful teaching, a variety of specific interactive behaviors that enhance learning and development can be used. Examples of these are presented in Table 2-1.

Skillful teachers display a broad repertoire of these—conversing, asking questions, modeling—often applying a mixture of techniques within a single play interaction. They can quickly assess a particular play situation in progress and determine on the spot just those approaches that will enrich children's activity. In this section of the chapter, "tools" for play intervention, those effective classroom behaviors used to enhance play, are presented.

Giving One-To-One Guidance

Teachers must make frequent, meaningful one-to-one contacts with children while playing with them. Children are more likely to retain information and complete tasks when they are approached in this manner (Stallings, 1975). All interventions described in this book, whether designed to promote math or reading competence or to enhance social skills, require individual teacher-child encounters. Effective one-to-one interactions include certain interpersonal features: Teachers place themselves at the child's level and establish eye contact rather than towering over their students from a standing position (Lay-Dopyera & Dopyera, 1987). Simple, clear language; positive, enthusiastic (though respectful) intonation; and warmth are also required for effective one-to-one guidance (Lindfors, 1987).

Table 2-1

Play Intervention Behaviors

Behavior	Example
1. One-to-one guidance	A teacher gets down onto a child's level, establishes eye contact, and responds to her request to share her drawing. "Tell me a story about your drawing," he says.
2. Question-asking	A teacher observes two children pretending to drive a car in the dramatic play area. He asks, "What will you do when you get to work?"
3. Modeling	A child sits alone and unoccupied at the writing center. The teacher sits next to her, takes out his own journal and begins to write in it. The child now writes also.
4. Warmth	A child has just said goodbye to her mother on the first day of school and shows signs of distress. The teacher puts an arm around her and asks in a gentle, reassuring voice if she would like to sit in his lap and listen to a story.
5. Encouragement	A child calls for a teacher to come look at a house he has just made of blocks. "Look at my house!" he says with enthusiasm. "I have been watching you build it. Who lives in the house?" the teacher says in an equally excited tone.

Effective teachers demonstrate conversational skills in their interchanges with individual children (Feeney, Christensen, & Moravcik, 1991). They engage in turn-taking, allowing students time to think about and respond to questions. They show children they are listening through eye contact, an enthused manner, and responses that are relevant to the child's comments.

Although effective teachers often initiate one-to-one interactions, they also encourage children to introduce their own topics for discussion. This requires that they position themselves close to children during free play so that these initiatives can occur. They move regularly in the classroom, "touching base" with all students (Brophy & Evertson, 1976).

The reader may be asking at this point how these one-to-one experiences can be managed with so many other needful students in the classroom also seeking adult contact. What are these other children doing while the teacher plays with an individual? How can a teacher conduct meaningful and on-going interventions while attending to an entire classroom group?

Classroom routines must be structured so that one-to-one interaction is possible. Three different plans for accomplishing this are commonly used in schools. Each plan is designed for the unique characteristics of a particular kind of classroom—a large day-care center, a small two-teacher preschool, or a traditional single-teacher public school program.

Large Day-Care Plan

In large programs several adults are responsible for many children. One strategy for assuring one-to-one contact in such centers has been dubbed the "zone defense" by a day-care director fond of sports analogies. In this plan each staff member, except one, is assigned a zone in the classroom. Teachers are responsible for observing and interacting with individuals within their zone. A teacher may linger in an interaction with an individual in this plan, knowing that children in other zones are well supervised.

The staff member who is not assigned to a zone serves as a resource person. This individual moves about the entire classroom resolving conflicts, providing needed materials, and generally overseeing the activities of the whole group. In one child-care center this resource person was identified with a colorful arm band. Children quickly learned to approach this individual with requests when other teachers were deeply engaged in one-to-one interventions.

Two-Teacher Preschools

Small preschool and day-care programs are frequently staffed by two adults, often a teacher and an assistant. In such programs one adult might be identified as the resource person, floating and observing as in the previous plan. The second adult would serve as the play facilitator, settling with individuals or small groups to administer specific interventions. Teachers might exchange these roles regularly so that each adult would have a whole-class perspective but also receive play intervention experience.

Traditional Single-Teacher Classroom

Public school teachers often find themselves alone in classrooms with large groups of students. Such arrangements are not ideal for learning generally and play intervention specifically. However, one-to-one guidance can still be provided in these classrooms. In some traditional Montessori programs a single teacher presents lessons to individual children while as many as thirty-five other students interact with the environment on their own. The secret is to provide activities that are totally self-absorbing.

When children are playing with modeling dough, pretending in a dramatic-play center, or building at the sand table, they require minimal adult support. Teachers can settle with confidence into ongoing and uninterrupted interchanges with individuals during such play. Activities that have one right answer, thus requiring adult checking, those which are uninteresting but have been imposed upon children (e.g., ditto sheets and other traditional "seat work"), or those which are too difficult for children to pursue independently, are inappropriate because they will certainly lead to interruption of teacher-child interactions.

Experienced solo teachers have been found to effectively balance movement throughout the classroom with in-depth intervention in individual children's play (Brophy & Evertson, 1976). These skilled teachers demonstrate superb timing, selecting just the right moments to engage one or several individuals and recognizing those times when a tour around the whole classroom is needed. They seem to have "eyes in the backs of their heads," monitoring the activities of all students while interacting with a few. They can anticipate trouble spots and move quickly to those areas of the classroom where they are most needed.

Teachers can provide one-to-one guidance in many ways. Several specific teacher-child interactions have been found especially useful—asking questions, modeling, and giving warmth and encouragement. Each will be considered below.

A skilled teacher can work with individuals while carefully monitoring play activities in other parts of the classroom.

Asking Questions

Perhaps the most effective play intervention tool is question-asking. Carefully phrased questions have been found to promote problem solving and the acquisition of knowledge (Forman & Kuschner, 1984; Kamii, 1982; Siegel & Saunders, 1979). Questions may enhance language acquisition (Newport, 1976) and have been found to nurture curiosity and exploratory behavior (Bradbard & Endsley, 1983).

The most important message from the question-asking literature is that not all types of questions lead to these positive outcomes. Teachers must phrase questions in such a way that thinking and learning are stimulated. In this section several specific classroom questioning practices are described. Although knowledge of how to phrase questions to facilitate development may be acquired in reading this chapter, it is only through much practice in real classroom settings that teachers can become competent at this inquiry approach (Siegel & Saunders, 1979).

Using Questions Instead of Giving Information

Children frequently approach a teacher for assistance or information. Sometimes a question is a more appropriate response to such bids than merely giving the requested information (Siegel & Saunders, 1979). The following vignette demonstrates this approach:

❖ ❖

Child:	(Holding up a seed pod) What's this thing?
Teacher:	What do you think it might be?
Child:	It's from out in the woods, I think.
Teacher:	How do you know?
Child:	Well, look. It grows on a plant or something. See the seeds? ❖

In this instance the child has done more thinking and has constructed his own understanding of the seed pod—an understanding that is more relevant and will be retained longer than if an adult had just given information to him (Bradbard & Endsley, 1983). When teachers answer questions by posing new ones, they promote self-discovery.

Asking Open-Ended Questions

The following two questions differ in the amount of thinking and language required to answer them:

1. What color is the stone?
2. What can you tell me about this? (holding up the stone)

In question 1 there is a single correct answer. Answering it requires superficial recall and a single word response. Question 2, in contrast, has many answers. Since the child must consider many different possible features of the stone simultaneously and make choices about which to mention, deeper thought processes are required to answer. More language may be used in responding to question 2 (e.g., "It's kind of roughish on this side, but not on the other side."). Answers to question 2 can be followed by further adult questioning and conversation (e.g., "What else can you tell me about it?").

Siegel and Saunders (1979) have argued that teachers should practice asking open-ended questions and should avoid "simple answer" inquiries—"yes/no" questions ("Did you like the story?") and "unison answer" questions (Teacher: "Does a plane go fast or slow?" Children in unison: "Fast!"). Simplistic questions can always be transformed into more useful ones ("What was your favorite part of the story?" or "How is a plane different from a car?"). Overall Siegel and Saunders argue that questions should not become verbal time fillers or methods of checking for comprehension, but tools for creating meaningful, two-way classroom dialogue.

Asking Cognitively Challenging Questions

Certain types of open-ended questions place particular cognitive demands on the listener. Asking these in the classroom can lead directly to students' intellectual growth. Siegel and Saunders (1979) recommend questions that create discrepancies for children; that is, conflicts between what they know and what is observed (e.g., "How can a blade of grass grow up through the sidewalk?") or between two external events (e.g., "Why does such an enormous piece of cork float, when a tiny stone sinks?"). Children attempt to resolve these conflicts and, in so doing, construct a more accurate understanding of the world (Piaget, 1971; Vygotsky, 1962).

Siegel and Saunders (1979) also recommend the use of "distancing" questions, those which require the child to think about objects or events that are not physically observable. If children are asked, "What would happen if we put the water table outside this winter?" they would need to separate their thinking from the immediate physical environment and use images and language to represent experience. Such separation of thought and reality is intellectually useful (Vygotsky, 1962).

Kamii (1982) specifies that teachers should ask questions that "encourage the child . . . to put all kinds of objects, events, and actions into all kinds of relationships" (p. 28). When a teacher asks a question like "How does the shell feel?" the child is required only to describe a physical property that can be directly observed. In contrast, when asked, "How are the two shells alike? How are they different?" the child must put the two objects into a relationship, a process requiring a more advanced form of reasoning.

Examples of other questions that stimulate this higher-level thinking are prediction, quantification, and causation inquiries (Kamii, 1982; Kamii &

DeVries, 1978). Prediction questions encourage children to reflect on future events (e.g., "What will happen when we drop the block into the water?"). In quantification questions, children are asked to make judgments about quantity using their own schemes, which may or may not include actual counting (e.g., "Who has the most raisins? How do you know?"). Causation questions challenge children to construct relationships between actions and consequences ("Why did your block building fall?"). Teachers should be alert for times in children's play when a well-formed question will challenge their thinking in these ways.

Responding to Answers

An important part of the question-asking process is responding to children's answers in ways that encourage them and stimulate their thinking. Three contrasting teachers' responses to children's answers are presented below. In each case the teacher has first asked how many beans are needed to fill twelve cups in a math game if one bean were placed in each cup. The child in each instance has answered, erroneously, ten.

❖ ❖
Vignette 1

Teacher:	No. Let's count together. (Points one at a time to the cups.) One, two . . . twelve. So how many do we need?
Child:	(Thinks a moment) Ten?
Teacher:	No. Twelve. Let's count again.

Vignette 2

Teacher:	Oh! Excellent! That was a terrific guess! So close! Really we need twelve.

Vignette 3

Teacher:	Okay. Why don't you get ten beans and put one in each cup.
Child:	(Counts out ten beans, begins to drop them in the cups; notices that there are not enough) Oh.
Teacher:	What happened?
Child:	Not enough. I'll get more. (Gets another large handful of beans. After placing one in each of the remaining cups, notices that there are many left over.)
Teacher:	That's interesting. Why did that happen?
Child:	There aren't enough cups. I'll put these back. (Puts the rest of the beans back in the container.) ❖

The first teacher is least encouraging in responding to the child's answer. He quickly corrects the child and guides her in a meaningless counting exercise. The interchange offers very little opportunity for thinking or further discussion and may discourage the child from ever attempting to answer another question. But is the teacher in the second vignette any more effective in creating a positive learning situation? She is certainly more positive, praising the child lavishly for a good guess. Still she provides the correct answer at the end of the interaction, giving the child that all-too-common message that right answers come only from adults; children's thinking isn't to be trusted.

The third teacher above turns the activity into a learning experience. He patiently works with the child, asking open-ended questions and providing an opportunity for the child to test his own thinking. Any answer that is meaningful to the child appears to be accepted by the teacher, so long as productive problem-solving has occurred. Generally the teacher of Vignette 3 displays several behaviors critical to the classroom inquiry approach—he allows "incorrect" answers, follows answers with more questions, and provides wait time.

Incorrect answers may be more useful for adult-child dialogue and subsequent cognitive growth than correct ones (Kamii, 1982; Siegel & Saunders, 1979). When teachers simply correct students, they miss opportunities to explore children's reasoning, to provide gentle challenges to misconceptions, or to stimulate intellectual processes. Teachers can follow up on incorrect solutions to problems in nonthreatening and stimulating ways (Siegel & Saunders, 1979). The third teacher above, for example, has created a concrete experience in which the child can observe firsthand the accuracy of his thinking. So, he can rethink an answer on his own without being told by an adult that he is wrong.

One effective way to respond to children's answers is to ask more questions. Through this technique teachers can challenge children to explain or clarify answers given or justify a particular position. Phrases like "Why do you think that?" "How did you figure that out?" or, as in Vignette 3, "Why did that happen?" require children to examine their own reasoning and to rethink a solution to a problem.

In order for children to think in depth about a question, they must be given time to answer. If teachers ask good questions but don't give students this thinking time, very little learning can occur. Research findings suggest that children be given several seconds of "wait time" to think about a question before answering it (Tobin, 1987). It is important to give this time to all students; in one study teachers were shown to give less answering time to less capable children than to their more able peers (Rowe, 1974).

Teachers should also wait several seconds before proceeding after a child has given an answer (Rowe, 1974). Sometimes children will have an afterthought or an additional insight to share that would be cut off by too prompt a teacher comment. Being careful not to cut off children's answers is part of an effective inquiry approach.

Modeling

Lay-Dopyera and Dopyera (1987) describe an incident in which a teacher sniffed and rubbed her eyes, because she had an allergy, while demonstrating a complex task to young children. Later, the children were observed sniffing and rubbing their eyes as they carried out this task, assuming that these behaviors were part of the procedure. This event illustrates how readily children will imitate adult behaviors (Bandura, 1986).

This powerful modeling effect can have negative consequences when children emulate the inappropriate behavior of a disruptive peer or an aggressive television character. Teachers can, however, make effective use of modeling in their play intervention. The process is quite simple: The teacher moves into a play area and models more complex play enactments, more pro-social interaction, or more organized, thought-provoking activity. Children will often imitate these more advanced actions.

If a child is involved in a simple "stacking and knocking down" behavior in the block area, for example, the teacher might sit down nearby and engage in an interesting and elaborate form of building. If children are choosing not to write in their journals at the writing center, a teacher might sit down and model writing by making an entry in an adult journal.

Modeling is more effective under certain conditions. Children are more likely to imitate models who are interacting in natural, real-life settings. This means that a teacher would be more successful modeling kindness by interacting warmly with children in a real play setting than by structuring a whole group puppet show about sharing. Models who are warm and nurturing are more likely to be imitated (Bandura, 1969; Yarrow, Scott, & Waxler, 1973). This suggests that a warm interpersonal style not only promotes a positive classroom climate but also assures that children will emulate their teachers' behaviors.

Children are more likely to imitate salient classroom behaviors than those that are less obvious or noticeable (Bandura, 1969). Teachers should perform behaviors to be imitated, then, in an exaggerated, though always genuine, manner (Forman & Kuschner, 1984).

The following episode reflects an effective modeling approach:

❖ ❖

It is a rainy day, so kindergarten children are unable to go out to the playground during outdoor time. Several students wander around the classroom without clear direction. A teacher brings a blanket to an indoor climber and proceeds to cover it, announcing to herself, "There! My tent is ready."

She goes inside and begins to set toy dishes and other pretend props under the enclosure. "It's almost time for supper," she states to no one in particular.

Her behavior quickly captures the notice of the wandering children. One enters her tent, watches a moment and then sets out dishes as the teacher is doing. "I'll help too, because we can't be late for supper," she exclaims in an adult-like voice. "Come here, Meagann, and help too. Let's say you're the maid."

Meagann now joins the group. The teacher continues her play acting, using gestures and noises to indicate she is now cooking over a fire. The two children imitate these actions, preparing a meal with her.

A third child now enters and all enjoy an imaginary meal, pretending to chew as the teacher is doing. "Meagann, you clean up now!" the first child directs.   ❖

This teacher could have used directive approaches to involve the wandering children. "Find something to do" would be a common adult response in this situation. Instead she models an elaborate and imaginative play theme. Children are quickly drawn into her imaginary world even though she makes no direct effort to involve them. She performs symbolic enactments—pretending with objects, assuming a make-believe role, creating an imaginary situation—and children imitate her. In so doing she has guided children toward more socially and intellectually useful forms of activity.

Warmth

There has been much debate about how affectionate teachers should be with their students (Lay-Dopyera & Dopyera, 1987). Montessori (1964) has argued that teachers can smother children with nurturance. When they hug, praise, or in other ways give attention to children who are deeply absorbed in classroom activities, for example, they may interrupt learning. Teachers are particularly cautious about touching these days because of a small number of highly publicized child-abuse cases in schools and centers that have created anxiety and suspicion among parents.

Most believe, however, that physical warmth is critical in early childhood education. Creating an affective bond between child and teacher may be the most important goal of programs (Honig, 1989). Warm relationships will lead to feelings of security and positive self esteem. From this perspective, teachers should hold and cuddle children. Warmth does not need to involve physical contact, however; some children prefer not to be touched. A friendly smile or well-timed nod of acknowledgement will also convey warmth and kindness.

Research findings indicate that a *moderate* amount of teacher warmth is most beneficial. In one investigation, positive, though not obtrusive, adult-child contact was associated with better peer relationships and greater involvement in classroom activities (Tzelepis, Giblen, & Agronow, 1983). In another, achievement was found to be related to the degree of warmth and enthusiasm exhibited by their preschool through third-grade teachers (Shipman, 1976). Pellegrini (1984), however, found that excessive teacher attention inhibited play.

Lay-Dopyera and Dopyera (1987) conclude from this research that teachers should display warmth but should be cautious not to overwhelm children with their nurturance. They might avoid making physical contact, for example, at inappropriate times (e.g., rubbing the back of a child in deep concentration). Care should be taken not to foster dependence while trying to be nurturing (e.g., carrying children around the classroom). On the other hand, when children need affection (when they are tired, feeling insecure, or simply desire warm physical contact) hugs and touches are extremely important.

Encouragement (Versus Praise)

Praising children seems to be a natural teacher response to positive classroom behavior. Phrases such as, "Very good!" or "I like the way you . . . " are common in classroom dialogue. Can teachers praise too much? Are some forms of praising more effective than others? These questions will be addressed in this section.

The teacher in the following episode uses excessive numbers of reinforcing statements:

A teacher moves over to three children painting at the art table. He looks over one child's shoulder.

Teacher: Oh, Matthew! What a wonderful picture!

Child: It's my father's house.

Teacher: Oh! It's beautiful! And I like the way you're working so quietly here too! (Moves to the next child.) Look at Meagann's painting! Did you all see hers? Simply beautiful! (Leaves the art area.)   ❖

Many teachers believe that praising students in this way will reinforce learning and shape desirable classroom behavior. It seems only logical that when an adult tells children that their behavior is "good" they will continue to behave in this way. Another belief about praise is that it will promote a positive self image. If children are told their classroom work is "excellent" they will, it seems, feel better about themselves.

In a review of research Hitz and Driscoll (1988) have raised serious questions about whether praise actually contributes to children's learning and self-esteem as most teachers have come to believe. They cite findings of numerous studies indicating that frequency of praising and achievement in school are not always related. Praising has, in fact, been associated with lower motivation, less effective problem solving, and dependence on adults (Martin, 1977; Stringer & Hurt, 1981; Green & Lepper, 1981). For some children praise is particularly ineffective (Brophy, 1981).

A warm smile or authentic conversation can be more encouraging than empty praise.

Hitz and Driscoll (1988) also conclude from this review of research that praise can actually threaten self esteem. One explanation of this finding is that praise is judgmental. When two of the three children in the vignette above are praised, but the third is not, the teacher has made an implicit comment about the latter child's work. Even the two receiving the praise have been given the message: "This is just how you should behave; no other way will please me as much." There is evidence that teachers who praise often also use more criticism (Brophy & Good, 1974; Miller, Bugbee, & Hybertson, 1985). Perhaps when teachers attempt to make many positive judgments they fall into a judgmental style, delivering more negative comments as well.

If praising is not appropriate, how does a teacher respond in a supportive way to children's accomplishments? Hitz and Driscoll (1988) recommend that teachers encourage, not praise. Encouragement, they specify, has the following unique features that distinguish this behavior from praise:

1. *Encouragement is specific.* The teacher in the vignette above makes general praising statements ("Simply beautiful!") In encouragement, a teacher makes a specific comment (not necessarily a judgement) about a particular activity: "I see you've chosen to add some yellow to your painting."

2. *Encouragement is delivered privately.* The teacher above publicly praises one child ("Look at Meagann's painting!"), risking embarrassment to the recipient and bad feeling among those not receiving praise. Encouragement is a private, personal interchange: (Quietly: "Matthew, tell me about this character in your painting.")

3. *Encouragement focuses on the process, not finished products.* In the above vignette the teacher evaluates completed projects ("What a wonderful picture!"), giving the message to all that this is how a painting should look when completed. In encouragement the teacher comments on process, without judging final outcomes: "You have been painting a long time. You must be very involved. Tell me about what you are doing."

4. *Encouragement is sincere and natural.* The reader may sense that the teacher's comments in the above example are forced and artificial. He is trying so hard to impart good feeling that he has missed an opportunity to discuss the subject of a child's drawing when it is mentioned ("It's my father's house"). In encouragement the teacher interacts with children naturally, without exaggerated intonation or affect: "Tell me about his house."

5. *Encouragement helps children to appreciate their own accomplishments.* When the teacher above praises children he gives the message that only adults can inform you if you have accomplished something important. Encouragement helps children to value their efforts independent of adult judgement: "You look excited about that painting that you've worked on so long. How do you feel about it now that you've finished?"

6. *Encouragement avoids competition and comparison.* The teacher of the vignette consciously compares Meagann's work to others' ("Did you see hers?"). In encouragement teachers comment on individual activity without comparison: "You have used a lot of red in your painting."

Learning to encourage instead of praise is extremely difficult; praising comes quite naturally to warm and caring people. Teachers can practice reforming less meaningful or empty praising statements into comments or questions that encourage children rather than judge them.

Summary

Teachers must make informed decisions when they interact with children at play. First, they must determine whether a particular play situation is one in which adult intervention would be useful. Sometimes staying away is the best strategy. Once a decision has been made to intervene, teachers have to decide how to enter the play setting and how to leave it without creating undue disturbance. A teacher must also determine what type of intervention to administer—parallel playing, co-playing, or play tutoring.

Regardless of the type selected, teachers must judge how much support to give to children so that direct help is provided for those tasks well beyond children's abilities, hints are given for those just above their mastery level, and no help is offered when children can perform independently.

Once they are playing with children, effective teachers demonstrate a range of play-intervention behaviors that enhance learning and development:

1. giving one-to-one guidance
2. question-asking
3. modeling
4. warmth and encouragement

Teachers can use one or several of these as they interact with children in the classroom. The remainder of this book will focus on how these general intervention guidelines can be applied in the classroom to promote development in specific learning areas.

Suggested Activities

1. Enter the play activities of children in an early childhood classroom. Make these entrances in at least three different areas of the classroom. Play with children for five minutes in each setting, then withdraw. Write an analysis of your entrances and exits, guided by the following questions:

   a. How did children respond to your entrances?
   b. To what degree were you able to enter the play activities already in progress? To what degree did your entrance alter play activities?
   c. How did children respond to your exits? If they protested when you withdrew, how did you handle these situations?
   d. How did children's play change after you exited the setting?
   d. Which were your "smoothest" exits and entrances? Why did these work so well?
   e. Which were your most disruptive exits and entrances? Why did these work less well?

2. Practice two different forms of play intervention—parallel playing and co-playing—with two different groups of young children. Write an analysis of them, guided by the following questions:

    a. How did children respond to your parallel playing? your co-playing?

    b. Compare parallel playing and co-playing. What are the advantages and disadvantages of each?

3. Work with an individual child on a particularly difficult problem (e.g., a math game or puzzle). Practice giving help as Vygotsky has suggested—directly assist on steps that are too difficult for the child, give hints on those just above the child's mastery level, and give no help on those steps the child has already mastered. Write an analysis of this interaction, guided by the following questions:

    a. How successful were you in giving just the right amount of help?

    b. What questions, hints, or other strategies could you have used to guide this child's learning more effectively?

4. Practice play tutoring in a small group of children by entering the dramatic play center and encouraging make-believe. (Model or prompt pretend play with objects or make-believe play situations.) Write an analysis, guided by the following questions:

    a. In what ways did you encourage make-believe?

    b. How did children's make-believe change when you were playing with them?

    c. How did it change after you left the play area?

5. Interact with children for at least a half hour, asking open-ended, cognitively challenging questions. Video or tape record your interactions. Write an analysis of your tape, guided by the following questions:

    a. How successful were you in asking open-ended, cognitively challenging questions? What kinds of responses did these elicit from children? What kinds of thinking were reflected in their answers?

    b. In what ways did you respond to children's answers (ask more questions, show enthusiasm and interest, correct "wrong answers," give simple praise)?

    c. How successful were you in giving children time to answer your questions? What effect do you think this wait time had on children's thinking?

6. Interact with a group of young children for a half hour, encouraging them in their activities but not praising them. Write an analysis of this experience, guided by the following questions:

    a. How successful were you in encouraging rather than praising?

    b. What impact did your encouragements have on children's play activities?

    c. If you caught yourself giving simple praise statements, what impact did these have? How could these have been rephrased to be more encouraging, as defined in the chapter?

Further Reading

Bradbard, M. R., & Endsley, R. C. (1983). How can teachers develop young children's curiosity? In J. F. Brown (Ed.), *Curriculum planning for young children*, pp. 118-130. Washington, DC: National Association for the Education of Young Children.

Garvey, C. (1977). *Play*. Cambridge, MA: Harvard University Press.

Hitz, R., & Driscoll, A. (1988). Praise or encouragement. New insights into praise: Implications for early childhood teachers. *Young Children*, 43(5), pp. 6–13.

Johnson, J. E., Christie, J. F., & Yawkey, T. D. (1987). The role of the adult in children's play. In J. E. Johnson, J. F. Christie, & T. D. Yawkey, *Play and early childhood development*. (pp. 21–43). Glenview, IL: Scott, Foresman and Company.

Lay-Dopyera, M., & Dopyera, J. E. (1987). Strategies for teaching. In C. Seefeldt (Ed.), *The early childhood curriculum: A review of current research* (pp. 13–34). New York: Teachers College Press.

Smilansky, S. (1968). *The effects of sociodramatic play on disadvantaged preschool children*. New York: Wiley.

Smilansky, S., & Shefatya, L. (1990). *Facilitating play: A medium for promoting cognitive, socioemotional, and academic development in young children*. Gaithersburg, MD: Psychosocial & Educational Publications.

CHAPTER
3

FACILITATING SOCIODRAMATIC PLAY

❖ ❖

A five-year-old girl hums to herself as she builds a platform out of large hollow blocks. She is so involved in her work that she does not notice a slightly younger child who is standing nearby watching. After many minutes of building this structure she stands back from her work and says, to no one in particular, "All right. The car's ready to go now."

She suddenly sees her classmate and invites her to play, "Lauren, let's go! The car's ready. You ride in my car too, okay?"

The younger girl, clearly eager to join the play, moves over to the block structure and asks, "Is this a car or a truck? I think it's a truck."

"No, a car," her older playmate responds. "Now I'll be the mother. Hurry, we'll be late! It will never do to be late!" She says this in a particularly serious, adult-like tone.

"It's a truck," the younger girl persists.

At this point the older child puts her hands on her hips and exhales, seemingly exasperated. "Now, honey, you get in here!" she commands, using her adult voice again.

"Okay," her playmate responds, "but it's a truck."

"Yeah, but let's say it's like a car-truck, all right?" the older child offers as a compromise. This seems to satisfy her playmate, who now sits down on the blocks.

"Now I'm the mommy and you're the baby," the older girl directs.

The younger child's predictable response is, "No! I'm not the baby! Let's say we're both mothers and this will be our baby." At this point she retrieves a doll from the nearby dramatic play area. "This is our baby Rachel." She speaks now to the doll, in a gentle, parental tone: "Rachel, you need to lay down and be good in our truck, 'cause we can't drive when you make all that noise."

"It's a car-truck," the older child corrects.

Off they go now in their pretend vehicle. The older girl drives, making gestures in the air to indicate a steering wheel. Her playmate cradles the doll and strokes its hair. At one point she reaches over and switches on a make-believe radio. "We need 98.3 FM," she explains.

The discussion now turns to their destination. "We're going to New York City, okay, sweetie?" the older girl says in her grown-up voice.

"Oh, no," responds her playmate. "It's so crowded there today! Let's go to McDonald's instead."

"Well, we'll go to McDonald's first and get our food. Then we better go to New York to the show."

A teacher has been observing these interactions from a distance. She has chosen not to intervene and now quietly moves away from this play area to join children in another part of the room.   ❖

❖ ❖

Later in the day two four-year-old boys stand at the mirror in the dramatic play center trying on various hats. They do not speak to each other. One child giggles as the other places a firefighter's hat on his head backwards; this is the extent of their interaction, however. Their silent activity goes on for several minutes.

A teacher observes their play. At one point she moves into the center and asks one of the children, who just now has put on a construction worker's hat, "What do you suppose a person does in a hat like that?"

The child wearing the hat says nothing, but his playmate answers quickly, "Oh, it's a working hat. For like working on buildings."

"Is that what you are getting ready to do? Are you a worker getting ready for work?" the teacher asks the child who has not spoken.

"Yeah. We're going to build something." he responds. Now he turns to his playmate: "Let's say we build something."

"I'll be a worker," the other child says, putting on a firefighter's hat. "You be a worker too," he says to the teacher, handing her a baseball cap. She puts on the cap and follows the boys over to a corner of the play area where a toy toolbox and plastic tools are stored.

"We need to get these tools," one child directs, pulling plastic screw drivers, hammers, and a drill from the box. "You have to wear these in your belt." He demonstrates by placing several of the tools into the waist band of his pants. "This is how we carry them."

The children now stand and study their tools. The momentum of the play has slowed. The teacher asks at this point, "So, what are you building today?"

"A house, I think. . . .No, a bigger building, like a tall one," one child answers.

"Yeah, really tall. Like a huge, huge building," the other child says. He gestures to indicate an immense structure, then laughs.

"Where is your construction site—the place where your building is being built?" the teacher inquires.

The children scan the classroom. One of them finally points to the block area, "Here. This is where we work. Come on." Quickly the children stack large hollow blocks into a tower. They then begin to use the tools to drive in make-believe nails and screws, making drilling and pounding noises.

As the children continue to interact with each other, the teacher backs away several steps and watches. Finally she states, "I'm going to take a break now; you keep working." The children do not seem to notice her departure from the play area.   ❖

Perhaps the most significant and enjoyable activity of childhood is sociodramatic play. In this type of play, illustrated in the examples above, children assume the roles of other persons, animals, or even objects, and play out make-believe situations that hold personal meaning. This is the most prevalent form of playful activity in early childhood; when young children are allowed to choose what they will do in the classroom or on the playground, they often spontaneously organize themselves into these role-playing episodes. The examples above show the highly creative, expressive, and social nature of sociodramatic play. Research has demonstrated that this form of playing contributes in many ways to children's development (Johnson, Christie, & Yawkey, 1987).

Young children's sociodramatic play is sometimes highly organized and involves much language, social interaction, and make-believe. In the first vignette above, for example, the two children engage in a highly elaborate play episode, discussing, negotiating, and then pretending. They exhibit many play skills and persist in this complex play theme without adult support. They are learning much about social interaction and are exercising symbolic thinking as they play. The teacher in this vignette wisely withdraws from their play setting, allowing them to interact without adult intrusion. The teacher could do little in this instance to enhance the value of this activity.

Some sociodramatic play is less elaborate. Children who perform highly repetitive, nonsocial, or less imaginative make-believe enactments, as illustrated in the beginning of the second vignette above, may not reap the full benefits of this form of play (Feitelson & Ross, 1973; Rubin, Maioni, & Hornung, 1976; Smith & Dodsworth, 1978; Smilansky, 1968; Johnson, Christie, & Yawkey, 1987). So, the teacher in this vignette has chosen to intervene to encourage greater social interaction and make-believe. She asks several questions which encourage her students to assume make-believe roles and to engage in complex enactments as they pretend. After this intervention the children interact with each other and use more language. They use play objects in highly imaginative ways and persist at a single play theme for many minutes. The vignette illustrates that in some instances teachers can enrich young children's make-believe.

The purpose of this chapter is to provide a rationale for facilitating young children's sociodramatic play. The developmental contributions of this form of play are considered first; guidelines for enriching this activity are then suggested.

The Value of Sociodramatic Play

The value of sociodramatic play has not always been recognized. Montessori (1964) argued that such activity is frivolous and often chaotic; she invented materials that actually discourage children from pretending. Even some modern-day public-school educators do not appear to appreciate the benefits of this activity. In a recent study, fifty percent of kindergarten teachers reported that no time in the day was devoted to this type of playing (Hatch & Freeman, 1988). Yet researchers have provided evidence linking sociodramatic play to many areas of development.

Sociodramatic Play and Cognitive Development

A number of studies have found that children who often engage in make-believe activity, or are encouraged by adults to do so, score higher on IQ tests or other measures of intellectual ability than do other children (Christie, 1983; Johnson, Ershler, & Lawton, 1982; Rubin, Fein, & Vandenberg, 1983). Others have found relationships between this play form and language or language-related abilities like reading (Athey, 1988; McCune-Nicholich & Fenson, 1984; Pellegrini & Galda, 1982).

It is easy to see in the first vignette above how sociodramatic play and cognitive development are related. The two girls engage in much high-level thinking as they plan and later embark upon a make-believe trip. They must use much language to negotiate the pretend elements of their play. They announce verbally what various play objects represent ("The car is ready!") or what will happen next on their make-believe journey ("We're going to New York City, okay, sweetie?"). They also use language to define make-believe roles ("Now I'm the mommy and you're the baby."). Without language, children would have a very hard time agreeing upon a shared meaning for the many symbols and pretend situations that make up this form of play (Garvey, 1977).

In sociodramatic play, children try out adult-like phrases and intonations as they enact their make-believe roles ("Now, honey, you get in here!"). Much representational thought is required, as objects are used to stand for things that are not actually present (e.g., using blocks to represent a car). Overall, the sociodramatic play setting is a safe and noncritical arena for exercising mental skills.

Sociodramatic Play and Social Development

Sociodramatic play also has been found to foster social competence and positive peer relations (Curry & Bergen, 1988; Connolly & Doyle, 1984). The interactions of the two children in the first vignette demonstrate why. This form of play often involves much negotiation. These playmates must agree about whether the vehicle is a car or a truck, what roles they will each play, and where they will go on their trip. They must persuade each another ("Let's go to New York City, okay, sweetie?"), explain their points of view ("It's so crowded there today. Let's go to McDonald's instead"), and compromise ("Lets say it's like a car-truck, all right?"). Children practice perspective-taking when they assume the roles of other people (Fein, 1984). This ability to put oneself in another's shoes is fundamental for positive peer relations.

Sociodramatic Play and Emotional Development

The contributions of symbolic play to emotional development and mental health have been described (Axeline, 1969; Schaefer & O'Conner, 1983; Trawick-Smith, 1989). Play is a vehicle for the expression and mastery of fears or concerns. The vignette below demonstrates how children re-enact in their play troublesome events in their lives:

Two six-year-old girls are playing in the dramatic-play area. They are busy setting a table with toy dishes.

Child A:	Now we have to set up for the party because Catwoman is coming over. Okay, Cheryl?
Child B:	Okay.
Child A:	So, let's set it up. It takes two to decorate. So let's get to work.
Child B:	(In a concerned tone) Oh, oh.
Child A:	What?
Child B:	Daddy's drunk again. I'll have to call the police.
Child A:	(Looks baffled) What?
Child B:	(Pretends to dial on a toy telephone. Whispers something inaudible into the receiver.) ❖

Child B above appears to be playing out family-related anxieties. Axeline (1969) has described how re-enacting such worries in a dramatic-play setting allows children to bring these to the surface and gain mastery over them. Stress is often reduced as children "play out" difficult experiences (Hyson, 1986; Trawick-Smith & Thompson, 1986).

Providing opportunities for rich sociodramatic play experiences will contribute, then, to children's development in numerous ways. For many children, providing space, props, and time for open-ended free play is sufficient to stimulate ongoing and highly organized make-believe. Some children, however, need adult support to initiate and maintain this form of playing (Smilansky & Shefatya, 1990; Johnson, Christie, & Yawkey, 1987).

The Role of the Adult in Sociodramatic Play

Sociodramatic play is a purely child-centered activity; children often re-enact their own personal feelings, experiences, and ideas as they pretend. Teacher interventions that interrupt ongoing play themes or redirect children's activities toward adult-selected purposes may destroy the personal and spontaneous qualities of make-believe. Some argue that adult-directed play may no longer be considered true play (Rubin, Fein, & Vandenberg, 1983).

Before the 1960s, child specialists advocated a strictly "hands off" policy in regard to adult intervention in children's play (Johnson, Christie, & Yawkey, 1987). It was argued that if children were allowed to play undisturbed they would resolve inner crises and master anxieties; adult involvement in these processes would only inhibit self-expression (Freud, 1961; Erikson, 1950).

Views on the adult's role in sociodramatic play have changed radically, however, since the publication (1968) of Sara Smilansky's now-classic study of low-income immigrant children in Israel. In this study she made extensive observations of children's play activities and conducted an experiment to see if adults could facilitate more frequent and complex sociodramatic play among these children. Four key ideas from her work have sparked great interest in adult play intervention:

1. Sociodramatic play is related to social and cognitive development and school success.

2. Not all children engage in sociodramatic play; some who do, perform play enactments which are less social, imaginative, verbal, or organized.

3. Absence of sociodramatic play abilities among children of low socioeconomic status may explain their academic difficulties in later childhood.

4. Adult intervention can increase the quantity and quality of sociodramatic play and enhance overall cognitive development.

Later studies have supported Smilansky's findings that sociodramatic play intervention leads to developmental gains (Christie, 1983; Smith, Dalgleish, & Herzmark, 1981).

Smilansky's Play-Intervention Program

Smilansky's overall approach to enriching young children's sociodramatic play has been used widely and with great success in preschool, childcare, and public-school programs (Smilansky & Shefatya, 1990). Her play-intervention strategy involves several steps; examples of each are presented in Table 3-1.

First, children are provided with rich experiences (such as field trips or stories) which they might later play out in the dramatic play center. This is an important step, she has argued, because sociodramatic play usually involves the re-enactment of previously acquired experiences; children who lack an experiential base may not be able to pretend.

Next, a special play area equipped with props related to these field trips or experiences is created in the classroom. After a trip to the grocery, for example, a make-believe store with empty cans and boxes, plastic produce, and a

Table 3-1
Steps in Smilansky's Play-Intervention Program

Step	Example
1. Provide experiences for children to play out.	A teacher takes children on a field trip to a local pediatrician's office.
2. Present props in the dramatic play area which relate to those experiences.	A make-believe doctor's office, which includes medical instruments, a cot to resemble an examining table, and a waiting area are created in the dramatic-play area.
3. Observe children's play; note children who don't pretend or need adult assistance in their play.	A teacher notices that one child only watches others play in the "doctor's office." She does not engage in make-believe.
4. Intervene in children's activities to encourage sociodramatic play or to enhance play abilities.	A teacher pretends to be a patient who has a cough and asks a child who only watches to listen to his lungs with a stethoscope. Once this child begins to pretend with other children the teacher withdraws.

Source: Adapted from Smilansky (1968)

cash register might be provided. Literacy props (e.g., pens and paper for making grocery lists, stickers for pricing make-believe produce) can be included. Props should be arranged within spacious play areas to allow maximum social involvement; play themes become more elaborate if more than two children are able to participate. Richer dramatic-play episodes result when space is enclosed on several sides by shelves or partitions (Moore, 1986). Although realistic dramatic-play equipment related to classroom themes should be provided, incorporation of a small number of nonrealistic raw materials (e.g., cardboard boxes, pipe cleaners, or blocks) can enhance (Trawick-Smith, 1990). Ideas for creating rich dramatic-play environments are provided in textbooks listed in the Appendix of Chapter 1 and in other resource materials (Frost & Klein, 1979; Johnson, Christie, & Yawkey, 1987; Weinstein & David, 1987).

The third step in Smilansky's program involves observation of children's play and identification of individuals who show play deficits. This is a controversial part of her strategy. Some teachers reject the notion that children can be deficient in their play; they believe that all playful activity is equally beneficial. Smilansky, herself, has urged respect for and acceptance of diversity in play styles. However, her research has shown that some critical components of sociodramatic play—components that are significant to children's development—are missing from the play of many children she has observed. Some do not interact with peers, for example; others rarely assume the roles of make-believe characters. Some children are unable to transform real objects or events into pretend ones. Others quickly switch from one role to another without developing elaborate themes or enactments. These children are then targeted for teacher intervention in Smilansky's program.

In the final step, teachers play with children and enhance these observed play deficits. In one instance a teacher might facilitate social interaction (e.g., "Jessica, would you like to join us for lunch at our restaurant?"). In another, a child might be encouraged to assume a make-believe role (e.g., "Susan, our patient needs surgery. Would you like to be the anesthesiologist?"). After a brief intervention the teacher withdraws from the play, allowing children to continue undisturbed.

Cautions and Guidelines

Teachers should use caution when applying this final step of Smilansky's program. Excessive or highly obtrusive interventions can interfere with play development (Bruner, 1980; Johnson, Christie, & Yawkey, 1987). Smilansky and Shefatya (1990) provide guidelines for giving just the right kind and amount of support for children's sociodramatic play:

1. Teachers should intervene in sociodramatic play only if children need support; much of the time children will enjoy rich benefits from this activity without adult assistance.
2. Teachers should not force themselves upon children as they play; they should honor their students' wishes to be left alone.
3. Teachers should intervene in ways that preserve children's own play themes; interventions that significantly interfere with activities in progress are inappropriate.
4. Teachers should intervene for a short while to enhance one or more play skills, then withdraw. The goal is to enrich self-directed play, not provide continuous adult-guided make-believe.

Teacher Behaviors That Facilitate Sociodramatic Play

Several tools for sociodramatic play intervention are question-asking, prompting, modeling, and providing props. Examples of each are presented in Table 3-2.

In question-asking a teacher first observes play and then inquires about children's activities in ways that facilitate verbal interaction, make-believe, or play complexity (e.g., "Why is your baby crying?" or "Where are we going on our trip?").

Prompting is a strategy in which the teacher gives direct suggestions or hints. Teachers can prompt children to use objects in make-believe ways, to persist at play themes, or even to include a new playmate in their activities (e.g., "Let's say this is our spoon," or "Let's have Dana be the older sister.").

Table 3-2
Sociodramatic Play-Intervention Techniques

Technique	Example
1. Question-asking	Two children pretend to be parents getting ready for work. A teacher asks: "Who cares for your babies while you are at work?" An elaborate discussion about child care ensues.
2. Prompting	A teacher plays with three children in a make-believe house. Two are very active, the third is not as involved. A teacher says, "Jeremy, why don't you come over and have some dinner with us? It's spaghetti!"
3. Modeling	A teacher plays with three children who pretend to care for imaginary pets. The teacher makes a gesture to indicate he is walking a dog on a leash: "My dog is on a leash. See? Now I can take her for a walk." The three children copy the teacher; each holds a make-believe leash.
4. Providing props	Two children are pretending to build with plastic tools. They notice that there are no pretend saws. A teacher hands them two long blocks and says, "Here are saws if you need them."

Source: Adapted from Smilansky (1968)

In modeling, teachers actually perform those play behaviors they want children to enact. Through this strategy teachers can demonstrate how to play a pretend character (e.g., "Welcome to our restaurant. Can I take your order, please?"), or how to create make-believe situations (e.g., "Oh, dear. My baby is ill. I'll need to call the doctor.").

One way teachers can enhance sociodramatic play is to provide theme-relevant props as children need them. When students initiate a hospital-related play theme, for example, teachers might introduce several medical props—syringes, stethoscopes, or gauze—for them to use. If children are pretending to cook dinner, the teacher might provide toy cooking utensils or even sticks to represent them. It is important for teachers to prepare rich and exciting environments before children begin to play. However, they must be vigilant for occasions after play has begun when the introduction of new play props would enhance play activities.

Sociodramatic Play Skills

Smilansky has identified several sociodramatic play skills that are significant to children's development—make-believe, social interaction, verbalization, and play persistence. Several other important play behaviors have been identified in later research—thematic-fantasy enactment and literacy play (Salz & Johnson, 1974; Christie, 1991). As teachers play with children they can enhance one or more of these; guidelines for facilitating each are provided below.

Verbalization

One reason sociodramatic play is so valuable is that it allows children to experiment with language. When they use make-believe voices to enact their characters or talk about play from outside their pretend world, children are learning about the sounds and structure of speech (Athey, 1988). As they verbalize in their play they come to discover the social uses of language and its power in influencing other people or resolving conflicts (Garvey, 1977; Rubin, 1980; Trawick-Smith, 1991). Some children use a lot of language while they play; others do not (Smilansky & Shefatya, 1990). Teachers can intervene to increase the verbal interactions of their students. Even children who talk often as they play can be assisted in learning advanced forms of language through adult intervention (Pellegrini, 1986; Sachs, 1980).

There are several types of important and unique verbal behaviors that are common in sociodramatic play. Pellegrini (1986) has observed that children frequently engage in *explicit language* as they pretend. This language conveys information to listeners with minimal reliance on concrete visual cues or gestures. When children refer to a tornado or a fire hose which is not actually present, or to a character who does not exist in reality, they are engaging in this important form of speech. This is challenging language; when using it children must describe with words things which are not present. This ability is related to success in many school-related areas including reading and writing (Pellegrini, 1986). Teachers can encourage this form of language by asking children to describe verbally their enactments. In the vignette below a teacher uses open-ended questions to promote explicit language.

❖ ❖

A six-year-old child is pretending to put a doll to bed in the dramatic-play area. A teacher approaches.

Teacher:	Why is your baby crying?
Child:	Oh, she's sick. She's been throwing up. She's got a horrible fever.
Teacher:	Oh, dear. How do you know she has a fever?

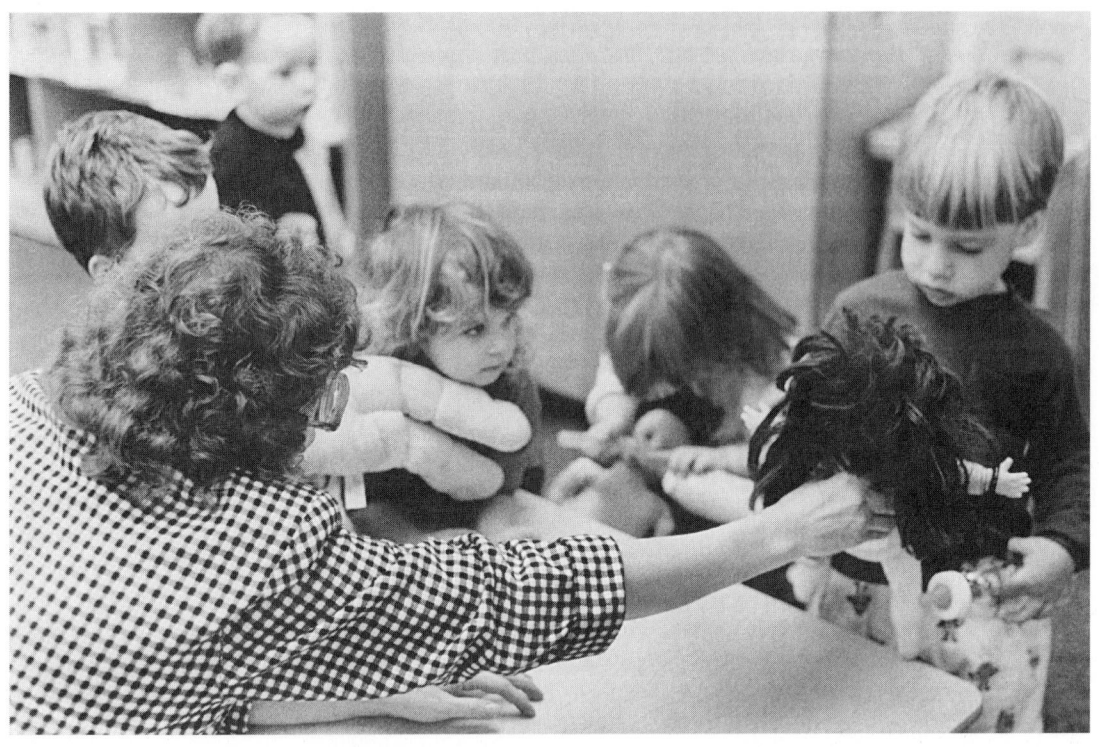

"Why is your baby crying?" Teachers can enhance verbal communication through question-asking.

Child:	Well, when you put your hand up to her forehead like this it feels all hot. (Demonstrates feeling the doll's forehead)
Teacher:	How did she get so sick?
Child:	Well, she went out onto the playground, you know? And she didn't have her jacket. And she got sick.
Teacher:	What will you do?
Child:	I'll call the doctor. (Makes gestures as though dialing an imaginary phone)
Teacher:	What is your doctor like?
Child:	Oh, he's very old.
Teacher:	Oh? What does he look like?
Child:	Well, he wears one of those white coats. And he has a white beard.
Teacher:	Oh. Well, what did the doctor say?
Child:	There's some medicine for the baby. We need to go to the doctor's office.

The child goes off to the "doctor's office"; the teacher quietly withdraws from the play area.   ❖

Through open-ended question-asking, the teacher of this vignette encourages the child to talk about things which are not physically present. The child uses many third-person pronouns and present, past, and future tense verbs—all prevalent features of explicit language. The child is particularly challenged by these questions; she is required to describe incidents and objects without the use of physical cues. This same language is required when children are asked in school to answer questions about stories they have read, to share their written work, or to describe experiences during "circle time."

Another language feature of sociodramatic play is *register-switching*, in which children shift from one style of language to another as they step in and out of their roles. Children might assume formal, adult-like styles when in character, then return to their own language styles when they are negotiating with a peer outside the play episode. Switching from one style of language to another is an important skill; in school, children must change registers frequently as they go from one context to another (Lindfors, 1987). They may use one style when talking with peers, another when giving an oral report, still another when reading aloud.

Teachers can enhance children's style-switching in sociodramatic play by encouraging them to speak within character and to change their intonation and language complexity as they do. One way to accomplish this is to model the use of voices, as demonstrated in the vignette below.

❖ ❖

Several five-year-olds are playing "house" in the dramatic-play area. They are all "parents" who are caring for their "babies"—several dolls. A teacher plays along with them.

Teacher:	(Talks to a doll he is holding, uses a parental tone) Now, honey, we need to make you some supper. I'm sure you are very hungry. (Makes gestures to show the doll is talking back to him, uses a high pitched "baby" voice) I don't want to eat now. I want to play. I'm not hungry.
Child A:	(Addresses the teacher's doll, uses an adult-like voice) No. You have to eat your supper. You will get sick if you don't eat a lot.
Teacher:	(Uses a parental voice again, addresses the child) What about your daughter? Is she hungry? Why don't you ask her?
Child A:	(Talks to her doll) Are you very hungry too, sweetie? (Now uses a high-pitched, child-like voice to answer) No! We're playing! We won't eat our supper! (Now addresses Child B) Suzanne, we're pretending our babies won't eat their supper, okay?
Child B:	Okay. My baby won't either.
Child A:	(Using an exasperated adult tone, addresses Child B) I don't know what to do with these babies. We need to get them to eat.
Child B:	(Responds to Child A) I don't know. Maybe no television today if they don't behave.

Other children join the play and also converse with their dolls in varied tones of voice. The teacher withdraws after a few minutes.   ❖

Through modeling, the teacher of this vignette has encouraged children to experiment with language registers. These students emulate the teacher's voices as they play and alternate among several registers—those of a parent talking to a baby, a parent talking to another parent, a baby talking to a parent, and a real-life child negotiating with another outside the context. Each register has distinct syntactical and phonological features.

Another aspect of language that is practiced in sociodramatic play is social discourse—interpersonal speech, which is used to influence peers, resolve conflicts, or articulate ideas. Garvey (1977) has shown that children spend a good bit of their playtime talking to one another—negotiating play themes, assigning roles, deciding who can play, or planning situations. As they interact they come to discover the power of language in establishing and maintaining positive peer relations. The role of language in making friends and gaining peer acceptance will be described in detail in the next chapter. An implication of these ideas for sociodramatic play intervention is that teachers should facilitate child-to-child dialogue as much as possible. The goal of language intervention in the dramatic play area should not be just to encourage children to talk, then, but to talk to one another. In the vignette below, the teacher facilitates child-to-child conversation.

❖ ❖

Two four-year-olds play parallel to one another in the dramatic play area. They play out their roles in detail, washing dishes, talking on the telephone, and dressing dolls. They rarely speak to one another, though, and do not coordinate their activities. A teacher enters the area.

Teacher:	(To child A) You have a lot of dishes to wash. This is hard work!
Child A:	Yeah. We just ate the dinner and I'm washing the kitchen.
Teacher:	Do you need any help? Maybe Jamal would help you.
Child A:	Yeah. Jamal can help.
Teacher:	You could ask him.
Child A:	Jamal, come on and wash the dishes. You have to help me 'cause there's too many.
Child B:	(Talking on the pretend telephone. Doesn't hear Child A's request, looks confused) What?
Child A:	Come on, Jamal.
Teacher:	He didn't hear you. You should ask him again. He's listening now.
Child A:	Jamal, come wash our dishes. We need to clean the kitchen.
Child B:	(In an annoyed tone) No!
Teacher:	(To Jamal) Why don't you tell Rebecca why you can't help. It looks like you're busy.

Child B: Yeah, Rebecca. I have to talk on the phone right now.

Teacher: (To Child A) Maybe he could help when he's done on the phone.

Child B eventually finishes his call and joins Child A. The two children begin to wash dishes together. The teacher withdraws.   ❖

In this vignette the teacher encourages child-to-child discourse. He prompts several verbal behaviors which are crucial to peer relations. He assists Child A in getting the attention of a peer and in making a friendly request. He encourages Child B to describe reasons for rejecting this request. Such behaviors are crucial for establishing positive peer relations (Dodge, 1983).

Social Interaction

Children play by themselves in very useful and enjoyable ways. It is not uncommon to see a single student playing "mother" or "father" to a group of dolls in the dramatic-play area or pretending with toy figures in the block center. Opportunities to play alone are particularly important in modern family life where children are in childcare with many peers for long hours. Isolate play may allow children to take a break from social stimulation. Playing alone may even contribute to intellectual development (Rubin, 1982a). It is important that teachers respect children's needs for isolate play.

Smilansky (1968) has argued, however, that some children never engage with peers and that this total absence of social interaction may deprive them of especially meaningful play experience. More recent research has confirmed that those who rarely engage in social pretend play may be at risk (Howes, Unger, & Beizer-Seidner, 1989; Rubin, 1988; Rubin, Fein, & Vandenberg, 1983). Children who engage in a great deal of solitary dramatic play are more likely to be disliked by peers and to have social skills deficits (Rubin, 1982b). Nonsocial pretenders are also less competent at perspective-taking and problem-solving (Rubin, 1985). These studies indicate that facilitating some social interaction in dramatic play is an important goal for teachers to pursue.

One way teachers can enhance their students' social interaction is simply by playing with them in open-ended ways. Adults are attractive playmates; children flock around enthusiastic and playful teachers when they enter the dramatic play area. Children who do not normally interact with one another may play together when a teacher plays along. A child who is often ignored or rejected by peers might now be included, a shy child might more readily enter a play situation with adult encouragement. The vignette below shows the impact on social interaction of a teacher's entry into the dramatic play center.

❖ ❖

A child sits alone in the dramatic-play center dressing and undressing a doll. She doesn't look at or interact with several other children who play near her. The teacher intervenes to promote social interaction.

Teacher:	Is your baby hungry? We could make her some dinner.
Child A:	(Says nothing, continues dressing the doll)
Teacher:	If she's hungry, let me know. We could make her a big meal at the kitchen. (Moves over to the kitchen and begins to pull out pans and dishes, plays parallel to Child A)
Child A:	(Moves over to the teacher) My baby is hungry.
Teacher:	Okay. Let's see. What should we make her?
Child A:	Baby food.
Child B:	(Moving over to the teacher) Here, I'll make the food.
Teacher:	Why don't you and Celeste work together? I'll rock the baby. (Rocks the doll)
Child C:	Can I play?
Child B:	No. We're making the supper, right, Celeste?
Child A:	(Nods, says nothing)
Teacher:	Why don't you cut vegetables, Sara?
Child C:	Okay. Celeste, can I have a knife?
Child A:	I'm using it. (Hands Child C another plastic knife) Here.
Child B:	What's your baby named, Celeste?
Child A:	Lawanda.
Child B:	Okay, Lawanda, your supper's ready.

All three children and the teacher sit down to eat. Children B and C direct questions and conversation to both the teacher and Child A. Child A nods or gives single-word responses. After a few minutes the teacher leaves the table. Child A sits with her peers for many minutes until cleanup time.   ❖

This vignette shows that sometimes all that is needed to promote social interaction is the presence of a warm and friendly adult. Two socially active children play with an isolate peer whom they had previously ignored, because a teacher is playing along. The children continue these interactions after the teacher has left the play area.

Sometimes a teacher needs to facilitate children's social pretend play more directly. In the following vignette a teacher assists a withdrawn child in entering a play setting and then actively orchestrates positive social interactions among the players.

❖ ❖

Two five-year-old children are playing "haunted house" in the dramatic-play center. Another child circles around them, watching their activities. He shows interest in their play, but his peers largely ignore him. A teacher enters the area.

| Teacher: | (To the two children who are actively involved) I see you've made a haunted house. Very spooky. |

Child A:	Yeah. I'm the guy who takes the tickets. These are the ghosts and they're real.
Child B:	Yeah. The ghosts are real. Not like pretend. They're real and they can eat you.
Teacher:	Oh, my. Well, I'd like a ticket to go through.
Child B:	It's real scary. But let's say the ghosts can't really eat you 'cause it's just pretend.
Teacher:	It's scary going through alone. Let me see if Lucy will go through with me. (To Child C, who is watching) Lucy, would you like to go through this haunted house?
Child C:	(Says nothing)
Teacher:	I really don't want to go through this spook house alone. Want to join me?
Child C:	(Nods "yes," moves over to the teacher)
Teacher:	Okay. Lucy and I are going through, all right, guys?
Child A:	Okay, Lucy. You come through too.
Teacher:	Do we buy our tickets here?
Child A:	Yep. That will be one dollar forty-four. (To Child C) Lucy, you pay me your money, okay?
Child C:	(Does not respond)
Teacher:	I'll buy my ticket. Why don't you pay Dennis for your ticket too, Lucy.
Child C:	(Quietly) Okay. (Pretends to pay Child A)
Teacher:	Okay, let's go through.

They begin to walk through a maze of large cardboard boxes. As they do, "ghosts" jump out with loud "boos." At one point Child C laughs. Later she says "boo" back to a ghost in a quiet way.

Teacher:	Oh, oh, Lucy. You sound like a ghost too. Are you one of the ghosts?
Child C:	Yeah. I scared you.
Teacher:	Yes. You did. You could pretend to be a ghost with Dennis and Christopher. You could hide like they do. Then I'll come through the spook house again.
Child A:	Okay. Lucy, you can be one of the ghosts. You come over here. (Points to a place behind one of the boxes) Now, you need to hide till the teacher comes through. Then you have to be very scary.
Child C:	Okay. (Joins the boys in their hiding places)
Child A:	Now be really quiet till she comes. Do you want to be a ghost or a witch?
Child C:	(Says nothing)

Child A: You be a witch. Hide down now, she's coming.

Child C: Okay. (Hides behind a box)

As the teacher walks through, all three children make spooky noises and jump out from behind boxes. Child C is an active, though quiet participant. The teacher goes through the spook house one last time, then excuses himself. The children continue to interact without him; Child C is included in the on-going play.   ❖

The teacher above has directly facilitated social interaction between an isolate child and her more social peers. He has modeled an effective play-entry strategy and has drawn her into the play with him. Later, he encourages her to join more fully in the play and prompts her peers to accept her. After he leaves the play setting they continue to interact without him.

Social interaction can be promoted across all areas of the curriculum. A full discussion of strategies for nurturing positive peer relations is provided in the next chapter.

In sociodramatic play children often transform the real into the imaginary. They use objects to stand for things which are not actually present (e.g., a doll used as a real baby). They transform themselves into characters ("I'll be a doctor, you be the patient."). Frequently children will use verbal descriptions to create pretend situations and to transform the real world into an imaginary one ("Let's say a hurricane is coming. We need to get in the cellar."). Because make-believe involves symbolic thought, creativity, and open-ended emotional expression, many feel that it is the most important dimension of sociodramatic play (Rubin, Fein, & Vandenberg, 1983; Simon & Smith, 1985). Teachers can structure the classroom environment and interact with children in ways that encourage them to pretend. Through focused interventions teachers can encourage the three types of which Smilansky has identified—in regard to objects, roles, and situations.

Make-Believe (Objects)

Using one object to represent another which is not actually present is a fundamental form of make-believe. When a child uses a toy telephone to stand for a real one or manipulates a long block as if it were a broom, complex and developmentally useful symbolizing occurs. The child uses the object as a "signifier" to stand for the missing object, very much as a writer uses printed words to describe the real world (Trawick-Smith, 1990). Encouraging children to transform objects in make-believe ways may promote the same kind of thinking required for language and literacy (Pellegrini, 1980).

Children vary greatly in their ability to transform objects. Some never do use objects to pretend (Trawick-Smith, 1990). Others perform only very simple pretenses in which one or a few realistic toys are used in their conventional ways as if they were real (e.g., drinking from a toy cup as if it were filled with liquid). Children who do not perform these simple pretenses can be encouraged to do so through play intervention. A teacher might at a critical moment provide a realistic prop that relates to a play theme in progress. If children are pretending to prepare for a dinner party but are using few objects in their play, for example, a teacher might produce a toy plastic telephone and encourage them to call and invite guests.

Very young children often use only one object for pretend. With development, children begin to incorporate several toys into their enactments (Rosenblatt, 1977; Watson & Jackowitz, 1984). Coordinating more than one object in a make-believe theme is quite difficult and developmentally useful; teachers can assist children in learning to do this. In the vignette below a teacher supports multi-toy make-believe.

❖ ❖

A four-year-old plays by herself in the dramatic play area. Her enactments are quite repetitive—she places a pan on the burner of the play stove, makes "sizzling" noises, then removes the pan. She repeats these steps many times. A teacher watches for a while, then intervenes.

Teacher:	(Sniffs) M-m-m-m! Smells good.
Child:	(Continues "cooking") Yeah.
Teacher:	Is this your dinner?
Child:	Yeah. It's macaroni and cheese. I'm cooking it.
Teacher:	(Retrieves a spoon from the toy sink) Will you need a spoon to stir the macaroni? I have a spoon here, if you need one.
Child:	Okay. (Takes the spoon, makes stirring gestures)
Teacher:	There are other spoons here. Also a fork. (Shows the child plastic utensils)
Child:	Oh. A fork, I think. (Takes a fork and now stirs with both the spoon and fork) It's hot.
Teacher:	Do you need salt or any spices?
Child:	What?
Teacher:	There is salt on the table. Also, some spices. If you want spicy macaroni.
Child:	Oh, yes. Some salt and pepper. (Takes empty spice jars and shakes make-believe spices into her pan)

The teacher now steps back and observes the child incorporate various objects into her play. After a few minutes she withdraws from the play area. ❖

The teacher of this vignette facilitates object play by suggesting the integration of several toys into a cooking theme. This intervention increases the complexity and make-believe quality of the activity as a whole. The child continues to play in this more elaborate way even after the teacher withdraws.

The most symbolic form of make-believe is when children use nonrealistic objects to represent things that are completely different (e.g., a wooden rod used as a broom) (Elder & Pedersen, 1978). Such abstract transformations require that children take greater "symbolic leaps" between the real world and an imagined one (Johnson, Christie, & Yawkey, 1987). In such transformations children must imagine the existence of certain features of objects (e.g., bristles at one end of the wooden rod) while ignoring others (e.g., that the rod is shorter and thinner than a real broom). When such transformations are performed with peers much language is necessary, as one child must describe for another what the object represents. Once children demonstrate frequent object pretense and begin to incorporate more objects into their play, teachers can encourage these abstract transformations. The vignette below illustrates one approach a teacher might use.

❖ ❖

Three five-year-olds are pretending to be firefighters. They wear fire hats and run around the play area making siren noises. A teacher watches this activity and finally intervenes.

Teacher:	Is there a fire?
Child A:	Yeah. We're putting it out.
Child B:	(Speaks at the same time as Child A) We're going to the fire!
Teacher:	What's burning?
Child A:	Oh. Somebody's house burned up.
Child C:	Let's put out the fire. (Makes more siren noises)
Teacher:	Where is the burning building?
Child B:	(Looks around the room) Here. It's burning here. (Points to a wall which borders the dramatic play area)
Teacher:	Is it a pretty bad fire?
Child B:	Oh, yes. It's all burned up.
Child C:	Well, it's burning. We need to stop it.
Teacher:	What will you use to put out the fire?
Child B:	Hoses. We need our hoses. (Looks puzzled, turns to his peers) Hey. We don't have hoses.
Teacher:	(Presents two short wooden rods) Could you use these as hoses?
Child A:	Yeah. Let me see. (Takes one of the rods and makes spraying noises) See?
Child C:	(Takes the other rod, walks to the "burning building," pretends to spray the make-believe fire) There. Put it out!

The three children take turns using the "hoses." The teacher disengages from the play theme as the children become more involved.   ❖

This teacher presents several nonrealistic objects and encourages children to incorporate them in their play. Providing these nonrealistic props creates opportunities for the children to make symbolic leaps and, generally, fosters more organized play.

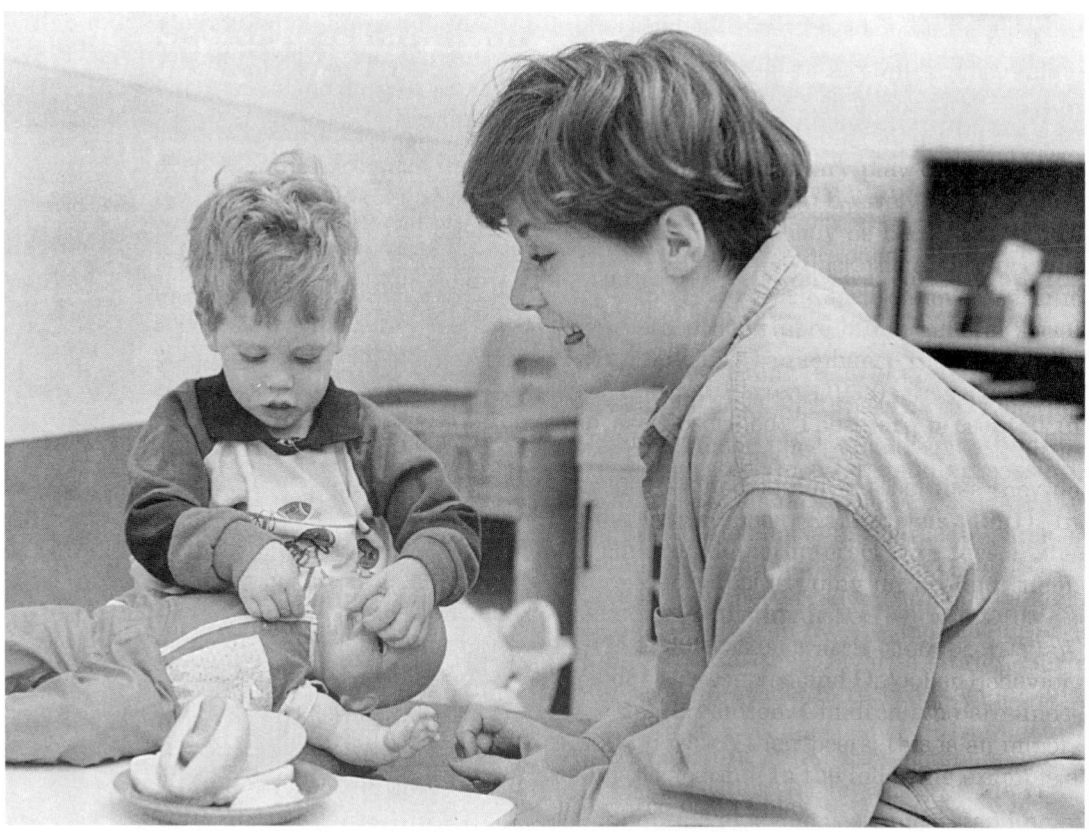

Teachers may need to assist some children in learning to play roles.

Make-Believe (Roles)

Children also transform themselves with imaginative roles in their sociodramatic play. They pretend to be powerful or significant adults, television characters, even animals or objects. Sometimes they will play themselves, but in highly imaginative contexts (e.g., playing oneself in the middle of an earthquake). Not all children will enact make-believe characters. Smilansky and Shefatya (1990) have suggested that adults may need to assist some children in learning to play roles.

Younger preschoolers engage in simple role enactments in which they play themselves performing certain routine behaviors (e.g., drinking from a cup, talking on the telephone). Even toddlers will pretend to sleep under a blanket or eat with toy dishes. This has been referred to as "self-as-agent" play (Watson & Jackowitz, 1984). As children get older they more often transform themselves into completely different imaginative characters. Older preschoolers also engage in more "other-as-agent" play, in which another make-believe person or even a doll becomes the agent of pretending. Rather than drinking from a toy cup themselves during this kind of play, for example, children have a doll, a stuffed animal, or even a playmate do the drinking (Watson & Jackowitz, 1984).

In the vignette below, a teacher assists children in enacting imaginative roles and in performing other-as-agent play.

Two six-year-olds are playing in a pretend hospital which has been set up in the dramatic-play area. They are giving dolls injections with plastic syringes. They do not interact with each other and show signs of losing interest in the play theme. A teacher intervenes.

Teacher:	I see you're giving shots.
Child A:	Yeah. (Points to the dolls) They're sick.
Teacher:	What kind of illness do they have?
Child B:	They have the flu very bad.
Child A:	And they need to have tubes in their ears.
Teacher:	Oh. Will they need to go into the hospital?
Child A:	This *is* the hospital. They're in the hospital right now.
Teacher:	Are you doctors?
Child B:	I'm a doctor.
Child A:	Let's say we're both the doctors. We don't have nurses.
Teacher:	Maybe he could be a nurse. (Holds up a doll) He could help you give injections and get the patients ready for surgery.
Child A:	(Hesitates) All right. (Pretends that the doll is holding the syringe, giving an injection. Uses a different voice to indicate the doll is talking) There you go. That didn't hurt.
Teacher:	Which of you is the surgeon? That's the person who performs the surgery, puts the ear tubes in.
Child B:	I know. I'll be the surgeon.
Child A:	(In a whiny tone) No, Brian.
Teacher:	(To Child A) You could be the anesthesiologist. That is a very important job. That's the doctor who makes the patient unconscious for the surgery.
Child B:	Yeah. I had that. He put a mask over me. (Demonstrates)
Child A:	Is that like a doctor?
Teacher:	Oh, yes. An anesthesiologist is a doctor.
Child A:	Okay.

The teacher plays with the children several more minutes, helping them to set up a surgery room. Then, as children begin to play out this hospital theme, he withdraws.   ❖

Here the teacher has encouraged children to clarify their make-believe roles and to take on more elaborate ones. He has also encouraged other-as-agent play by suggesting that a doll become a nurse who administers injections. After these interventions children stay within these new roles for a long period of time and engage in more elaborate enactments.

One goal in enhancing role playing is to encourage play diversity. Children often enact the same role time and again. Regularly pretending to be a particular significant adult may meet important emotional needs; assigning children new roles in a directive way is not appropriate. Some children, however, may enact only one or several roles because of limited play experience or an inability to invent new characters (Trawick-Smith, 1987). Occasionally children are limited in their role choices by a preoccupation with their favorite television shows (Carlsson-Paige & Levin, 1987). Children may be observed playing only popular superheroes on the playground or in the dramatic play area (a full discussion of this problem is provided later in this chapter). When teachers observe this, they can encourage children to try out diverse roles in a unobtrusive way through modeling or prompting. The teacher in the above vignette demonstrates a nondirective approach to promoting role diversity (e.g., "You could be the anesthesiologist.").

Another way teachers can enhance role playing is by promoting role complexity. Some children will enact a role with much flourish, using make-believe dialogue and performing detailed enactments in character. Other children perform less complex roles, exhibiting simple and repetitive enactments as they pretend. Through question-asking, modeling, or prompting, a teacher can increase the complexity of children's role playing (Trawick-Smith, 1987), as demonstrated in the vignette below.

❖ ❖

A pretend airport has been constructed in the dramatic play area. A four-year-old sits behind the controls of an airplane made out of a cardboard box. He makes loud jet-engine noises and rocks back and forth; these are the only enactments he performs. After watching this activity a few minutes a teacher intervenes.

Teacher:	Do you need a co-pilot?
Child:	What?
Teacher:	Sometimes pilots need a co-pilot to help them fly the plane. I could help you with the controls.
Child:	Okay. Sit here. (Points to another seat in the box)
Teacher:	(Squeezes into the box) Should I check the dials to see if we have enough gas?
Child:	No, I'll do it. (Looks at dials painted on the cardboard plane, makes noises and gestures indicating that he is pushing buttons) There. We have some gas.

Teacher:	I'll check the radar to make sure we're going in the right direction. It's very cloudy out. We can't see very well.
Child:	Where's the radar? This? (Points to a painted dial)
Teacher:	Sure, that could be our radar. Do you want to check it?
Child:	Yeah. (Again pretends to push buttons and turn dials) Oh, oh. We're going the wrong way, I think.
Teacher:	Maybe we should call the control tower at the airport.
Child:	Okay. (Talks to the "control tower" through a pretend radio) We need to land but we can't see. Can you help us?
Teacher:	What did the people in the tower say?
Child:	They said come land. We're going right.
Teacher:	When will we land?
Child:	I'll land it. (Makes engine noises, makes gestures to indicate landing) Here we are.
Teacher:	Great. I think I'll get off here. (Moves out of the play area)
Child:	Okay. (Makes engine noises, pretends to take off again. Manipulates dials and talks on the radio) ❖

Before the teacher of this vignette intervenes, the child performs only two basic enactments—making engine noises and rocking the airplane back and forth. The teacher encourages the child to elaborate on his role, suggesting that he check the gas level and radar and call the control tower. When the teacher disengages, the child continues to display these more detailed enactments. Such complex role playing has been found to be related to overall play development (Trawick-Smith, 1987).

Make-Believe (Situations)

Another kind of make-believe in sociodramatic play is children using verbal descriptions to create imaginary situations or dilemmas. For example, children might warn peers that there will be a flood, that many guests will be arriving for dinner, or that a baby is ill and in need of a doctor. These make-believe situations are often created so that some kind of a problem is posed for the pretend characters to solve (Trawick-Smith, 1987). A great deal of collaboration among players often results as children discuss, plan, and negotiate how they will resolve a particular dilemma. These make-believe contexts lead to social interaction, verbalization, and complex role enactment.

Some children do not create make-believe situations in their play, however (Smilansky, 1968; Smilansky & Shefatya, 1990). Teachers can assist children in learning how to develop pretend-play contexts; the following vignette illustrates one approach.

❖ ❖

Two five-year-old children are pretending to be pirates; they rock back and forth in a wooden boat on the playground. They shout out to peers who pass by. A teacher watches these interactions.

Child A:	(Speaks in a make-believe voice to two children walking past) We're pirates! Stay away from our ship!
Child B:	Let's go, Seth. We need to rock harder.
Child A:	Not too hard. We'll fall in the water. I'm falling! (Demonstrates by toppling out of the boat)
Child B:	Seth! Get back in. (Now sees the teacher watching, addresses her) Come see our ship. We're pirates.
Teacher:	I see.
Child A:	Do you want to get in the ship?
Teacher:	Oh, I don't think I would fit. Where are you going in the boat?
Child A:	We're pirates.
Teacher:	Yes. Where are you headed?
Child B:	Going in the water. I don't think we're going anywhere, are we, Seth?
Child A:	(Says nothing)
Teacher:	How is the weather? Is the weather bad?
Child B:	The weather? Oh, it's pretty bad. It's raining, right, Seth?
Teacher:	Oh, oh. I hope it's not a typhoon. Sometimes there are typhoons at sea.
Child A:	What are those?
Teacher:	A typhoon is like a terrible storm. The winds blow hard, the waves crash. Your boat could even tip over if you're not careful.
Child B:	Okay. A typhoon is coming. Hold on, Seth. (Steps out of character and addresses his playmate in his regular voice) Let's say a typhoon is coming and we have to fix the ship so it won't sink, all right, Seth?
Child A:	Okay. How do we fix it?
Child B:	Oh, we fix the sails like this. Look. (Makes gestures to indicate he is working on the ship)
Child A:	The wind is blowing already. The typhoon is here, I think. (Begins to rock the boat)
Child B:	And let's say if we tip over, the sharks could eat us, all right, Seth?

As the children become absorbed in this make-believe situation the teacher moves away. ❖

When the children of this vignette invite the teacher to play with them, she offers an idea for a make-believe situation—a typhoon is coming. They readily adopt her suggestion and elaborate on it, adding sail-fixing and shark-watching to their play enactments. This new make-believe situation rejuvenates the play and enhances its complexity.

Literacy Play and Thematic-Fantasy Enactment

There has been a growing interest in how sociodramatic play can enhance literacy development. In the past, researchers have focused on indirect ways that make-believe facilitates reading and writing (Cazden, 1976; Pellegrini, 1980; Vygotsky, 1978). In more recent research it has been found that children engage directly in literacy-related activities as they pretend (Christie, 1991). When children play school, for example, the "teacher" often reads to "students." In grocery store play, children write shopping lists. Often children will re-enact in their sociodramatic play stories that have been read to them.

The discovery that children engage in literacy-related activities in the dramatic play center has led some play specialists to devise new literacy interventions. In one strategy teachers provide literacy props—books, writing implements, wall signs, and other print-related materials—and then prompt or model their use in make-believe contexts (Morrow, 1991; Neuman & Roskos, 1991; Vukelich, 1991). Such interventions have been found to increase the quality and quantity of children's spontaneous literacy activities. Children have also been discovered to engage in more peer tutoring, often helping each other learn about print, as a result of these interventions. An example of a teacher facilitating literacy play is presented in the vignette below.

❖ ❖
Two four-year-olds are playing in a pretend post office which has been created in the dramatic play area. They mail envelopes in a mail box provided. A teacher moves into the center.

Teacher:	(Speaks to no one in particular) I haven't written to my mother in so long. I think I'll jot her a note. (Places stationery, envelopes and markers on the table; begins to write) Let's see. I think I'll write, "Dear Mom."
Child A:	(Approaches the teacher) Can I write one?
Teacher:	Sure. Who will you write to?
Child A:	(In a pretend, adult-like voice) Well, I need to write to my daughter. She has moved away and I need to write her. Come on, Maria. Let's write to our daughters, okay?
Child B:	How old are they?
Child A:	Let's say they're teenagers.

Child B: Okay. We can write 'em and mail 'em. (Points to the make-believe post office)

The two children write and discuss their letters. The teacher continues to write with them. Finally the children place their letters in envelopes, address these in "scribble writing" and mail them at the post office.

Child A: Let's say I'm the daughter now and I get your letter, okay? (Takes an envelope from the mail box, now assumes a different voice) Oh. A letter! What does this say? (Shows the letter to the teacher)

Teacher: You could ask your mother. (Points to Child B) She wrote it.

Child B: (Takes the letter from Child A, runs her fingers along the scribbles which are the words) Dear Daughter, Please come home now. Aren't you scared by yourself? Love, Mommy.

The children continue to play mother and daughter, writing more letters and mailing them. The teacher leaves the play area.   ❖

The teacher in this vignette facilitates literacy play by providing props and modeling their use. When one child has trouble "reading" the other's letter, the teacher encourages peer tutoring. These interchanges lead to self-directed reading and writing after the teacher has withdrawn.

Another literacy-related intervention involves encouraging children to re-enact stories (Salz & Johnson, 1974). This is a controversial strategy; some believe this is not real sociodramatic play intervention because it is adult-directed. Children are read a story in this approach and then encouraged to re-enact it. Teachers provide story-related props, assign roles, and actually play along. Children are encouraged to play out the story several times; on each occasion the teacher becomes less involved in the play. Later, the teacher might facilitate children's spontaneous re-enactment of the story in the dramatic-play center or on the playground. In the vignette below a teacher demonstrates this last step, facilitating the re-enactment of a story which was read earlier.

❖ ❖

Five four- and five-year-old children are running across a swinging bridge which is part of a playground playscape. A teacher crouches under the bridge.

Teacher: (In a scary voice) Who's that walking on my bridge?

Child A: (Stands in the middle of the bridge) What?

Teacher: Who's that walking on my bridge?

Child A: (Giggles, backs away, addresses the other children) Oh! The troll! There's the troll under the bridge. We're the goats, okay?

Child B: (Walks to the middle of the bridge) It is I, the little billy goat. I'm too little to eat. Wait for my big brother.

Teacher: Hmm. Well, okay. Where's the big brother?

In line, each child crosses the bridge assuming the character of one or another of the Three Billy Goats Gruff. Each attempts to recreate and elaborate on the dialogue of the story.   ❖

Because the teacher selects the play theme and assigns roles in this type of intervention it should be used sparingly. Too much thematic-fantasy play intervention can deprive children of opportunities to pursue their own play interests.

Persistence

A final element of sociodramatic play which Smilansky (1968) has identified is play persistence. This is the ability to continue in a single play theme for an extended period of time; this play dimension has been found to be related to overall play complexity and to attention and perseverance in non-play tasks (Sylva, Roy, & Painter, 1980; Trawick-Smith, 1987). Some children cannot maintain make-believe roles for very long; they switch quickly from one role to another or leave the dramatic play area altogether after only a few minutes. Teachers can intervene to encourage children to persist at their make-believe themes.

Often when a teacher enters a play setting, the life of the play theme is extended; the mere presence of a playful adult creates new interest and excitement. If the teacher suggests novel enactments or situations which enrich or expand the theme in progress, children are even more likely to persist. Such interventions have been found to lead to greater persistence at play when teachers are no longer present (Smilansky, 1968; Smilansky & Shefatya, 1990; Sylva, Roy, & Painter, 1980).

An elaborate sociodramatic play theme takes a long time to organize and play out. Children who have special difficulty sustaining their play involvement may not enjoy the benefits of this activity. Based on their research, Johnson, Christie, and Yawkey (1987) have suggested that typically developing preschoolers can persist at sociodramatic play for 5 minutes or more; kindergartners can sustain episodes for longer than 10 minutes. Those children who are unable to play for this long might be targeted for play-persistence intervention.

A Final Word on Facilitating Play Skills

It is obvious from the vignettes presented that all the play skills described by Smilansky are interrelated. Although she has suggested targeting one or only several of these in play intervention depending on an individual child's needs, when one behavior is enhanced others are as well. When make-believe with objects is encouraged, for example, children are more likely to take on imaginative play characters. When social interaction is facilitated, verbalization will be enhanced. When literacy props are introduced children will persist longer at play themes. Promoting a single play behavior, then, can enrich all aspects of children's play.

Sociodramatic Play in a Technological Age

Concerns and issues have been raised about the influence of technology on children's play. Two technological advancements that predominate modern life—television and microcomputers—are considered here.

Television

Two children are pointing gun-shaped objects, which they have made out of plastic construction toys, at each other. They make shooting noises and take turns collapsing on the floor. A teacher suddenly appears in the area.

Teacher: No guns in school.

Child A: Oh. These aren't guns. These are our fire hoses.

The children quickly change their play theme and begin squirting a make-believe fire.

Teacher: Well, remember. You can't play guns in school.

Child A: Okay.

Several minutes after the teacher has left the play area the two children resume their gun play.   ❖

A major dilemma facing teachers is what to do when children's play is predominated by television-related themes. Through interviews with teachers and school administrators, Carlsson-Paige and Levin (1987) have discovered that television has a profound influence on the play themes that children select. This is troubling for several reasons. When children play the same television-related roles over and over again, their play is limited to a very narrow range of themes. They may perform the same enactments, use the same dialogue, or even play with the same children each time they enter the dramatic play area or playground. Another concern is that television programming for children is becoming more violent (Eron & Heusmann, 1987)); violent play related to favorite television shows often appears in children's activities (National Association for the Education of Young Children, 1990). Violent war play may nurture militaristic and authoritarian sociopolitical concepts

(Carlsson-Paige & Levin, 1987). When children have G.I. Joe shoot the "bad guys" in their play, just as they have viewed on television, they and their playmates may be constructing less than positive perspectives on conflict resolution.

For these reasons some teachers have adopted a rigid rule that television-related play—particularly that with violent content—is not allowed in school (Schneiderman & Sousa, 1986). Teachers of this perspective intervene in such play and actively redirect children into other roles or even terminate the play altogether. Other teachers allow television play but restrict it in some ways. Some will permit war play, for example, only on the playground and only if it's performed with make-believe, nonrealistic toy weapons (Carlsson-Paige & Levin, 1987). Some have recommended that it be allowed only in acceptable locations—such as in wide-open areas free of obstacles—and only at certain times of the day (Kostelnik, Whiren, & Stein, 1986).

A number of authors have raised concerns about efforts to restrict children's play in these ways (Carlsson-Paige & Levin, 1987; Wolf, 1984). They argue that television-related war or superhero play is the result of watching violent television or, more generally, living in a world where guns and violence are a regular part of life. The play is not the cause of violent behavior, they contend, but a way of expressing feelings and ideas about the war and violence that they witness on their favorite shows or the evening news.

Some believe that television play has developmental benefits (Carlsson-Paige & Levin, 1987; Kostelnik, Whiren, & Stein, 1986). Such activity may give children feelings of power and mastery. Since they are relatively powerless in real life, children may enjoy feelings of strength, wisdom, and courage when they assume the roles of supernatural heroes or powerful warriors. When children play out the roles of television characters they may be experimenting with important distinctions between reality and fantasy which are as yet unclear in early childhood (Carlsson-Paige & Levin, 1987). Sutton-Smith (1986) has concluded that restricting children's play is a form of censorship, which deprives them of an outlet for emotions and ideas.

Teachers are faced, then, with a dilemma: How can they nurture kindness and a distaste for violence on the one hand and yet allow freedom to choose one's own play themes on the other? Carlsson-Paige and Levin (1987) offer a solution: Teachers can permit such play but actively intervene to help children construct understandings of war and violence. Through play intervention, teachers can encourage children to think about alternatives to violence in solving problems ("Why did you shoot Shredder? How could you get him to talk to you?") They can identify children's concerns or anxieties about war ("The bomb is dropping on our house? What do you think will happen? What do you think about bombs really?"). They can clear up misconceptions about violence and war ("If you shoot him he will die. Do you want to kill him?") and ease the anxieties of children who are confused about fantasy and reality ("You know that Jason isn't really a bad guy"). They can encourage children to broaden their roles and make their characters more humane ("Where do the star-fighters go when they are done fighting? Do they have a home?") or encourage role diversity ("Who is the navigator of the spaceship?"). They can enhance the imaginativeness of play, encouraging less stereotypic enactments ("How else can we stop the monster besides just shooting him? Do you have any special powers?"). In these ways children are able to select play themes that are meaningful to them but at the same time receive accurate information and alternative viewpoints about violence and war. In the vignette below a teacher demonstrates Carlsson-Paige and Levin's approach.

❖ ❖

Three five-year-old boys are playing superheroes in the dramatic play area. They kick and chop in the air, making grunts and groans. A teacher enters the setting.

Teacher:	It looks like quite a battle here.
Child A:	Yeah. We're the Ninja Turtles. Randy is Shredder.
Teacher:	Why are you fighting him?
Child A:	He's the bad guy. Didn't you know?
Teacher:	Why is he bad?
Child B:	(Hesitates) I don't know. He just is. The Ninja Turtles fight with him.
Teacher:	Does that kicking hurt him?
Child A:	No. He's the Shredder. He doesn't get hurt.
Teacher:	Let me check. (Addresses Child C in a make-believe voice) Are you hurt, Shredder? Did their kicks and punches hurt you?
Child C:	(Collapses to the ground) They hurt me. I can't walk. I can't fight. (Begins to moan)
Teacher:	Oh, no. Do you have a home where you can go to rest? Where do you live?
Child A:	Let's say he lives over here. (Points to a corner of the play area) And the turtles live down here in the sewer. (Points to another area)
Child C:	Okay. I'll go to my home. (Moves over to his appointed corner, begins piling pillows in a circle to make a hideout. Addresses the "turtles") Let's say you can't see me when I'm here.
Child A:	Okay. We'll make our hideout here. (Joins Child B in making a circle of large hollow blocks)

As the children set up their hideouts, the teacher slips out of the play area. ❖

"Are there other ways to stop the monster besides shooting it?" Through play intervention teachers can redirect violent television play.

The teacher of this vignette has not disrupted the children's television-related play theme, but helped to extend it. She expresses, as a character, her concern about injuries suffered in a fight. She helps children assign human qualities to the characters, even to the "bad guy." She has facilitated more varied, less stereotypic enactments—building a hideout, discussing the Shredder's injuries. She has given subtle messages in her interventions—that "bad guys" are human, that fighting can lead to injuries—without being judgmental or interfering in the children's play.

Microcomputers

Elkind (1987) has characterized the use of microcomputers in early childhood classrooms as "miseducation." He raises concerns about the abstract nature of computers and how they can distract children from useful forms of play. In response Shade and Watson (1990) argue that, "when used appropriately, with good software and teacher guidance, computers can be more active than television, less static than picture-books, and more open-ended than crayons" (p. 379). They suggest that microcomputer play enhances social and emotional as well as cognitive development.

Wright and Samaras (1986) propose that children view the computer as a "remarkable toy" and follow a typical sequence of toy-use when using one—first exploring, then problem-solving, and ultimately engaging in make-believe enactments. They have provided evidence that children pretend while working with computers; the following vignette, drawn from their research, illustrates this "high-tech" sociodramatic play (Wright & Samaras, 1986, p. 80).

Joe and Phil were sharing one monitor. Joe brought two puppets to the computer to let each one "have a turn using it." Phil began moving his cursor to pursue Joe's.

Joe: Come on, the puppet doesn't know how to do that. This puppet wants to practice!

         ❖

Through informal intervention teachers can encourage pretend play on the computer. Further, they can enhance sociodramatic play skills outlined above. Through question-asking, for example, they can elicit social interaction and verbalization (e.g., a teacher says to the puppet in the vignette above: "Can you tell Joe and Phil what you would like to play on the computer?"). Make-believe in regard to objects or situations can be promoted (e.g., a teacher says to two children who pretend to "sew" by crossing lines back and forth on a screen: "I see you are sewing. Tell me about what you are sewing"). Teachers can support children's role playing at the computer (e.g., a teacher says to the two children in the vignette above: "Are you the puppet's teachers? What are you helping him learn today?").

Computer play not only enhances problem solving and creativity, then, but may serve as an ideal context for enhancing make-believe. Selecting open-ended, developmentally appropriate software and intervening in informal, unobtrusive ways are key ingredients to fostering pretend play at the microcomputer.

Summary

Sociodramatic play promotes cognitive, social, and emotional development. Some types of play are more elaborate and social than others and so lead more directly to these important areas of growth. Teachers can support children who do not perform these more complex forms of play through carefully formulated interventions.

Sara Smilansky has provided guidelines for such interventions. An important aspect of her play-enrichment program is targeting and enriching specific play abilities that are related to development—make-believe, social interaction, verbalization, persistence, and literacy enactment. As teachers play with children they can select one or more of these behaviors to enhance. This approach has been found not only to increase play abilities, but also to lead to language and intellectual development, social competence, and emotional well-being.

Sometimes children are limited in their play to enactments of television-related roles which often contain violent content. Rather than restricting this play, teachers can enrich and extend it, so that children gain new perspectives and information about war and violence.

Although the microcomputer has been viewed as a threat to high-quality play, some new software is open-ended and conducive to sociodramatic play. Teachers can intervene at the computer terminal to support and encourage make-believe.

Suggested Activities

1. Observe children interacting in the dramatic play area of the classroom. Make notes about ways this activity leads to learning and development. Write a discussion of your observations guided by the following questions:

   a. In what ways did children learn language or cognitive skills as they played?

   b. What social learnings occurred during your observation?

   c. In what ways did children benefit emotionally from this play experience?

   d. Which children seemed to benefit most from the play? Why do you think so? Which children did not seem to benefit? Why?

2. Play with a group of children in the dramatic-play area of a classroom. As you play, attempt to facilitate several of the play behaviors reviewed in this chapter—make-believe, social interaction, verbalization, play persistence, literacy enactment. After a short while withdraw from the play and observe what happens. Write a discussion of your experiences guided by the following questions:

   a. Which play behaviors were you able to enhance in your interventions? How successful were you at enriching play in these areas?

   b. What happened after you left the play area? Was children's play more elaborate in some way? Less so? Why do you think the play changed, if it did?

    c. Which children did you interact with most in your play interventions? Why did you select these particular children? Which children needed less support in their playing?

3. Intervene in children's television play either in the dramatic-play area or on the playground. Try to enrich or extend this play in ways described in this chapter without disrupting it. Write a discussion of your experiences guided by the following questions:

    a. In what ways were you able to clear up misconceptions or provide information about violence, war, or other controversial topics?

    b. In what ways did you "humanize" characters?

    c. In what ways did you promote more complex and diverse roles?

    d. How did children's play change after your intervention?

Further Reading

Bergen, D. (Ed.). (1988). *Play as a medium for learning and development.* Portsmouth, NH: Heinemann.

Christie, J. (Ed.). (1991). *Play and early literacy development.* Albany, NY: SUNY Press.

Hughs, F. P. (1991). *Children, play, and development.* Boston: Allyn and Bacon.

Johnson, J. E., Christie, J. F., & Yawkey, T. D. (1987). *Play and early childhood development.* Glenview, IL: Scott, Foresman and Company.

Smilansky, S. (1968). *The effects of sociodramatic play on disadvantaged preschool children.* New York: Wiley.

Smilansky, S., & Shefatya, L. (1990). *Facilitating play: A medium for promoting cognitive, socioemotional, and academic development in young children.* Gaithersburg, MD: Psychosocial & Educational Publications.

Trawick-Smith, J.W. (1985). Developing the dramatic play enrichment program. *Dimensions, 13*(4), 7–11.

4

PROMOTING SOCIAL COMPETENCE

❖ ❖

Two five-year-old boys sit on a large hollow block structure they have just built, rocking back and forth and making eerie noises. One talks to the other in a radio-like voice, as though speaking through a transmitter. He even makes crackling sounds to indicate static. "Get the lasers ready. Enemy ahead. Lasers ready, Justin?"

"Okay, lasers ready," his playmate replies in the same sort of voice.

Suddenly their play is interrupted by a third child who runs noisily into the play area. He is wearing a firefighter's hat and making loud siren noises. He addresses his peers in a commanding tone: "Hey! We're firemen. You're a fireman, you're a fireman and I'm a fireman. Get on the fire truck." With this he pushes one of the other boys forward to make room for himself on the block structure.

"Adam!" this child protests. "Get off!"

The intruder pushes the child again, knocking him off the blocks. He shouts in a hostile tone: "This is the fire truck! *You* get off!"

The two original players move away from this child quickly. They retreat to the adjoining dramatic play area to continue their outer space theme undisturbed. A teacher hears the commotion and moves into the area. She approaches Adam who now sits on the blocks alone. "Adam, you sound so angry," the teacher comments.

"Yeah. 'Cause they didn't want to play. This is my fire truck."

"You're angry because they won't play with you?"

"Yeah."

The teacher pauses a moment, then asks: "Adam, did you see what happened when you pushed Seth?"

"They didn't want to play." There is still anger in Adam's voice.

"Did you see how they moved away from you? They didn't want to play with you when you pushed and yelled at them. If you want to play with them you have to think of a way to join them without yelling."

"But they didn't want to play fireman." Adam is quieter now.

"Why don't we join them on their spaceship? We could be astronauts too," the teacher suggests.

Adam hesitates, then responds: "Yeah."

The teacher and Adam now move into the dramatic play area where the two other children have fashioned a new spaceship out of three chairs placed in a row. "Adam can't play," one of the boys says immediately when he sees Adam and the teacher approaching.

The teacher assumes a make-believe voice: "We're astronauts like you are. We have an important message from earth."

"Are you going to play too?" one of the boys asks the teacher.

"Yes. Adam and I have just traveled from earth."

"Yeah. We got a message," Adam adds.

"What is it?" one of the two original spacemen asks, now playing along.

Adam looks puzzled and turns to the teacher: "What is it?"

"We have a message that something dangerous is coming. We saw something, didn't we, Adam?" the teacher asks.

"Yeah. There are monsters," Adam offers.

"Right. Monsters. What will we do?" The teacher uses an animated voice.

"What kind of monsters are they, Adam?" one of the boys asks. "Are they meat-eaters?"

"They are killer monsters. They can kill you. We need to fight with them," Adam says loudly. He starts to climb onto a chair that is part of the new spaceship.

The teacher quickly intervenes: "Wait, Adam. This is their spaceship. Let's ask them where we should sit." Now she addresses the two other boys: "Can we sit on your ship? Will you save us from the monsters?"

"Come on, sit here," one of the children says in a serious tone, indicating that they may sit on the back chair. Adam sits there; the teacher crouches behind him.

"Okay, we're ready," the teacher announces.

The three children recite a countdown, then make loud rocket noises and wiggle this way and that. They play together for many minutes.

The teacher is fortunate to have an assistant teacher who can manage the rest of her class while she spends time playing with Adam. She chooses to stay in the area for an extended period to give Adam assistance in interacting with his peers. She continues to redirect Adam's angry and aggressive reactions to his two playmates and to demonstrate prosocial ways to participate in the play. Eventually, she leaves the play area for a short while and watches from a distance. The three continue to play in a cooperative way until lunch time.   ❖

This teacher has promoted social development in several fundamental ways. She has helped Adam to identify his angry feelings and to determine where they come from. Too, she has assisted him in analyzing the undesirable outcomes of his hostile and aggressive behavior ("They didn't want to play with you when you pushed and yelled at them"). Later, she demonstrates a successful approach to joining others at play, prompting Adam to make interesting contributions to the play theme already in progress ("We have an important message from earth"). Finally, she continues to give Adam support in order to provide an extended positive experience with peers.

In short, the teacher above demonstrates play intervention that promotes social competence. This chapter will provide guidelines for such interventions into the social worlds of children. Specific techniques for enhancing social skills, peer acceptance, and the formation of friendships will be considered.

❖ ❖ ❖

What Is Social Competence?

The term *social competence* refers to two interrelated social aspects of human development—being liked by others and having skills to interact effectively in social settings. Both positive peer relationships and social skills in the early years are good predictors of overall happiness and mental health in later life (Hartup & Moore, 1990; Parker & Asher, 1987). Children who are disliked by peers, deficient in social abilities, or aggressive and impulsive in their interactions in the preschool years are more likely to become psychologically troubled adults (Parker & Asher, 1987; Rubin, Hymel, LeMare, & Rowden, 1989). Teachers can assist children in acquiring social skills and making friends; these may be the most important goals of early childhood education.

Popular, Rejected, and Neglected Children

Some children have a very hard time interacting with peers; others are quite competent at making friends and winning acceptance and respect from their playmates (Hartup & Moore, 1990). It is important for teachers to identify both types of children. They must determine if there are less effective children in the classroom and give them assistance in forming positive peer relations. Identifying socially capable children is also important; by observing their behaviors and interpersonal styles teachers can learn a lot about what it takes to be well-liked and accepted in the classroom. Also, by observing highly competent children, teachers can identify potential peer models who might be paired with less effective children in order to enhance social abilities (Selman & Demorest, 1984).

There are several ways to determine whether children are socially competent. Teachers can observe their classroom interactions over a period of time and in a variety of settings; students who are cooperative, friendly, verbal, and skilled at getting needs met by peers are likely to be socially well-adjusted. Those who rarely interact with others, fight and argue frequently, or engage in annoying and bizarre behaviors may need special adult support (Dodge, McClaskey, & Feldman, 1985).

Another way to determine children's overall social competence is to assess how well they are liked by their peers. Teachers can informally observe whether students are accepted by others in the class. Children who are often invited to play, both inside and outside of school, or who generally receive lots of peer attention, are usually quite competent socially. Those who are regularly ignored by peers, or even actively rejected when they attempt to enter play groups, are in need of social skills intervention (Dodge, 1983).

A final way to determine whether children are successful in peer relations is to assess whether they have friends. Socially competent children are likely to have one or several peers with whom they play often and give particular attention, and whose liking and attention are reciprocated by these individuals. Those who have no friends may be less competent and even at risk (Hartup & Sancilio, 1986). Even children who are generally ignored by classmates but have one friend are likely to be well-adjusted socially (Gottman, 1983).

Relying on these methods of determining social competence—direct observation, assessments of peer liking, and number of friendships—researchers have been able to identify three distinct types of children: popular, rejected, and neglected children (Dodge, 1983).

Popular Children

Popular children are those who are very well liked by peers and who have many friends. These children have been studied extensively by researchers who have sought to identify the specific social skills or interpersonal styles that lead to such great success in peer relations. These researchers have suggested that the social behaviors of popular children become target skills to enhance in social intervention strategies (Mize & Ladd, 1990).

Why are popular children so well liked? Generally, they are very active socially (Trawick-Smith, 1992). They often initiate contact with peers and are energetic in directing play activities. Overall, they are leaders who make many play suggestions and structure the activity of others (Scarlett, 1983; Trawick-Smith, 1992). The behaviors of Child A below illustrate this active leadership style.

❖ ❖

Child A:	Now, Lauren, it's time to bathe our babies, okay? Can you come over here and help us? Let's bathe 'em 'cause they're very filthy. So let's really scrub 'em. And I'll be the mamma, you be the older sister, okay? Now you come over now, all right?
Child B:	All right. (Moves over to Child A)
Child A:	Let's say we set up for the party, okay? Some guests are coming at 5 o'clock. (Now addresses Child C) And let's say you come help too, Susan.
Child C:	(Says nothing, joins Child A in the dramatic-play area)
Child A:	Now we need to set the table. You have to put the forks just the right way. Here I'll show you. (Demonstrates how to set the table) Now you do it, okay, Susan? Oh. There's the phone. (To child B) Will you answer that, honey? ❖

Child A is exceedingly active in directing peers. Although her playmates have trouble getting a word in edgewise, they seem very pleased to be able to play with Child A and do as she directs. Such active leadership has been found to enhance one's status in a peer group (Scarlett, 1983).

Children who are popular are usually those who can use language effectively in social situations (Ladd, 1981). In the following vignette, Child A demonstrates such verbal skill, adjusting the phrasing and tone of his language three different times until he finally persuades a peer to help him build with blocks.

❖ ❖

Child A:	(Building with blocks, addresses Child B in a friendly tone) Help me build my boat, Jason.
Child B:	(Says nothing, does not look up from his own blocks)
Child A:	(In an angry tone) Jason! Help me build it!
Child B:	(Also angry) No!
Child A:	(In a friendly tone again) Jason, let's say this is our boat. (Points to his block structure) Let's say we build it, all right?
Child B:	Okay. But I'll do the long blocks. (Helps Child A stack blocks) ❖

In this example, popular Child A uses subtle changes in phrasing and intonation to persuade a peer to do what he wants. When his angry demand does not work he tries a request for joint action ("Let's say we build it, all right?") which leads to success. The child appears to be experimenting with language, trying out options until hitting upon a phrasing that works. Such verbal skill is common among well-liked children.

Popular children are friendly and positive in their interactions with peers. They are rarely aggressive or bossy (Dodge, 1983). They more often give positive feedback, attention, and affection to their classmates. Overall, they are very pleasant children to play with; this positive style is illustrated below.

❖ ❖

Two children are making puzzles at a table. One of the children is having trouble; she's chosen a puzzle that is too difficult. Popular Child A assists her.

Child A:	Can't you do it?
Child B:	No. It's too hard.
Child A:	Here, make this one instead. (Hands her another puzzle)
Child B:	(In an annoyed tone) No, Jennifer! I need this one.
Child A:	Should I help you do that one? I can help you. (Begins to look over Child B's puzzle pieces)
Child B:	I can do it! (Pushes Child A's hand away)
Child A:	I'm just going to point to the pieces you need, all right? I'll point to the pieces and you put them on there.
Child B:	Okay. What goes right here? (Points to her puzzle)
Child A:	Oh, it's this one. (Gives child B a piece)
Child B:	(Places the piece on the puzzle) It fits.
Child A:	(In an enthused tone) You got one! ❖

In this vignette Child A demonstrates helpful, friendly behavior. She does not become angry or aggressive when Child B rejects her offer for assistance; in a tactful and friendly manner she suggests a way she can help. She gives enthusiastic encouragement when her playmate succeeds.

Popular children can be assertive and are not "led about" by peers. A moderate amount of the time they reject the play suggestions or initiatives of their playmates (Trawick-Smith, 1992). When they reject others' ideas, however, they do so in a tactful manner (Hazen, Black, & Fleming-Johnson, 1984). Often they will give a reason for rejecting another's ideas and may offer an alternative course of action to the one suggested. This diplomatic style is profiled below.

❖ ❖

Child A:	(Placing plastic farm animals in a block structure) I'm building a farm here. Let's say this is a farm.
Child B:	(Building with blocks) No, this is a museum where paintings are. See, Joseph?
Child A:	No! It's a farm!
Child B:	No, 'cause there's not enough room for a whole farm. Let's say it's a museum where farm animals can go. They can go to the museum, okay? See? (Begins placing farm animals in his structure)
Child A:	Okay. But those animals might make a mess at the museum. (Joins Child B's play theme) ❖

Here Child B has rejected Child A's suggestion, but has given a reason for the rejection and offered an alternative play theme. His rebuff of Child A's ideas was not harsh or hostile and did not result in a dissolution of the play.

Popular children are quite competent at resolving conflicts; they often do so in friendly, nonaggressive ways (Asher & Renshaw, 1981; Trawick-Smith, 1988). They are more likely to compromise when disputes arise, as illustrated in the vignette below.

❖ ❖

Child A:	(Climbs on a tractor tire on the playground) This will be our shark ship, okay? Get on quick, Jeremy! The sharks will eat you!
Child B:	No! This is my police helicopter!
Child A:	Well, okay. We're police. But we need to chase the sharks, okay? I see the sharks way down there! Come on!
Child B:	Okay. Let's get 'em!

Both children begin to make helicopter noises and swat at make-believe sharks with plastic garden tools. ❖

Here Child A displays an effective mixture of leading and following, adopting another's suggestion but at the same time winning acceptance of his own. Such give-and-take is quite common among popular children.

One thing young children must learn in order to be effective with peers is how to enter a play group (Putallaz & Wasserman, 1989). Children tend to be quite protective of play themes already in progress; they often reject bids by newcomers to join their activities. Popular children are quite savvy at gaining entrance into play-in-progress; they have acquired social skills that win their acceptance in groups (Putallaz & Wasserman, 1989; Ramsey, 1989a). They seem to know just what to say and do to get in. Child B of the vignette below demonstrates one effective approach.

❖ ❖

Two children are playing on an indoor climber. A third child approaches and tries to enter the play setting.

Child A: You can't play, Robert.

Child B: (In an excited tone) But a tornado's coming!

Child A: What?

Child B: A tornado's coming! Quick! Help me get inside, Seth!

Child A: Okay! Come on! (Pulls Child B inside the climber)   ❖

The child of this vignette has demonstrated several techniques which are effective in gaining entrance to play groups. He does not ask to play, but simply starts playing along, making an interesting contribution to the play theme. He addresses one of the children by name. These strategies have been found to be very successful among preschool-age children (Ramsey, 1991).

One last characteristic of popular children is that they can accurately "read" social settings (Crick & Ladd, 1987; Asher & Renshaw, 1981). They seem to be aware of the needs, motives and behaviors of their peers and of the effects of their own behaviors. They are better able to identify the outcomes of particular social initiatives, for example. They know that pushing or hitting can lead to retaliation or that some children will do what you ask if you are friendly (Trawick-Smith, 1992). They can more accurately name the intentions of peers (Dodge, 1980). This ability to monitor one's social behaviors and those of others may explain why popular children are able to select those strategies that are most successful—they have come to learn which ones work well with peers and which ones don't.

In summary, popular children demonstrate certain specific social skills and behaviors which may account for their popularity. In a later section of this chapter, strategies for teaching these skills to less effective children will be suggested.

Rejected Children

Rejected children are those who are actively avoided by peers. These children are named most often when students of a given class are asked to identify those they would least like to play with (Dodge, 1983). They are disliked because they display anti-social behaviors that are often extremely obvious and disruptive. They are often quite aggressive. They can respond to the slightest frustration or disagreement with uncontrollable violence. Often they are impulsive and unpredictable in their aggression; they can surprise their play-mates with violent outbursts.

The vignette below illustrates the aggressive and unpredictable behaviors of a rejected child.

Three children are looking at books in the library corner. Each is absorbed in his own reading; all is quite peaceful for awhile. Without warning Child A kicks another who has moved too close. He then grabs this child's book.

Child A: (Pulling the book from Child B's hands) Give me this!

Child B: No. Give it back, Philip!

Child A: (Moves toward Child B in a threatening way, uses an angry tone) You better not touch me.

Child B: (Covers his head, expecting to be struck)

Child A: (Pushes Child B) This is my book. You give it to me. (Now turns to Child C who is watching, snatches his book as well) You better give them to me.

Both Child B and C quickly retreat from the library corner to find a teacher. Child A sits down by himself and continues to read.   ❖

The child in this vignette becomes suddenly aggressive for no obvious reason. He bullies both boys, in spite of the fact that such aggression will drive them from the play area. He seems content to be on his own after they have left.

A characteristic of rejected children is an inability to read social situations or to understand the feelings of peers (Asher & Renshaw, 1981; Dodge, 1980). For example, rejected children often erroneously interpret the actions of peers as intentional and hostile. The following vignette demonstrates this tendency to assign hostility to a nonhostile act.

A child has accidently bumped into another's blocks, toppling a portion of the structure. The latter child immediately attacks, striking her peer several times before a teacher can intervene.

Teacher:	(In an alarmed tone) What is happening here?
Child A:	He kicked over my blocks.
Child B:	(In tears) I didn't mean to.
Child A:	He tried to kick 'em. If he kicks 'em again (turns to Child B) I'll hit you harder.
Child B:	(Sobs loudly, moves toward Child A and the teacher) But it was not on purpose!
Child A:	(Kicking out at Child B) You better get away from me. Stay outta my blocks! ❖

Here the child has reacted angrily, assuming that Child B's action was deliberate. Even Child B's movement toward her is interpreted as a threatening gesture. This tendency to assign negative intentions may explain why rejected children so frequently strike out, seemingly without provocation.

Some rejected children are also isolates; they choose to play alone and push or hit when others move near them (Asher & Dodge, 1985). Such children may be most at risk because they not only are difficult to play with but show no desire to be with peers at all. Most rejected children suffer low self-esteem, although some hold exceptionally positive and unrealistic views of self (Boivin & Begin, 1989). Some rejected children, for example, report that they are very well liked when in fact they are not. This is another sign of their inability to interpret social circumstances accurately. How do children first come to be rejected? They may begin life with a negative inborn temperament (Hartup & Moore, 1990) and are more likely to have parents who are punitive and authoritarian (Sroufe & Fleeson, 1986). When they come in contact with peers a vicious circle emerges: Rejected children push, hit, or display negative affect and their peers move away from them or refuse to play. This rejection angers them and threatens positive feelings of self. They respond with even more aggression; acting-out behavior escalates. Such children are at special risk and are in most need of adult intervention to enhance social relationships.

Neglected Children

Neglected children are those who are largely ignored by their peers; they often go unnoticed by teachers as well. The predominant characteristic of neglected children is isolate behavior. They tend to be loners who rarely initiate contact with others and often retreat when initiatives are directed toward them. Some neglected children choose to be alone (Scarlett, 1980). Many, though not all, neglected children are shy (Dodge, 1983; Honig, 1987).

Observations of neglected children's interactions with peers reveal that they are quite inept in social settings. They lack the social skills to enter a play group, to capture the attention of peers, to persuade others, or to respond appropriately to others' initiatives—the very skills that account for the popular child's high peer-group status (Honig, 1987). In the following vignette a neglected child is profiled.

❖ ❖

A child swings by herself on the playground. Several peers come over to join her; one initiates a conversation.

Child A:	Can you swing as high as this, Emma? (Demonstrates)
Child B:	(Says nothing)
Child A:	Emma? Can you swing this high? Look.
Child B:	(Shakes her head "no," says nothing)
Child C:	I can, Sharon. Look. I'm higher than you.
Child A:	Uh-uh. I'm higher.
Child B:	(Stops her swing, climbs off, leaves the area) ❖

In spite of repeated initiatives by a peer, neglected Child A does not respond. She does not appear interested in social interaction and leaves the area in response to her classmate's friendly advances.

A moderate amount of shyness is typical; most children are shy at one time or another in the early years (Honig, 1987). Most shy children will make friends and interact with peers. Children who are shy but socially competent will display many social abilities, but may do so in only certain classroom settings or with particular peers. Observations across situations and areas are necessary, then, in assessing peer neglect. A quiet but friendly social style does not always lead to low peer status.

Children who never interact with others and are, thus, unable to make friends may be at risk, however—particularly as they get older (Rubin, Hymel, LeMare, & Rowden, 1989). If a child never initiates contact with peers, adult assistance may be needed.

Neglected children may have been born with a "slow-to-warm-up" temperament which leads to quietness and wariness; caution and timidity in entering into new relationships may be a fundamental aspect of their personalities (Honig, 1987). A circular relationship between temperament and peer interaction emerges: They are so quiet and cautious that they are ignored. They are not invited, then, to participate in play activities and so miss opportunities to refine social skills and gain confidence in peer relations. They may grow comfortable with isolate play. They further isolate themselves and, thus, are noticed less and less.

Early learning of social skills may reduce later rejection or neglect by peers; teachers can facilitate social skills among their neglected students. Strategies for achieving social skills will be considered next.

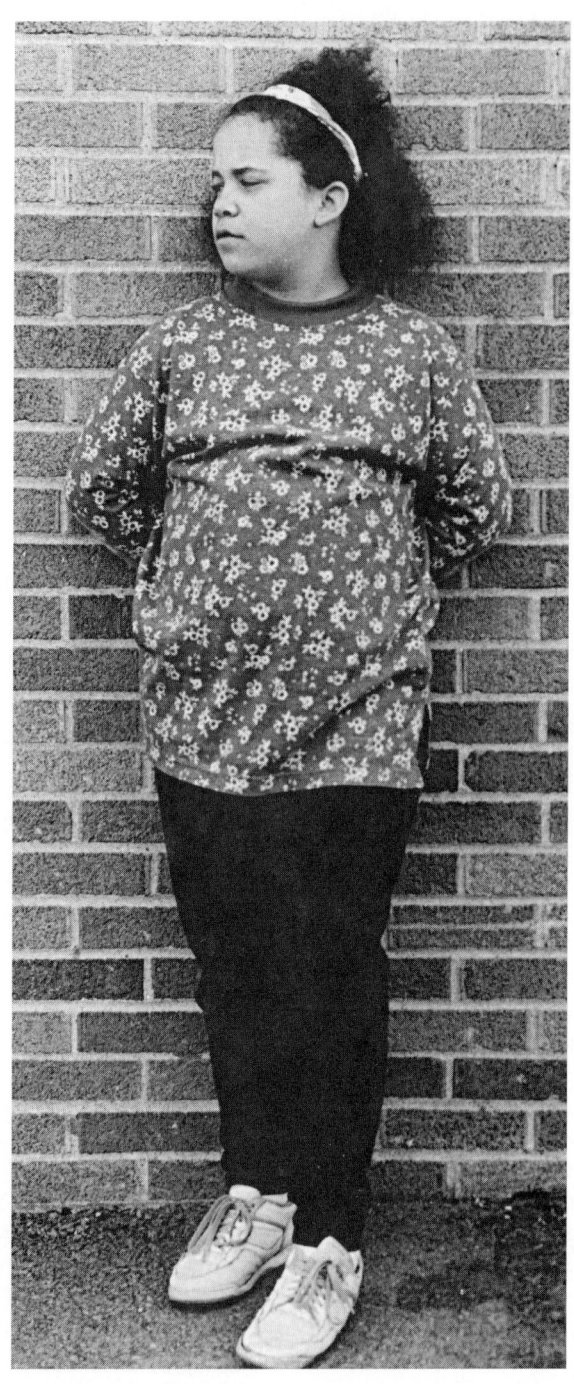

Neglected children are often loners who rarely interact with peers.

Facilitating Social Skills

Early and positive experience with peers can lead to the acquisition of social knowledge and skills (Hartup & Moore, 1990; Howes, 1987). Providing many opportunities for children to interact with one another in play settings is the most important way teachers can facilitate social competence. A growing body of research suggests, however, that adults can play an active role in promoting social skills. Teachers can facilitate social development through informal interactions in which they model or prompt specific social skills and nurture friendships (Mize, Ladd, & Price, 1985). Such interventions have been found to enhance the peer-group status of children (Ladd & Mize, 1983). In this section, guidelines for social skills intervention are presented.

General Guidelines

When should teachers intervene to enhance peer relationships or social interaction? Which children need such support? How much assistance should be given? There are no easy answers to these questions. For this reason social skills intervention requires much teacher reflection and sensitivity to the needs of children.

Who Needs Support?

A first step in social skills intervention is to decide which children need help in acquiring social competence. All students might benefit from occasional interactions with a teacher which help them to learn new social behaviors or to make friends. Those who are truly rejected or neglected by peers are most in need of adult assistance. Profiles of the children presented above can serve as guides to assist teachers in deciding who to help. Through careful observation teachers can note those who would benefit from adult involvement in their interactions.

Which Social Skills Should Be Enhanced?

Once children who need help are identified, teachers can analyze their play to determine which behaviors or skills should be enhanced. One child might need assistance simply in interacting more often with others. Another might benefit from interventions that teach effective social language. Still another might require support in entering play groups. In their interventions, teachers might focus on some of the social skills highlighted in the profile of popular children above—behaviors which appear to lead to successful friendship formation and peer acceptance.

How Much Help Should Be Given?

Vygotsky's work (1978), discussed in Chapter 2, is helpful in deciding how much assistance to give students. He has argued that in some cases children need much support from adults; direct guidance is very appropriate when a problem facing a child is insurmountable. If a social problem arises which a child cannot begin to resolve alone, then, a teacher might directly suggest solutions. This direct guidance is illustrated in the example below.

❖ ❖

A teacher observes that four-year-old Child A, who rarely plays with others, has tried to join a group of peers in the block area. They have rejected his requests to join in. The teacher intervenes.

Teacher:	Why don't we go over and start building our own house? (Takes Child A's hand and walks over to the block area. Begins to build with him)
Child A:	(Quietly, to the teacher) I'm going to build a house for this family. (Points to a set of plastic people)
Teacher:	You should tell Joseph what you're doing. Say, "Joseph, I'm building a house for these people."
Child A:	I'm building a house for these guys, Joseph.
Child B:	(Looks up from his building) Okay. I'll build another house 'cause there isn't enough room in your house. Some of them can live over here.

Child B begins to interact with A. The teacher withdraws after a few minutes. ❖

In this vignette the teacher has directly taught a group-entry strategy, even offering specific language the child might use. Until this child has acquired skills to enter groups on his own, according to Vygotsky, the teacher should continue with this direct guidance.

After much of this direct assistance has been given, children may be able solve social problems with only minimal adult support. At this point teachers might give hints or subtle prompts that help children to interact with peers more independently. The vignette below demonstrates this hint-giving approach.

❖ ❖

Child A of the above vignette has now been given much support from the teacher and has become more competent at interacting with peers. He attempts to enter a group in the dramatic-play area. The teacher now uses a different approach in helping him to get in.

Child A:	They won't let me play.
Teacher:	Did you ask them?

Child A:	Yeah. And they said no.
Teacher:	So asking didn't work? What else could you try?
Child A:	You come over with me.
Teacher:	I can't come over right now. What could you do by yourself to join them?
Child A:	I could eat the dinner with them.
Teacher:	Right. You could just join them at the pretend dinner. What could you say to them when you join them?
Child A:	I'm hungry.
Teacher:	Yes. "I'm hungry. Could you please pass the asparagus?" That might work. Try it.

The teacher watches as the child tries his strategy. He is successful; his peers accept him into the play theme.   ❖

In this instance the teacher chooses to guide the child indirectly in solving his own problem. She does this by asking questions and suggesting refinements to the child's approach. She coaches the child in choosing and implementing his own entry strategy.

As children become more competent at solving problems, according to Vygotsky, teachers should give over all responsibility to them. In the following vignette the teacher encourages a child to solve a social problem without any assistance.

Child A of the above vignettes has become quite effective in entering play groups. He approaches the teacher once again with complaints about being excluded. The teacher encourages him to solve the problem without assistance.

Child A:	(Points to the water table) They won't let me play.
Teacher:	I know you can figure out how to join them. I've seen you do that before.
Child A:	Should I just go play with them?
Teacher:	That might work. You figure this out on your own.

The child invents his own strategy—he begins an interesting water experiment in a corner of the water table; children eventually include him in their play.   ❖

Here the teacher has been encouraging, but has given full responsibility for solving this problem to the child. From Vygotsky's perspective the key to effective social skills intervention is to decide when to guide directly, when to give hints, and when to leave children alone to solve their own social problems.

A Caution

A word of caution is in order when determining which children to assist and how much help to give. Children cannot all become "social butterflies." Some are quiet and less social, others more active and outgoing. Some are less positive in affect and are slow to warm up to others. Such children may still be successful in making friends and interacting with peers; teachers should accept and appreciate these social differences among students. They should not tamper too vigorously with unique social styles. Social skills intervention, as with all play intervention, should be administered in a nonimposing way. Children should never be forced to play together or interact in ways they do not choose. The goal is to assist children in learning social skills when this assistance is needed and desired.

Group Dynamics

Every class is different; experienced teachers frequently marvel at the "chemistry" of a particular group of students. Individual children may be more or less neglected or rejected by peers depending on how others in the class respond to them. In some groups they might be accepted readily into play activities, in others their initiatives might be regularly ignored or rebuffed. Group composition, then, is a critical determinant of success in peer relations (Putallaz & Wasserman, 1989). Thoughtful placement of children with social skills deficits into positive classroom groups is important. If these children can play often with accepting, prosocial peers they have a better chance of acquiring social skills and forming friendships.

Children are usually assigned to a particular class because of age, academic achievement, or pure luck, however. The resulting classroom grouping may not create the ideal social context for less competent children. In this instance teachers must intervene to enhance positive group dynamics; in essence they must create a positive classroom chemistry. They can nurture among the whole group a sense of belonging and caring which will lead ultimately to more positive social interaction and acceptance of socially less competent students.

Group meetings in which children share ideas or raise concerns will go a long way toward enhancing positive group dynamics. Children might be asked to discuss real classroom problems and to consider alternative solutions to them. Activities in which children respond to social dilemmas (e.g., what to do when a peer won't play with you) are particularly effective (DeVries & Kohlberg, 1990). The most potent approach is to facilitate prosocial behaviors among all students through informal play intervention (Oden, 1986). Teachers can assist all children, for example, in making contact with and accepting the initiatives of less-accepted peers. Although the following sections focus on facilitating social skills among less competent children, it is important to remember that these interventions are necessary for all students in the class. The ultimate goal is to assist all children in entering into warm and meaningful relationships with others.

Social Participation

As stated in earlier chapters, playing alone can be valuable; children learn to entertain themselves and to experience the comfort of being alone. When children spend long hours in large classroom groups, solitary play can provide a peaceful respite from active classroom life. Some children rarely interact with peers, however. In the case of rejected children this may be because they are actively avoided by playmates; neglected children may lack the ability or willingness to join play groups. It is futile to try to teach such children specific social skills until they are interacting with others more often; general social participation must be encouraged before teachers can enhance refinements in social behavior. In the classic work of Mildred Parten (1932), stages of social participation among young children are described. These are presented in Table 4-1.

The first two stages have been excluded by some authors because they do not involve social interaction (Feeney, Christensen, & Moravcik, 1991). In "Unoccupied Behavior," for example, children do not interact with toys, materials, or peers; they show little interest in what is going on around them. "Onlooker Behavior," Parten's second stage, is distinguished by an interest in what others are doing; children in this stage often watch their peers play. Although there is little that is social about Unoccupied and Onlooker Behavior, these may serve as departure-points for intervention. Children who are unoccupied might first be encouraged simply to watch their peers; this is an important step toward more involved social participation. In the following example a teacher assists an unoccupied child to watch others play.

A six-year-old who rarely plays with others sits at a table in the math center, resting her head on her hand and staring off across the room. Several other children play a game of dominoes; the isolate child does not appear to notice them. A teacher approaches.

Teacher:	Did you see that Polly and Roberta are playing dominoes?
Child:	(Doesn't look up) What?
Teacher:	Polly and Roberta are having quite a game. Listen to them giggle.
Child:	(Glances over at the two girls, then stares off again. Says nothing)
Teacher:	Why don't we watch them for a while. Let's see who wins.
Child:	Okay. (Turns now to face her peers)

The teacher and child watch for several minutes. The teacher comments enthusiastically on the events of the game and what the two children are doing. The isolate child begins to watch more intently. She smiles and even laughs once at something silly her peers have said.   ❖

Table 4-1
Parten's Stages of Social Development

Stage	Example
1. Unoccupied behavior	A child stares off across the classroom, not looking at anything in particular.
2. Onlooker behavior	A child watches a group of classmates playing with blocks. She smiles and shows delight when they begin to giggle and get silly. Still, she makes no attempt to join them.
3. Parallel play	A child sits right next to several others in the sandbox. She makes a mound of sand on her own. Now and then she looks over to see what the others are doing. She continues to work on her own project.
4. Associative play	A child sits at the art table working with modeling clay. Several other children sit beside him. Although he works with his own ball of clay, he converses with the others often and shows them what he is working on. He shares cutting and modeling tools with his playmates.
5. Cooperative play	A child builds an airport with two others in the block area. Each child adds blocks to the same structure. They plan together how they will build it and negotiate when there is a dispute over design.

Source: Parten (1932)

In this vignette the teacher does not attempt to facilitate actual social contact; this onlooking child would have rejected such an initiative. Instead, the teacher simply tries to stimulate her student's interest in what others are doing. It might take many weeks of watching peers before this child will be ready for actual social interchanges.

Children show they are interested in peers' activities when they begin to watch or hover around them. Teachers might now attempt to promote the next of Parten's social play levels, "parallel play." In this form of activity a child plays side-by-side with others but rarely interacts. Still, children in parallel play enjoy the close proximity to others; this is significant social experience. In the following vignette the teacher encourages a child to play parallel to others.

Four five-year-olds are playing in the sandbox on the playground. A child stands for a long time watching them. A teacher moves into the area.

Teacher:	Why don't you make a sand pie too. Come on with me, I'll help you. (Takes the child's hand and walks to the sandbox)
Child:	(Says nothing, walks with the teacher)
Teacher:	(In an enthused tone) Now I'm going to make a huge pie. (Begins to make a mound of sand)
Child:	(Says nothing. Begins to make his own sand mound. Occasionally stops to watch the teacher and other children as they work)

The teacher continues to converse with the child and work with the sand. After several minutes she withdraws from the sandbox. The isolate child continues to play with the sand and to watch his playmates. No interaction among the children occurs. ❖

The teacher of the vignette is encouraging parallel play. There are two important reasons she is doing this. First, her intervention leads the isolate child to a more social level of play than before—the child now plays right next to others and watches, even copies their actions. Second, parallel playing is an excellent way to enter a play group. The teacher is helping the child to learn a behavior that will come in handy later as he desires to join more fully the play of others.

Once a child is regularly playing parallel to others the teacher can begin to facilitate general interaction. Following Parten's (1932) framework the teacher might first strive to enhance associative play. In this form of social play children pursue their own individual play themes but interact often. They might talk to one another about what they are doing or even share materials. In the next vignette a teacher demonstrates how associative play can be encouraged.

Three five-year-old children are drawing in silence. They rarely speak to one another; they each use a single crayon rather than selecting other colors available in a large container on the table. A teacher sits down and converses with them.

Teacher:	Tell me about your drawing, Jeremy.
Child A:	Oh, this is the sun. See? (Points to a place on his drawing)
Teacher:	Oh, yes. I can see that. Is the sun shining down on someplace special?
Child A:	This is my house. See, my cat's getting outdoors. She's not supposed to be outdoors.
Child B:	Can I see?
Teacher:	(To Child A) Why don't you show Alex your drawing?
Child A:	Okay. (Holds up his drawing)

Child B:	Let's see. (Moves over to look at Child A's drawing) I have a cat.
Teacher:	Do you? Tell me about it.
Child B:	My cat can go outside.
Child A:	(Now speaking to Child B) My cat can't. But he's sneaking out. See? (Points to his drawing)
Child C:	(Takes another piece of paper) I'm going to draw a guinea pig. That's my pet. He's going to sneak outside.
Teacher:	Oh, my.
Child C:	I need a brown crayon.
Teacher:	You could ask Jeremy to pass you the container.
Child C:	Jeremy, give me the brown.
Child A:	(Throws the crayon to her)
Child B:	(Talking to his peers, rubbing a yellow crayon back and forth across his drawing) Look! There's a fire. It's burning the houses. The people better get out.
Child A:	(Shows his drawing to peers) Now my cat is running into the road. These are cars coming.
Child C:	Yeah. He could get run over. My guinea pig isn't getting run over. See? (Shows Child A her drawing)
Child B:	(Addressing his peers) There's a fireman coming now to put it out.

The children continue to work on their own individual projects but now converse with each other.   ❖

Before the teacher intervenes the children of this vignette are playing parallel to one another. By encouraging communication among these young artists she has raised their social participation to a higher level—associative play. They begin discussing their individual projects, although they each comment on their own drawings more than they respond to their peers' work. They also share materials. Their play is not as yet fully coordinated; but much social interaction is occurring.

The most complex form of social activity—cooperative play—often emerges in the older preschool years. Children who are playing associatively may need assistance from adults in playing cooperatively. In cooperative play children adopt a single coordinated play theme; they plan, negotiate, and differentiate roles in pursuit of a shared goal. In the vignette below a teacher transforms associative play into cooperative play.

❖ ❖

Two four-year-olds are playing with dolls in the dramatic-play area. They each dress and care for a "baby"; although they speak to one another about their activities, they do not coordinate their play in any way. A teacher enters the area.

Child A:	(Dressing a doll) I'm getting ready to go shopping. I need to bundle her 'cause it's cold.
Child B:	My baby won't stop crying. (To her doll) What is it? Are you sick or something?
Teacher:	(To Child B) Maybe you should take her to see a doctor.
Child B:	Yeah. She might need some medicine.
Teacher:	(To Child A) Are you going to drive your car to the store?
Child A:	Oh, yes. This will be the car. (Points to two chairs)
Teacher:	Maybe you could give Jennifer and her baby a ride to the doctor's office.
Child A:	Okay, Jennifer. This is my car, see? You come over and ride with me.
Child B:	Okay. Where do I get in?

The two children begin to drive to town with their dolls. They discuss the illness and what the doctor will do. They decide to go together to the doctor, then do grocery shopping. ❖

In this vignette the teacher has successfully encouraged the children to merge their similar play themes into a single coordinated one. Once the children cooperate fully in their dramatic play the teacher withdraws.

Facilitating Friendships

Most preschool children have at least one reciprocated relationship with a peer (Matheson & Wu, 1991); those who maintain long-term friendships tend to be more competent socially (Howes, 1983, 1987). Some children lack friends. Teachers can help them enter into meaningful relationships with others; this is an important goal for a number of reasons. A single friendship can insulate a child from some of the negative effects of being rejected or neglected by other peers (Hartup & Moore, 1990). It may be that having a friend is reaffirming; it shows children that they can be successful and liked, even if by only one other child.

Friendships are very useful for social skills intervention. Studies have shown that friendships provide unique social opportunities for children. Conflicts among friends are less heated and more likely to end in compromise (Hartup, Laursen, Stewart, & Eastenson, 1988); a child is more likely to be accepted into a play group when one of the players is a friend (Ramsey, 1989b). When playing with friends, less-effective children can try out new social skills and enjoy greater success. So, an especially opportune time for teachers to facilitate social skills is when children are playing with their friends.

Teachers can begin by observing classroom interactions to identify pairs of students who show signs of mutual interest or compatibility. A teacher might note, for example, that a particular student makes many initiatives toward an isolate peer who has no friends. Another student might be observed regularly approaching an aggressive peer who is generally rejected in the classroom. Once potential friends have been identified, teachers can make arrangements for them to spend time together in informal, non-threatening settings. A teacher might approach parents and encourage outside-of-school contacts, for those families who can manage this. A teacher can bring the children together in the classroom by asking them to help with tasks or projects or by encouraging them to enter joint play activities. Once a teacher observes a "spark" between two potential friends, interventions for enhancing social interaction among the two can be implemented.

A teacher might carefully pair a neglected child with one who is very social and kind. A rejected child could be paired with one who is socially competent, confident, and assertive. The major criterion for creating such pairs, however, is mutual liking; children should never be forced to play together when one or the other does not wish to enter into the relationship.

In some cases, interaction between two children will be temporary, lasting only the duration of a particular play activity or perhaps extending for a day or two (Howes, 1983). These contacts are still very important to the rejected or neglected child who normally has very little positive social contact. If an ongoing friendship emerges, the intervention will have been particularly meaningful—facilitating a reciprocal relationship may be one of the greatest successes a teacher can have (Selman & Demorest, 1984).

Teaching Social Behaviors

Once children are participating to some degree in social activities and have established a friendship or two, teachers can assist them in learning specific social skills. Several important skills identified in research are presented in Table 4-2.

Strategies for enhancing each will be presented in this section.

Play Leadership

Popular children tend to be leaders within play groups; they often take initiative in guiding peer activities (Trawick-Smith, 1988). This willingness to lead makes them attractive playmates (Mize & Ladd, 1990); one reason isolate children are more likely to be ignored is that they rarely direct the play of others (Scarlett, 1983). Children can be coached in leadership behaviors through informal play intervention.

The teacher below guides an isolate child in leading a peer group.

❖ ❖

Three five-year-old children are playing in a pretend hospital set up in the dramatic-play area. Child B, who rarely plays with others, mainly watches the other

Through play intervention, teachers can teach social skills such as leadership and conflict resolution.

two. She is directed by her peers to give them objects and to perform medical procedures on doll "patients." A teacher intervenes.

Child A: Now, Sara, you have to come over here with that doll. That's a patient too, you know.

Child B: (Says nothing, walks over to Child A with a doll)

Child C: Yeah. Let's say we need to give him surgery, okay, Cheryl? Sara, give me the patient. We need to put him to sleep.

Teacher: Oh, my. He needs surgery? Will Sara be the surgeon? (To Child B) Would you like to be the surgeon, Sara?

Child B: (In a timid voice) Yeah.

Child A: No. I'm doing the surgery.

Teacher: Well, we need several surgeons if this is a serious operation.

Child A: Okay. Come on, Sara. (Lays doll on a cot, spreads out medical instruments)

Teacher: Sara, what sort of surgery does our patient need?

Table 4-2
Target Behaviors for Social Skills Intervention

Social Skill	Sample Teacher Intervention
1. Leadership	A teacher plays with four children cooking a pretend meal. One child, Dana, is quite withdrawn and uninvolved. The teacher suggests, "Why don't we let Dana decide what we'll make for dinner? Dana, what should we cook?"
2. Socially effective language	A teacher overhears a less competent child meekly invite a peer to ride on a pretend car. This child ignores him. The teacher suggests, "Tell Marcus where you'd like to go in the car. Maybe he'll join you if you tell him where you're going."
3. Nonaggressive conflict resolution	A child, Sheila, has just hit Marie. A teacher intervenes: "Sheila, you can't hit. What is another way to let Marie know that you are angry?"
4. Tactful rejection	Sean wants to build a mall out of blocks. Ben does not and says so with a loud "No!" A teacher intervenes: "Ben, why don't you tell him why you don't want to make a mall? Can you give him a reason? Do you have another idea for what you can build?"
5. Compromising	Two children are arguing over what to play. One wants to pretend to be a "Ninja Turtle," the other wants to play "Batman." A teacher asks, "Is there some way you could play both of those things? How could you play Ninja Turtles *and* Batman?"
6. Entering play-groups	A child wants to play with two others who are pretending to work in a restaurant. He asks them if he can play and they say no. A teacher assists: "Why don't you try this — say, 'Julie, I want to order a hamburger for lunch.'"
7. Monitoring the outcomes of social initiatives	One child has just pushed another. The teacher intervenes: "What happened when you pushed Sally? See how she moved away from you? She didn't want to play with you any more when you pushed her."

Child B: (Quietly) He needs to have some tubes put in.

Child C: Oh yeah, Sara. Those tubes in his ears, right?

Child B: (Nods, says nothing)

Teacher: (To Child B) What instrument will you need first in our surgery? We can assist you.

Child B: Um. That one. (Points to a plastic medical instrument)

The teacher plays with the children for several minutes. As Children A and C continue to hand Child B instruments she requests, the teacher withdraws.   ❖

In this vignette the teacher gives a neglected child an opportunity to direct the play. Her peers accept her leadership in this case; her initiatives are mostly successful. Research has shown that such interventions will increase the confidence of isolate children and the frequency with which they lead (Scarlett, 1983).

Socially Effective Language

Popular children use language effectively in social situations. They display a broad repertoire of verbal strategies to get peers' attention and to communicate play ideas. Teachers can model or prompt effective use of language in social settings. In the following example a teacher helps a child learn phrases for getting another's attention.

Two six-year-olds are building with blocks. One of the two, Child A, is quite aggressive and generally rejected by peers.

Child A: (Pointing to his block structure, in a loud tone) Noah! Look!

Child B: (Does not look up from his block building, says nothing)

Child A: (In a loud, angry tone) Noah!

Teacher: (Quietly to Child A) Why don't you talk to Noah in a quiet voice? Say, "Noah, look at what I built."

Child A: (In a quieter voice) Noah, look.

Child B: (Looks up briefly) Yeah. (Returns to his work)

Teacher: Maybe you could tell him what you made. Say it in a quiet voice. Say, "I made this airport. See?" Maybe he'll listen if you say it like that.

Child A: Noah, this is the airport, see?

Child B: (Looks at Child A) Oh, yeah. Where are some planes, though?

The two begin to discuss the airport; the teacher withdraws from the block area.   ❖

Here the teacher has encouraged a rejected child to soften his tone and to phrase his bid for attention in a more interesting way. Although not all interventions work out so smoothly, in this case the teacher has assisted Child A in successfully engaging his playmate. This experience shows Child A the power of softer, requestive language.

Nonaggressive Conflict Resolution

Aggressive behavior leads to peer rejection (Dodge, 1983). Through teacher intervention, aggressive children can be shown the futility of their forceful initiatives and can be taught alternatives to violence in solving social problems (Mize & Ladd, 1990). This can be done at "circle time" through the use of literature, puppet shows, or games. A more effective approach to reducing aggression is to intervene in real-life classroom conflict and to model prosocial behaviors.

Modeling specific prosocial skills may be the most effective technique. When a teacher is warm, kind, and friendly, shares materials, and gives help, children are more likely to behave in these ways themselves (Bandura, 1986). Through informal interventions teachers can promote positive conflict resolution. Helping children learn skills for resolving disputes can reduce classroom aggression, particularly among older preschool or primary grade children (Yeats, Schultz, & Selman, 1991). A question such as, "Can you think of a way we could all play with the blocks?" gives children opportunities to explore nonaggressive and mutually satisfying resolutions to social conflicts.

Pointing out the consequences of children's aggressive acts might gradually lead to an understanding of the negative social outcomes of violence (Ladd & Mize, 1983). For example, when a teacher responds to an act of aggression by pointing out its impact on the victim (e.g., "Look at how Sara is crying. You really hurt her. Do you see?"), an aggressive child might come to realize the adverse effects of such acts.

Redirecting children's angry interactions with their peers has also been recommended as a way to reduce aggression (Hendrick, 1992). By showing children verbal alternatives to aggressive behavior, for example, teachers demonstrate more appropriate expressions of anger. "Don't hit; use words if you are angry," is a common and effective response to aggressive incidents in early-childhood classrooms. The vignette below illustrates this technique.

❖ ❖

Two three-year-olds are playing in the sandbox on the playground. Child B has just stepped on a sand mound which Child A has made. Child B begins to hit her; a teacher quickly intervenes.

Teacher:	No, Susan. You may not hit her. You look very angry. If you're angry, tell her. Use words.
Child A:	(In an angry tone) She stepped on my sand.
Teacher:	You can tell her with words. Say, "I don't like that!"
Child A:	(To Child B) I don't like that! You stepped on it! I don't like that!

The children now resume their play without further incident.   ❖

The teacher above has helped the child to express anger in a nonviolent way. Studies have shown that when teachers give specific verbal alternatives to young children, classroom aggression is reduced (Caldwell, 1977). As children get older, the teacher can encourage them to think of their own strategies for dealing with conflict (e.g., "What is another way to tell Melissa you are angry?") (Carlsson-Paige & Levin, 1987).

Tactful Rejection

Popular children are skilled at saying "no" to peers' play suggestions in ways that don't hurt feelings or lead to an end to the play theme. They display a tactful approach to rejecting others' initiatives (Trawick-Smith, 1988). Teachers can encourage children to be more diplomatic by suggesting that they do two things when rejecting another's ideas: 1.) tell why the suggestion is being rejected, and 2.) give an attractive alternative course of action (Hazen, Black, & Fleming-Johnson, 1984). The teacher in the example below prompts a child to perform these rejecting behaviors.

Two four-year-old children are playing with large cardboard boxes on the playground. One child wants to pretend that they are animals who must hide in their "caves" from hunters. The other child doesn't want to play this. As a dispute erupts a teacher moves over to them.

Child A:	Come on, Seth. I want to play animals.
Child B:	(In an whiny tone) No!
Child A:	(Now angry) Seth!
Teacher:	My, you both sound angry. What's up?
Child A:	Seth won't play. I want to be animals and he won't.
Teacher:	Seth, maybe you could tell Jeremy why you don't want to pretend to be an animal. Can you tell him?
Child B:	I don't want to get in the box. That's not how you play with these.
Teacher:	Oh. So you don't want to play animals, because you don't want to get inside the boxes?
Child B:	Yeah.
Teacher:	Do you have another idea about what you could play if you don't want to play animals?
Child B:	Let's roll 'em. (Begins to roll one of the boxes down a hill) See? They roll down.
Child A:	(In an enthusiastic tone) Okay.

The children begin this new game, rolling the boxes down the hill and leaving the teacher behind. ❖

Here the teacher has prompted tactful rejection. She encourages Child B to explain why he has rejected A's idea and to suggest an alternative. In this case the strategy was successful. Instead of ending in a falling-out between the two and a dissolution of the play, the disagreement was amicably resolved with assistance from the teacher.

Compromising

Popular children also compromise quite often in disputes, negotiating with peers and even giving in now and then. This give-and-take style of interaction is associated with being well liked by peers (Trawick-Smith, 1988). Teachers can facilitate compromise in play settings; the teacher of the vignette below illustrates one approach.

Two six-year-olds are arguing over what to do in the science area. One child wants to use the float-and-sink tub, the other a balance. A teacher assists them in resolving the dispute.

Teacher:	Can you think of a way to use both the float-and-sink tub and the balance?
Child A:	No. I want to do the floating and sinking. Come on Rosie.
Child B:	Can we play float *and* weigh?
Teacher:	Can you think of a way to do both?
Child A:	Oh. We can weigh the things and then sink them.
Teacher:	Some of the objects might get ruined if they get wet.
Child A:	Let's take out the things that can't get wet. Then we can sink the other ones. Then we weigh them. (Begins to take objects out of a container)
Child B:	But we have to weigh them first, okay, Anna?
Child A:	All right.

Once the two have come to an agreement, the teacher exits.   ❖

The two children of this vignette have reached a compromise with adult assistance. They have managed to combine their play interests; each seems satisfied with the plan they have worked out. With guidance from a teacher, children can become quite skilled at resolving conflicts (Trawick-Smith, 1988).

Entering Play Groups

It is not uncommon in play-based classrooms for several children to begin a play theme and then exclude all others who wish to join in (e.g., "We're building a house and you can't play, Jason."). Being an active member of a peer group requires an ability to join in these play settings; popular children employ complex and savvy methods for doing this.

Many common group-entry strategies are ineffective. Simply asking to play almost always results in rejection (Ramsey, 1989a). (It is interesting that some teachers will suggest this strategy when their students complain of being excluded.) Another ineffective method has been called "hover and wait" (Ramsey, 1989a). In this approach the child stands watching in hopes of being invited to play. Other unsuccessful strategies include taking toys and objects away from group members or trying to forcefully take control of play activities.

Several research studies have identified more effective techniques. The best approach may be to join in the play in progress without drawing attention to oneself (Ramsey, 1989a). If others are playing restaurant, for example, the child wishing entry might sit at a table and quietly eat lunch. If children are building with blocks, a child might begin constructing a building parallel to them. Once this unobtrusive entry has been made, the child might make interesting comments that enhance, rather than disrupt the play (e.g., "I'm making an office building."). Calling individual playmates by name is another effective way to be included in ongoing play (e.g., "Joseph, can I order a hamburger?").

If children are having a particularly difficult time being accepted in groups, a teacher can model these successful entry strategies. Initially a child might be directed to play situations where there is a greater likelihood of success. For example, it is much easier to enter play with another single child than with a group. A teacher might guide an isolate child, then, to an individual peer when teaching entry approaches. Play groups that include a friend of the entering child are more likely to allow entrance. An isolate child can be guided toward groups in which a friend is involved. Again, friends can be extremely useful for facilitating social skills.

In the following vignette a teacher demonstrates strategies for facilitating entry skills.

❖ ❖

A four-year-old has just come to a teacher on the playground to complain that two peers will not play with her. The teacher studies the play-setting this child wishes to join, then assists her in getting in.

Teacher:	It looks like they're playing house. Why don't we pretend to be mail carriers and deliver an important letter?
Child A:	Okay. (Follows the teacher over to a climber where the two peers are playing)
Teacher:	(Quietly to Child A) Why don't you knock on the door and tell Sheila that you have an important package?
Child A:	(Knocks on the climber) Sheila. We're the mailmen. We have a very important package.
Child B:	(Stops interacting with Child C, looks over at Child A) What is it?
Child A:	(Looks at the teacher) What will it be?

Teacher:	What do you think?
Child A:	It's some food you ordered.
Child B:	Oh. Some food? Great; bring it here.
Child C:	Food doesn't come in the mail.
Child A:	This is special food. It's from the Chinese restaurant.

The children begin to interact. Once Child A is fully included in the play the teacher exits.   ❖

This teacher has prompted a child to use several effective group-entry techniques. He suggests that she simply begin playing in an unobtrusive way and that she add an interesting new element to the theme in progress. Further, he encourages her to call one playmate by name. In this case the children readily accept her into the group.

Monitoring Outcomes of Social Behaviors

Performing the above social skills may not ensure that children will be effective in peer groups. Children must know when and with whom to use these various strategies in order to be fully competent. To learn which behavior is right for a particular play context, children must notice the consequences of their actions (Crick & Ladd, 1987). They must observe that aggression leads to rejection in many situations, for example, or that compromising results in mutually satisfying resolutions to conflicts in others. Popular children are very good at monitoring their own social initiatives and observing outcomes. In this way they learn quickly which behaviors work best in which settings. Other children may need adult assistance in making such observations.

As children interact with peers, teachers might directly point out or ask questions about the consequences of their initiatives.

In the vignette below a teacher demonstrates a question-asking intervention to encourage reflection on the outcomes of social behavior.

❖ ❖

Two five-year-olds are playing with modeling clay at the art center. One child wants more clay; the other refuses to relinquish any. A teacher enters the area.

Child A:	(In an angry tone) Aaron! Give me some of yours. Look how much you have and I don't have any!
Child B:	(Also angry) No!
Teacher:	(Quietly to Child A) You're very angry, Samantha.
Child A:	He won't give me any of his clay. Look at how much he has.
Teacher:	What happened when you yelled at him to give you more?
Child A:	He wouldn't give me any.
Teacher:	Did yelling at him work?

Child A:	What?
Teacher:	Did it work to yell at him?
Child A:	No. He didn't give me any.
Teacher:	What would be another way to get some clay from Aaron?
Child A:	I could say it quiet. (To Child B in a quieter voice) Aaron, give me some clay.
Child B:	All right. (Pinches a minuscule portion of clay from his huge ball and hands it to Child A)
Child A:	No!
Teacher:	What happened here? Did he give you some when you asked quietly?
Child A:	No. Just a little.
Teacher:	What else could you try?
Child A:	*You* tell him to give me some.
Teacher:	I'd like you to work this out. How about saying, "Let's play with the clay together, all right, Aaron?" What will happen then?
Child A:	Okay. (To Child B) Let's play with clay together, all right?
Child B:	(In an exasperated tone) Oh, all right. (Hands Child A a sizable chunk of clay)
Teacher:	What happened?
Child A:	He gave me clay. But he didn't want to. ❖

Child B finally gives Child A some clay only because she wears him down with incessant requests. In spite of the less-than-positive outcome of this interchange, the teacher is able to assist Child A in analyzing the social situation and monitoring the effects of her efforts. Such interventions lead to overall social competence in young children (Ladd & Mize, 1983).

It is particularly important that aggressive, rejected children receive this kind of adult assistance. Studies indicate that highly aggressive children often are not aware that their violence leads to peer rejection (Crick & Ladd, 1987). As discussed above, teachers can point out consequences when an aggressive interchange has occurred.

❖ ❖

A seven-year-old has just struck another while on the playground. A teacher moves in quickly.

Teacher:	You may not hit, Andy. That really hurts. Do you see how you hurt Sean? See? He's crying, isn't he?
Child:	Yeah. But he was bothering me.
Teacher:	What happened when you hit him?

Child:	He's crying.
Teacher:	Yes. And what did he do?
Child:	He went away.
Teacher:	Right. He doesn't want to play with you when you hit him. He just moved away from you.
Child:	Yeah.
Teacher:	And what else happened when you hit him?
Child:	You came over here.
Teacher:	Yes. I became angry. Adults and children get angry when you hit. ❖

This teacher has helped the child to see three negative outcomes of aggression—peers get hurt, they no longer want to play, and adults as well as children get angry. Over time this child may come to recognize the futility of such actions.

Teachers can point out to children the consequences of their aggression.

Summary

Peer acceptance and formation of friendships are extremely important in the early years. Young children who are not well liked or who are ineffective with peers are at risk. Those who are actively rejected by peers because of aggressive or annoying behavior and those who are neglected by others because they are shy or nonsocial need special support in forming peer relationships. Adults can assist these less effective children by enhancing their social skills.

Which social skills should be promoted? Studies of highly popular children indicate that certain behaviors enhance one's status in a peer group. Leadership, language competence, and tact are characteristics of more popular children. Skills at compromising, resolving conflicts in nonaggressive ways, and entering play groups are also important in peer relations. These behaviors may be promoted through informal play intervention in the classroom. Through modeling, question-asking, and prompting, teachers can help children acquire the skills of friendship.

Suggested Activities

1. Observe children interacting in an early-childhood classroom. Identify a child you assume is popular, one who is likely to be rejected, and a third who appears to be neglected by peers. Write a description of each child guided by the following questions:
   a. Which social interactions led you to believe each child was popular, rejected, or neglected?
   b. Which social skills described in this chapter were you able to observe in the popular child? Which skills were lacking in the two less effective children?
   c. What recommendations would you make for social skills intervention?
2. Play with a group of children and, as you do, try to increase general social participation in the group. Write a description of your experiences guided by the following questions:
   a. How successful were you in increasing general social interaction? Which of your techniques were most effective?
   b. Describe the level of social participation (see Parten's stages, Table 4-1) both before and after you played with children. In what ways, if at all, did the level of social play change?
3. Play with a group of children in an informal way. After observing the group for a while, select one child you feel could benefit from social skills

intervention. Briefly enhance one or more of the following social behaviors: leadership, social language, nonaggressive conflict resolution, compromising, entering play groups, tactful rejection, or monitoring the social situation. Write a description of your experiences guided by the following questions:

a.   Why did you choose this particular child for intervention?
b.   Which skill or skills did you focus on? Why did you select these?
c.   How successful were you in teaching these skills?

Further Reading

Greenberg, P. (1992). Positive peer relations. *Young Children, 47*(4), 51–59.

Hartup, W. W., & Moore, S. G. (1990). Early peer relations: Developmental significance and prognostic implications. *Early Childhood Research Quarterly, 5,* 1–17.

Hazen, N., Black, B., & Fleming-Johnson, F. (1984). Social acceptance: Strategies children use and how teachers can help learn them. *Young Children, 39*(3), 26–36.

Honig, A.S. (1987). The shy child. *Young Children, 42*(4), 54–64.

Melson, G. G., & Fogel, A. (1988). The development of nurturance in young children. *Young Children, 43*(3), 57–65.

Mize, J., Ladd, G. W., & Price, J. M. (1985). Promoting positive peer relations with young children: Rationales and strategies. *Child Care Quarterly, 14,* 221–237.

Rogers, D. L., & Ross, D. D. (1986). Encouraging positive social interaction among young children. *Young Children, 41*(3), 12–36.

Roopnarine, J. L., & Honig, A. S. (1985). The unpopular child. *Young Children, 40*(6), 59–64.

Trawick-Smith, J. W. (1988). Let's say you're the baby, OK?: Play leadership and following behavior in young children. *Young Children, 43*(5), 51–59.

5

PROMOTING LANGUAGE AND LITERACY

❖ ❖

A four-year-old sits at the writing center composing a story. In a blank book made from construction paper he has drawn a large head with legs sprouting from it. He now produces a set of zig-zagging scribbles that are the words.

A teacher moves over to him and asks about his project.

"A book," the child responds proudly, holding up his unfinished work.

"I see. You're writing a book," the teacher replies, expanding his shorter utterance into a full sentence. "Could you read to me what you have written so far?"

As he runs his finger along his scribbles, the child reads the following story in very serious, adult-sounding, book-like language:

"Once upon a time there was a monster that just loved to eat up little boys." The child pauses.

"Oh, dear!" the teacher responds, enthusiastically. "Read more! I want to hear about this monster."

"Well, it's got big teeth and it's very meanish!" he reads.

"Why does it just eat little boys, do you suppose?"

"Well, because it's meanish and they don't let him into 'Quick Stop' to buy food." the child explains.

After further discussion, the teacher asks the child to predict the ending of the story and encourages him to write more pages. He then leaves the child and moves on to talk with another young author.   ❖

The teacher in this example has performed several play intervention strategies found effective in promoting language and literacy development. He accepts the child's early inventive writing and, in fact, encourages him to write on his own. He expands and elaborates upon the child's utterances and keeps the conversation going. He responds with enthusiasm to all of the child's oral and written initiatives. This chapter demonstrates how a classroom teacher might employ such techniques in order to encourage the language development of young children.

Facilitating Oral Language

Early childhood educators have traditionally had a "romance with language" (Evans, 1975, p. 139). Verbal abilities have been viewed as being central to school success, general intellectual development, and social competence (Lindfors, 1987). During the earliest days of Head Start in the late 1960s, language kits and instructional materials were developed to enhance verbal skills.

These were often designed to meet the special needs of disadvantaged children, who were believed to suffer language deficits (Bereiter & Engelmann, 1966). One such program that is still widely used is the Peabody Language Development Kit (Dunn & Smith, 1965). The kit includes presequenced, teacher-directed language enrichment activities.

Language specialists have come to question whether such formalized approaches are really needed in early childhood classrooms (Cazden, 1972; Lindfors, 1987). They have argued that these kits create artificial and meaningless contexts for language use. Real-life conversations, from their perspective, would serve as better vehicles for teaching verbal abilities. Lindfors (1980) describes this informal, naturalistic approach:

> We know that language grows best in meaningful situations, that is, situations that are meaningful and interesting *to the child*. . . .Involving a child in a veritable language bath all day every day in the rich and meaningful activities that fill our classroom is the best possible way that we can enhance the child's growth of language structure. (p.79)

Verbal Elaboration

The approach of most language kits is to present advanced language forms to children, encourage them to imitate them, and then praise appropriate imitations. Many studies have shown that this is not how children learn to talk (Bloom, Hood, & Lightbown, 1974; Brown & Bellugi, 1964; Brown, Cazden & Bellugi, 1969; Ervin, 1964; Kemp & Dale, 1973). Nelson (1973) found, in fact, that in homes where parents performed this positive reinforcement strategy, children acquired language more slowly.

Chomsky (1965) has argued that children will acquire linguistic rules on their own if they are "bombarded" with adult language within naturalistic settings. An effective strategy for teaching language, then, is to comment on children's classroom activities in an elaborate manner. When doing so, the teacher is providing rich adult language samples from which children can construct linguistic rules.

A teacher might elaborate on children's block play, for example, by stating, "I see you have put the longest blocks down first, and now you are adding some very tiny ones to your building." Smothergill, Olson, and Moore (1971) found that children whose teachers used this elaborative style performed better on verbal tasks. In another study it was found that if adults used new words to comment on children's activities, these words were learned more quickly (Bloom, 1983). Teachers should converse with children regularly, then, about what they are doing.

Several types of verbal elaborations are effective:

Describing the Physical World

Children learn new vocabulary when adults use labels or descriptive words to comment on meaningful objects in the environment (Nelson, 1973). As children manipulate objects, teachers can overlay descriptive language: "That sparrow's nest is so rough and prickly. I wonder if the baby birds are uncomfortable sitting in it."

In such interactions, the adult is taking advantage of a teachable moment, modelling rich descriptive speech and providing labels for objects that, at this point in time, are of extreme interest and importance.

Describing Physical Actions

In most early childhood programs, children spend much time outdoors engaged in running, climbing, and riding. Although teachers frequently choose to observe during these playground periods, such physical activities might provide an ideal context for language intervention. Adults can comment on children's actions using descriptive speech: "When you swing you really kick your legs far out in front of you. You're going incredibly high!" In such verbal elaborations the adult is coding the child's action in language, translating real experience into a verbal description. There is evidence that when adults do this they promote the acquisition of grammar and word meaning (Schickedanz, Schickedanz, & Forsyth, 1982).

Providing Interpersonal Language

Children learn language so that they can communicate effectively with others. Garvey and Baldwin (1970) have found that children acquire linguistic rules within naturalistic social settings. Teachers should conduct language interventions, then, during highly social activities. They can model interpersonal language by commenting on children's social interchanges. Statements such as, "You look very upset. Did Jeremy annoy you?" help children acquire language to express feelings.

Other interventions might focus on language that makes one more effective with peers: "Adam, you screamed at Susan. Did you see how she walked away from you when you did that? If you want her to get on the climber, ask her. Say, 'Susan, do you want to ride on my fire engine?'" Such strategies not only teach word meaning and syntax, but demonstrate socially effective intonation and style.

A distinction should be made between verbal elaboration and overbearing teacher talk. The verbally elaborative teacher converses with children, commenting, asking questions, taking a turn in a discussion, then listening as children take a turn. Lindfors (1987) has observed that in preschool and elementary classrooms, teachers do most of the talking. Care should be taken, she argues, to avoid dominating the language environment. Teachers can comment on activities using elaborate language, then allow turn-taking among students.

Responding

In the previous section, teachers were encouraged to initiate conversation. Research suggests that responding to children's own verbal initiatives is also important. Wells (1981) found that children whose parents responded quickly and with enthusiasm to their verbalizations were advanced in language acquisition. These parents displayed greater interest and physical warmth and encouragement when their children spoke to them. They also responded verbally to their children's comments more often.

Why do such responses lead to language growth? Enthusiastic adult reactions encourage children to continue talking. The children come to recognize the power and importance of language when they see its positive impact on parents and teachers. Verbal responses to children's initiatives present new examples of adult language from which they may discover linguistic rules. When adults respond to children's utterances, they are showing how conversations work—that when one person talks the other listens, that speakers take turns talking, and that one's utterances must be relevant to the conversation in progress.

Samples of appropriate responding behaviors are listed in Table 5-1. Each of these responses communicates the teacher's genuine interest and desire to further the conversation.

It should be noted that brief praising statements (e.g., "Uh-huh," "That's interesting," or "Very good") are missing from this list of appropriate responses. These phrases do not encourage children to continue talking; children have been found to "see through" and become annoyed with such empty responses (Chandler, 1981; Ohanian, 1982).

Also absent from the list in Table 5-1 are responses in which children's language usage is corrected. Teachers should respond to the content of children's verbalizations, not to grammatical correctness. Nelson (1973) found that highly competent children had parents who accepted their children's language and responded to its meaning rather than to its form. Her study suggests that pointing out children's language errors can actually delay language growth.

Although research suggests that parents should respond quickly to their children's initiatives (Wells, 1981), this is more difficult to accomplish within a school setting. Even the most responsive teachers will experience periods in the day when they are confronted with many simultaneous bids for attention and cannot quickly respond. The responsive teacher, unable to meet these needs immediately, clearly articulates a desire to respond and regret at the inability to do so: "Marie, I would love to come look at your drawing, but I have to finish reading to Joshua first. I will come over and see you in a few minutes."

In order to respond, teachers need to be in close proximity to children throughout the day, particularly during free-play periods. They must move regularly throughout the classroom so that all students have access to them for questions, sharing of accomplishments, and other verbal bids (Brophy & Evertson, 1976).

Table 5-1
Appropriate Responses to Children's Verbal Initiatives

Responding Behavior	Example
1. Showing interest through body language (Getting down on a child's level, establishing eye contact, warmly touching)	When a child asks a question, a teacher gets on her knees and looks right into his eyes, nodding with interest as the child talks.
2. Asking questions	After a child has related a family problem, a teacher asks, "What did you say to your sister when she got so angry with you?"
3. Adding to the conversation	After a child describes something he saw on a nature walk, a teacher states, "Something else I saw were tiny buds on the trees. Why do you think those are appearing?"
4. Sharing relevant personal experiences	After hearing a child's troubling story, a teacher states, "I had that happen to me one time too. Our dog ran away for two days! I know how sad you must feel."
5. Giving assistance	A child has just explained that she has been left out of a play group. The teacher suggests, "Why don't you go over to their pretend restaurant and order lunch? Maybe Tina and Mary will play with you then."
6. Expressing emotions	After listening to a child's joke a teacher laughs heartily, then says, "That is such a funny joke. I loved the part about the snake!"
7. Recognizing feelings	A teacher responds to a sad story by saying, "You must be very sad, and your mother must be very sad too."

Before teachers can respond, children must be allowed to initiate some of the conversation. In their informal interchanges with young children, teachers can avoid asking all the questions or picking all of the topics for discussion. Children will gradually make verbal initiatives to teachers who have an "approachable manner" (Endsley & Clarey, 1975).

Teachers should demonstrate an eagerness to listen, even to the most egocentric meanderings of discourse that are so prevalent in early childhood (Piaget, 1971). They should patiently allow "thinking time," characterized by "um-um-ums" and other disfluencies. Asking children to start over, slow down, or speak more clearly will discourage them from using language and will be counterproductive to the language-learning process.

Expansion and Expatiation

A responding technique receiving much attention in the language acquisition literature is "expansion"—the practice of recasting a child's less mature utterance into a more advanced, correct, or complete form:

❖ ❖

Child: Red paint!

Teacher: Oh. You need more red paint to use on your painting.   ❖

In laboratory studies, this verbal intervention has been found to advance the acquisition of certain language features (Farrar, 1987). Cazden (1972) warns that expansion will be ineffective in the classroom if teachers are not "tuned in" to the idiosyncratic language features of their students who may be of different cultural and dialectical backgrounds. To use this technique effectively, she suggests, teachers must be cautious not to misinterpret a child's utterance and expand it in an incorrect direction:

❖ ❖

Child: (Having just spilled red paint all over another child's expensive overalls) Red paint!

Teacher: Oh. You need more red paint to use on your painting. I'll get you some more!   ❖

In this instance the expansion may confuse the child (and lead to even more disastrous results!) rather than assist in language learning.

Cazden also argues that teachers may overuse this technique to the exclusion of other, more meaningful and stimulating responses:

❖ ❖

Child: (Holding up a drawing she has just completed) This a man, hurt my mother.

Teacher: Yes. That is a man who is hurting your mother.   ❖

Here the child clearly has a message to convey, but it is overlooked by the teacher who is overapplying the expansion strategy.

Cazden studied a technique called "expatiation," as well—a response strategy in which the teacher furthers the discussion of the topic initiated, using especially elaborate language, without making an effort to restate the child's original utterance. The following is another example of this technique:

❖ ❖

Child: Red paint!

Teacher: Are we out already?

Child: Yeah, 'cause I used some on my picture.

Teacher:	You must have had quite a bit of red in your drawing.
Child:	Yeah. I made apples. See? (Holds up painting) ❖

In Cazden's (1972) study, expatiation was found to be slightly superior to expansion in promoting language acquisition. This research suggests again that teachers are most successful when they respond in rich, descriptive language to the content of children's verbalizations, rather than attempting to teach adult forms directly. Expansion should not be used at the expense of meaningful discourse.

"Parentese"

Chomsky (1965) has stated that children can learn the rules of language from the most disfluent and error-ridden speech of adults—from mere "scraps" of adult verbalization. From his perspective, children learn to speak when bombarded with language of any sort.

Other psycholinguists have suggested that certain kinds of adult language are especially facilitative of language learning. Many studies suggest that experienced parents speak a developmentally useful form of language called "parentese" or "adult-to-child language" (Cross & Morris, 1980; Gleitman, Newport, & Gleitman, 1984; Jacobson, Boersma, Fields, & Olson, 1983).

Generally, "parentese" provides simpler, clearer language samples for children to analyze. This form of speech may make their discovery of linguistic rules easier. Some features of "parentese" are listed in Table 5-2. An adult who is speaking this language form uses shorter sentences, enunciates more clearly, speaks more slowly, pauses longer between words and phrases, and exaggerates intonations. Fewer disfluencies and other errors are made.

One important feature of "parentese" is that it is composed of sentences at a syntactically complex level just above that of the child's own language. As children get older, their parents will naturally adapt speech directed to them, so that it will be increasingly complex and remain slightly above the child's competence level. So, adults will speak a simpler language to a child at two years old than at five years old. Psycholinguists believe that this gradual adaptation of communication to the developmental level of the child may be critical for teaching language.

An implication of this theory is that teachers should try to match their language in the classroom to the level of the children they are teaching. They should use this simpler speech form and increase verbal complexity as their students learn more language rules.

Of all the play-intervention behaviors described in this book, speaking "parentese" is perhaps the most difficult to learn. No amount of isolated practice at shortening sentences or slowing one's speech will be effective. One must become skilled at changing one's language to meet the developmental needs of particular children. Experience in speaking to children of diverse language

Table 5-2
Features of Parentese That Contribute to Language Learning

1. Phonological Features (Speech Sounds)

Exaggerated intonation
Clearer enunciation of speech sounds
Stretching words or syllables out into longer utterances
Longer pauses between words
Higher than normal pitch
Slower speech
Exaggerated, dramatic stress and emphasis
Absence of disfluencies

Sample:

As a teacher discusses a story he is reading with a child in the library corner, he varies his intonation and the pacing of his language. He begins by asking a question in a slow, suspenseful style: "What...on earth...do you think...will happen next?" After the child makes a prediction, he responds with a louder voice, more rapid pacing, and a burst of enthusiasm: "Oh, ho! So, you think he will be able to eat all of that food?!"

2. Syntactic Features (Grammar)

Shorter sentences
Less complex syntax (e. g., fewer embedded clauses)
Sentences just above the complexity level of the child's own language

Sample:

A teacher uses short sentences and simple, clear language to teach the rules of a game at the math center: "Let me show you how to play. You spin the spinner. First, one player spins. Then that player moves along the board. He moves the number of spaces it says on the spinner. Let me show you (demonstrates). Then the other player spins. He moves the number of spaces it says on the spinner. He moves his marker along the board like this (demonstrates)."

3. Semantic Features (Word Meaning)

Fewer semantically complex words (e. g., use "car" instead of "automobile")
More general terms for objects, actions, or feelings (e. g., use "computer" instead of "IBM clone")

Sample:

A teacher talks with a child who is having difficulty completing a puzzle. She uses a more simple and general term, "sad," to mean "frustrated" or "confused." She says: "You look very sad. Are you sad?" (The child nods, says nothing.) "Sometimes I get sad when I can't do things. Everyone feels like that sometimes."

Sources: Lindfors (1980); Reich (1986)

abilities may be the best way to learn this form of language. Several research studies have shown, for example, that experienced teachers and parents are more effective in speaking "parentese" than those who have not spent much time around children (Gleason, 1975; Sachs, Brown, & Salerno, 1976; Weist & Stebbins, 1972). This suggests that readers of this book who are preparing to teach young children should spend as much time as possible communicating with students of all ages.

There are ways that both new and experienced teachers can enhance their "parentese" while engaging in conversations with children. Careful monitoring of students' responses to one's statements and subsequent adjustment of language based on this feedback will assist in learning this speech form. In one study, it was found that young children were most attentive to speech just above their own productive language (i.e., "parentese") and tended to "tune out" that which was either too simple or too complex (Snow, 1972). If teachers note that children are inattentive to their verbalizations, then, they might adjust language to a more or less complex level and note student reactions.

Friedlander (1970) found that children are more likely to attend to "bright" than "flat" intonation. Teachers might respond to the inattention problem by injecting a more lively, enthusiastic intonation into their speech, as well.

Shipley, Smith, and Gleitman (1969) have reported that children respond more appropriately to directions given in "parentese." When students show difficulty in following directions, a teacher might try simplifying verbal instructions, using clearer, more exaggerated intonation, and adapting other language features as indicated in Table 5-2.

Sometimes children provide more direct feedback about whether a teacher is using an appropriate language form, as the following vignettes reveal:

When teachers use rich, descriptive words and phrases, children learn language rules.

❖ ❖
Vignette 1

Teacher: (A student teacher) Okay, now how we'll play this game is that all of the players from team one will be responsible for hiding the oranges from their opponents. . .

Children: (Talking at once) What?

Teacher: Okay, now team one will take all the oranges and hide them in various parts of the room. Then team two will search for them.

Child A: (In an annoyed tone) I don't think we understand this game!

Teacher: Okay. Let me try again. Here's how we'll play. I'll give team one five oranges. (Hands them to team members) You'll hide them. You can hide them all around the room; anywhere you want! Team two will hide their eyes. (Demonstrates; continues to give instructions)

Child B: (After the student teacher has given instructions) Oh. Well, why didn't you tell us that?

Vignette 2

Teacher: The choo-choo moved up and up the hill.

Child: (In an angry tone) That's not a "choo-choo"—that's a train!   ❖

In Vignette 1 the student teacher has been told in no uncertain terms that he is not communicating well. He eventually breaks his instructions into shorter, less semantically complex statements. He employs physical demonstration as he talks. In Vignette 2 the teacher appears to have annoyed a four-year-old by using too simple a term for "train." As teachers receive such feedback and practice adapting language, they become increasingly skilled at speaking in just the right form to maximize communication with students.

It is important to make a distinction between "parentese" and "baby talk." "Baby talk" includes extremely exaggerated, high-pitched intonations, use of infantile vocabulary (e.g., "bye-bye" for "goodbye"), and substitution of third-person for first-person pronouns (e.g., Mrs. Johnson instructs her students, "Bring Mrs. Johnson your drawings."). Such language has been criticized as disrespectful of children and lacking in instructive value (Feeney, Christensen, & Moravcik, 1991). Although "baby talk" is often heard in natural infant-parent conversations, parents frequently abandon these features by the time their children reach three years of age (Lindfors, 1980).

Teachers should speak simplified, but adult forms when interacting with children. Dale (1976) summarizes this linguistic style:

> Talking in baby talk to a child for the first five years of his life would surely hinder his learning, but so would speaking the language of an encyclopedia or a diplomatic treaty. (p.144)

Question-Asking

In Chapter 2 and elsewhere in this volume, question-asking has been described as a powerful tool for promoting cognitive development. Much research indicates that questions stimulate children's thinking (Siegel & Saunders, 1979), promote an understanding of the world (Kamii, 1982), and nurture curiosity (Bradbard & Endsley, 1983). Less attention has been given in the literature to the effects of adult question-asking on young children's language development. There is evidence that adult questioning and communicative competence are linked.

In one study, children whose mothers frequently asked questions were found to learn language at a rapid pace. In contrast, those whose mothers most often issued imperatives (e.g., "Take your plate to the table") were slower to learn linguistic rules (Newport, Gleitman, & Gleitman, 1977).

Why does questioning promote language? First, questions are more interesting and complex language samples to interpret (Siegel & Saunders, 1979). A comparison of the two utterances listed below reveals that decoding a question requires the application of many more linguistic rules:

Utterance 1:   Your brother broke the train.
Utterance 2:   Why did your brother break the train?

At least three language rules not used in Utterance 1 are needed to speak or understand Utterance 2: a "wh- question rule," an auxiliary verb ("did") insertion rule, and a tense-marker rule ("break" instead of "broke"). Simply stated, Utterance 2 provides a far more sophisticated and challenging language sample for the child to analyze than would a mere restatement of Utterance 1.

Another reason that questions facilitate language is that they elicit child speech. Answers to questions provide practice in communicating. Not all types of questions provide opportunities for communication, however. "Yes/No" and "unison answer" questions, for example, that do not promote high levels of thought (see Chapter 2), are not as useful for language practice either. When a teacher asks, "Did you like that story?" children can answer with a nod of the head without any verbalization at all. Teachers should strive to ask open-ended, cognitively challenging questions. Table 5-3 presents samples of less effective questions and how these might be rephrased to facilitate language use. In each instance, much more language (as well as thought) is required in response.

Question-asking is a powerful teaching tool. When teachers ask children about their self-directed play activities in unobtrusive ways, they not only guide learning but create a context for meaningful discourse in which language rules are learned.

Table 5-3
Transforming Questions from Low to High Level

Low-Level Question	High-Level Alternative
1. Did you enjoy the story?	What part of the story did you like best? Why?
2. What did the boy in the story see when he looked out the window?	Tell me about a time when you saw just what the boy in the story saw.
3. How did the girl in the story feel?	Why did the girl feel the way she did?
4. What did the boy do about his problem?	What would you do if you were the boy?
5. How did the story end?	How do you think the story will end?

Interventions at the Book and Writing Center

There has been growing interest over the last ten years in the literacy development of young children. Although earlier work on children's reading and writing has focused on acquisition of "readiness skills," current researchers have been examining the ways children read and write within naturalistic settings. These authors have documented similarities in the processes of oral and written language-learning and the important role that children themselves play in their own acquisition of written symbols (Graves, 1983; Goodman 1986; Smith, 1983). Their work has given rise to the "whole language" curriculum, in which children are exposed to meaningful print and encouraged to write on their own at a very young age (Schickedanz, 1986). This section of the chapter will present specific play-intervention strategies that enhance the emergence of literacy.

Lap Reading

The cornerstone of a "Whole Language" program is the "shared language experience" (Goodman, 1986; Schickedanz, 1986; Smith, 1983) in which teachers and children engage in cooperative language and literacy activities. One such experience—booksharing—is illustrated in the following vignette.

A teacher invites two four-year-olds to read a book with him in the library center. He sits in a rocking chair; the two children squeeze in on either side of him. As he begins to read; the children rest against him and listen intently. At one point in the story a monster is introduced; a discussion begins about whether this is the same creature as one presented earlier in the book.

Child A:	(Interrupts the teacher's reading) Wait. I have to see if this is the same thing as before. (Flips back in the book several pages to look at an illustration)
Teacher:	You think this creature is the same one as before?
Child B:	I think he's the same monster. (Pages ahead to where they are currently reading) See? He's got this funny hair.
Child A:	(Studies the illustration) I think . . .okay, he's the same. Let's read some more.
Child B:	Wait. Look! He's got teeth sticking out. He isn't the same guy.
Teacher:	So, do you think this new monster is another creature?
Child B:	Yep. He's a bad one too.
Teacher:	The new monster? How can you tell?
Child B:	Look. See, he's not even smiling.
Teacher:	I'll read some more of the story. (In a suspenseful tone) We'll just find out about this monster and whether he's the same or a new one. We'll find out if he's bad. (Resumes reading)

These children are enjoying a warm personal contact with a teacher. In addition, their interactions include rich conversation and many opportunities to learn about books and how print works. They make predictions about the story that they will test out by following the plot line carefully. Such meaningful interchanges may not have taken place in a whole-group story-reading session.

Through booksharing with adults and subsequent independent experiences with familiar books, young children learn to make sense out of print. Schickedanz (1982) has shown, for example, that children come to learn "by heart" those stories read over and over to them. Later, through independent reading, they begin to map their oral story across print, thus discovering much about how books work. Some children begin to read through this process without any formal instruction.

In most early childhood classrooms, whole-group bookreading is a daily experience. "Big books" are commonly used so that children may get a close look at print. Another important way children experience books is by sitting in the laps of teachers who read aloud to them. Such lap-reading has the following advantages over whole-group reading:

1. Children can see print close up.

2. Children can interrupt the story at any time to ask questions, relate events of the book to their own lives, or turn back a few pages to review an earlier episode (such interruptions in a whole group setting would lead to protests from other listeners).

3. Children can handle the book, turn its pages and find its beginning and ending.

4. Children can enjoy quiet, warm, and individual physical contact with the adult.

Teachers can regularly initiate one-on-one reading experiences with young children during free-play periods. They can interact with those already looking at books in the library center, but should also invite those playing in other classroom areas, who rarely look at books, to join a lap-reading session. Children should never be coerced, of course, into a shared book experience. If a selection of high-quality children's literature is available in the reading area, a teacher can involve a child in story reading with minimal persuasion.

Schickedanz (1978) suggests that records of these reading sessions be kept for each individual child. Teachers might record the number of lap-reading sessions children have participated in, and titles of their favorite stories. Such information is invaluable in assuring that all students receive regular and meaningful experiences with print.

Good lap readers are dramatic in their reading; they draw listeners into a story with an enthused tone and animated gestures. They ask just the right sorts of questions—those that guide children's enjoyment or understanding of the story without distracting from the plot. They allow children to have some control over the reading experience and are patient when long discussions or disagreements arise mid-story. The following vignette illustrates this effective lap-reading style.

❖ ❖

A teacher enters the library center. She offers to read to a five-year-old; he rejects her book selection, however, and suggests another. She sits next to him and begins to read. She uses a suspenseful tone in reading the narration and assumes different voices when reciting the dialogue of various characters. She holds the book so that the child can always see the pictures and encourages him to turn the pages. Occasionally she makes comments about the illustrations or points out where she is reading in the text. At one point she chooses to ask a question.

Teacher: How do you suppose Martha was feeling when George poured out the soup she made for him?

Child: She must be angry at him. And you know what?

Teacher:	What?
Child:	Sometimes my mother makes a lot of food I don't like. And you know what?
Teacher:	What?
Child:	I say, "I don't like this awful stuff." And you know what? You know what she says?
Teacher:	What?
Child:	She just yells, "Eat that supper or you won't have any more." (Laughs) She gets angry.
Teacher:	Yes. Do you think Martha feels like that?
Child:	Yeah. 'Cause she worked and worked on that soup. And you know what?
Teacher:	What?
Child:	She's gonna get a little angry, I think.
Teacher:	Let's read the rest of the story. ❖

The teacher of this vignette demonstrates many effective lap reading strategies. A number of these have been found to promote literacy. In the following section these strategies are described in detail.

Giving Children Choices of Reading Material

An underlying principle of the Whole Language philosophy is that children will learn to read from books that are meaningful to them (Goodman, 1986). Since children's tastes and life experiences are diverse, it is important to encourage children to make their own story selections during lap reading. If two or three children are being read to, the ensuing disagreement over that book to read can be most useful (Kamii, 1982). In such clashes of opinion, children learn social skills and clarify their own book preferences.

Teachers sometimes worry that children will not select the most appropriate or developmentally useful reading material when given this autonomy. It is the teacher's responsibility to assure that a diverse collection of high-quality literature is included in the library center. Books with predictable language patterns and those dealing with themes significant to children's lives have been found to be particularly facilitative of literacy (Harris, 1986; Holdaway, 1979).

Children should also be allowed to end the reading before the story is finished, and to select another book. Although this behavior can be annoying to teachers (who often would like to learn themselves how the story comes out in the end!) and can cause clashes among children with differing opinions about the book, such autonomy assures that children will experience books that capture their interest and hold meaning for them.

Reading the Same Books Over and Over

Reading to children can be a most pleasant teaching activity. When a child requests that a particular book be read again and again, however, lap reading can become tedious. There is research to suggest that teachers should honor these requests to the degree that patience will allow. As Schickedanz (1986) has demonstrated, children come to know the story lines of books that have been repeatedly read to them. Eventually they will begin to "read" these by heart, recreating with extreme accuracy not only the precise language of the author but the intonations of the adults who have read to them.

This by-heart reading is a significant accomplishment in learning to read. Children will sometimes "map" the oral story across the printed words. When the story and print don't match, children must reanalyze the print and formulate new hypotheses about how the book works. Sometimes they seek help from adults to clear up these confusions. One child was heard exclaiming: "This book's not working right!" (Schickedanz, 1982). Eventually, by-heart reading and story-print matching can lead to conventional reading without specific skills instruction.

Encouraging Children To Handle Books

Most teachers have worked with students who have little experience with books. These children may not even know how books work; they may be observed paging through them from back to front or turning several pages at a time. When read to, these children sometimes close the book before the story is over, particularly if the final pages contain no illustrations (Schickedanz, 1982).

While reading to children, teachers can encourage them to handle books. They might begin by asking, "Can you find where the story begins?" They might ask children to turn the pages, using gentle reminders such as, "Oops! You turned the page before I was finished reading!" or "You turned two pages. You only turn one page at a time when you read. Let me show you," when overzealous page-turning occurs. Such interchanges show the child that certain parts of a story appear in certain parts of the book and that words come from the print, not the illustrations.

Pointing Out Print

In a "whole language" classroom, helping children construct the meaning of a story is emphasized. Specific print lessons aimed at teaching sound-letter associations or sight vocabulary are not usually included. As teachers read to children, however, they can point out informally where print is and how it works. For very young preschoolers, simply noting now and then where the words of the story come from facilitates print awareness (Schickedanz, 1982): "Look. It says here (moving a finger across the print), *The Very Hungry Caterpillar*."

As children get older, the teacher might occasionally ask questions about the text: "Can you find where it says 'Bump'?" Schickedanz (1986) has found that children who are read to often will begin to ask their own questions about print (e.g., "Where does it say 'Joseph'?").

Although teachers should initiate conversations about print, these should never interfere with understanding of the story. Deriving meaning and joy from books must continue to be the ultimate purpose of lap-reading experiences.

Asking Questions/Discussing the Story

Children ask questions and share insights throughout a booksharing experience. Unfortunately, when a teacher is attempting to hold the interest of a whole group of children, such comments about the story are often met with a response like, "That's interesting. But it's my turn to talk now. You can have a turn when I am finished with the book." Children's inquiries and commentaries about a book reveal that they are thinking, imagining, and relating the story to their own lives as they listen. Such discussion should be encouraged, not discouraged. During lap reading, a teacher has the luxury of lingering in a conversation with a child about a story. The teacher can not only provide an enthusiastic response to comments, but promote and enhance these discussions.

One way to elicit such conversations is to ask open-ended questions about the events of a story. Questions that encourage children to predict what will happen next are particularly important (Holdaway, 1979; Pflaum, 1986). Examples of this question-asking approach are shown in Table 5-3.

The teacher should also respond with enthusiasm to a child's comments during story reading. Following guidelines provided earlier in this chapter, the teacher should provide responses that show his interest in the child's viewpoint and a desire to further the dialog.

Encouraging Story Recitation

Children enjoy "reading" stories by heart and may be observed presenting their favorite books to peers or even dolls and stuffed animals. In these recitations children often recreate verbatim both the words and intonations of adults who have read to them. As described above, children will often attempt to match their memorized stories to print; story recitation can contribute to literacy development. Occasionally, teachers can ask children to read to them in this manner. A child may decline such a request. Schickedanz (1986) notes that even children who are proficient at independent reading wish to be read to now and then. Some children relish an opportunity to read to a teacher, however. During these experiences, teachers can engage in the same kinds of interactions recommended for adult-reading sessions.

As children recall or reinvent these stories, teachers should refrain from correcting inaccuracies in the retelling. Corrections have the same negative consequences in reading development as they do in oral language learning (Schickedanz, 1986). The purpose of this by-heart reading experience is to empower children to construct their own meaning from books. Negative responses lead children to question their reading competence.

Teachers can encourage children to "read" favorite stories "by heart."

Encouraging Independent Reading

Since children reread on their own books that have been read to them by teachers, ample time should be given for independent book-looking during free-play periods. Teachers should stay away from the book area at times so that children can engage in their own form of reading undisturbed. Teachers must make judgements, then, about when to intervene, when to share a book with a child, and when to withdraw. They should avoid dominating reading experiences or spending too much time in the book center. Schickedanz (1986) reports that children are more likely to interact with books when teachers make moderate rather than frequent numbers of visits to the book area.

Interpreting Environmental Print

The book area is not the only place where children encounter print. The world is filled with rich text for children to interpret; signs, food labels, even junk mail provide opportunities for children to see and construct meaning from written words. The following vignettes demonstrate how children attempt to interpret print that occurs naturally in the world around them.

❖ ❖

Vignette 1

A three-year-old stands with his mother in a line at the bank. He spots a sign announcing the latest rates for certificates of deposit. Running his fingers along the print he "reads" in a voice loud enough so all in the bank can hear: "No one's allowed to rob this bank."

Vignette 2

An adult asks a child to read the text on a toothpaste tube. With much confidence the child runs his fingers along the tube and "reads:" "If you don't brush too much your teeths fall out."   ❖

Although these children have not accurately read the printed messages; they have actively constructed meaning from print. Their constructions are logical; one child interprets a message related to banks, the other to toothpaste. As children encounter environmental print in this way, they learn about the forms and functions of written language (Harste, Woodward, & Burke, 1984).

Teachers can facilitate literacy by providing rich environmental print. They can place written signs throughout the classroom (e.g., labels for where materials are to be stored, instructions for using equipment, or listings of scheduled events). Children's names can be displayed prominently on cubbies, attendance rosters, or individual art work. Teachers can point out these printed messages and help children to construct their meanings as illustrated in the vignette below.

❖ ❖

At clean-up time, a child puzzles over where science materials are to be stored. A teacher moves over to assist him.

Teacher:	I see you're having trouble figuring out where the magnets go.
Child:	Yeah. I didn't get them out. Where should I put them?
Teacher:	One way to figure out where things go is to read these labels. (Points to labels on shelves) See? This one says "shells."
Child:	Oh. This says "water stuff." (Points to a shelf where eyedroppers are stored)

Teacher:	And what do you think this one says? (Points to a shelf with plant-care materials)
Child:	(Runs a finger along the print) It says, "water the plants . . . water plants with these." I think that's what it says.
Teacher:	There's an empty shelf here. What do you think this says?
Child:	Maybe it says "magnets."
Teacher:	Yep. And that's where the magnets go. ❖

The teacher in this vignette encourages the child to construct his own personal meanings from environmental print. Had she insisted that labels be read correctly she would have discouraged his independent reading. Instead she accepts his early reading, knowing that through experiences like this he will come to read more and more like an adult over time.

Empowering Children to Write

A traditional view of writing is that children must develop certain readiness skills before they are able to actually compose written work. Programs adhering to this perspective emphasize skills training in such areas as naming and copying letters of the alphabet, holding a pencil, or writing one's name in correct adult form. Teachers with this traditional view stress neatness, correct formation of letters, and spelling in early writing exercises so that children will not learn poor handwriting habits. The role of the teacher, from this perspective, has been to directly teach adult-level writing competence.

Some authors have suggested that early language programs should emphasize the meaning of children's stories and the connections among oral and written language and experience (Ashton-Warner, 1963; Allen & Allen, 1968). Excessive attention to correct form, they contend, will inhibit true writing—that is, the process of expressing ideas in print. They have warned that children of different dialects and cultures would be especially impeded in writing development by being asked to write in the prescribed form of standard English.

These authors have promoted a different kind of classroom strategy—called the language experience approach—in which teachers serve as scribes for early writers, recording their stories on paper for them. Since the purpose is to promote the development of the child's own unique language and an ability to express thoughts, Language Experience teachers write down exactly what children say without correction or editing of misstatements or grammatical errors.

This approach is still widely used today in early childhood programs, in part because it focuses on the meaning rather than the form of children's stories, and allows more creative, noncritical, and developmentally appropriate writing experiences. However, an underlying assumption of this approach—that very young children cannot write on their own and so adults must do this for them—has been recently challenged.

A growing body of literature indicates that children can and do write by themselves in naturalistic settings (Harris, 1986; Harste, Woodward, & Burke, 1984). Calkins (1986) argues that asking children to dictate may actually inhibit writing development by sending the message that only adults can write in an appropriate form.

In a new approach to writing introduced by Whole Language theorists (Calkins, 1986; Harris, 1986; Harste, Woodward, & Burke, 1984), children are provided with meaningful opportunities to write on their own, even in the early preschool years. Children are given journals in which they may record their own thoughts and feelings. Writing centers are developed in which various writing media are displayed and where children may write whatever and whenever they wish. In this approach, writing experiences are often incorporated into other areas of the classroom—writing pads are provided in the block area to make signs or in the dramatic play area to be used as make-believe shopping lists. The microcomputer is a new, although controversial, addition to the writing curriculum in many classrooms; even preschoolers may be observed independently composing with word processing programs. (For a listing of classroom writing ideas see Schickedanz [1986].)

Children's early writing may appear to be "scribbling" to adults. These scribbles represent real ideas, however. Zigzags might stand for a whole story, for example, that a child can "read." As children write in this way without restriction, they gain confidence in their ability to express ideas in written form. They write more often and their written products gradually approximate adult content and form. Their writing progresses in stages from scribbling to prephonetic writing, to invented phonetic spelling, to conventional writing (Sulzby, 1986). Adults facilitate this development by empowering children to write—by nurturing the belief that their own unique writing is acceptable and important and can convey meaning to others (Calkins, 1986).

Obviously the role of the teacher in the writing process is quite different in this approach than it was in earlier methodologies. The teacher should no longer serve as an instructor of correct form, as in the traditional approach, nor as a scribe who writes for children, as in the Language Experience model. The modern Whole Language teacher facilitates independent writing within meaningful and natural contexts. This section of the chapter will present specific ways teachers can interact with children as they engage in this naturalistic writing.

Reacting to Writing As One Reacts to Oral Language

Research has demonstrated that writing develops in a way that is similar to oral language learning (Harste et al., 1984; Schickedanz, 1986). Teachers should respond to children's writing, then, as they would to verbalizations or any other form of creative expression. Just as adult criticism of oral language can impede communication and linguistic development (Nelson, 1973), so it can stifle children's writing. The following two vignettes illustrate this point:

❖ ❖
Vignette 1

Child: (Presenting a note composed in "inventive spelling") Look! I wrote a letter to Jennifer. It says, "I don't like you because you are so mean. Love, Rebecca."

Teacher: What does Jennifer do that is so mean?

Child: She says I can't be the mother. She always wants to be the mother. (In an angry tone) She always says, "You be the baby!"

Teacher: Why don't you write that in your letter. You could tell her how much you hate being the baby. Then maybe she would let you be the mother sometimes.

Child: Oh . . . (Begins to write more in her letter)

Vignette 2

Child: (Presenting a letter composed in "inventive spelling") I wrote a letter to the army. You want me to read it?

Teacher: The army? Yes.

Child: It says, "Stop making those bombs, so you won't kill some people."

Teacher: That's excellent! Your writing is so neat! Let me show you something, though. See this word ("stp")? If you put an "o" in that word it will say (sounding out the word) "st-o-p." Let me show you (erases the "p" for the child).   ❖

In the first vignette, the teacher responds to the meaning of the letter. The child is given a message that what she has written is important and that writing is one way to communicate feelings and persuade others. She is eager to continue her letter after this interaction.

In Vignette 2 the teacher responds only to form. Although the message of the letter conveys important ideas and may signal a worry, the teacher chooses to talk about vowels. This child receives a very different message—the content of one's writing is irrelevant; writing is merely a tedious and meaningless struggle to write just like adults.

Guidelines presented in an earlier section for responding to oral language should be applied when reacting to children's writing. As children write, adults should comment on and ask questions about the content of the work, not its form. With much writing practice, experiences with books and other print in the environment, opportunities to share their stories with teachers and other children, and encouraging and meaningful adult responses, children will gradually discover the rules of adult writing. They do not require constant critique of their efforts (Harste et al., 1984). Table 5-4 presents some examples of appropriate responses to children's written efforts.

Table 5-4
Responses to the Content of Children's Writing

Response	Example
1. Encouraging predictions	"You've written such an interesting beginning! How do you think the story will come out?" (Child answers.) "Will you come read it to me when you're finished?"
2. Asking questions about the content of the story	"Why does the monster in your story get so angry at the children?"
3. Being persuaded	"In your letter you say you don't like the games we play at circle time. What activities would you like to do instead?"
4. Relating life events to the story	"I remember when something like what you wrote about happened in our classroom. Do you remember?"

Encouraging Autonomous Writing

Very young children truly believe that they can write and that adults can interpret what they have written (Pflaum, 1986). All experienced teachers have had an encounter, such as the one below, that demonstrates this:

❖ ❖

Child:	(Holding up a piece of paper with horizontal lines of scribbles written on it) Look! Read this!
Teacher:	Oh! Interesting! Read it to me!
Child:	You read it!
Teacher:	Well . . . I'd like you to read it to me.
Child:	No. You read it!
Teacher:	Since this is your own story, in your own writing, I'd like you to be the one to read it.
Child:	(Sighing in exasperation) It says right here, "No other people allowed in the blocks." ❖

This strong conviction that one's writing has communicative power will lead to continued efforts to learn about and experiment with print. Teachers should build on this belief by giving the message in every writing experience: You can write and your written messages hold meaning.

Phrases such as, "You can write it in whatever way you wish," or "You can use your own personal writing," will encourage autonomy in writing. When children ask a teacher to write for them (perhaps this is a remnant of a previous Language Experience classroom), a reply such as, "It's your own story. You can write it on your own and in your own words," is appropriate. As children learn more about print, they will ask how to spell words. Encouraging autonomy is, again, the best way to promote writing development: "You can spell that word in any way you wish. See if you can figure it out." Harste and colleagues (1984) have demonstrated that very young children invent logical and rule-governed ways to spell words and that this inventive spelling is an important exercise in the process of learning how to write.

Some children will have already come to doubt their own writing competence. They will respond to a writing experience with statements like, "I can't write," or "You write it for me." Such children need much encouragement. Perseverance pays off: A kindergarten teacher recently reported that it took six months of nurturance to encourage one student to engage in scribble-writing. Once he had overcome his doubt, however, he became one of the most prolific writers in the class.

There are common classroom practices that discourage autonomous writing. Evaluation of written work is one such practice. Awarding grades, or even stars or smiling faces, moves the emphasis of the experience away from writing's true purpose; children will be more concerned about writing in a form that is valued by adults than in communicating ideas. Even praise can inhibit autonomous writing. As discussed elsewhere, a well-intentioned statement such as, "I love that story," serves as an adult evaluation and can inhibit self-expression. Discussing a story's meaning (e.g., "Why does the monster eat up little boys?") is a more appropriate way to encourage independence at the writing center.

Another practice that may restrict children's writing is suggesting that children dictate. Experience stories and other dictation experiences are very common in early childhood classrooms. Even some "whole language" advocates recommend this practice (Harris, 1986). Calkins (1986) has argued that dictation reduces confidence in one's own writing; Harris (1986) reports that when given a choice, children will choose to write on their own rather than have teachers write for them.

Encouraging Children to Share Their Stories

Writing is a means of communication. Children come to understand writing's true purpose if given opportunities to convey meaning to others through their written work. A number of teacher-guided whole-group programs, such as the "Author's Chair," have been recommended (Graves & Hansen, 1983). In such experiences children share a story with others in the class. Discussion, questions, and comments follow. Informal sharing should also be encouraged during free-play time (McGee & Richgels, 1990). A teacher might approach two young authors who have just finished books and suggest, "Why don't you read your stories to each other? There's a cozy corner where we can sit." Initially the teacher should sit in on these sessions, encouraging each child to read independently and facilitating discussion afterwards. As children become used to sharing their writing, a teacher might initiate story-reading sessions and then withdraw, allowing children to read to one another undisturbed.

Teachers can also encourage children to write to one another. When disagreements arise, for example, a teacher might encourage a child to write down feelings or solutions to conflicts in a letter to the peer with whom the conflict has arisen. Since preschool-age children (and even some primary-grade students) will use very personal scribble or inventive writing, the teacher should encourage them to read their own letters to others. The teacher can also ask students to express complaints about the classroom in the form of written grievances. Generally, the teacher should regularly encourage written communication, even among the very youngest preschoolers.

Incorporating Writing Into Children's Play

As teachers intervene in children's classroom activity, they can create spontaneous opportunities to write (McGee & Richgels, 1990). If children are pretending to shop for groceries in the dramatic-play area, for example, a teacher might present small writing pads and encourage them to make shopping lists. When children are waiting for a turn at the water-play table, a teacher might produce a sheet of paper and explain, "This will be our sign-up sheet for the water table. If you are waiting a turn, put your name on the sheet—write it in your own way. When it is your turn you can cross your name off the list."

Paper and markers might similarly be provided in the block area so that children can create signs for their play cities or communicate messages to others in the class ("Keep your hands off" is a favorite!).

Writing with Children

As shown in Chapter 2, an important way that children learn is by observing and emulating adult behavior (Bandura, 1969). When children observe their parents reading, for example, they are more likely to read themselves (Durkin, 1966). It is logical that teachers should also model writing to show that it is an important, "grown-up," and powerful way to communicate. During free play periods teachers might sit briefly at the classroom post office, joining children in writing letters to other class members. Teachers might write and share journals along with children at the writing center. Such modeling is very different from writing for children, as in the language experience approach. Teachers are writing their own ideas, while children write theirs.

Teachers can encourage children to write in every area of the classroom.

Summary

Language and literacy cannot be taught to children directly. It is through informal verbal intervention in children's self-chosen play activities that teachers most effectively facilitate communicative competence. Children should be "bathed" in oral and written language in the classroom. Several strategies have been found effective in promoting oral language—verbal elaboration, question-asking, and responding. Through these techniques, teachers should continually present rich samples of "parentese," an adjusted form of adult language that is clear and simple. "Parentese" must be distinguished from "baby talk," however. Only respectful adult language forms should be used; infantile vocabulary or exaggerated, high-pitched intonation should be avoided.

Teachers should respond to young children's written efforts much as they do to oral language initiatives. They should ask questions or make comments about the content of children's writing, not its form. Children should be encouraged to write any way they wish. Opportunities can be provided for sharing writing with others.

Teachers can expose children to high-quality literature through lap reading. By reading one-to-one with children, encouraging independent selection of books, discussing the story, and commenting on print, teachers can informally foster the emergence of literacy while reading to children.

Suggested Activities

1. Video or audiotape a conversation between you and one or more young children. Listen to the tape and write an analysis of your verbal behavior, guided by the following questions:

   a. In what ways did you elaborate verbally on children's activities? How would you assess the amount of language that you used? How rich and descriptive were your verbalizations?

   b. How successful were you in responding quickly to all child utterances? To what degree were your responses enthusiastic and encouraging? Which of your questions succeeded in extending the conversation? How did you show that you were listening (e.g., body language, eye contact)? To what extent did you respond to the content of children's language, not its form? At what points did you catch yourself correcting errors or disfluencies?

   c. Which were your most open-ended, cognitively challenging questions? Which were "low level" questions?

   d. Analyze your verbalizations for signs of "parentese." Which language features listed in Table 5-2 did you display in your dialogue with children? Which, if any, of your verbalizations reflected "baby talk"?

2. Read several books to one or more children as they sit in your lap. Write an analysis of this experience, guided by the following questions:

   a. In what ways did you allow children to have some choice and control over reading experience (e.g., encourage them to choose the books, allow them to end a story before it was finished, honor their requests to have the same book read again, ask them to handle the books and turn pages)?

   b. What signs did you observe that children noticed the print and understood how it works (e.g., pointing to words or asking what certain passages say)?

    c. Describe any by-heart "reading" that you saw. How accurately did children recreate the story or your own reading intonations as they "read" by-heart?

3. Interact with three different children who are engaged in open-ended writing. Write an analysis of this experience, guided by the following questions:

    a. How did the children differ in their willingness to write independently? If children asked you to write for them or spell out words, how did you respond? If children told you that they could not write, how did you encourage them? In what other ways did you encourage them to write independently?

    b. In what ways did you encourage children to share their stories with you? With peers? How eager were they to read their work to others? If children asked you to read their stories, how did you respond?

    c. Describe your discussions of children's stories. What questions did you ask? To what degree did you discuss content of these stories, not form?

Further Reading

Ashton-Warner, S. (1963). *Teacher*. New York: Simon and Schuster.

Calkins, L. M. (1986). *The art of teaching writing*. Portsmouth, NH: Heinemann.

Christie, J. F. (Ed.). (1991). *Play and early literacy development*. Albany, NY: SUNY Press.

Goodman, Y. (1986). Children coming to know literacy. In W. H. Teale, & E. Sulzby (Eds.). *Emergent literacy: Writing and reading*. (pp.1–4). Norwood, NJ: Albex.

Graves, D. (1983). *Writing: Teachers and children at work*. Portsmouth, NH: Heinemann.

Harste, J., Woodward, V., & Burke, C. (1984). *Language stories and literacy lessons*. Portsmouth, NH: Heinemann.

Lindfors, J. W. (1987). *Children's language and learning* (2nd ed.). Englewood Cliffs, NJ: Prentice-Hall.

Pflaum, S. W. (1986). *The development of language and literacy in young children* (3rd ed.). New York: Merrill/Macmillan.

Schickedanz, J. A. (1986). *More than ABCs: The early stages of reading and writing*. Washington, DC: National Association for the Education of Young Children.

6

PROMOTING LOGICO-MATHEMATICAL REASONING

A teacher has planned a self-directed math activity in which tiny cars are parked in garages made from fruit baskets. If a child parks just one car in each garage, a one-to-one correspondence between the two sets of materials will have been created. A child sits in the math center examining the new activity; the teacher moves over to guide him.

Vignette 1

Teacher:	What you do here is count out just the right number of cars so that one car goes in each garage. Let me help you get started. How many garages do we have?
Child:	One, two, three . . . nine. (Makes an error, counting one garage twice)
Teacher:	Oops! You counted this one twice. Let me help you. I'll point to each garage and you count them as I do. (Points to each garage)
Child:	One, two, three . . . eight.
Teacher:	Very good. We have eight garages, so how many cars will we need?
Child:	Eight.
Teacher:	Okay. Can you count out eight cars and drive them over to the garages?
Child:	Okay. (Accurately counts eight cars and drives them one by one, with screeching tires and roaring engines, into the garages)

Vignette 2

Another teacher demonstrates a very different approach when interacting with a child playing this car-and-garage game:

Child:	(Sitting with the game materials) How do you do this?
Teacher:	You need to get just enough cars so that there is one car for each garage.
Child:	How many?
Teacher:	Just enough so that you can park one car in each garage.
Child:	Okay. (Studies the garages for a moment. Goes to a bin of cars and gathers a large handful. Spills them out on the table) There! That's enough!
Teacher:	Do you think you have enough for each garage?
Child:	Yep! (Begins parking the cars. Quickly realizes that she has brought too many)
Teacher:	Oh, oh! What's wrong here?

Child: There aren't enough garages!

Teacher: We don't have any more garages. What can we do?

Child: (Studies the situation) I know! (Gathers up all but seven cars and returns them to the bin.) There! That's how you do it. (Parks the cars and notices the one empty garage. Pausess a moment, then drops this eighth garage under the table) There!   ❖

The teacher of the first vignette appears at first glance to have been more successful at promoting mathematics learning. He has guided the child in using a conventional mathematics skill, counting. The child eventually arrives at the correct answer. A careful analysis of this first interaction, however, reveals that very little mathematical thinking is occurring at all. The child is told directly how to solve the problem; he does not have an opportunity to study the dimensions of the task, reflect on alternative courses of action, and invent his own solution.

Although the child does count, his inaccuracy in counting the garages suggests that he does not fully understand number and is unable to use counting as a reliable tool for solving problems. The counting strategy suggested by the teacher may hold no true meaning for the child, then, except as a rote memory recitation—much like a nursery rhyme (Kamii, 1982)—which pleases adults and allows him to arrive at the correct answer.

Although the child in the second vignette does not appear to engage in what could properly be called mathematics, she is actually engaging in a great deal more thinking and problem solving. She has designed her own meaningful solution to the problem, making a rough visual estimate of the number of garages and then collecting an equivalent handful of cars. Her actions, no matter how primitive, come closer to true quantifying than an adult-imposed, rote-memory counting strategy.

The teacher guides the child in independently testing the accuracy of her thinking ("Do you think we have enough for each garage?"). She discovers on her own that she has brought too many cars. Since the teacher has not corrected her response or directly proposed a more accurate solution, the child can rethink her approach and design an alternative course of action (e.g., putting some of the cars back). When, after this, there is still one garage left over, she adopts perhaps the most creative solution of all—she drops this last garage under the table. To adults this may seem to be inappropriate. This rule-bending, however, is a common way that young children solve problems, and reflects logical thought (Kamii & DeVries, 1980). That the teacher encourages such creative actions shows her commitment to independent problem solving.

The teacher of Vignette 2 is facilitating a form of thinking that is critical for solving problems and understanding the world: logico-mathematical reasoning (Kamii, 1982). It is through careful intervention—posing just the right sorts of questions, interacting at just the right times—that she has encouraged the child to think in this high-level way. In this chapter, guidelines for play-intervention strategies that challenge children's thinking are provided. Specific interactions that stimulate autonomous problem-solving and true logico-mathematical reasoning are considered.

Logico-Mathematical Knowledge

Piaget (1965) and his students (Kamii, 1982; Kamii & DeVries, 1980) have described three distinct kinds of knowledge: social, physical, and logico-mathematical. These differ in the manner in which they are acquired. Social knowledge is learned directly from other people through instruction or modeling. When a child is taught to say "please," to recite a nursery rhyme, or to name the months of the year, social knowledge has been acquired. Children can't learn these facts by observing the physical world; there is no observable or logical reason that September is called "September," for example. Social knowledge comprises mainly social conventions. Rote-memory counting of number words is a form of social knowledge (Kamii, 1982); children frequently recite numbers as they would the words of a poem without attaching any underlying meaning to them.

A second type of knowledge is acquired through observation. When children note, for example, that a shell is hard, heavy, rough, or cold, they have acquired physical knowledge. The emphasis of the science curriculum in early-childhood programs is often on the observation of physical attributes of natural phenomena (Smith, 1987).

A complex form of knowledge that is essential to problem solving and ongoing learning is logico-mathematical knowledge. This is knowledge of *relationships* among objects, events, or actions. The understanding that two shells are different from one another is an example of logico-mathematical knowledge. In this instance, "different" is not a property which can be observed in one shell or the other. Nor can "different" be transmitted to a child directly, although adults will sometimes attempt this (e.g., Teacher: "The two shells are *different*. Can you say that?" Child: "Different"). True understanding of the differences between two shells must come from the child's mental comparison of the objects. The child must thoughtfully place the shells into a relationship. Logico-mathematical knowledge, then, is very personal and internal (Kamii, 1982). One child may determine that two shells are different (e.g., One is rough; one is smooth); another may conclude that they are alike (e.g., They are both the same size).

An implication of Piaget's work is that children must create relationships among objects, events, or actions *on their own* (Kamii, 1982). It is not enough for children to be told about or to directly observe the world. Children must be encouraged to think about what they observe and to create mental relationships from these observations. A teacher can facilitate this internal reflection by phrasing questions or posing challenges in such a way that logico-mathematical knowledge, rather than simple social or physical knowledge, is obtained.

Kamii (1982) provides specific intervention guidelines, urging that teachers "encourage children to be alert and put all kinds of objects, events, and actions into all kinds of relationships" (p.28). Several examples of such adult interventions will clarify her approach:

❖ ❖

1. Encouraging children to put all kinds of objects into all kinds of relationships.

Two children have just completed a make-believe theme in the dramatic-play area. They have used many different props—dress-up clothes, pots and pans, dolls, plastic tools, and wooden blocks. They begin to clean up.

Teacher:	I know a game we can play while cleaning up. Can you put the toys away so that things that are alike go together?
Child:	You mean like dishes over here?
Teacher:	You can put the toys away wherever you like. But try to put things that are alike together.
Child:	Oh! I know! Like put the biggest things over here. (With another child he places large toys in one corner, "medium-sized" equipment in another, and very small items in a third)

In this episode children were encouraged to put objects into relationships, using their own judgements about what things are alike. This interchange would have been very different if the teacher had merely noted, "The toys are scattered all over the floor!" (which would lead only to physical knowledge) or had reminded, "When you finish playing you always put things back where they belong so others can find them" (which would impart social knowledge). The teacher instead seems committed to promoting more advanced thought processes. His commitment is particularly impressive given the mess his intervention has created in the dramatic play area!

2. Encouraging children to put all kinds of events into all kinds of relationships.

A child has built a block structure that towers at least two feet over her head. She places one last block, a long one, on her building; it teeters, then collapses.

Child:	Oh! (Looks surprised, upset)
Teacher:	Why did your building fall, do you think?
Child:	(Angry tone) These stupid blocks!
Teacher:	You sound angry. What do you think happened?
Child:	It was too high. (Pauses) This one was too heavy. (Holding up the last block she placed)

In this episode the teacher encourages the child to create relationships between two events. The child must mentally associate building too high and placing the long block on the structure with the collapse of the building. This interaction could have led to less advanced thinking if the teacher had only said, "That is a very long block you put on" (which would contribute to physical knowledge), or had scolded, "We have a rule in this class. You can only build as high as your own head" (which would have led only to social knowledge). The teacher did not try to teach the child directly about the relationship between these events (e.g., "If you build that any higher it will fall"). Logico-mathematical knowledge is acquired only when children have discovered such relationships on their own.

3. Encouraging children to put all kinds of actions into all kinds of relationships.

Children are standing beside a slide on the playground, rolling rocks and noting how they land on the ground.

Teacher: What would happen if you rolled one from the very top of the slide?

Child: It would go faster!

Teacher: Do you think it would land farther away from the slide?

Child: Yeah. It would probably go way out there! (Climbs the ladder to the top of the slide. Rolls a rock down) Oh. Look how far it went!

Teacher: Why do you think it went farther?

Child: Because it starts higher so it goes faster. I'll do another one!

Teacher: What if you really pushed the rock hard down the slide?

Child: It would really go! (Pushes a rock down) Yep. See?

The teacher continues to challenge these children to change their actions and note the outcomes (e.g., "What if you dropped the rock down on the slide?"). Children then begin experimenting on their own; the teacher moves away.

In this episode the teacher has encouraged children to modify their actions and interpret the results. Again, an internal relationship must be created between the method of dropping and how far from the slide the rock lands. Such relationships would not have been constructed if the teacher had simply said, "Listen to the sound the rocks make when they roll" (which would contribute to physical knowledge), or had instructed, "You can't use the slide this way. Slides are only for sliding down on your bottoms" (which leads to social knowledge).   ❖

Through play intervention, children may be encouraged to engage in logico-mathematical reasoning. An important example of this is helping children to think about number.

Promoting an Understanding of Number

Teaching children how to count has been a goal of most preschool and kindergarten programs (Castaneda, 1987). There is evidence, however, that even primary-grade students use counting in a superficial, rote-memory way (Gelman & Gallistel, 1978; Fuson, Richards, & Briars, 1982; Cobb, 1985). In fact, children younger than age seven who are able to count will often not choose counting to solve real-life problems, relying instead on more primitive forms of guessing and estimation. Kamii (1982) explains these findings by noting that understanding number is an instance of logico-mathematical knowledge. Although children have been taught successfully to count number words through social transmission (e.g., counting games and exercises), they don't know what numbers mean. The following episode illustrates this:

❖ ❖

Teacher:	Can you count the chips?
Child:	One, two . . . twelve.
Teacher:	Great! So we have twelve?
Child:	Yeah. It's this one. (Points to the last chip counted) ❖

In this episode the child appears to be naming objects using number words, but does not clearly conceptualize "twelveness." To understand number, this child must mentally put these objects into relationships. For example, the child must determine that, when counting, the number "5" represents objects "1," "2," "3," and "4," which have already been counted, as well as "5." According to Kamii (1982), no amount of counting instruction can impart this understanding to children. They must construct this knowledge independently; through play intervention, adults can assist them in doing so.

Kamii (1982) offers general guidelines for promoting number understanding in young children:

1. "Encourage the child to quantify objects logically and to compare sets (rather than encouraging him to count)" (p. 30). A teacher will often encourage children to count when solving problems. If these students do not understand number and cannot use counting as a reliable tool, they will engage in rote-memory recitation of number words. This exercise will not contribute to learning what numbers mean. What is required for intellectual growth is the opportunity to quantify—that is, to make autonomous judgements about amounts. In quantifying, children make their own estimates about the number of objects or the amount of liquid in a container, using whatever strategy is meaningful to them. The following are some non-counting strategies children will choose if allowed to select their own solutions to number problems:

a. Children are trying to decide who has the most blocks. They examine each pile of blocks and make a rough guess about who has more.
b. Children are trying to decide who has won a card game. They line cards up in rows and ascertain whose row of cards is the longest.
c. A child is trying to set out enough game pieces so that every child who is playing a board game will have one. She nods at her playmate, states her name, "Jessica," and puts a piece down on the board. "Joseph," she states, looking at the next child and placing another piece down. She continues until enough markers have been provided.

Although this rudimentary quantifying appears unrelated to counting and more conventional mathematical operations, such actions will eventually lead to an understanding of number. Kamii (1982) specifies that teachers should intervene in such situations and ask questions that encourage these self-chosen quantification strategies, but should not require counting, per se: "Did you get as many as I did?" "Who has the most?" "You have more than Rachel. What can we do?" When teachers suggest counting, they give the solution away and run the risk of promoting rote-memory recitation.

2.   "Encourage the child to think about number and quantity when these are meaningful to him" (p. 31). Throughout the day, many opportunities arise for quantifying. Children may puzzle over how many granola bars to make for a snack, which child has used the most blocks, or whether there are enough mail slots in the classroom post office for each student to have one. At these times teachers can intervene to encourage quantification.

Again, open-ended questions that do not give away the solution can be asked (e.g., "Who has the most? What can we do so that we all have the same?"). These interventions should not be confined to a certain part of the day or a particular classroom area. Whenever and wherever judgements about quantity are needed to solve problems, children can be encouraged to employ their own forms of quantification to solve them.

3.   "Encourage children to make sets with moveable objects" (p. 31). Young children learn best when provided "hands-on" materials (Barron, 1979). It is not simple manipulation of these objects that leads to learning, however, but acting upon them in thoughtful ways. Teachers can encourage children to think about these objects and put them into relationships (Williams & Kamii, 1986). One particularly useful intervention is to request that children generate sets of objects. Although problems such as "find a set of eight objects" are frequently posed in classrooms, a more effective approach is to encourage children to create equivalent sets: "Can you find enough balls so that everyone has one?" The problem posed in the latter question has many possible solutions; children can quantify in any way they wish while solving it.

4.   "Encourage the child to exchange ideas with peers" (p. 40). One of the most meaningful quantification experiences is that of arguing with a peer

about who has more. Such "clashes of opinion" are useful for several reasons. When the fair distribution of materials or the outcome of a game is in dispute, a child is far more motivated to quantify than if asked to do so by an adult. Teachers' challenges to the accuracy of a child's thinking lead to doubt and a belief that only adults have the right answers. When a peer disputes a child's solution to a problem, however, useful confrontation between two equal-status thinkers results. Each must defend a position and possibly rethink the solution. Such teacher interventions as, "Do you all agree that Jason won the most cards?" or "Did you get as many crackers as Sean?"—behaviors that are often avoided by teachers who fear conflicts—may actually stimulate logico-mathematical thought. The following vignette demonstrates the value of peer conflicts and the role teachers can play in guiding these in productive directions:

❖ ❖

A four-year-old has just distributed "goldfish" crackers to a group at snack time. One child clearly has received more crackers than the child sitting next to her.

Child A:	Jill has more!
Teacher:	How do you know?
Child A:	Look! (Places her plate of crackers next to Jill's)
Teacher:	What do you think, Jill? Do you think you have more?
Child B:	(Eats quickly. Says nothing)
Child A:	I want more!
Teacher:	There are no more crackers. Why don't you and Jill divide your crackers so that you each have the same amount?
Child A:	Yeah. (Takes a handful from Jill's plate)
Child B:	(In an angry tone) No! (More calmly) Wait. I'll do something. (She lines her crackers up on the table) Here. Give me yours to make a line. (Takes Child A's crackers and lines these up next to hers. Takes crackers from her line and places them in Child A's so that the lines look equivalent) There.
Child A:	(Studies the lines carefully. Says nothing)
Teacher:	Are you both satisfied?

Both children nod and begin eating.   ❖

Teachers can promote an understanding of number, then, by encouraging children to make autonomous judgements about quantity throughout the school day. The math center is an obvious place to challenge children's thinking in this way.

Interventions at the Math Center

Math centers or other activity areas can be found in many early-childhood classrooms. Activities that involve matching, counting, number recognition, or sorting are often included; group games are also sometimes provided in these areas. Many of these materials are ideal for encouraging quantification. Others may be less useful if used in the ways intended by their manufacturers, but may be adapted through informal adult guidance to be more developmentally appropriate. Through play intervention, children may be encouraged to think about number as they use math center materials.

Asking Quantification Questions

The primary purpose of intervention in the math center is to challenge children to think at high levels, not to elicit correct answers (Kamii, 1982; Kamii & DeVries, 1980). Through the kind of question-asking approach illustrated in the vignettes below, a teacher can guide a child in meaningful quantification.

❖ ❖

Vignette 1

Matching games in which children must create one set of objects to match another set (e.g., matching cars to garages) are common. In this episode two children match flowers to fifteen flower pots.

Teacher: Can you find just the right number of flowers so that one goes in each pot?

Child A: Should I count them?

Teacher: Figure it out in any way you like. You need one flower to go in each pot.

Child A: (Attempts to count flowers) One, two . . . No wait, I got mixed up.

Child B: (In an annoyed tone) No! Here. Just bring all the flowers out. (Pours all available flowers—twenty-five of them—onto the table) This is how you do it. (Lines up flowers and pots in one-to-one correspondence. Notices that many flowers are left over)

Teacher: What happened?

Child B: There are too many. See?   ❖

In this vignette, the teacher does not insist that the children count, but encourages them to select any meaningful solution. One child, perhaps remembering that adults like counting, asks if this should be the approach. The teacher reiterates that the children may use any method. Eventually they choose a strategy that they can understand—they put flowers and pots into two lines and compare them.

Vignette 2

Dominoes are common in math centers for obvious reasons. Children quantify when they attempt to match a domino with six dots to another with the same number. Dominoes are also movable objects themselves. In the following episode, the teacher challenges five-year-olds to compare sets of dominoes as they play a traditional version of the game.

Teacher:	(In a playful tone) Oh! I have to draw more dominoes from the "bone pile." (Draws until a domino that he can play is selected) I wonder if I have the most dominoes left in my hand.
Child A:	No. I've got the most. (In a silly voice) I'll never get rid of these!
Teacher:	Are you sure you have more?
Child A:	Of course! Look. (Makes gestures over his own pile to indicate a large amount, then over the teacher's pile to show a smaller number) See? I've got the most.
Child B:	Count 'em. (Counts the teacher's pile, then Child A's) He's right. He's got twelve, you've got . . . wait. (Counts the teacher's again) You've got nine. That's not as much.
Child A:	(Nods) I told you already I had the most!

This vignette demonstrates how an open-ended question can lead to different quantification strategies by students at two different levels of development. One child makes a gross estimate of amount, the other counts accurately. Each is encouraged by the teacher to trust his own unique solution.

Modifying Activities

A particular math activity may not meet the developmental needs of all children. Some students may be unchallenged by a math material; others completely overwhelmed by its complexity. Kamii and DeVries (1980) recommend that a teacher "modify a game so that it will be in harmony with the way children think" (p. 202). In informal interventions at the math center, teachers can suggest modifications to an activity in progress—creating a more or less difficult task for students by adding materials or taking them away, changing the rules or encouraging children to change them, or giving hints or information that will make a solution easier or more difficult to come upon.

Some common math activities are too simple. An example of a material that does not challenge all children to think is a puzzle in which pieces with the same number of pictures are matched to each other (e.g., two butterflies are matched to two clowns). True quantification may not be required for such activities; they may be solved at a glance without reflection. This is because children can *see* which pieces have two and which have three. Piaget (1965) has explained that children can perceive "twoness" and distinguish it from "threeness" because these numbers—called perceptual numbers—are so small. Children may extract "two" from a puzzle piece just as they extract "red" from an apple, by simply observing and noting physical properties.

When math activities require children to judge the quantity of sets of five or more objects, internal reflection is stimulated. In such activities, the child must put the objects into relationships; they cannot be solved at a glance. An implication is that teachers might modify activities so that more than five objects are being considered. One approach is to add objects to a game in progress as the need arises. The following vignettes illustrate this strategy.

❖ ❖

Two children are engaged in the car and garage matching activity described at the beginning of this chapter. A teacher sees that they are solving this task perceptually, judging at a glance that four cars need to be selected to park in the four garages on the table.

Teacher: I'm going to give you some more garages. (Places fifteen plastic meat trays on the table)

Child: Those are funny-looking garages.

Teacher: (Laughs) Yes, they are. Now, can you get just enough cars so that one can park in each of these funny garages?

Child: (Studies the stack of meat trays) Whew! Give me a break!

The children place the trays in a line. One child points to the first tray and counts "one"; his playmate takes one car from the bin and places it on the table. The first child points to the next tray and counts "two"; the other child retrieves another car. They continue with this cooperative and novel counting procedure until they believe they have enough cars.

Child: Okay. Let's drive 'em in. (They park the cars, noticing that they are two cars short)

Teacher: What happened?

Child: Wait a minute. (Thinks a moment) Let's do that again. (Puts all the cars back, and he and his friend repeat the entire procedure)   ❖

In this vignette, the matching activity has been transformed from a simple perceptual exercise into a challenging task. Had the teacher not intervened the play would have ended quickly and without much reflection. The teacher has determined that materials need to be added to make the task more challenging. By increasing the number of objects that these children must think about, the teacher has elicited greater reflection.

Sometimes games must be modified because they are too difficult. In the following example both materials and rules are altered to allow younger, less advanced thinkers to play.

Teachers can modify number activities to make them more challenging.

❖ ❖

Two young four-year-olds are playing "Concentration." They have spread out a large number of cards face down on a table and are now taking turns searching for "matches." They are unable to find any—there are simply too many cards for them to manage.

Teacher:	It's hard to remember where all of those cards are!
Child A:	I know. We can't do it.
Teacher:	Let me show you a way to play that makes it easier to find matches. (Removes half the matching pairs from the table) Try it now.

The children begin to play. A child turns up one card, then lifts a second. When they don't match he quickly puts the second card down and tries a third. Failing to match again, he picks up still another card.

Child B:	(Angry) No! You only do it once!
Child A:	But I can't find any!
Child B:	(Still angry) But you can't just look and look and look!
Teacher:	Should we make a rule that you can look more than once?
Child A:	Yeah. 'Cause you can't find them.
Teacher:	How many times should we say you can look?
Child A:	Three times.
Child B:	(In an annoyed tone) Okay. But that's not really how you play. ❖

In spite of Child A's protests, the children are generally satisfied with these modifications to the game. It allows them to be successful and play until all cards have been matched. When a group of five-year-olds plays the game later in the day, this modification is not needed. They are better able to think about a large number of cards.

In spite of careful planning in creating developmentally appropriate materials, activities at the math center will not necessarily meet the wide range of developmental needs represented in an early-childhood classroom. Teachers can modify tasks so that individual students are challenged just the right amount.

Inventing New Games

There has been great debate over whether classroom materials ought to be designed so that they can be used in one correct way (DeVries & Kohlberg, 1990; Montessori, 1964). If activities can be structured so that only one use is possible, some argue, the precise intended benefits are realized (Montessori, 1964). Students of Piaget (Kamii & DeVries, 1980; DeVries & Kohlberg, 1990) take great exception to this position: "The surest way to defeat our objectives for children to become autonomous, exchange views with peers, and be mentally active is to make them play in the 'correct' way" (Kamii & DeVries, 1980, p. 202).

Children may create a novel action that is far more meaningful to them than the object's intended use (DeVries & Kohlberg, 1990). In the following vignette a teacher intervenes to enhance the value of an invented game.

❖ ❖

Two six-year-old children sit at the math center snapping plastic shape tiles onto boards. Although students are to be creating patterns and shapes with these materials, these children have instead invented a racing game. The rules are simple: Whoever fills up his board with tiles first is the winner. A teacher notes that there are not enough tiles to fill both boards.

Teacher:	Do you think you can *both* fill your boards?
Child A:	I'll do it first!
Teacher:	Are there enough tiles for both of you to fill your boards?
Child A:	Sure! Look. (Runs his hand through a bin of tiles)
Child B:	(Pauses) Are there enough, Jason?
Child A:	(Still filling his board) I'm winning!

The game continues. As the children place more tiles on their boards and the supply in the bin diminishes, the children begin to wonder if they will have enough pieces for either to win.

| Child B: | Oh, oh, Jason! (Points to the bin) We don't have enough. |

Child A:	I'm still winning. (Pauses for the first time) Let me see. (Tries to count pieces in the bin, then spaces left on his own board. He has great difficulty with this because there are so many tiles and they fill varying-sized spaces on the board) Well . . . I think I have enough.
Teacher:	You have enough so that *both* of you can fill your boards?
Child A:	(Pauses again. It is clear from his expression that he has only considered the amount needed to fill his own board. He looks puzzled) Maybe if I finish real fast.

They continue to play until all tiles have been used. Neither child has filled his board.

Teacher:	What happened?
Child B:	(Laughing) I told you we didn't have enough.
Child A:	We need about this many more. (Roughly measures the space left unfilled on his board with two fingers)
Teacher:	So, who won the race?

The children discuss this at length, trying various solutions—who used the most pieces, who covered the most area. The teacher quietly leaves the play area.

The children in this vignette are not using this material in ways intended by its manufacturer. The race they have invented, however, leads to many opportunities to think about quantity and area. The teacher recognizes these opportunities and enters the children's self-chosen game to enhance learning.

Sometimes children will use a material over and over in its conventional way until it is no longer challenging. When children are observed completing previously mastered tasks without much thought or enthusiasm, teachers might actually model the invention of new games. The following vignette demonstrates this type of intervention:

❖ ❖

A child at the math center places pegs in a pegboard. She is not particularly absorbed in her activity and looks often at what other children are doing in another part of the room.

Teacher:	Tell me about what you're working on.
Child:	(In an unenthused tone) I'm making a birthday cake.
Teacher:	Tell me about it.
Child:	These are the candles. (Points to the pegs)
Teacher:	What if there were three people who had birthdays today? What would we need to do?

Child:	On the same day? Well . . . you'd need three birthday cakes.
Teacher:	Like these? (Produces two more pegboards) Let's say all three people are the exact same age.
Child:	They would be, like, twins?
Teacher:	Yes. All three would be the exact same age. Like triplets.
Child:	Triplets. Like twins, only three!
Teacher:	Yes. Let's say these people are very old.
Child:	Like 10 years old?
Teacher:	Maybe even older. Now, can you put all these candles on the three cakes (points to a bin of pegs) so that each person has the same number of candles?
Child:	Yeah. 'Cause they're the same age!
Teacher:	Right.
Child:	So they need the same candles.
Teacher:	Right.
Child:	Should I use all the pegs?
Teacher:	Sure! All of them. These people are very old!

The child works for many minutes on this task, using visual estimation to create equal sets of pegs on each of the pegboards.   ❖

Here the teacher has brought new life to a set of familiar materials, inventing a stimulating and challenging game which leads to greater reflection. It is important to note that the make-believe element of this child's original activity—making birthday cakes—is preserved in this interaction. The teacher has introduced a new task within this same theme.

Interventions in Group Games

Kamii and DeVries (1980) assert that group games are ideal for eliciting quantification and other kinds of mathematical thinking. Children are highly motivated to quantify when competing with others. Challenges to their thinking come from peers rather than adults; resulting "clashes of opinion," as described in earlier sections, are useful for social and cognitive development. Making and adhering to (and breaking!) rules lead to greater understanding of social conventions and the perspectives of others and to an ability to negotiate with peers. In this section interventions in group games which promote cognitive growth are considered.

Setting Up the Game

Kamii (1982) suggests that preparing to play a game may be more educational than the game itself. She provides the example of a teacher initiating a game of musical chairs: If children decide how many chairs they need to play, they make judgments about quantity; if the teacher sets up the chairs, they do not. A question like, "Can you get enough chairs so that we all have one?" (She argues that young children prefer the game when everyone has a chair and no one is eliminated) poses a complex problem for children to solve.

In most games materials must be distributed equally among players. In the vignette below a teacher takes advantage of this process to promote quantifying.

Three children and a teacher have just decided to play a board game.

Teacher:	What do we do first?
Child A:	Pass out the cards.
Teacher:	How can we pass them out so everyone has the same number?
Child B:	Here. Like this. (Deals one card to each player until all cards are distributed. However, he has forgotten to deal himself cards)
Teacher:	(Pauses a moment) Do we all have the same amount?
Child A:	I think so. Let's play.
Child B:	Wait a minute! Wait! I don't have any!
Teacher:	What can we do?

The child tries to take a few cards from every other player so that he has enough. This does not work well, so he eventually collects all the cards and re-deals. ❖

These children take more time passing out materials than playing the game. But it is time well spent—much thinking and discussion about number occur. The teacher recognizes the value of this interchange and patiently encourages children to resolve these problems on their own. She intervenes with questions which encourage quantifying.

When preparing to play a game, children often discuss rules. Kamii and DeVries (1980) suggest that teachers allow children to change the rules, so long as all players agree. If there is conflict, the resulting discussion will be intellectually useful. These authors predict that children will follow rules they have invented more conscientiously than those imposed upon them by an adult. Teachers can intervene in game preparation to encourage clarification of rules. In the vignette below a teacher encourages children to negotiate about the rules of a board game and, in so doing, provokes much useful thought.

❖ ❖

Two seven-year-old children sit down to play a traditional board game. One child requests that the rules of the game be modified slightly.

Child A: Now we're going to play like I do at home. When you get one of these bad cards, you know, you don't have to go all the way back.

Child B: No, Cheryl! That's not how you play!

Child A: (In a whiny tone) No! We need to play like I do at home!

Teacher: Why do you want to change the rules?

Child A: 'Cause if you go all the way back to "start" it's too far back. You can't ever catch up!

Child B: But, Cheryl, you have to go back when you get a card! That's how you play.

Teacher: Can you change the rules so that you don't go all the way back to start? Just a little way back? What do think?

Child B: Yeah. Like you have to go back nine spaces?

Child A: No! You never catch up!

Teacher: Cheryl, how far back do you think we should go when we get a bad card?

Child A: Um . . . let's say three, maybe.

Child B: No. Then you catch up the next turn. Let's say (demonstrates on the game board with her marker) one, two, three, four, five.

Child A: Okay.

Both children agree and begin the game.   ❖

In this episode, children are faced with a quantification problem: How many spaces are just the right number to go back, so that the player who is penalized can still catch up? If the teacher had urged children to follow the conventional rules of the game, the high-level thinking and social negotiation involved in solving this problem would never have occurred. He urges children to think about and discuss the controversy until it is resolved.

Playing the Game

Group games afford many opportunities for effective adult intervention. Teachers may judiciously pose quantification questions, for example, as children compete: "Who's winning so far? "How many more spaces do you have to move until you win?" "Are there more cards left on the floor or more in your hand?" "How do you know that Jeremy only needs one more turn to win?"

One way to stimulate logico-mathematical reasoning in games is to encourage score-keeping (Kamii, 1982; Kamii & DeVries, 1980). In some games, such as bowling or bean-bag tossing, a score sheet can be kept. If children are given paper and markers and encouraged to keep score while playing, they will invent a way that is meaningful to them. Younger children may make simple marks or scribbles. Near age five, as Kamii (1982) has documented, children will write numerals that correspond to the number of pins they have knocked down or bean bags they have tossed through the hole. They do not at this age add up their cumulative score as they record the results of each turn; they record their current performance only. At six or seven, Kamii observes, children will attempt to add up their scores in a number of creative ways.

The following episode illustrates the effect of a teacher's suggestion that children keep score:

❖ ❖

Two six-year-olds are playing a bowling game on the floor of the math center.

Child A: (Having just bowled) There! I got a lot of 'em!

Teacher: (Sets paper and markers down at a nearby table) If you want to keep score in your game, you can use these.

Child A: Okay! I'll put down how many. (Counts the number of pins he has knocked over) Four! (Writes a 4 on a sheet of paper)

Child B: It's my turn. (Bowls once, knocks over three pins. Gets the ball back and quickly bowls again, knocking down four more. Standing up close to the pins he rolls a third time, and the remainder of the pins fall)

Child A: C'mon! It's my turn!

Child B: (Ignoring child A, making his own score sheet) Okay. I'll put a three. (Writes this on paper)

Teacher: Ah. You wrote a three?

Child B: Yeah. I rolled it once, and I rolled it again, and I rolled it again. Three.

Teacher: I see. It took you three times to knock them down?

Child B: Yeah. (To his playmate) It's your turn!

The children continue to bowl and keep score in their own separate and unique ways.   ❖

Ending the Game

Asking children to discuss the outcome of a game is certain to create "clashes of will" and may lead to quantification. In some cases, in fact, the game itself is not as engaging as the process of figuring out who won (Kamii, 1982). Playing the traditional card game, "War," for example, may not be as useful as discovering the winner at its conclusion. When playing, children must compare numerals or dots printed on cards—these are not movable objects. At the end of the game, however, players must act upon concrete, movable pieces—the cards themselves. They might stack each player's cards in a pile, place them in lines, or count—whichever strategy is most meaningful—to determine the winner.

Teachers can also challenge children's thinking while they put the game pieces away, as the vignette below reveals.

❖ ❖

Teacher:	(To children who are putting a board game away) Did you put all of the markers back?
Child:	Yep. (Points to the box where they are stored)
Teacher:	How do you know?
Child:	We put them all back!
Teacher:	Can you think of a way to check?
Child:	Oh. I can put them out. (Places markers back onto the game board, each onto its own separate starting square. She can tell that some are missing) Oh, oh.
Teacher:	How many more do we need to find?
Child:	Well . . . (Silently counts the empty squares) Three more. (Looks around) Here are two.
Teacher:	How many do we still need?
Child:	Hmm . . . one. Oh, here! Polly was sitting on it! ❖

Reducing the Intensity of Competition

Although games can motivate children to think at high levels, they can also cause anxiety and restrict autonomy when competition becomes too great. Teachers can watch for signs of unpleasant interaction between "winners" and "losers" and intervene to reduce tensions among children. Kamii and DeVries (1980) suggest that when adults respond to winning in a casual way (e.g., "Well, Brenna won that time. What shall we play next?") and avoid "fanning children's boastfulness or the importance they attach to winning" (p. 199), the intensity of a competition is diminished. Two practices which create too severe a tension in games are giving prizes to winners and eliminating "losers" as the game progresses (e.g., the traditional version of musical chairs) (Kamii, 1982; Kamii & DeVries, 1980).

In spite of teachers' best efforts, some children will still become upset when losing. Direct conversation about how games must have winners and losers and that losing does not reflect on a child's overall competence can be initiated. The following vignette is an example.

❖ ❖

A game has just ended. A teacher notices that one child is rubbing his eyes and showing other signs of being upset.

Teacher:	You look upset, Jeremy.
Child:	(Turns away) No.
Teacher:	Are you sad because you lost the game?
Child:	(Holding back tears) I couldn't get enough of the cards! I couldn't play it very good.
Teacher:	Do you know why Jessica won?
Child:	(Sniffles) She got more cards.
Teacher:	Yes. But that's because she was very lucky. You just have to be lucky to win that game. Do you know why you lost?
Child:	(Chuckles) Lucky?
Teacher:	(Laughs, rubs child's shoulder) Yes! Or unlucky! It's all luck. You played just as well as Jessica did.
Child:	(Moves over to the blocks) I can build an airport.
Teacher:	Do you want me to help? ❖

In this vignette the teacher reduces the bad feeling through a casual manner and a light-hearted and humorous discussion about what it takes to win a game. He has helped the child to maintain a sense of competence by pointing out that he has played as well as the other children and that winning is usually a matter of chance. When the child wishes to demonstrate his abilities in the block area—perhaps to regain a general sense of competence—the teacher responds with enthusiasm and spends time assisting him in succeeding at this new task.

The solution to such adverse reactions to losing is not to remove games from the classroom (see Kamii & DeVries, 1980, for a rationale). However, some individuals may be unable to handle competition emotionally. These children may so doubt their own abilities and react so intensely to "failure" that the risk of losing does not outweigh the benefits of a game. Teachers can intervene as these children play and modify games so that competition is eliminated altogether.

An approach suggested by Kamii (1982) is to discuss with a group as they set up a game whether children want to play competitively or not. If the group wishes to play without winners and losers, the teacher can guide children in a modification of the rules. Perhaps only one marker will be used in a board game so all would move the same piece and win when it arrives at the finish. All children might pool their matching pairs in a "concentration" game and would win together when all cards have been matched. A teacher might also intervene in a competition in progress to reduce the impact of losing. Right after one child has won, a teacher could state, "Let's keep playing and see who wins next!"

Quantification in Everyday Classroom Life

Children can be encouraged to think about number as they engage in self-chosen activities throughout the classroom. In the dramatic play center, "waiters" and "waitresses" can be challenged to get enough utensils so that all "customers" have them. A make-believe mother might be asked if she has purchased enough fruit bars at the store for her many and assorted children (dolls, stuffed animals, plastic dinosaurs, and one real playmate). At the water and sand tables, children can be encouraged to think about continuous quantity, comparing amounts held by various containers or considering the size of sand mounds. As a child is experimenting with an eye dropper and baby food jars at the water table, for example, a teacher might ask, "Can you squirt the water so that all five jars have the same amount?"

Intervention in classroom disputes can lead to quantification. When a large group on the playground cannot decide whether to be aliens or "Ninja Turtles," a teacher might suggest a vote. The most challenging part of classroom voting is interpreting the outcome: "Who won?" In a group of five or more the answer to this question requires quantification.

Transition times pose quantification problems for children. At clean-up time, children can be asked, "Are all the blocks back?" "How many are missing?" "Do we have most of the blocks put away?" "If we each put one more block back will we be done?" On any occasion when materials are distributed, quantification can be encouraged with the right question: "Can you pass out the raisins so that everyone has the same amount?"

Teachers can be alert for situations throughout the day when they may encourage children to think about quantity. To reserve number activities for a certain "math time" creates an artificial separation between mathematical thinking and other kinds of problem solving, and gives children the message that quantifying is a purposeless activity that is required at only one time of day.

Interventions in the Block Area

Much logico-mathematical reasoning occurs in the block center. As children build with blocks they must place objects into relationships. Table 6-1 reviews mathematics concepts that can be learned through play with blocks. In this section, block play interventions that lead to mathematical thinking will be described.

According to Leeb-Lundberg (1984), the primary role of the teacher in the block area is to observe and appreciate the developmental value of self-directed block building. Children will benefit most when they can design, create, modify, and eventually destroy block structures on their own without adult interference. Occasionally, adults might enrich block play experiences, so long as they do not interrupt self-directed building. As adults play with children they can encourage them to think about spatial relationships, area, length, equivalence, and number.

Table 6-1
Mathematics Concepts Learned Through Block Play

Concept	Example
1. Number	A child attempts to determine if her block structure contains as many blocks as that of a peer.
2. Spatial relationships	A child notes that some plastic farm animals are inside and some are outside a block enclosure.
3. Area	A child must determine how many blocks are needed to make a roof to cover an entire building.
4. Length	A child makes a set of stairs for a building, deciding which block will be the next, slightly shorter step.
5. Equivalence	A child who has used up all rectangular blocks creates a needed shape by piecing together two triangular pieces.

Source: Adapted From Leeb-Lundberg, 1984

Spatial Relationships

Many teachers view block play as an ideal context for teaching the names of geometric shapes (Pitcher, Feinburg, & Alexander, 1989). As children play, teachers may ask, "What shape is the block that you are using?" or "Can you hand me a triangular piece?" Although children can learn to name and identify block shapes in this way, these are instances of social and physical knowledge. Children can recognize a triangle just as they can identify the color of an apple. They can name the shape "triangle," just as they can name a peer or recite a rhyme. However, it is well documented that young children have only a vague understanding of shapes, how they are constructed, and what their properties are (Leeb-Lundberg, 1984; Piaget & Inhelder, 1963; Reifel, 1984). They cannot accurately construct shapes, for example, or solve problems that require detailed understanding of shape features (Piaget & Inhelder, 1963).

Children only gradually come to learn geometric concepts. First they must acquire an understanding of very basic spatial relationships. If teachers wish to promote knowledge of geometry in the block area, they must intervene to enhance these basic understandings rather than simply asking students to name shapes.

Preschool-age children think about space in terms of the arrangement of objects and the relative position of one object to another. They adopt very primitive and approximate understandings of the position of objects, such as "close to," "far away from," "inside," "outside," or "surrounded by" (Piaget, 1963). Teachers can ask about these relationships when it is meaningful to the child to do so. There are frequent opportunities during block play to comment on the relative position of objects (Leeb-Lundberg, 1984; Reifel, 1984), as the following vignettes reveal.

❖ ❖

Vignette 1

Child:	Hand me those blocks!
Teacher:	Which blocks?
Child:	(Points) The ones there.
Teacher:	The ones that are closest or the ones that are the farthest away?
Child:	Closest.
Teacher:	These? (Holds up two blocks)
Child:	No. I mean fartherest.

Vignette 2

Child:	(Points to plastic farm animals that lie outside a block enclosure which the child has built) These animals are cold!
Teacher:	Why?
Child:	It's winter.
Teacher:	Well, are these animals cold? (Points to plastic animals that lie inside the structure)
Child:	No. They're warm 'cause they're inside. These are outside. (Pointing) They're outside 'cause they're bad. ❖

After age five, children develop more advanced notions about space and the relationships among the objects within it. They also acquire a clearer understanding of the precise properties of geometric shapes. They can construct straight lines, angles and most shapes. In kindergarten and primary-grade classrooms, teachers can intervene to help children think about the properties of geometric forms:

❖ ❖

A child has built an enclosure, but at one corner the blocks have not been brought together into a tight angle—a large space remains in the structure.

Child:	The animals are in the fence. Now they can't get out unless the farmer lets them.
Teacher:	Are there any openings where they can sneak out?
Child:	(Studies structure) Well . . . here. (Shows the opening in the corner by running a finger through it)
Teacher:	Can they get out through there?
Child:	Yep. (Quickly brings the corner blocks tightly together. Creates a new opening in the side of the enclosure while doing this)
Teacher:	Is your fence completely closed?

Child: Oh. (Sees the new opening) How did that get there? (Works with the blocks for several minutes widening the angle of these corner blocks in order to add a block to the side to fill this new opening)   ❖

This teacher has not asked the child simply to name shapes in this interchange, but to solve geometric problems. The child first solves a problem involving angles, discovering that lines must be brought together to form tight corners, then experimenting with the degree of this angle so that a new block may be accommodated in the structure. Such interactions will contribute more to children's later understanding of geometry than simple shape-naming activities.

Area

As children play with blocks, they gradually form an understanding of area. Although precise judgments about amount of space are not possible until later in life, younger children do make rough estimates of area as they play (Leeb-Lundberg, 1984). Children may comment, for example, that the block area is "too crowded" or that there is "a lot" of space to build on the table top. Frequently children will compare the area created in one structure to that of another: "More people can live in this house than in that one."

Teachers can pose geometric problems for children to solve as they build with blocks.

As teachers intervene in children's block play they can encourage them to think about area. One ideal situation for such intervention is when children are building enclosures—"fences" or "walls" which are so prevalent in young children's constructions:

❖ ❖

Vignette 1

A child has created two enclosures—one large, one small. Each has a floor made of blocks.

Child:	These are the houses for these guys. (Points to plastic people)
Teacher:	Can all of these people live in these houses? (Points to the multitude of plastic figures) Is there enough room?
Child:	Well, it's pretty crowded, I think. And they have to take turns using the bathroom!
Teacher:	Yes. Will more people live in this one (points to one structure) or this one (points to the other)?
Child:	This one, of course! (Points to larger building)
Teacher:	How do you know?
Child:	Look how many blocks there are on this floor. One, two, three . . . (Counts all the blocks in one floor, then the blocks in the floor of the other building) There are twelve here and only nine in that one. I'll show you how much room there is. (Stands a plastic figure on each block of the floor of the largest enclosure. Counts them) See? Twelve people can live in this one.

Vignette 2

A child has built an enclosure and is preparing to create a roof—long blocks laid across it.

Teacher:	Will you need a lot of blocks?
Child:	About fifteen or so.
Teacher:	Fifteen! Wow! That's quite a few.
Child:	Or maybe not too many. (Studies the structure) Maybe only five blocks. (Begins to add the roof. Five blocks do not cover the enclosure) Oh, maybe six blocks, I think. (Adds a final block to complete the roof) ❖

In these interchanges, children were encouraged to reflect on space. Detailed computation of area is developmentally a long way off for these children; but they are making early, meaningful judgments about the amount of space created in their block structures. Teachers have prompted these judgments by asking interesting questions that relate to their activities.

Length

When children compare the length of blocks, they are engaging in logico-mathematical reasoning. A child comparing three buildings (e.g., "This is the tallest; this is next tallest; this one is the shortest") is placing objects into relationships (Leeb-Lundberg, 1984). Children make many judgments about length as they build; teachers can encourage them to think and talk about how long or short their structures are.

❖ ❖
Vignette 1

A child is building a bridge between two blocks which are balanced on end, parallel to one another.

Child: I have to make a bridge so I can drive my cars across.

Teacher: Which block will be long enough?

Child: (Pauses) This one?

Teacher: What do you think?

Child: Okay. I'll try it. (Attempts to place the block between the two upright ones. It is not quite long enough to span the two) Wait. I can do something. (Moves the two uprights closer) There. Now it fits!

Vignette 2

A child has just constructed an "office building."

Teacher: How do the people get into the building?

Child: (Studies the structure) Here. This is a door. (Points to part of the building) But I need to make steps!

Teacher: Can I hand you the blocks that you will need?

Child: Sure! I need some more. I need a long one.

Teacher: Will this one work? (Holds up a very short one)

Child: (Laughs) No! That's way too short for now. Look. (Places this small block on the "steps") See how little? We could use this when we get up to the top. I need one that's kind of long. Like this. (Gestures with arms to show the desired length)

Teacher: Like this one?

Child: Just right!   ❖

In these interchanges, children are encouraged to compare lengths to solve real-life, meaningful problems. In each instance the teacher challenges the child to make estimates of length and then test out her thinking independently.

Equivalence of Volume

Standard unit blocks, which are found in most early-childhood classrooms, were designed to hold certain mathematical properties (Winsor, 1984). When all larger blocks have been used on a particular construction, children can create equivalent-sized substitutions by piecing smaller blocks together. When two medium-length blocks are placed end-to-end they make up the same volume as the largest blocks; four of the smallest units equal the volume of one of these medium-sized pieces. Triangular solids or "ramps" may be combined to create the precise volume of rectangular shapes. Children may be observed experimenting with equivalence of volume in this way as they engage in self-directed building (Leeb-Lundberg, 1984).

There are times when a teacher can encourage children to think about equivalence. An opportune moment to do this is when children complain that all the largest blocks are gone, as in the following vignettes.

❖ ❖

Vignette 1

Several children are working on individual structures in the block area. One child protests that all the longest blocks have been taken; she needs these to complete a high wall she is constructing.

Child:	(In a whiny tone) Emile and Marcia have all the long ones! I need some!
Teacher:	Well, they are using those blocks. Can you think of how to finish your building without them?
Child:	I need them! I need to have long blocks to go all the way across. See? (Gestures toward her building.)
Teacher:	Here are some shorter ones. (Holds up smaller unit blocks) What could you do with these?
Child:	They're not long enough! (Pauses) Let me see. (Takes the small blocks from the teacher, places four of them end-to-end. Notices that they create the desired length) There!

Vignette 2

A child has built an enclosure and now is creating a "floor" of blocks inside of it. He runs out of medium-sized blocks and all rectangular blocks are being used.

Child:	Well! I can't finish my floor. (Points to plastic figures) These people will fall through to the ground!
Teacher:	Can you finish the floor with these? (Holds up triangular pieces)
Child:	Nope. Not the right kind. They don't work. Look. (Places a triangular piece in the enclosure)

Teacher: What if you used a few of these blocks?

Child: Well, let's try it. (Discovers that by pairing triangular pieces he can make rectangular ones) There. Now the people won't have to stand in the dirt!

                                                                             ❖

In these vignettes, children have been encouraged to think about equivalence at a time when it is meaningful to them. Indeed, without creating equivalent volumes they would be unable to complete their buildings.

Number

Children quantify continually as they build with blocks. Blocks are in essence discrete concrete objects; block buildings are sets of these to be created and compared. Teachers can enhance the quantification that occurs in the block center by asking the right sorts of questions (Kamii, 1982).

Although the block center is the site of much cooperative play behavior, disputes can sometimes arise. Children frequently clash over such issues as who has more blocks, whose road is longest, or whether one playmate is using too many of the toy cars. Teachers can intervene in such arguments to promote quantification, as well as independent social problem solving, as the below vignette reveals:

❖ ❖

Child A: Sharon has all the blocks! I need more for my building!

Child B: I was here first! I need these for my tunnel!

Teacher: I think there are enough blocks for everyone, James. Look at all of these still on the shelf!

Child A: That's not enough. Sharon still has more!

Teacher: I'll bet if you used all the blocks on the shelf you'd have as many as Sharon.

Child A: No. I don't think so. Let me see. (Pulls all remaining blocks from the shelf and piles them in a tight group next to Child B's pile of unused blocks) Oh. I do have more!

Child B: No you don't! We both have the same. Look. (Measures the width of her pile with her arms. Keeping her arms fixed to represent her pile's width, she now places them over Child A's pile in comparison. It appears that the piles are the same width using her primitive measure) See? We have the same.   ❖

Teachers can also encourage children to think about quantity as they work alone. One strategy is to elicit estimates of how many blocks it will take to complete a certain project. Leeb-Lundberg (1984) suggests that young children will often respond with primitive quantity measures that are meaningful to them: "a lot," "a bunch," "a pile":

❖ ❖

Child:	Now you can help me with this building, okay? It's a two-person building!
Teacher:	A two-person building! Okay. What do I do?
Child:	Hand me the blocks for the road.
Teacher:	How many will you need?
Child:	Oh. A lot. Nineteen or so. This many. (Gestures with arms)
Teacher:	I'll put the blocks out for you one by one. You tell me to stop when you have just the right number.
Child:	Okay. I'll count 'em! (Counts as the teacher puts down blocks. Gets confused and stops counting) Okay. Okay, that's just right!

In another situation the teacher encourages the child to create a set of blocks to match a set of plastic dinosaurs:

Child:	(In a make-believe voice) The flood is coming! Get on the islands. (Begins placing plastic dinosaurs on blocks)
Teacher:	Are the animals trying to get out of the water?
Child:	Yeah. They have to stand on these islands. (Points to blocks) So they won't drown.
Teacher:	Do you have enough islands so each dinosaur can stand on one?
Child:	Well . . . (Places dinosaurs on "islands" and discovers there aren't enough blocks) There aren't enough. The dinosaurs need to share. (Places several of the figures on a single, remaining block) ❖

Clean-up time in the block center affords many opportunities for quantification:

❖ ❖

Teacher:	(To children cleaning up blocks) How many blocks can you carry at once?
Child A:	A lot! (Gathers up a load) Look!
Child B:	(Also gathers a stack) Look at me!
Teacher:	Do you have more than I do?
Child A:	Yeah. Put yours down. (Puts her stack next to the teacher's) Yep! I've got more.
Child B:	*I've* got more! (Stacks her pile next to the others) ❖

Note that in all examples teachers do not ask children to count. As Kamii (1982) recommends, they pose real-life problems which relate to what children are doing and that require autonomous judgments about quantity.

A Word about Microcomputers

The microcomputer is a relatively new and controversial addition to the mathematics curriculum in many schools. Opinions—both positive and negative—abound regarding the impact of this technology on logico-mathematical reasoning as well as other areas of learning. A prevalent view is that microcomputers are very expensive math worksheets; they provide highly abstract, passive, and purely visual experiences which may not lead to true understanding (Hendrick, 1992). Certainly the criterion of Kamii (1982), that meaningful mathematics experiences involve physical action on movable objects, are not met by much of the software available today. Some have argued that microcomputers inhibit social interaction; they provide young children with another opportunity to "tune in" to visual media and "tune out" human interaction.

Microcomputer enthusiasts have argued that developmentally appropriate software does exist. Such programs enhance logico-mathematical reasoning (as opposed to mindless counting or computation) and facilitate cooperative interaction among children (Woodill, 1987). Programs that involve true problem solving can be identified. These are interactive; the user must adapt actions in relation to computer feedback. In essence children are encouraged to "put all kinds of actions into all kinds of relationships" (Kamii, 1982, p. 28). Teachers should be very cautious in selecting software, microcomputer advocates warn, but should not be fearful of the technology altogether (Woodill, 1987).

Once again, it is the nature of teacher-child interactions that will determine if microcomputer experiences are meaningful. Through question-asking, prompting, or modeling, teachers can enhance logico-mathematical reasoning at the computer. As in group games, teachers can facilitate useful "clashes of wills" during computer play (e.g., "Jason, why don't you tell Maria why you don't want to move the cursor?"). Social interaction can be enhanced (e.g., "Robert and Hannah, why don't you work on the computer together rather than taking turns?"). Helping children to analyze their "errors" (for example, to "debug" a Logo program) by asking them to reflect on the causes of problems and to invent alternative strategies for solving them will foster causal thinking. With cautious selection of software and thoughtful teacher intervention, the microcomputer can become a valuable learning tool in the mathematics curriculum.

A Reminder about Excessive Intervention

A reminder must be given about the negative consequences of excessive intervention. The reader may get the sense from reading the many classroom vignettes described in this chapter that teachers should continually interrupt—even pester—children with challenges to their thinking. As discussed in

Just the right amount and kind of intervention is needed to promote logico-mathematical reasoning.

earlier chapters, too much intervention destroys the pleasure of the game and its child-centered quality. Kamii and DeVries (1980) urge that teachers intervene "sparingly, and posing the right question at the right time. . . .If a teacher too often asks, 'How did you guess?' the question will become boring and will make the game distasteful" (p.210).

The reader is reminded, then, that the variety of interactions described here are not to be employed all at once within a single activity—perhaps not even within a single day. Only one or several of these interchanges are initiated, then the teacher withdraws. Only when a question, an observation, or the provision of new materials are meaningful to the child and are directly related to a self-chosen activity will these interventions effectively promote development.

Summary

Children acquire several types of knowledge in early childhood classrooms. When they learn the words to a song or the names of their classmates, they have acquired social knowledge. When they notice that leaves are green or that ice is cold, physical knowledge has been learned. A type of knowledge that is critical for later learning is logico-mathematical knowledge—the knowledge that relationships exist among objects or events. When a child discovers that a pumpkin seed is smaller than an acorn, she has acquired logico-mathematical knowledge. Such knowledge is constructed from within; children must come to understand on their own that the acorn and pumpkin seed can be related in this way. A teacher cannot teach "smaller than" directly; children must acquire it by thinking about these objects as they handle them.

Teachers can help students to construct logico-mathematical knowledge through play intervention. They can pose questions and challenges which encourage them to "put all kinds of objects, events, or actions into all kinds of relationships" (Kamii, 1982, p. 28).

One type of logico-mathematical knowledge that teachers may enhance is the understanding of number. By intervening in children's games, activities at the math center, or other everyday experiences, teachers can encourage children to quantify. Quantifying is different from rote counting. It requires children to make judgments about quantity in any way they find meaningful. Children may make gross estimates about amounts rather than counting; teachers should encourage this. It is only through this independent reflection that children will gain an understanding of number.

The area of the classroom where much logico-mathematical reasoning occurs is the block center. Although teachers should mainly encourage children to build with blocks on their own, they can occasionally intervene to promote understandings of space, area, length, equivalence, and number.

Suggested Activities

1. Play with three groups of children in three different areas of a classroom. As you interact, ask questions that encourage children to put objects, events, or actions into relationships (e.g., "How are these alike? different?" "What will happen if . . .?" "What happened when . . .?" "Can you make . . .occur?"). Write an analysis of this experience, guided by the following questions:

   a. To what degree were you successful in phrasing the questions in open-ended, challenging ways? Describe any difficulties you had in inventing and asking such questions.

   b. Which of your questions led to the most thinking or problem solving? Which didn't lead to much thinking at all?

   c. To what degree did children interact with their peers as they answered your questions? Were there discussions or disagreements among children about the answers? How did you help resolve them?

2. Spend half an hour at the math center of a classroom. As children play with materials there, ask quantification (not counting) questions. Write an analysis of the experience, guided by the following questions:

   a. To what degree were you successful at asking quantification, but not counting questions?
   b. Which of your questions led to the most autonomous quantification?
   c. Describe the different strategies children used to quantify in response to your questions (e.g., counting, one-to-one correspondence, visual estimation).

3. Play a game with a small group of children. Ask quantification questions while you guide children in setting up the game, playing it, ending it, and putting pieces away. Write an analysis guided by the following questions:

   a. In what ways did you engage children in quantifying? Which of your behaviors led to the most quantifying?
   b. Describe any "clashes of will" among children that you observed. How did you respond to them?
   c. Describe children who reacted negatively to the competition. How did you deal with this problem?
   d. In what ways did children bend the rules of the game? How did you respond?

4. Spend half an hour with children in the block area. Intervene in children's play and ask questions that encourage mathematical thinking. Strive to enhance several of the following areas: spatial relationships, area, equivalence, length, and number. Write an analysis of this experience, guided by the following questions:

   a. Which areas of math learning were you able to promote?
   b. Which questions stimulated the most mathematical thinking? Which questions didn't appear to lead to much thinking?
   c. How did children react to your interventions? Did they enjoy your participation or prefer that you leave them alone? Did your interventions ever disrupt block play in progress?

Further Reading

Castaneda, A. M. (1987). Early mathematics education. In C. Seefeldt (Ed.). *The early childhood curriculum: A review of current research* (pp. 165–182). New York: Teachers College Press.

Hirsch, E. S. (Ed.). (1984). *The block book.* Washington, DC: National Association for the Education of Young Children.

Kamii, C. (1982). *Number in preschool and kindergarten: Implications of Piaget's theory.* Washington, DC: National Association for the Education of Young Children.

Kamii, C., & Devries, R. (1978). *Physical knowledge in preschool education.* Englewood Cliffs, NJ: Prentice-Hall.

Kamii, C., & DeVries, R. (1980). *Group games in early education*. Washington, DC: National Association for the Education of Young Children.

Reifel, S. (1984). Block construction: Children's developmental landmarks in representation of space. *Young Children, 40*(2), 61–67.

Williams, C. K., & Kamii, C. (1986). How do children learn by handling objects? *Young Children, 42*(1), 23–26.

7

SCIENCING WITH YOUNG CHILDREN

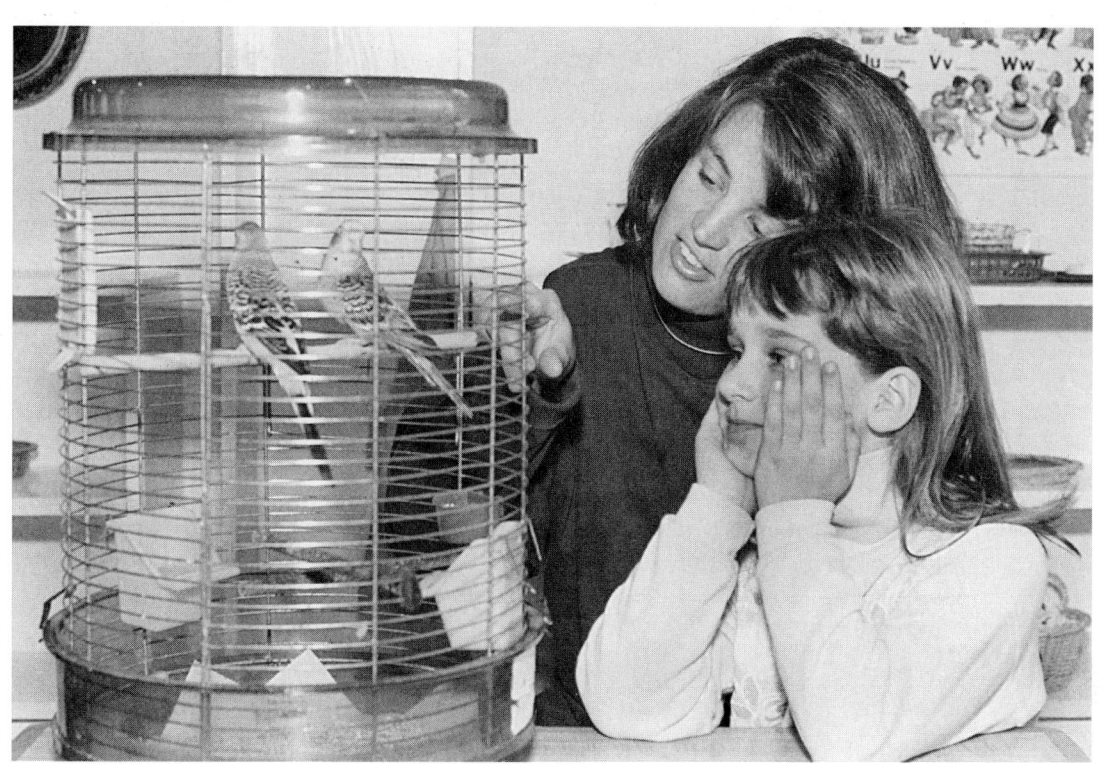

❖ ❖

Two seven-year-olds are arguing about whether plants breathe. Their discussion becomes quite loud and draws the attention of a teacher.

Teacher: This sounds like quite a discussion.

Child A: Matthew says that plants can breathe. That's not true, is it?

Teacher: That's an interesting question. You don't think plants can breathe?

Child A: No, 'cause you can't see 'em. They don't breathe in and out, in and out. (Demonstrates breathing, inhaling and exhaling in an exaggerated way)

Child B: They do too breathe! My kindergarten teacher told me. They have to breathe air or they die.

Child A: They don't breathe air! They're just plants!

Teacher: How can we figure out whether plants need air to live?

Child B: (Points to a plant by the window) We could cover this plant with a blanket. Then take it off and it would be dead.

Child A: But you can breathe through a blanket!

Teacher: Also, if we cover the plant with a blanket it wouldn't get any sun either.

Child B: Oh, yeah.

Teacher: I'm going to give you two plant cuttings. Why don't you do an experiment with them? You can give both of them water and light. You could give one air, but not the other one.

The teacher produces plant cuttings, water, jars, and lids. With his assistance the children prepare an experiment, placing one cutting in a jar with water but no lid and the other sealed tightly in a similar jar. The teacher then provides two small notebooks from the science center.

Teacher: Why don't you write down your hypothesis about what will happen. A hypothesis is a guess about how things will come out.

Child B: Okay. I'll write that this one (points to the sealed cutting) will turn brownish and deadish.

Both children write their predictions in their own invented spelling. Each day the teacher encourages the children to observe and compare the plants. They may write notes or draw sketches if they wish. As the days pass, both cuttings turn yellow. The one in the sealed jar also develops brown patches. The following exchange occurs about a month after the experiment has begun:

Child A: (Holds up jar to show the teacher) Look! They both died!

Teacher: So, what do you think happened?

Child A:	I think plants die when you cut them off.
Teacher:	Do you want to write about that in the journal?
Child A:	(Nods, begins to write)
Child B:	They aren't dead! They're yellow! One got brown spots, see? I thought they'd get brown.
Teacher:	Why do you think it turned brown?
Child B:	Well, the plant needs air to stay green, I think . . . (hesitates) or yellow, maybe. When it doesn't get air it turns brown.
Teacher:	You can write about that.

Both children record their interpretations of the outcome of the experiment. The jars remain in the classroom for the entire year. Both these and other children regularly examine the cuttings and interpret their observations. ❖

The reader may ask: Have these children learned science at all from this experiment? They seem to know as little about what plants need at the end of the experience as they did at its beginning. Perhaps the teacher could have better structured the activity so that the outcome would be clearer—so that the plant without air would die. If he put just the right amount of water in the jars, placed them in just the right light, used the correct sized container to avoid a "terrarium effect," wouldn't children come to better understand the importance of air in sustaining life? Maybe the teacher should have told the children the correct answer at the onset: Plants do need air to live.

Had the teacher imparted specific botanical facts in these ways, however, he would have removed from the activity the most important processes of science—observing, predicting, designing experiments, and interpreting their results. He has chosen to encourage children to pursue answers to their own scientific questions, rather than imposing his own. He has guided them in designing an experiment to resolve a problem and has urged them to make independent predictions, orally and in writing, about the outcome. He allows children to interpret results and accepts these personal interpretations without criticism.

In short, this teacher has chosen to let children become scientists themselves, to do what scientists do. The teacher is "sciencing" with children, rather than teaching them about science (Cain & Evans, 1990). This act of self-discovery is far more useful for the development of scientific thinking and general cognition than merely hearing about what adult scientists have already discovered (Bredderman, 1982).

❖ ❖ ❖

Sciencing Versus Learning about Science

"Read and recite" science programs that focus on learning scientific facts in abstract, adult-directed fashion are common in kindergarten and primary grade classrooms (Forman & Kaden, 1987). Even play-based preschools and day-care centers often focus on learning scientific information about the physical world—seasons, weather, or animals, for example. There is a great deal of research suggesting that approaches focusing on these end-products of science (i.e., specific facts that have already been discovered) are less useful for young children than those in which scientific processes are emphasized.

Discovery-based programs in which children experiment on their own have been found to foster process skills—observing, measuring, interpreting data—but also to lead to greater mastery of science content than direct instructional approaches (Bredderman, 1982). Thinking processes acquired in discovery-based classrooms appear to generalize language, reading, and mathematics learning (Bredderman, 1982; Shymansky, Kyle, & Alport, 1982). Creativity may be enhanced through activity-based science (Bredderman, 1982); children in these programs express more positive attitudes toward science as a discipline (Bredderman, 1982; Shymansky, Kyle, & Alport, 1982) than do other children.

Cain and Evans (1990) conclude that children should be "sciencing," not learning about science in early childhood. The orientation of this book is toward science as a way of thinking and acting rather than as a body of knowledge to be imparted to young children. Interventions within children's informal, self-directed play activities that engage children in scientific processes will be stressed in this chapter. Specifically, ways teachers can engage children in the Scientific Method will be presented. Steps in the method are listed in Table 7-1 and will be discussed in-depth in the following sections.

Observing and Reflecting upon Nature

A critical step in the scientific method is observing. Scientists make regular observations of the physical world. They do not just look at nature, however, but think about what they observe and place observed events or phenomena into hypothetical relationships. If children are to become scientists in the classroom they must be assisted in observing in this reflective way.

Young children are not always alert and attentive observers. In the following vignette, a particularly unobservant five-year-old is profiled.

Table 7-1
Steps of the Scientific Method

Step	Example
1. Observing and reflecting	A child handles two shells. A teacher asks, "How are the two shells different?" The child responds, "This one is flat. But this one is all curly; it goes round and round (demonstrates) . . . I think it must have had a worm living inside."
2. Asking scientific questions	A teacher asks many questions about Fall during a nature walk. Children begin asking questions, as well. A child asks, "Why didn't the leaves fall off this bush? All the other leaves are falling off."
3. Formulating and testing hypotheses	A child is quickly touching a magnet to each object at the science table to determine which objects it will attract. A teacher suggests, "Before you touch an object, make a guess: Do you think it will stick or not stick?" The child looks at a sheet of foil. "Uh . . . it will stick," she guesses. She tests her hypothesis. "Nope!"
4. Interpreting results	A child has placed a cup of water outside in winter to see what will happen. Before the school day ends he retrieves it; it is solid ice. The teacher asks, "What happened?" The child provides an elaborate interpretation: "See? The water really went away, 'cause all that's left is ice. It's so, so cold that the water goes away."

A preschool class takes a walk through a forest near the school. One child walks along with his head down, scanning the ground for treasures. During the walk the sky grows dark and threatening and a fine mist falls, causing a premature end to the experience. Back at school the following conversation occurs between the downward-looking child and the teacher.

Child: Why did we have to come back? I found some things out there! (Produces stones and acorns from his backpack)

Teacher: Well. Did you see the sky?

Child: (Shakes head, "no," and continues looking at collected objects)

Teacher: Did you see how dark it was?

Child: Was it going to rain?

Teacher: It did rain! Didn't you notice? (Laughs)   ❖

Children like this one need adult support to become observant scientists. Teachers can encourage students to use all senses in their observations by asking questions ("Do you smell anything here?") and pointing out significant or puzzling phenomena ("Look at that cloud that just rolled across the sky. See how different it is from the others?") (Smith, 1983). Children can be guided in attending to all areas of the visual field (e.g., "Let's all lie down on our blankets for a moment and look up," or "Let's turn around and look at where we've been").

Simple observation is not enough, however, for constructing an understanding of the world. Seeing, smelling, and touching will lead to physical knowledge, as described in the last chapter (Kamii, 1982). Scientists must also put objects, events, or actions into relationships as they observe, a process that requires advanced logico-mathematical reasoning. Children must reflect upon natural phenomena, not just look at or touch them.

In the following vignette, children are given opportunities to note physical features of objects at a science center, but are not challenged to look for relationships among them. Their observations become superficial and brief.

❖ ❖

Two children examine various nuts displayed on the science table. Their interest appears to be waning; a teacher intervenes.

Teacher:	(Holding up a nut) How does this one feel?
Child A:	Bumpy.
Child B:	(Unenthused) Yeah. Bumpy.
Teacher:	Anything else?
Child B:	Nope. Bumpy.
Teacher:	(Produces a second nut) How about this one?
Child A:	Hmm . . . bumpy too.
Child B:	Yeah. C'mon, Rachel, let's play in the housekeeping corner.

The two children leave the science center; the teacher shrugs and returns the nuts to the display.   ❖

These interactions did not lead to scientific thinking as the teacher had hoped. In fact, the children's interest was not sustained. Science centers often get less use in classrooms than other areas (Rosenthal, 1974) in part because they contain much to look at but little to think about and act upon.

The teacher in the vignette below is far more successful in engaging two five-year-olds:

❖ ❖

Teacher:	(Points to a container of all different kinds of seeds gathered from a field behind the school) Look at all these seeds. Can you find any that are alike?

Child A:	(Sifts through the seeds. Picks out two different types) Yeah. These are smaller.
Child B:	Yeah, but look. (Holds up two other seeds) These are all prickly. See?
Teacher:	(Produces several meat trays) If you'd like, you could put seeds that are alike together in these trays.
Child A:	Okay. (Begins sorting the seeds with Child B) ❖

As teachers interact with children, they can encourage more reflection, as the teacher in the above vignette has done. They can pose challenges or questions that encourage comparison, categorization, or transformation. These processes may be elicited in the science center, other areas of the classroom, or outdoors.

Promoting Reflection in the Science Center

A table full of fascinating objects from nature can stimulate much scientific thought or can lead to meaningless manipulation, depending upon the kind of adult support provided. Handling a sparrow's nest, examining stones with a magnifying glass, or attracting iron filings with a magnet does not necessarily involve reflection. When teachers intervene in these activities to encourage children to put events and objects into relationships, they nurture true scientific thought (Kamii, 1982).

Comparing

Teachers can encourage children to put objects into relationships by asking: "How are these alike? How are they different?" In response, children must consider common and dissimilar attributes of these objects and engage in internal reflection. When several children interact to solve these problems, useful conflict can arise as children attempt to reach consensus and defend their ideas about "sameness" and "differentness." Questions such as "How does this feel?" do not produce the same effect, since they result only in physical knowledge. Although questions like "Which is bigger?" stimulate more thought, they still do not allow children to select their own ways of comparing objects—the attribute to be used in comparison is assigned to them. Open-ended comparison questions create more opportunities for logico-mathematical thought.

In encouraging comparison, a teacher might suggest that "scientific instruments" be used. In the following interaction, a teacher has recommended that children use a balance, a magnet, and a nutcracker to determine how objects are alike and different.

❖ ❖

Two children are examining a collection of objects—stones, "Indian corn," nuts, seed pods, shells, and leaves—at the science center. A teacher intervenes.

Teacher: I know something you can do with these things. Are these two alike or different? (Points to a stone that one child is holding and a small piece of corn held by her playmate)

Child A: Hmm. . . . Well, this is corn.

Child B: And this is a rock.

Teacher: So are they alike or different?

Child B: I don't know.

Child A: Oh! (Pointing to the corn) 'Cause this has more colors!

Teacher: Yes. You could use some things here to check whether they're alike or different. (Retrieves a magnet, balance, and nutcracker from the table) What could we do with these?

Child B: I don't know.

Child A: Well, the magnet doesn't work. (Demonstrates that it doesn't attract either object) See? They don't stick.

Teacher: So are they alike or different?

Child B: Well, they both don't stick.

Teacher: Yes. Now, how could you use the balance?

Child A: Oh! Put them both on! (Places an object on each side of the balance) Look. This side goes down. (Shows how the corn tips the balance down sharply)

Teacher: So what does that tell you?

Child B: So now they're different. This one's . . . heavy. (Points to corn)

Child A: This one's the heavy one. (Points to the corn) This one's the not-heavy one. (Points to the stone)

Teacher: (In an enthused tone) How about the nutcracker?

Child A: That can squish things.

Teacher: Yes. Can we use it to decide if these are alike or different?

Child A: We could see if they both squish. (Laughs)

Child B: (Laughing) We'd break the things!

Child A: Not the rock; just the corn.

Teacher: You can try it.

Child A: (Giving a hesitant, "are you sure this is okay?" look) All right. (Crushes the piece of corn)

Child B: I can do the rock! (Squeezes the nutcracker on the rock several times) Oh. It doesn't work.

Teacher: So what do you think?

Child A: Not alike. The corn breaks.

Teacher: Why don't you test some other things?

The children continue to experiment with the nutcracker, remarking on how some things break and some do not. The teacher withdraws from the area.   ❖

In this interaction the teacher guides children from simple manipulation toward thoughtful action. The introduction of several instruments, each of which has a different effect on the objects, encourages them to consider alternative attributes and to rethink many times the solution to the problem of sameness and differentness.

Categorizing

One task of scientists is to categorize natural phenomena, to put things that are alike together. Categorization requires the comparison of a collection of objects, each of which must be compared to all other items based on selected criteria (Inhelder & Piaget, 1958). When a child places sticks and leaves in one pile and never-living objects in another, complex comparison is occurring— each new object must be considered in terms of its "living" or "non-living" features.

Categorization may be encouraged in the classroom by asking children to put things that are alike together. The problem must be posed so that the teacher does not suggest the attribute to be used in the categorization. "Put all the big shells here," gives the solution away. As Smith (1983) warns, "children must decide on their own classification schemes; otherwise they are not constructing the relationships themselves" (p.148).

Within early childhood classrooms, very different classification methods, representing various levels of cognitive functioning, will be observed. Some children may put all the objects in a single pile. This is a useful and logical way to categorize—children in this instance are still creating relationships, they are simply not able to hold the categorization criteria constant:

A child puts one brown nut in the container, then a brown shell. Now he selects another shell that is not brown, and still another shell that is green. Now he places green objects into the container—leaves and plant cuttings.   ❖

Although adults do not often view this as true categorization since only one category has been created, the child is engaging in precisely the kind of internal reflection that is critical for later, advanced scientific thought.

Other children will create categories that are very different from the ones adults would create (Inhelder & Piaget, 1958):

"Can you put the things that are alike together?" This is the best way to encourage children to categorize objects independently.

❖ ❖

A child is asked to categorize objects she has collected on a nature walk. She creates two categories—"nails" and "not-nails."   ❖

Primary-grade children will use more complex schemes for categorizing; a few may even use multiple dimensions in their sorting (e.g., putting large green objects in one pile, small green objects in another). By posing categorization problems in an open-ended manner, the teacher ensures that children will be able to solve them in ways that are developmentally meaningful.

More complex interventions in which categorization containers and other new materials are provided are illustrated in the vignette below.

❖ ❖

Two six-year-olds are examining a collection of objects displayed on a large table.

Teacher:	Would you like to help make a museum in our classroom?
Child A:	Sure. Museum?
Child B:	This is like a museum 'cause there is a lot of old stuff here.
Teacher:	You're right. We could move the objects around so that the things that are alike go together.

Child A:	Why?
Child B:	At a museum all the rocks go one place, and the fossils somewhere else, and the gift shop is in the front.
Teacher:	Right. So we could put the things that are alike together just like at other museums.
Child B:	How should we do it?
Teacher:	(Producing large meat trays) You can use these to put objects in if you want. You could put things that are alike in each one.
Child A:	Like all the shells here. (Begins placing shells in a tray)

The teacher observes as the children begin placing objects together. She then briefly intervenes again.

Teacher:	Sometimes museums label objects. A label tells what is displayed. We could make labels to tell what each of your trays holds.
Child A:	Like shells. (Points to the shell tray)
Teacher:	Right. (Provides markers and labels made from cardboard pieces) If you want, you can use these to make a label for each pile. You can write what is in the tray in any way you want.

The children finish categorizing, then use inventive spelling to label categories. ❖

Here the teacher has integrated scientific and literacy experiences. After several days, the labels are removed and another group is encouraged to create a museum using their own very different categorization scheme.

Transforming Objects

Piaget (1971) has argued that knowledge of the world can only be constructed by understanding how things change. Scientists regularly think about change, predicting and testing what will occur over time, how one phenomenon will alter another, or whether what is changed will eventually return to its previous form. Forman and Kuschner (1984) assert that most early-childhood programs focus only on the static features of objects. Looking at pictures or examining objects as they currently exist are common in the early science curriculum; children must have more opportunities, they argue, to witness the transformation of objects from one state to another.

Teachers can encourage children to transform objects as they play with them. Questions such as, "What will happen if we add more ice cubes to the cup of water?" are useful because they encourage children to think about change before it occurs and then to cause the transformation themselves. A follow-up challenge, such as "Can you make the water level like it was before?" encourages the child to reverse the transformation (e.g., remove some of the ice cubes with a spoon and observe that they melt).

In the vignette below, a teacher helps children move beyond simple observation of static properties to active transformation of objects.

Two four-year-olds are examining stones, shell, twigs, leaves, and other objects from nature. A teacher sits down with a bowl of water and eye droppers.

Teacher:	How do you think these things would change if they got all wet?
Child A:	They'll be all wet!
Teacher:	Yes. Will they look different?
Child A:	Yeah. Wet.
Child B:	And darker, too.
Teacher:	Why don't you squirt some water on each object and see what happens?

The children put drops on each object and discuss changes in their appearance. Before they finish their experiment, several stones and twigs have dried, returning to their original color.

Teacher:	Look at these! What's happening?
Child B:	They went back.
Child A:	Here. (Adds more water to them)

The children continue to transform the objects with water until their container of water is empty.   ❖

The teacher in this vignette helps children act upon objects rather than just observe them. They make predictions, test them, then observe the objects return to their previous states.

Varying Actions and Observing Results

The foundations of physics can be laid in the early years when children are encouraged to act upon objects and observe their reactions (Kamii & Lee-Katz, 1983). Children do this quite naturally on the playground or in the classroom. When a child throws a half-full milk carton very hard into the trash bin and observes the resulting explosion, simple physics has been studied. When a group varies the speed and strength with which they bump into a playground fence and note differences in sound (and their teacher's reactions!), they are studying physics.

Teachers can guide such experimentation through question-asking. Kamii and Lee-Katz (1983) suggest two types of questions that lead to scientific thought—those in which children are encouraged to anticipate the outcome of an action (e.g., "What will happen if you . . .?") and those in which they are asked what they might do to produce a particular result (e.g., "What could you do so that . . . occurs?"). Although questions such as these should be posed in all areas of the classroom, the science center is a good place for such interventions. In the following vignette, a teacher creates a physics demonstration from a simple, repetitive motor activity:

A five-year-old child is sitting at the science center, rolling a ping pong ball off the table and watching it bounce.

Teacher: What would happen if you stood up and dropped the ball from up high? (Demonstrates, holding the ball over his head)

Child: Well . . . Let me try it. (Drops the ball) It bounces up more.

Teacher: What if you stood on a chair and dropped it?

Child: Oh! Then it would really bounce! (Stands on the chair and drops the ball) Oh. That's not too much higher. (Tries again) Oh.

Teacher: How could you make the ball bounce higher?

Child: I'll really throw it down. (Throws the ball to the ground) Oh. It really bounced.

Teacher: (Assembles a collection of objects from the table) Do you think these things will fall the same way?

Child: Oh. No, some of these won't bounce. I think some will just, like, crash. (Begins dropping objects from the chair)

Another child joins him; the teacher withdraws from the area. ❖

In this, as in all other vignettes of this section, the teacher has provoked internal reflection. The child must, in this instance, put actions into relationships, associating the mode of dropping with the height of the bounce.

Promoting Reflection in Nature

Processes such as comparing, categorizing, transforming, or varying actions can also be fostered by intervention in children's outdoor nature experiences. Walking in the woods on a beautiful day may or may not involve scientific reflection, depending on the kind of adult support provided. Children might collect objects or observe nature without deep thought; or they might be induced through teacher interventions to think at high levels, as in the following vignette.

❖ ❖

A teacher and a small group of six- and seven-year-olds hike along a trail on a warm day. They begin in deep woods, then suddenly come upon a clearing.

Teacher:	(Standing in the clearing) Come stand here!
Children:	What? (All gather in the meadow)
Teacher:	How is this different out here than it was when we were walking before?
Child A:	It's hot!
Teacher:	Why do you think it feels that way?
Child B:	Because the sun.
Child A:	(Speaking at the same time as B) There's no shade!
Teacher:	Why?
Child C:	Oh! There's not trees. The trees keep the sun out.
Teacher:	Yes! (Pauses) How else is it different out here?
Child C:	Well, look at all the grass we're standing in. We didn't have to walk through this before.
Child B:	(At the same time as C) The weeds!
Teachers:	Why didn't weeds grow in the woods?
Child A:	(Thinks a moment) Maybe they like it hot.
Teacher:	Ah. They grow in the meadow because they like it hotter?
Child D:	No. They like the sun. They need sunshine. And the rain can fall on here. (Demonstrates with fingers how rain falls on the meadow)
Teacher:	Interesting. Is there anything else that's different out here?
Child E:	(Has wandered a few yards away from the rest of the group) Look at the grasshoppers!
Child A:	Oh! Grasshoppers? Did we have grasshoppers in the woods?
Teacher:	Do you remember?
Child B:	I think grasshoppers like the rain too.
Child A:	Can we go back and check?

They walk back into the forest and search for grasshoppers. Here they make further comparisons, with teacher guidance, between woods and meadow—how the smells, the feel of the soil, the texture of the vegetation differ.   ❖

This vignette shows how eager children are to construct relationships among natural phenomena. With several well-framed questions, the teacher has engaged children in a thoughtful comparison of two distinct ecosystems. He has also encouraged speculation about causal relationships—why grasshoppers choose to live in the meadow; why only moss and ferns grow on the forest floor. Resulting thought and discussion go well beyond mere observation and description of physical properties.

Asking Scientific Questions

A step in the scientific method that is often ignored—even in discovery-based science curricula—is asking questions. Adult scientists must raise significant questions about what they have observed. Such questions serve as the basis for further scientific experimentation. In an effort to engage children in scientific processes, teachers will frequently select, themselves, the questions to be researched. Studies in science education suggest, however, that children will think at higher levels and learn a good deal more when allowed to ask and answer their own scientific questions (Kuhn, 1974).

When children ask in the course of playful experimentation, "What would happen if . . .?" or "Why is it that . . .?" teachers can encourage them to seek answers on their own. Children will pursue these with greater interest and vigor and will retain answers longer because the questions are more meaningful to them and match more closely their current level of understanding (Forman & Kaden, 1987).

Not all children ask questions (Endsley & Clarey, 1975). Encouraging them to do so requires more than simple adult praise for inquisitive behavior. Genuine curiosity about the world must be fostered. In a comprehensive review of research on curiosity and question-asking, Bradbard and Endsley (1983) identify factors that are related to curiosity in young children. Several specific teacher behaviors are identified—responding, nurturing, and modeling. Teachers can perform these behaviors as they intervene in young children's science activities.

Responding

When teachers and parents respond with enthusiasm to young children's questions, they will ask more of them (Bradbard & Endsley, 1983). Statements such as, "What an interesting question!" or "How do you think we can find out?" give the message that children's questions are valued and that they, themselves, may seek solutions to them. The effects of responsiveness are well illustrated in the vignette at the beginning of this chapter. Had the teacher been less responsive to children's inquiries about plants and air, very little sciencing may have occurred. Because this teacher encouraged children to continue investigating answers to their questions, ongoing and meaningful research took place. The vignette below serves as another example of responsive science teaching.

❖ ❖

A five-year-old is experimenting with a magnet in the science center. She is now watching children play at the water table.

Teacher:	It looks like you are thinking about something.
Child:	(Smiles) Oh . . . Do magnets work under water? (Laughs)
Teacher:	Do you think so?
Child:	I don't know.
Teacher:	How can we find out?
Child:	(Points to the water table) We could go over there.
Teacher:	Good idea!
Child:	(Takes a magnet to the water table) Should I try it?
Teacher:	Sure!
Child:	(Puts magnet in the water and attempts to attract plastic measuring cups) Nope!
Teacher:	Why didn't it work?
Child:	(Pauses for several seconds, thinking) Oh! Wait a second! (Retrieves paper clips from the science table; drops these in the water) Now let's try. (Attracts the paper clips) Ah! Now it works! See? The cups aren't metal. ❖

Because of this teacher's enthusiasm and encouragement, the child persists in seeking an answer to her question, finally constructing an understanding that the properties of magnets are the same under water. Concepts learned will hold more meaning and be retained longer than those selected and directly taught by adults (Kuhn, 1974).

Nurturing

Children display more curiosity and ask more questions when in the presence of warm and friendly adults (Moore & Bulbulian, 1976). This is explained by the fact that asking questions is risky. Some children have been given the message for too long that their interests and ideas are not important; it is only adult questions that are worthy of discussion and experimentation. Teachers can counteract this belief by responding to children's questions with warmth (e.g., a hug or pat), acceptance (e.g., "I don't think that's a silly question! That's very interesting!"), and friendliness (e.g., "Can I work with you in solving that problem?"). When children receive support from teachers they will take risks, think autonomously, and ultimately think at high levels.

Modeling

In other chapters of this book, teacher questions have been extolled as potent educational tools. Adult question-asking serves yet another function, however: When teachers ask questions they are modeling inquisitiveness. Children will

Responding to children's questions with enthusiasm will enhance curiosity and exploration.

explore more and ask more questions when they observe their teachers doing so (Bradbard & Endsley, 1983). The effects of adult questioning on young children's curiosity are illustrated in the following vignette.

❖ ❖

Two four-year-olds are examining seed pods at the science center. Very little discussion is occurring; interest appears to be waning.

Teacher:	(Points to the remaining segment of stem still attached to a pod) Hmm . . . I wonder what this is?
Child A:	Oh. That's where it attached, I think.
Teacher:	Oh, yes. (Pauses) Now here's something interesting. What do you think this part is for? (Points to the pod itself)
Child B:	That's where the seeds are. See? But I wonder what this stuff is for? (Pulls a seed from the pod and points to the silky strands attached to it)
Teacher:	What do you think?
Child A:	And what's this? (Points to the tiny seed itself)

The discussion continues, with children raising questions about the function of each part of the pod, then inventing their own answers to them.

In this case, two adult questions served as the framework for an entire inquiry. Children imitated the teacher's general approach and raised their own scientific questions.

Formulating Hypotheses

Many of the questions children ask may be answered through empirical experimentation. Teachers can guide children in designing an experiment; the more input children have in creating the research methods, the more they are behaving as true scientists. Before any experiment is conducted, however, children can be encouraged to predict outcomes. Scientists often formulate hypotheses; prediction involves advanced logico-mathematical reasoning (Kamii & Lee-Katz, 1983).

As teachers intervene in children's scientific exploration, they can elicit guesses about how things will turn out. "What do you guess will happen?" and other encouragements will lead to the formulation and testing of hypotheses. Children can be challenged to make predictions in any area of the classroom. When a teacher asks, "What do you think will happen when you put that last block on your building?" or "What will happen next in the story?" scientific predictions are encouraged. Many opportunities for making predictions arise in the science center as the vignettes below reveal.

❖ ❖
Vignette 1

Two four-year-olds are using flashlights to test which objects at the science table light can shine through.

Teacher:	Have you found some objects that light shines through?
Child A:	Yep. This. (Holds up a section of newspaper)
Teacher:	What if we folded that paper in half? Would light shine through it then?
Child A:	Sure. (Folds paper and tests his hypothesis) Look. Goes right through.
Teacher:	How about if we fold it again?
Child B:	No! Now it won't.
Child A:	Oh . . . I guess it will. (Tests these hypotheses. It shines through) I was right.

Teacher:	What about this? (Holds up a large sponge) Will light shine through this?
Child A:	Um . . . yeah.
Teacher:	Why do you think so?
Child A:	It's got holes all in it.
Teacher:	Let's see.
Child A:	(Tests hypothesis) Oh! It didn't!
Teacher:	Isn't that interesting? You can make guesses about these other objects as well. You can guess first, then check and see if you're right.

Children continue experimenting, guessing and then testing their predictions. The teacher leaves the area.

Vignette 2

Two six-year-olds drop objects into a float-and-sink tub.

Teacher:	Would you like to see a new way to do this float and-sink experiment?
Children:	(In unison) Yes.
Teacher:	(Produces two containers) First look at each object. Make a guess: will it float or will it sink? If you guess that it will float, put it in one box. If you think it will sink, put it in the other box.
Child A:	Then do we drop 'em in?
Teacher:	Sure. But first you could make guesses.
Child B:	Yeah. This is a different way to play.
Teacher:	Yes. Let's start with this one. (Holds up a small piece of cardboard) Will it float or will it sink?
Child B:	Float!
Child A:	Yeah. Float.
Teacher:	Okay. So where should we put it?
Child A:	In the water?
Child B:	No. Put it here first. In this box. (Places the object in a box)
Teacher:	What about this thing? (Holds up a bar of soap)
Child A:	Um . . . sink.
Teacher:	Why do you think so?
Child A:	It's heavy. So let's put it here. (Places it in the other box)

The children continue to make predictions; the teacher withdraws. Then they test their hypotheses on their own, dropping one object at a time in the water. When a hypothesis is not confirmed, they move the object to the other box. ❖

In both vignettes, the teachers have integrated an additional step in the experimentation—making guesses about how things will turn out. In the first vignette involving young preschoolers the prediction is informal, a quick guess is made and children proceed with the experiment. In the second, the teacher encourages older children to commit themselves, formally, to a set of hypotheses before continuing. More complex social negotiation and categorization are involved. In other situations, primary-grade children may be encouraged to write down predictions—something that adult scientists often do. Literacy is, thus, integrated into sciencing.

Interpreting Results

A threat to true scientific experimentation often occurs at the conclusion of a science experience, when even the most enlightened, discovery-oriented teacher will suffer from an uncontrollable *temptation to tell* (TTT). TTT surfaces in most adults at one time or another. It is fueled by a desire to give children a clear and accurate interpretation of the world, and by a concern that misconceptions that they draw on their own will be a source of ongoing confusion. It is not uncommon for a teacher to allow great autonomy in asking questions or experimenting, but to assume a direct-instructional mode when it is time to discuss what has been discovered. The following vignette illustrates the power of TTT.

❖ ❖

Several four-year-olds have been experimenting with magnets. A teacher watches and asks stimulating questions. To this point the activity has involved pure self-discovery.

Teacher:	Okay. So what do you know about magnets?
Child:	They stick to all these things. (Points to a pile of objects on the table)
Teacher:	What else do you know?
Child:	Well . . . They don't stick to these. (Points to another pile)
Teacher:	(Laughs) Right. But why do they stick to these?
Child:	(Thinks a moment) They're so . . . so . . . so powerful. It's powerful. And they stick right together.
Teacher:	It's magnetic, isn't it?
Child:	(Looks puzzled, says nothing)
Teacher:	But why does it stick to these, and not those?
Child:	These are so powerful.

Teacher:	Also, these are made out of metal.
Child:	What?
Teacher:	Metal. Magnets stick to metal.
Child:	(Picks up a penny from the "no-stick" pile) Is this metal too?
Teacher:	Right. But it's not the right kind of metal. The metal has to be iron or nickel or . . . something else to stick.
Child:	(To another child) Jason, do you want to play in the blocks? ❖

The teacher has clearly fallen victim to TTT. The experience has been meaningful as a process, but the child cannot possibly sort out the ambiguities of magnetism at this age. Yet the teacher cannot resist imparting information about magnets directly.

Children acquire scientific knowledge by *"con*struction" not by *in*struction (Kamii & Lee-Katz, 1983). They must create an explanation of observed phenomena or the outcomes of experiments internally—an explanation that holds personal meaning. To the child in the vignette, the interpretation, "magnets stick because they are so powerful," is logical and useful. It represents an impressive early construction of how magnets work. Explanations beyond this are useless.

Teachers can encourage preschool and kindergarten children to interpret findings verbally:

❖ ❖

A five-year-old child is placing objects on a balance and comparing weights. She has just compared a small stone and a large shell.

Teacher:	That's interesting. What do you think?
Child:	(Pointing to the large shell) This one's bigger.
Teacher:	How do you know?
Child:	Well, look. It's bigger. And it, like, pushed it down. (Points to the balance) It's bigger.
Teacher:	That's interesting. Will you test some other things?
Child:	Yeah. This. (Removes the stone and places a leaf on the balance. The leaf is larger than the shell; the shell still weighs more) Oh. The shell is bigger.
Teacher:	The shell is bigger than the leaf?
Child:	(Hesitates) Oh . . . (Leans over and studies the leaf) Well . . . the shell's fatter. So it tips it down. ❖

In this vignette, the teacher resisted the urge to explain concepts of weight versus size. Had the teacher stated, "The leaf is larger, but the shell weighs more," the child would not have engaged in autonomous interpretation of results. She might have come to doubt her own thinking and would likely have been confused by the explanation. The teacher avoided TTT and posed, instead, thought-provoking questions that gave gentle challenges to her thinking and allowed her to rethink her initial explanation.

❖ ❖

Children have placed carrot tops in water and have been observing changes in them each day. Two six-year-olds observe the early green shoots sprouting from the carrots.

Teacher: What do you think?

Child A: Well. It's growing.

Teacher: (Produces small spiral notebooks) You could start journals if you want. You could make sketches in here and write about what happens to the carrots.

Child B: Like, write about these green things?

Teacher: Sure. Anything. You could write about what you think is happening.

One of the children chooses to play elsewhere; the other draws a sketch in one of the notebooks. He then writes an interpretation of his observations in invented spelling. After a short time the teacher returns to the area.

Teacher: Have you been writing about the carrots?

Child B: I'll read it. (Runs finger along invented spelling) It says, "The carrots are turning into grass. No more carrot."

Teacher: Interesting. You should come over on other days and look at the carrot and write more in your journal.   ❖

Had the teacher in this vignette corrected the child (e.g., "No. It's still growing into a carrot plant. One kind of plant can't grow into another kind"), true sciencing would have been impeded. With experience and development—perhaps even during the course of the carrot-tops experiment—the child will eventually come to construct an accurate understanding of plant life.

Summary

Sciencing and learning about science are two different things. In sciencing, young children behave as scientists do. They observe, ask questions, formulate and test hypotheses, and interpret data. Right answers and scientific facts, the end-products of scientific discovery, are not important in the early years. The act of discovery is far more important than what is discovered.

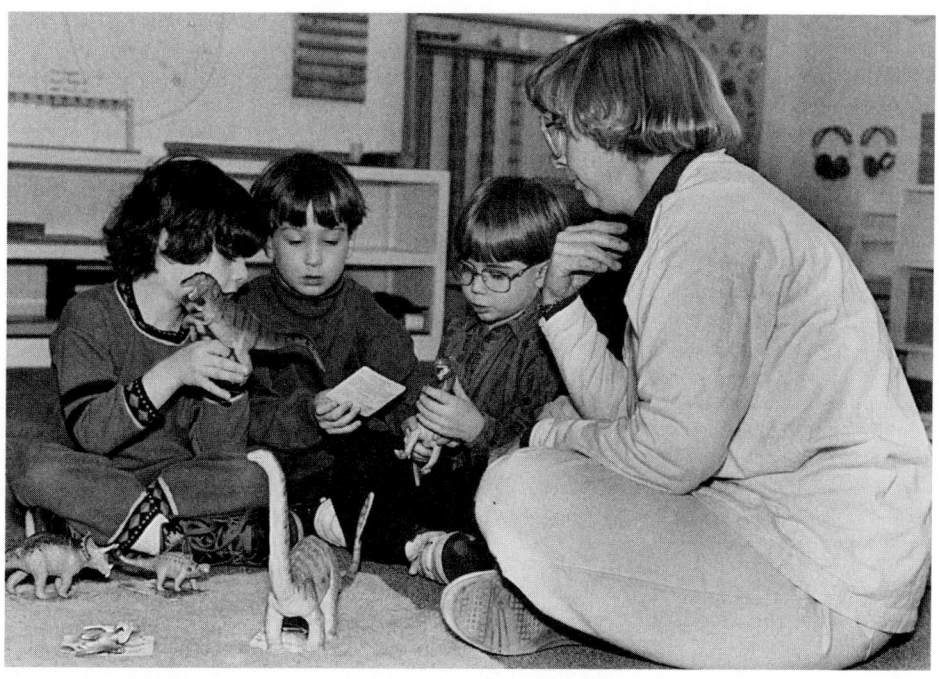

Avoiding the "Temptation to Tell" is a challenge for teachers.

Teachers can engage children in sciencing through informal classroom intervention. Through questions, they can guide children in using all their senses to observe and to reflect meaningfully on these observations. Teachers can stimulate curiosity by asking questions themselves, and by responding with warmth and enthusiasm to children's inquiries. Teachers can encourage children to formulate hypotheses throughout the classroom, to make guesses about the outcomes of any action. When scientific experimentation is complete, children can be asked to construct their own interpretations of the results. Teachers should resist TTT (Temptation To Tell). Children acquire scientific knowledge through *con*struction rather than *in*struction.

Suggested Activities

1. Present a collection of interesting objects from nature and a set of "scientific tools" (e.g., a magnet, a balance, or water for immersion) to a small group of children. As children handle them, ask questions or pose problems that encourage them to reflect upon the objects, not simply observe them. Write an analysis of your experience, guided by the following questions:

    a.   In what ways did you encourage children to compare objects? How successful were children in selecting their own criteria for comparing? How did they use tools to compare objects? Describe any clashes of opinion that occurred while children were comparing.

    b.   In what ways did children categorize objects? What questions did you pose to encourage categorization? What categories, if any, did they create on their own?

    c.   In what ways did children transform objects? What questions did you pose to encourage these transformations? What predictions did children make before transforming objects?

    d.   In what other ways did children act on the objects? In what ways did you encourage them to vary their actions and note the results?

2. Take a nature walk with a small group of children. Model scientific question-asking as you walk. Write an analysis of the experience, guided by the following questions:

    a.   What open-ended, cognitively challenging questions did you ask? To what degree did you get children to reflect on nature and put observed phenomena into relationships?

    b.   How did children respond to your question-asking approach (e.g., ask more questions, explore more intently)?

3. Intervene in children's activity in at least three areas of a classroom (including the science center, if there is one). While playing with children, encourage them to formulate hypotheses about events (e.g., predict what magnets will attract, what will happen if another block is added to a block building, or how a story will come out at the end). Write an analysis of the experience, guided by the following questions:

    a.   In which areas of the classroom were you able to elicit hypotheses? Describe predictions children made in both science and non-science activities.

    b.   In what ways did children immediately and independently test their hypotheses?

4. Participate in a scientific experiment with young children. This could be an informal activity (e.g., using flashlights to check on what light shines through) or more formal (observing melting icicles brought in on a winter day at the water table). Encourage children to formulate hypotheses (for older children these could be written). At different points during the activity ask children to interpret results. Write an analysis of the experience, guided by the following questions:

    a.   How willing or able were children to form their own conclusions about the experiment's outcome? If children were reluctant, why do you think they were?

    b.   If children made "inaccurate" interpretations of results, how did you respond? To what degree were you able to avoid TTT?

    c.   Describe clashes of opinion, if any, about the outcomes of the experiment. How did you respond to them?

Further Reading

Bradbard, M. R., & Endsley, R. C. (1983). How can teachers develop young children's curiosity? In J. F. Brown (Ed.), *Curriculum planning for young children*. Washington, DC: National Association for the Education of Young Children.

Bredderman, T. (1982). Activity science: The evidence shows it matters. *Science and Children, 20*(1), 39–41.

Cain, S., & Evans, J. (1990). *Sciencing* (3rd ed.). New York: Merrill/Macmillan.

Forman, G., & Kaden, M. (1987). In C. Seefeldt (Ed.), *The early childhood curriculum: A review of current research* (pp. 141–161). New York: Teachers College Press.

Kamii, C., & Lee-Katz, L. (1983). In J. F. Brown (Ed.), *Curriculum planning for young children* (pp.171–176). Washington, DC: National Association for the Education of Young Children.

Shymansky, J.A., Kyle, W.C., & Alport, J.M. (1982). How effective were hands-on science programs of yesterday? *Science and Children, 20*(1),14–15.

8

ENHANCING ARTISTIC
AND MUSICAL EXPRESSION

On his very first visit to an early childhood classroom, a freshman practicum student sits down at the art table with a group of five-year-olds who are drawing with markers. As he chats with them about their work he picks up a marker himself and begins to doodle. He makes a "stick figure" person and a flower made of a line stem and huge exaggerated round petals. He notices that all the children at the table now have stopped their drawing and are studying his work. One child hands her own paper to the college student and asks, "Can you make a flower for me?"

"Sure," the student responds and reproduces his flower on the child's paper. Now others make the same request; soon he is swarmed by five-year-olds waving their drawings before his face. He realizes he may be in some trouble here; he makes an attempt to remedy things: "Wait. Why don't you draw your own flowers. Let's all draw our own pictures."

"I can't draw a flower," one child responds. "You draw one for me." As the turmoil continues, the student looks across the room to the head teacher and gives her a desperate look. She moves in quickly for the rescue.

She addresses the student teacher gently: "Let me show you a way you can help children to work on their own drawings."

She now asks the children, "I'd love to see your drawings. Will you show me what you have been working on?"

One child holds up her work: "Yeah. Look at this. This is a giant who can eat these trees. See?"

"I see."

Another child responds: "Yeah. I'm going to make a bigger giant. You know, like in that book?" He begins to work again on his own drawing.

As the children continue to discuss their work, the college student joins the head teacher in interacting with them. Following the teacher's lead, he begins to ask questions about their creations and responds with enthusiasm to their discussions. Once the children have settled into working on their own drawings again, the head teacher gives the college student an encouraging smile and leaves the area, knowing that a valuable lesson has been learned.   ❖

The ways that teachers intervene in children's artistic activities have a powerful effect on creative expression and self-confidence (Seefeldt, 1987). If adults insist on deciding what or how children will draw, for example, they may inhibit artistic development. If an adult presents models of finished products, as the college student in the above example has done, children may come to doubt their own artistic abilities and become dependent on adults to draw for them. On the other hand, adult encouragement is necessary in artistic development. When the head teacher of the above vignette asks children about their drawings, for example, she inspires them to continue with their own work and stimulates more imaginative representations. This chapter provides guidelines for positive intervention in children's visual and musical arts experiences. The focus will be on promoting open-ended, purely creative expression with these media; cautions about heavy-handed and product-oriented approaches will be given.

What Is Art (and What Is Not)?

True art involves open-ended self-expression with a particular medium. Examples include easel painting, finger painting, collage, dough and clay sculpture, and woodworking (Hendrick, 1992). Even activities such as block building or writing, discussed in earlier chapters, can be considered art if children engage in these in purely creative ways. Musical experiences can also involve open-ended self-expression. When children use their bodies creatively in dance, invent words to a song, or create imaginative rhythms with instruments, they are engaging in true art.

The term "art" has erroneously been assigned, however, to other kinds of school activities. When children are presented with pre-cut shapes to piece together in only one correct way (e.g., making a clown face from teacher-cut shapes) or are asked to color in predrawn forms (e.g., coloring dittos or coloring books)—activities that often have been referred to as "art"—they will not engage in true artistic expression. Clemens (1991) has argued that "projects of this sort are designed to please adults. What they teach children is that their own work is not valuable" (p.5). In this book, such activities will not be considered art at all. Only those experiences in which children maintain full control of a medium, deciding for themselves how it will be used and what outcomes will result, will be referred to as art.

Artistic and Musical Development

Children's development in the visual arts and music progresses in stages; opportunities for authentic and self-directed expression will foster growth in these areas.

Visual Arts Development

Studies of young children's artistic development show how important true art experiences can be (and why product-oriented projects should be avoided). Seefeldt (1987) documents young children's progression through specific stages of visual artistic expression, beginning with scribble stages and advancing to more representational drawing levels. Descriptions of stages of drawing development are presented in Table 8-1.

In toddlerhood and the early preschool years, children often scribble. These scribbles become more controlled as children develop, often containing more circular strokes and discrete shapes. Eventually children name their scribbles or tell stories about them. Even in the early preschool years, then, there is an awareness that art can be used to symbolically represent the real world. Children must advance through scribble stages before they are able to produce more representational work. Product-oriented crafts or instruction in art "gimmicks" (e.g., teaching stick-figure drawing) will not promote scribble development and may, in fact, inhibit it (Di Leo, 1982).

In the later preschool years, children often begin to create simple representations of people and things that are important to them. Heads predominate drawings in this period. As children progress they draw stick arms and legs that protrude, at first, right from the heads of their figures and are later attached to bodies drawn below the heads. Other representational figures emerge in children's drawings as they develop into the early primary-grade

Table 8-1
Stages of Drawing in Early Childhood

Stage	Approximate Age	Description
Scribbling stage	Fifteen months to three or four years	Large zig-zagging lines give way to more controlled and circular markings later in this stage. Eventually, discrete shapes appear. Children begin to name their scribbles as they approach the next stage.
Preschematic stage	Three or four years to six or seven years	Early representations are drawn. For the first time, adults can recognize what children have created. Names of drawings stay the same over time. Early drawings are composed of heads with basic features. Over time, arms, hands, legs, arms, and detailed facial features emerge.
Schematic stage	Six or seven years to nine or ten years	Whole scenes that include houses, trees, a sun, as well as people are created. Figures "float in space" and are out of proportion early in this stage. Later, figures may be anchored to a ground line with a shading of blue at the top of the page representing the sky.

Source: Adapted from Di Leo (1982), Lowenfeld (1947), and Seefeldt (1987)

years. Trees, houses, animals, clouds, or the sun may appear, although these are often drawn out of proportion to one another or may be shown floating through space. In the elementary years, elaborate scenes are created; there is a greater degree of correspondence between drawings and the real world. The figures now are often anchored to a ground line; a patch of blue sky may be added above (Di Leo, 1987).

These advancements come only through continual self-directed artistic expression (Seefeldt, 1987). Coloring shapes that are pre-drawn or pre-cut by adults, or assembling collage materials into "cute" finished products following teacher directions, will not contribute to artistic development. Indeed, these projects may cause children to question their artistic competence and discourage creative expression (Schirrmacher, 1986).

When adults engage children in discussions about their art, encourage them to regularly represent their understandings of their world through various media, and give ample time for long-term art projects, children's development in the arts is significantly advanced (Schirrmacher, 1986). Adults are generally astonished, for example, at the representational quality found in the artistic efforts of children in early childhood programs in Reggio Emilia, Italy (New, 1990). Even preschoolers in these centers are found to create highly representational figures. There, self-directed representation of the world is central to the curriculum. Children are regularly encouraged through drawings, paintings, or sculpture to express their own personal perspectives of school themes, field trips, or interpersonal experiences. These projects can take many hours, days, or even weeks, and are often collaborative efforts among several students. Although adults give guidance on how media are used, children direct their own experimentation with media. The result is that children of Reggio Emilia display far more elaborate, detailed, and representational art work than would be predicted for children of this age.

Musical Development

Young children's musical development also progresses in stages. Wolf (1992) describes changes in children's singing during the early years. Singing stages are presented in Table 8-2.

Infants and toddlers engage in musical babbling. Over time, toddlers attempt to sing along with others, although they often lag behind or "tag on" to the end of songs. In the early preschool years children can talk/sing simple songs that have a narrow range and uncomplicated rhythms. At four years, singing accuracy has increased; children may sing simple songs with the same accuracy as adults. In the elementary years, children begin to sing accurately in groups. This singing development advances when children are encouraged to sing on their own or in groups with an adult; instrumental accompaniment is not necessary (Wolf, 1992). Although recorded music may contribute to this development, practice and singing along with other human voices may be most useful.

Table 8-2
Stages of Singing in Early Childhood

Stage	Description	Example
Musical babbling stage	Music-sounding babbles are produced in response to singing or recorded music.	A caregiver rocks and sings to a baby; in response the baby coos in a melodic tone.
Tagging on stage	Children show great interest in a song. They sing along only to some parts, often lagging behind the singer.	A teacher sings with a group of toddlers; they smile and bounce along to the rhythms. They sing bits and pieces of the song, especially the repetitive chorus. They each sing at a different point in the song and lag behind the teacher.
Talking/singing stage	Children sing or talk along with the singer; they are more willing to join in group singing.	A teacher sings with three-year-olds during group time; some join in, others just "tag on." A few talk the lyrics; others only join in on the chorus.
Increased accuracy stage	Children sing lyrics and notes with more accuracy than before; they often sing whole songs with a group.	A teacher of four-year-olds introduces the song "Wheels on the Bus." Children follow along well, particularly on the chorus, and use appropriate hand movements. There are still many "missed notes" and much "lagging behind the group."
Accurate singing alone stage	Children sing simple songs alone with near-adult accuracy.	As a five-year-old plays in the sandbox, he hums the tune "Twinkle, Twinkle Little Star," without missing notes or stumbling over lyrics.
Accurate singing in groups stage	Children sing simple songs in a group with accuracy and coordination.	A group of six-year-olds sing a remarkably coordinated version of "She'll Be Comin' 'Round the Mountain." All singers are well coordinated in timing, pitch, tune, and lyrical accuracy.

Source: Adapted from Smale (1985) and Wolf (1992)

Other aspects of musical development have been studied: beat competency, creative movement, musical perception, and music appreciation (Andress, 1991; Hitz, 1987; Wolf, 1992). Research suggests that children advance in these areas when authentic, open-ended, and child-centered musical experiences are provided. Encouraging children to sing just like adults, to sing the "correct" lyrics, or to perform elaborate adult-pleasing musical programs in front of large groups (all are product-oriented approaches) will not contribute to musical development (Andress, 1991).

The Role of the Adult in Artistic Development

Although research suggests that child-centered experience in the arts is most useful, adults do have a role to play in enhancing artistic expression. This section presents guidelines for intervention in the visual and musical arts.

Observing Children's Visual Art

Although early childhood teachers have long valued children's art, they do not always take the time to actively observe artistic activities in progress (Dyson, 1988). Children's artistic efforts are a "window" to development; they reveal aspects of children's language and literacy development, social competence, even sociodramatic play abilities. When teachers take a close look at children drawing together at the art table, for example, they are likely to see conversation, interpersonal negotiation, writing, make-believe, exploration, and possibly singing, as well as drawing.

Teachers can observe children's symbolic thought as they paint, draw, or sculpt (Gardner, Wolf, & Smith, 1982). It is not enough to examine finished products; it is what children do while they are drawing that reveals symbolization. If a child tells a story while drawing or shares the theme of a painting with a peer or teacher, symbolizing can be directly observed. Even scribbles are highly symbolic if they represent ideas or stories (Gardner, 1980).

Some children may be observed "playing a story" as they create (Dyson, 1988). The following vignette demonstrates this common childhood activity:

❖ ❖

A child sits by himself at the art center making circular marks on paper (he has been making representational figures for many months, but now chooses to scribble). He talks to himself in an animated voice: "Look out! The earthquake is shaking the ground!" He scrawls long scribbles back and forth across the paper at this point in his enactment. He now selects another sheet of paper and continues to draw. "The people are going down inside the crack!" he exclaims in a make-believe voice. "Run!" He persists at this theme for many minutes using eight different sheets of paper.   ❖

Dramatic play behaviors may be observed in such play; the child in the vignette creates make-believe situations and uses make-believe voices as he draws. His use of scribbles to represent persons, objects, or events is not unlike the make-believe transformations in dramatic play that were described in Chapter 3.

Emergent literacy is often evident in children's art activities. Some view art itself as a form of writing (Hipple, 1985). When children draw an elaborate scene or tell a story about a clay sculpture, for example, they show an ability to represent ideas graphically. Children also begin to write as they draw, weaving print into their artwork. Inclusion of scribble writing or letters to stand for text in a painting or drawing is common even in the preschool years (Dyson, 1988). Children frequently write their own names on their work.

Hendrick (1992) suggests that art is often highly social and collaborative, as the following vignette illustrates:

❖ ❖

Two four-year-olds sit at the art table creating collages from paper, buttons, beans, and other scrap materials. A third child approaches.

Child A: We're making a design.

Child B: Yes. A design.

Child C: I'm going to make a design too.

Child B: No, Alice, there isn't room. See? (Makes a gesture showing how small the table is)

Child C: I'll just be on this little space here. (Shows a small corner of the table where she will work)

Child A: No, 'cause we need that space for our buttons. (Quickly slides a container of buttons over to that corner of the table)

Child C: Now there's room here. (Pulls a chair up to an empty space where the button container had been. Before her peers can respond she speaks to them in an enthused voice) I'm making a lov-e-ly flower. It will be a bea-u-ti-ful flower. (Giggles)

Child A: What?

Child C: Oh, it will be lovely. Are you making one too?

Child B: No, I'm making a design.

Child A: (Pointing to her collage) I have a flower.

The children continue to work together and converse about their creations. ❖

Here one child solves a common social problem—how to gain acceptance into a play group. Generally, the art center affords many opportunities for resolving conflicts, negotiating, sharing materials, and collaborating (Hendrick, 1992).

The primary role of the teacher in the visual arts, then, is to observe and learn as much as possible about children's artistic, symbolic, linguistic, and social development. Careful observations are critical for selecting appropriate interventions to promote development in these areas.

Talking with Children about Their Artwork

Engaging children in authentic conversation about their artwork may be the most effective way to enhance artistic development. The following vignette demonstrates the power of such interactions.

❖ ❖

Two children are molding clay at the art table; a teacher stands near by, but says nothing. She smiles as she looks upon their work. A child speaks first.

Child A:	Do you think I should add a long tail to my snake?
Teacher:	That would be interesting. How would you do that?
Child B:	No, Rachel. Snakes can't have tails, 'cause they are like tails. They're just like tails. That's all.
Teacher:	Snakes do look like long tails, don't they? Can you think of how you might add a tail to a snake, Rachel?
Child A:	Sure. You can just put another tail on. See? (Begins to add a second tail to her clay snake)
Teacher:	Yes. A two-tailed snake.
Child B:	How about a three-tail one? (Begins making a third tail)
Child A:	Are there really snakes that have three tails?
Teacher:	What do you think?
Child A:	No.
Teacher:	But you can certainly create one with the clay.
Child B:	Yeah. It's like imagination. But let's add a lot of tails, all right, Rachel?

By the end of the morning, the children have added twelve tails to their snake sculpture, using all the clay from the bin.   ❖

The teacher of this vignette demonstrates genuine interest in what children are creating. She asks questions and converses about the content of their work; such interactions encourage highly creative expression.

Talking with children about their artistic efforts in progress is a tricky business. Just the right sort of interchange will enhance artistic expression; some kinds of comments may actually inhibit it. Schirrmacher (1986) identifies several ineffective approaches to discussing art with children. He cautions against a "correcting approach" in which teachers provide criticism of children's work in order to assist them in learning to draw. The vignette below shows the deleterious effects of such an interaction.

❖ ❖

Child:	(Holds drawing up to the teacher for approval) Look! I made a squirrel.
Teacher:	I see. What color is that squirrel?
Child:	Oh. Red. It's a red squirrel.
Teacher:	Have you ever seen a red squirrel?
Child:	What?
Teacher:	What color are squirrels usually?

Child: (Says nothing, looks away to another part of the room)

Teacher: Alex? What color is a squirrel?

Child: I think I'm going over there. (Leaves the art center to join other children in the block area)   ❖

Obviously this interaction does nothing to assist the child in developing as an artist. In fact this harsh insistence on realistic representation drives him from the art area; he may think twice before returning there.

According to Schirrmacher (1986), when teachers give positive judgements about children's artwork in an effort to reward their efforts or finished products, they also may stifle creativity. A comment such as, "Oh, beautiful work, Julio," may give the message to other children that their work is not as worthy. It may also implicitly communicate to Julio that it is only the sort of product he has just created that will win adult praise. Generally, empty praise

Smiling or studying children's art in a reflective way will show interest and enthusiasm without forcing children to talk about their work.

statements give children a sense that art is something one does for adult approval, not for personal expression or gratification.

Asking children to tell what they are creating in their drawings or paintings may also discourage artistic efforts. Questions such as "What is that?" or "Is that a car?" imply that the adult cannot recognize what is being represented; such inquiries cause children to question their own artistic competence (Smith, 1983). Further, these interactions imply that children must always draw "something." How might children answer such questions, Schirrmacher (1986) asks, if they are merely experimenting with media and not attempting to represent anything specific? The vignette below demonstrates the less than positive outcomes of such interchanges.

❖ ❖

A four-year-old is painting at the easel. She paints thick horizontal lines across the paper and studies the paint trails as they drip downward. A teacher approaches.

Teacher:	What is it you are making, Rosie?
Child:	Um . . . I don't know.
Teacher:	This looks like the sky to me. (Points to a blue horizontal line near the top of the paper)
Child:	Okay.
Teacher:	That's the sky?
Child:	Okay.
Teacher:	Or maybe this is just a blue design.
Child:	All right, it's a blue design.

❖

This child acquiesces to the teacher's suggestion that her painting "be something," even accepting his designation that her experimental streaks of blue paint are the sky. When the teacher offers an alternative label the child accepts this new interpretation with resignation. Will this child feel as comfortable experimenting with media after this interaction? Has the message been given that children should paint or draw only those things that adults can recognize or name?

Many art educators recommend open-ended question-asking approaches. "Tell me about your drawing" or "Can you tell me a story about your collage?" are examples of less restrictive interventions at the art center. Although such questions do promote language and emotional expression, they can also inhibit children's activity (Schirrmacher, 1986). Some children may not wish to discuss their paintings. They may feel that their artistic effort speaks for itself and that no further description or storytelling is required. In the following vignette, a teacher may be too obtrusive in eliciting a child's discussion about her drawing.

❖ ❖

A six-year-old is drawing a detailed representation of four people and an animal-like figure. She sings to herself as she draws. A teacher sits down with her at the art table.

Teacher:	Can you tell me about your drawing?
Child:	(Shakes head "no," says nothing)
Teacher:	Why don't you tell me a story about your drawing?
Child:	(In an annoyed tone) Why do you always want us to tell these stories?
Teacher:	You don't like telling stories about your work?
Child:	No. This isn't a place for talking and talking. It's for drawing.

The teacher grasps this not-too-subtle message and withdraws.   ❖

Here the child is assertive enough to reject the teacher's initiatives. Her drawing is a private effort; she wants to keep its message to herself. Fortunately the teacher of the vignette is sensitive to her needs and exits the setting.

Schirrmacher (1986) recommends an intervention in which teachers quietly position themselves near children who are engaged in art. Saying nothing at first but merely smiling or studying a child's work in a reflective way will show interest and enthusiasm but will not impose upon children as they create. Also, this moment of quiet observation will allow the teacher to come to understand what children are doing and to determine what, if any, intervention is needed. He suggests that children be allowed to talk first; if they say nothing perhaps this is not the appropriate moment to initiate conversation.

When children initiate conversation about their work, teachers may respond with comments or questions regarding the media (e.g., "I see you've used some of this rough material in your collage."), the theme of the work (e.g., "Where are the fire fighters going in their truck?"), or the composition itself (e.g., "I see you've made an interesting border around the baby. Tell me about that."). It is sometimes appropriate to ask questions that elicit discussions of feelings (e.g., "So, the little boy is about to get a shot? How do you suppose he feels about that?"). Children often reveal anxieties in their artwork; they also convey aspects of their lives that are exciting or meaningful (Nickerson, 1983). An informal, child-initiated discussion about artistic efforts can be an ideal context for helping children understand and master feelings.

The teacher below demonstrates Schirrmacher's approach.

❖ ❖

Two five-year-old children are drawing with markers. A teacher joins them at the art table.

Teacher:	(Says nothing, sits and watches the children working)

Child A:	I'm making a ghost.
Teacher:	A ghost. I see.
Child A:	See, the ghost is pretty scary. (Laughs)
Teacher:	Yes.
Child B:	Is he scaring someone?
Child A:	Yes—see, this is the guy he's scaring. (Points to a place on his drawing)
Teacher:	What will that guy do?
Child A:	Oh, he's not afraid. He's not afraid of ghosts. They're not real.
Teacher:	He isn't afraid of ghosts?
Child A:	Well, only if it's dark.
Teacher:	It can be scary in the dark.
Child A:	It's only scary if your mom or dad aren't there.
Child B:	Yeah. Then that's real scary. (Laughs)
Teacher:	So, is the guy in your picture scared?
Child A:	Yeah. I think so, 'cause his mom's not around.

The teacher continues to discuss the fears of the character in the drawing for several more minutes, then withdraws from the area.   ❖

The teacher of this vignette discusses a child's drawing in an unobtrusive way. The child initiates the conversation; the teacher follows his lead. She finds an opportunity during the discussion to explore fears of ghosts and the dark.

Providing Media

As children engage in artistic expression, they encounter many challenges with the media they are using. They may find that the paint is too thick to allow detailed representation, for example, or that the paste is too dry to make beans stick. Perhaps the buttons they are using in a collage are too heavy and fall off before the glue has dried, or a tool is needed to make cuts in a clay sculpture they are working on. Occasionally, children show signs that they simply want new and different media to incorporate into a project. At these times a teacher can enhance artistic expression by providing new materials.

A teacher can provide media in a way that enhances problem solving and creativity (Clemens, 1991). If children are experiencing the problem of overly heavy buttons on a collage, the teacher might guide them in solving the problem independently. Rather than simply providing smaller buttons and instructing children in how to glue them, a teacher might ask: "Why do those buttons keep falling off, do you think? What can we do about that?" If children at this point come upon the solution of using lighter buttons the teacher could now provide them. If not, the teacher might follow up: "What could we use instead of these big buttons?" or "Can you think of anything that would stick on better?"

Sometimes children show signs of losing interest in standard art materials. A less than enthusiastic manner at the art center or avoidance of the area altogether are sure signs of boredom. Some children are quite direct in expressing their lack of interest in available materials: "I don't want to just draw some more. I've been drawing since I was a baby." When interest wanes, a teacher might present unusual and enticing new media. They can be presented in an open-ended way: "What could we do with these things?"

The following vignettes demonstrate the positive impact of providing new materials at the art center.

❖ ❖

Vignette 1

Child:	(Paints on an easel with large brushes, displays an annoyed expression)
Teacher:	Samantha, is something wrong?
Child:	(Stares intently at her painting) I can't get this flower right.
Teacher:	No? What's the problem?
Child:	See, I have to draw tiny little lines on here. (Points to the petals she has painted) But if I try, all the paint will get all mixed.
Teacher:	The black paint would run together with the yellow, wouldn't it? I have an idea. (Retrieves a tiny brush from a water-color set) You might try a very small brush. It might be easier to make tiny lines with this.
Child:	(Begins to make black lines on her drawing) That's easier.
Teacher:	Yes. You can make very thin lines with that brush.

Vignette 2

Child:	(Works with modeling dough. Sees the teacher passing by and seeks assistance) I need something to cut this. (Points to his sculpture)
Teacher:	What could we use?
Child:	Not these popsicle sticks. They just mush it.
Teacher:	Mush it?
Child:	Yeah. Like just mush it down. (Demonstrates how the sticks don't make a clean cut)
Teacher:	What else could we use?
Child:	A sharp knife. (Laughs)

Teacher:	I'm afraid you'd cut your fingers.
Child:	How about scissors?
Teacher:	Let's try. (Retrieves a pair of scissors, hands them to the child)
Child:	Yep. Look. (Shows how they cut the dough)
Teacher:	Those cut very well, don't they?

In these vignettes, the teachers have encouraged children to try new media to solve problems they have encountered at the art center. In one case, a direct suggestion leads to greater control over a painting, in the other, a question guides experimentation with a new artistic tool.

Encouraging Invention of New Projects

As well as providing new media, teachers might encourage children to use familiar art materials in new and creative ways.

Encouraging experimentation with standard media such as markers and paper, scissors and glue, collage materials, or paint will allow children to study in depth the properties of these materials and to become proficient in using them (Clemens, 1991; Seefeldt, 1987).

Open-ended questions may be the best way to encourage experimentation and invention. As children appear to lose interest in materials, a teacher might ask: "What else could we do with these?" A teacher could also pose problems that stimulate creative invention, using the media available:

A five-year-old child is drawing with crayons but seems unengaged and uninterested. He gets up to leave the art area.

Teacher:	Can you make a drawing that is life-size?
Child:	What's life-size?
Teacher:	It's when you draw something as big as it is in real life.
Child:	(In an amazed tone) Huh? Like I could draw a person this big? (Gestures over the table to indicate a huge area.)
Teacher:	Yes. You could draw a person. Or anything else.
Child:	How could we get him on the paper?
Teacher:	One sheet of paper is too small, isn't it? What could we do about that?
Child:	Use lots of paper. Put it together, see? (Demonstrates, placing many pieces of paper on the table. Now calls to another child) Darryl, c'mon. We're making a real size person.

At the children's request, the teacher provides tape so that they can assemble smaller pieces of paper into one large sheet. As they begin to draw their life-size person, they are confronted with many challenges. The taped pieces of paper are very hard to draw on. Each child takes a turn holding individual sheets in place so the other can work. Crayons are particularly difficult to use on this project; they don't mark well over tape or crumpled paper. The children experiment with various markers until they find those that work best.

The teachers leaves the children, but checks in now and then to see how the project is progressing. He asks occasional questions to engage children's thinking (e.g.,"How do you tell if your drawing is as big as a real person?"). The children work on their drawing until the end of free-play time. They return to the project on the next day; the work is not complete until the end of the week.   ❖

By posing a challenge, this teacher has prompted highly creative and collaborative artistic expression. He could have provided large pieces of butcher paper for the project, but recognizes the many problem-solving opportunities that have been created by allowing the children to proceed with their own plan.

Enticing Reluctant Artists

All teachers of young children come across students who do not wish to work with art media. Although gentle invitations to watch or participate at the art center are appropriate, children's unique play preferences should be respected. Teachers should never force such children into art activities. Most children will find outlets for self-expression, if not at the art center, then in the block area, dramatic play center, or writing table.

Hendrick (1992) suggests that some children refrain from art projects because of concern about getting messy. Such children may enjoy and benefit from art activities, but will not allow themselves to participate. Hendrick suggests reassuring these students (and their parents) that getting painty or sticky is permissible. Another strategy is to entice such children into the art center by presenting "dry" art materials first—markers, crayons, or scissors, for example. Once children feel comfortable with these art media, teachers gradually can demonstrate "messier" materials.

Several other strategies for encouraging children to feel comfortable with the messiness of art are illustrated in the following vignettes.

❖ ❖
Vignette 1

Two children are fingerpainting. A third child shows great interest in this activity, but holds back. She has been a child who is reluctant to get messy. A teacher approaches.

Teacher:	Look at how they are painting. Isn't it interesting how their fingers make swirls in the paint?
Child:	Yeah. It's pretty.
Teacher:	Yes. Would you like to try?
Child:	(Shakes head "no")
Teacher:	You know, a problem with fingerpaint is it feels sticky on your hands. So, do you know what I do? I always bring a bowl of water and a paper towel right up to the art table with me, so I can wash my hands right away if I want.
Child:	Yeah. It gets all sticky.
Teacher:	(Brings water and a towel to the table. Speaks to the two children who are fingerpainting) Here. If you need to wash your hands you can wash them right away. (Now to the reluctant child) Would you like to try?
Child:	All right. (She slips into a smock. Then she dips one finger into the paint the teacher has provided. She makes circular marks on paper, then stops and quickly washes her finger) There.
Teacher:	You made a swirl. The paint is very thick, isn't it?
Child:	Yes. (Now puts her whole hand into the paint and begins to smear it on the paper. She washes her hands after each stroke)

Vignette 2

A child has shown reluctance to engage in messy art. He watches others at the art table but does not join their activities. A teacher approaches with a tub of soapy water.

Teacher:	Marcus, would you like to help me clean up this art table? I haven't scrubbed it in a while.
Child:	(Hesitates at first, then speaks) Yeah.
Teacher:	(Squeezes suds from a sponge onto the table) See? You can use your hand to scrub it around and around. (Demonstrates making strokes with her hand) Would you like to try it?
Child:	(Cautiously dips hand into the suds) Look.
Teacher:	I see. You're giving it a scrub!
Child:	Put some more suds down. (Begins to "paint" with the soap suds more vigorously) ❖

The teachers in these vignettes have found noncoercive means to encourage children to try messy art. In each instance, the child eventually enjoys the feel of the media and persists. Over time, such experiences may lead them to experiment with varied and ever more messy materials.

Helping Children to Persist in Projects

Teachers should respect children's decisions to stop work on a particular art project or to change activities altogether. However, some children rarely persist in artistic efforts; they briefly "dabble" in one medium, then another, without becoming fully absorbed in elaborate artistic expression. Some children are eager to begin art projects but lose interest quickly. Teachers can occasionally intervene to enhance persistence in the art center; the following vignette demonstrates one method.

A five-year-old child enters the art center and pulls out a huge sheet of butcher paper, several nature magazines, scissors, and paste from the shelf. He cuts one small photograph from the magazine, pastes it in a corner of the enormous sheet, then gets up to leave. A teacher who is working with other children in the center intervenes.

Teacher:	Goodness, Robert. This looks like quite a project. Tell me about what you are doing.
Child:	Oh, it's just a thing where I fill up all this space with pictures. (Gestures to indicate he will cover the entire sheet with photographs) But I'm kinda tired.
Teacher:	Well, no wonder. It will take a lot of hard work to make such a huge collage.
Child:	Yeah. It's a lot of cutting and cutting. You paste these things. (Demonstrates by cutting another photograph and carefully pasting it on the paper) See? It looks pretty good.
Teacher:	Yes. Sometimes when I'm working on a big project like this I get help. I ask a friend to help out.
Child:	Oh. Like have Alex help me?
Teacher:	You could ask him.

The child goes over to his peer in another part of the classroom. Both return to the art center and work together on the collage for many minutes. ❖

Here the teacher is encouraging persistence by asking questions about the child's project and facilitating collaboration with a peer. The child becomes more fully engaged in the media as a result.

Showing Respect For Children's Art

The best way to demonstrate respect for children's artistic efforts is to engage in authentic conversation with them about their work, as described above. There are other ways teachers can give a message that children's efforts are appreciated. Handling children's artwork carefully (e.g., rolling paintings rather than folding them, or waiting until collages dry and all materials are firmly attached before moving them) shows that the teacher values these creations (Clemens, 1991). Taking care not to crush finished work into cubbies or backpacks to take home also demonstrates respect. Avoiding throwing away children's work (even the simplest scribbles) without consultation is important. If teachers must discard very old works, they should not do so in the presence of the children who have created them.

Another demonstration of respect is to exhibit children's art in the classroom. A controversy surrounds the degree to which children's work should be displayed. Montessori (1964) argued that classroom environments should be simple and aesthetically pleasing, free from clutter and overly complex stimuli. Montessori teachers often choose not to display children's art for these reasons. This no-art-in-the-classroom policy is tempting to teachers for a variety of reasons. Classrooms can become so cluttered with children's efforts that one artwork cannot be distinguished from another. When only artwork that is aesthetically pleasing from an adult perspective is displayed, children may be given the message that only certain kinds of finished products are acceptable. The child whose painting has turned from yellow to orange to gray as each new color was added may become distressed if a teacher declines displaying this work.

Clemens (1991) argues that displaying children's work can enhance creativity if done cautiously and respectfully. She urges that exhibits of children's work reflect the diversity of artistic efforts and media used; she advises against displaying many examples of the same type of project together. This approach assures that comparison among artworks will not occur and that diversity, not conformity, is celebrated. Children might each be given their own display space in which they may present one or two works; they make decisions about which creations will go there, how long they will be displayed, and when they will be replaced with newer works. This system helps avoid the cluttering concern raised by Montessori.

Several cautions must be heeded in displaying children's work. Any artistic effort must be exhibited, regardless of its aesthetic qualities from an adult perspective; display opportunities must be provided equitably among all children. Children should be given autonomy to choose how they will hang works. In the following vignette a teacher empowers a child to take responsibility for an exhibit.

❖ ❖

A four-year-old child has just finished a drawing and holds it up to show her teacher.

Child:	Look. This is my house.
Teacher:	Yes. Is this where you live?
Child:	Yep. Can I hang it?
Teacher:	Certainly. Where would be a good place to put it?
Child:	Right here. (Points to a book shelf)

Encouraging children to display their work is one way teachers show respect for their artistic efforts.

Teacher:	That looks good. Here, I'll tape it. (Reaches for the child's drawing)
Child:	I can do it. (Takes the tape from the teacher, tears off a tiny piece. Tries to put up the drawing but it immediately falls to the floor)
Teacher:	Oops. What happened?
Child:	Not enough tape. (Now the child runs an enormous line of tape across the front of her drawing, sticking this work to the bookshelf only a few inches from the floor)
Teacher:	Is that where you'd like it?
Child:	Yeah. It's kind of low, but you can still see it. ❖

In this vignette, the teacher gives the child an opportunity to choose how and where her work will go up. Even though the drawing is displayed in an unusual way from an adult point of view (with tape across the front and only two inches above the floor), the teacher accepts her effort.

Teachers must also respect children's wishes not to have art displayed. Often children wish to keep their work a private matter or desire to take it home to share with family members. There should be no pressure to display art; expectations that children will always present their work publicly may limit children's efforts to "exhibition-quality" work. Story scribbles, experimentation with media, or other private projects may be inhibited.

Facilitating Collaboration

Hendrick (1991) has noted that art experiences are often quite social: "Children who are working side by side often develop a spirit of camaraderie" (p. 317). Teachers can intervene at the art center to facilitate social interaction and conversation. Sometimes teachers can encourage children to collaborate with peers to solve problems. The following vignette illustrates this approach.

Three four-year-olds are making collages at the art table. A teacher sits down and watches them work.

Child A:	(Struggling with paste and small pieces of paper) I can't get this paste to work.
Teacher:	What's the problem?
Child A:	(Waving his hand to disengage a piece of paper sticking to his finger) See? It sticks to my hand.
Teacher:	(To Child B) Hannah, are you having that problem?
Child B:	No. See? No paste on my hands.
Teacher:	What's your secret? How do you get the paste to work? Maybe you could tell Benjamin.
Child C:	No, I'll tell him, 'cause my paste is working too. See, Benjamin, you just use a little. (Demonstrates, dipping one finger into the paste)
Child A:	That's what I did, but it didn't work.
Teacher:	(To Child B) What do you think, Hannah? Have you got a suggestion for Benjamin?
Child B:	Yep. Just put a little, Benjamin. See? Just dip your finger in. (Demonstrates) Now do it.
Child A:	(Dips finger in paste, tries to put it on a piece of paper) See? It's still sticking. (Holds up a paste-covered hand with his piece of paper sticking to it)

Teacher:	Maybe we could wash off some of that paste. (Hands the child a damp towel to clean off the excess paste)
Child A:	(Cleans hands) There. Now I can paste it. (Successfully pastes paper on his collage)
Child C:	You stuck it on, Ben. Didn't you?
Child A:	(Does not look up; pastes another piece of paper on his work) Yep. ❖

Here a teacher encourages children to interact and solve a problem together. The art center is an ideal context for facilitating cooperative learning and nurturing social skills.

Integrating Art Throughout the Curriculum

Artistic expression does not just take place at the art center. If children are encouraged, they will create drawings and other artistic representations in almost any area of the classroom. They might add drawings to their stories at the writing table or recreate scenes from their favorite books with clay, paint, collage materials or other media. Sketch pads and other materials might be provided in the science center to allow children to record the results of experiments graphically (e.g., sculpture and drawing can be integrated into a soil erosion experiment in which children sculpt sand land forms, pour water over them, and create "before and after" sketches).

As part of a thematic unit in geography, children can draw maps of the classroom or create "treasure maps" on the playground. Such activities promote an understanding of map space even among very young preschoolers (Hinitz, 1987). At the water table, various media (e.g., paper, clay, styrofoam and toothpicks, or foil) can be provided for creating boats. In the math center, children can make sketches to indicate the number of pins they have knocked down in a bowling game. As children get older, they may be observed integrating drawing and other kinds of media into their block building (Johnson, 1984).

Artwork can even be included as part of outdoor play. Easels can be moved outdoors on some days; children can decorate large cardboard boxes or other play materials with chalk, markers, or paint. Painting on warm, sun-baked sidewalks with water and paintbrushes creates an interesting effect.

In early childhood classrooms of Reggio Emilia, Italy, artistic representation is incorporated into every aspect of children's learning (New, 1990). If children are studying shadows, they are encouraged to draw figures with shadows cast from them. When exploring dinosaurs as a class, children are given materials to collaborate on building life-size sculptures. Through this symbolic representation, children more readily construct knowledge about the world (New, 1990).

Teachers can intervene informally to encourage artistic expression throughout the classroom. In the following vignette, the teacher provides materials that stimulate drawing at the science center.

❖ ❖

One of the field mice kept in a cage in the science area has become pregnant. There has been much interest in this among students in the class; many challenging questions have been posed to the teacher. Two children now study this pregnant mouse quite closely. A teacher joins them.

Child A:	She's getting kinda bigger.
Child B:	Yeah, of course, 'cause she's got a baby mouse inside.
Child A:	She's got a lot of babies in there.
Child B:	She was pretty little but now she's big and fat. (Laughs)
Teacher:	She's changing pretty quickly, isn't she? How much bigger do you think she'll get?
Child A:	Oh, a whole lot bigger, I think.
Child B:	I think so.
Teacher:	How will she look when she has her babies?
Child A:	Kinda sick and tired?
Teacher:	(Laughs) Yes. What else?
Child B:	She'll be really small again.
Teacher:	Sometimes scientists watch animals and record how they change over time. They make little sketches on each day to show how the animals have changed.
Child A:	Yeah, like a drawing or something.
Teacher:	Right. I have notebooks here. Would the two of you like to make drawings of the mother mouse? You could make a drawing each day until she's had her babies.
Child B:	(In an enthused tone) And we could draw her after those babies when she's little again.
Teacher:	Here are the notebooks and some markers. You could draw her every day and show how she changes.

The children make elaborate initial drawings. On subsequent days, they diligently return to the area for further sketches.   ❖

Not only has this teacher promoted artistic expression, she has also encouraged children to more fully understand natural processes and to reflect on change over time. The drawings later will allow children to reconstruct their observations and to share them with others.

Facilitating Musical Development

Hitz (1987) has argued that musical experiences for young children should reflect the same kinds of open-ended, creative processes as visual arts activities. Music, from his perspective, provides many opportunities for problem solving and critical thinking; when children are encouraged to use their bodies or voices to express themselves creatively, they develop not just musically but intellectually. The following vignette illustrates open-ended, process-oriented music.

❖ ❖

A kindergarten teacher sits in the music center with three children. He strums on an autoharp; the children compose lyrics to go with his chords.

Child A: (Singing) The man fell from up a tree, up a tree, up a tree. The man fell from up a tree and fell down to the dirty ground.

Now the teacher and two other children sing again the words Child A has composed.

Teacher: All right. Now what will be our second verse?

Child B: I've got one. It's kind of silly, though.

Teacher: Fine. It'll be a silly song.

Child A: No, let's not make it silly.

Child C: We could have some silly ones and some not silly ones, all right?

Teacher: Yes. Some verses could be silly, some not.

Child B: Okay, so here is the song. (Sings; the teacher accompanies him on the autoharp) The man flew back around the tree, around the tree, around the tree. The man flew high up to the tree, to see what he could see.

Teacher: Okay . . .

Child B: (Interrupts) Wait! It's not done. (Sings) To see what he could see, to see what he could see. The man flew like a . . . like a airplane to see what he could see.

The teacher and other children do their best to sing Child B's verse. The group composes several more verses before ending their musical session.   ❖

This teacher has demonstrated the same responses to children's musical creations as were recommended in the previous section on the visual arts. He shows interest in children's work, but does not evaluate. He converses with them about their song and facilitates collaboration and social problem solving. He does not expect or encourage finished end-products; the song is a purely child-centered composition. This section examines interventions that promote spontaneous and creative music-making.

Creating Music During Free Play Time

Most think of music as a group experience in which the teacher leads children through songs, finger plays, or movement experiences. Perhaps the most creative music occurs, however, as children go about their play activities in the classroom. Children sing or hum, listen to music, or experiment with rhythms as they play; music occurs spontaneously in almost every classroom area. Teachers can encourage and enhance this open-ended music-making. Simply allowing children to sing or tap rhythms while engaged in classroom activities is a first step. When teachers insist upon absolute silence while children are "working," not only are social interaction and verbalization reduced but children are deprived of significant opportunities to engage in personal musical expression. In active, play-based classrooms, children are free to move, dance, or sing when the need or desire arises.

Singing Along with Children

Teachers can enrich these spontaneous musical experiences. When children hum or sing, teachers can join in or encourage others to do so. Below is an example.

A six-year-old child sits at the art table. As she draws, she hums to herself a song just sung at group time. Now and then she sings a few words. A teacher sits near her. After a time the teacher begins to hum along with her in an unobtrusive way. The child looks up from her drawing, smiles, then returns to her work. A moment later a second child sitting at the table picks up the tune as well; both children and the teacher now hum in unison. The teacher now sings a verse; the children join her, still working on drawings as they do. The teacher eventually leaves the art center; the music continues from that corner for a long time.   ❖

In this interchange, the teacher has not only sanctioned singing as an integral part of the art experience, but has encouraged a second child to sing along. This spontaneous music-making without accompaniment may be the best way to foster singing accuracy and creative musical expression (Wolf, 1992).

Sometimes children will invent their own songs during play activities. Teachers can respond with encouragement and enthusiasm to such inventions (e.g., "My favorite part of your song is where you sing about the water 'pouring, pouring, pouring, out of the bottle.'"). Teachers can model the creation of songs or encourage students to do so. One particularly musical kindergarten teacher, for example, would make up a new song each day to sing at cleanup time. After a number of weeks of this, he encouraged children to make up songs to sing (e.g., "What can we sing today when we clean up? Can anyone make up a new song?"). He reported that children displayed remarkable creativity in these spontaneous compositions.

Singing standard childhood favorites throughout the school day will also enhance musical development. Singing with children while swinging on the playground, during nap time, or while cleaning up for snack provides positive and meaningful musical experiences. Music can also be woven throughout the curriculum.

Special projects around themes can include singing, instrument making and playing, or movement (Wolf, 1992). As part of a multicultural study of harvest festivals, for example, a kindergarten teacher showed examples or illustrations of basic instruments (e.g., drums, stringed instruments, horns) found across cultures. During free play she presented raw materials (e.g., sticks, boxes, rubber bands, wood blocks, beans, gourds, styrofoam, paper mache materials, cardboard tubes, wooden drawer knobs, sandpaper) in the art center and encouraged children to invent instruments of the basic types discussed. Throughout the day, the teacher facilitated spontaneous music making, playing music of various cultures, and joining children in inventing songs with the instruments they had designed.

Experimenting with Rhythm and Beat

Teachers can facilitate spontaneous experimentation with rhythm and beat. Opportunities for play with instruments allow children to discover about these musical elements (Wolf, 1992; Hitz, 1987). Andress (1991) has recommended a music and movement center in which instruments, musical props (e.g., scarves, toys, and puppets), and recorded music are made available to children every day as a way to foster this experimentation. Full-length mirrors along several sides of the center would allow children to observe their own performances. Teachers might intervene regularly in this area to encourage or facilitate creative experimentation (e.g., "Can you make an interesting beat with all three of the drums?" or "How could we use the xylophone in your song?"). In the following vignette, a teacher introduces a variation on a traditional childhood game in order to foster experimentation with rhythm and beat.

❖ ❖

Two six-year-olds sit in the music center playing teacher-made drums (various wooden containers and barrels with rubber stretched across the rims). A teacher observes for a few minutes, then initiates a game.

Teacher:	I know an interesting game to play with drums.
Child A:	Okay. How do you play?
Teacher:	Well, you may have played this game before. It's called "Riddly-Ree." But I know a special version of the game we could play here in the music center.
Child B:	Oh, we played that! We did that at group time, I think.
Teacher:	Yes. But this is a different way to play. Let me show you. (Selects a drum, then recites a poem in an animated tone) Riddly, riddly, riddly, ree. Do what I do after me! (Plays an interesting beat pattern on the drum)

Both children attempt to imitate the teacher's beat.

Teacher: Now we'll make it harder. Riddly, riddly, riddly, ree. Do what I do after me. (Plays a complex beat)

After playing several rounds with the teacher inventing the beat to be copied, the children are encouraged to take turns saying the poem and presenting beats to one another. Once the game is fully under way, the teacher withdraws.   ❖

Listening and Responding to Music

Playing recorded music during the school day will nurture an appreciation and an awareness of musical diversity. Music of all types (e.g., children's music, folk, jazz, classical, soul, rock, and music representing many different cultures) should be presented. Music that matches the activity level appropriate for a particular time in the school day can be selected (e.g., soothing classical music at nap time; lively dixieland jazz in the large motor area).

As music is played, children will display movement responses that signify their appreciation of a rhythm or beat and reveal their feelings toward the music. Andress (1991) has argued that teachers might facilitate these movement responses in three ways—modeling, describing, and suggesting. In *modeling*, the teacher moves freely to rhythms in order to demonstrate that adults enjoy music and express their feelings or ideas about what they hear through movement. The goal is not to entice children to imitate adult movements but to convey a message that swaying to rhythms, bouncing or tapping to a beat, are enjoyable, adult-sanctioned behaviors. Andress (1991) describes "tactile modeling" as modeling in which adults come into contact with children in their movements. For example, a teacher, dancing to a song, might extend two fingers for a child to grasp as an encouragement to dance along. The child might accept the teacher's fingers and join in, but may release at any time. The following vignette demonstrates this modeling strategy.

❖ ❖

A teacher sits with a four-year-old child on her lap in the book area. They have just read a story and now take a "breather" from classroom activities to enjoy a warm moment sitting together quietly. Classical music is playing in another part of the room. The teacher begins swaying back and forth to the music; the child rocks with her. Now the teacher extends her arms forward around the child and displays her open hands in front of him. He takes her hands and guides her in making rhythmic side to side sweeps with their arms in a gesture resembling a symphony conductor. Together they continue this "dance," the child taking the lead, until the piece has ended.   ❖

Describing is a strategy in which the teacher comments in elaborate ways on the movements children have displayed in response to music (Andress, 1991). The following is an illustration of this approach.

❖ ❖

Children are dancing with scarves to lively jazz that is played from a tape recorder out on the playground. A teacher watches for a time and then intervenes when one piece has ended.

Teacher: Look at all the twirling. You're all spinning 'round and 'round.

Child A: Yeah. Look at me. (Twirls, then dramatically falls to the ground)

Teacher: (To other children) Did you see Jeremy twirl and twirl . . . then fall down?

Child B: Yeah. I'm twirling and then I fall. (Demonstrates)

Teacher: Yes. You fall when the music stops.

Child A: Yep. Fall down at the end.

The next piece begins; twirling resumes. The children observe one another's dancing and now and then comment on new movements. The teacher withdraws from the area.   ❖

This intervention not only encourages creative movement to music but facilitates language learning, as well (Smothergill, Olsen, & Moore, 1971).

A final intervention that Andress recommends is *suggesting*, in which the teacher actually poses movement problems for children to solve in response to music. The teacher of the following vignette employs this technique.

❖ ❖

Two children are listening with headphones to a song on the tape recorder. It is early morning and children are just arriving at the day-care center; a teacher encourages them to unplug the jack so that the music fills the classroom.

Teacher: This is one of my favorite songs on the album.

Child A: Yeah. It's about garbage.

Teacher: It's funny. What does this song make you want to do? Is there a special way you like to dance when you hear it?

Child B: I feel like throwing out the garbage. (Makes a throwing gesture) Like that.

Teacher: Great. Every time they shout that word you can throw it out. (Imitates the child's movement)

Child C: (Approaching from another area of the classroom) I'll do it. Look. (Makes a new throwing gesture)

Teacher: That's a new one. What are some other ways we could throw the garbage away?

Numerous children have now entered the area. Each adds a variation to the "garbage throwing" dance. The teacher rewinds the tape and plays the song again.   ❖

Teachers can make music
with children at any time
of the day and in any area of
the classroom.

Group-Time Musical Experiences

The focus of this section has been on facilitating spontaneous musical expression in children's play activities. Many of the principles presented above apply to planned, whole group musical experiences as well. Hitz (1987) has argued that group-time music is very important; he urges that an open-ended, problem-solving approach be taken even in these more teacher-directed activities. He suggests that divergent questions be posed regularly, for example, so that children interject their own ideas into these experiences (e.g., "What are some other ways we could make the spider go up the water spout?" or "We've sung all about the wheels on the bus and the driver and the windows. What are some other things on a bus we could sing about?").

Musical experiences involving open-ended movement can be planned. Teachers can apply Andress's (1991) strategies for encouraging movement reactions to music described above (e.g., "Did you see how Melissa skated around the chair? That was very creative. What are some other ways we can go around the chair as we sing?").

Language and literacy might be incorporated into planned musical experiences. Children can be encouraged to write or dictate words to standard or invented songs; they can read the lyrics to predictable songs that are presented on experience charts (e.g., "She'll Be Comin' 'Round the Mountain") (Hitz, 1987). Whenever possible, group-time discussions about themes or topics under study in the classroom can include music.

Although whole group music affords important opportunities to sing, play instruments, dance, and react to recorded music in a group, elements of individual, open-ended self-expression should be maintained. It is genuine creative expression with music and movement which is most important in early childhood (Hitz,1987).

It is this author's experience that some classrooms—particularly traditional public school classrooms—are quite amusical. One reason for this may be that teachers feel incompetent in music themselves, or believe that only trained music teachers can appropriately engage children in these experiences (Wolf, 1992). A regular infusion of music into the classroom is critical, however, not just for musical development, but so that children will acquire positive dispositions toward music (Andress, 1991).

Summary

True art involves open-ended creative expression. When children are encouraged to experiment with media, invent their own art projects, and decide for themselves what the finished outcomes will be, artistic development is fostered. Projects that require children to use media in only one way or that lead to a single adult-selected finished product cannot be considered true art. Even musical experience is most useful for children if individual, creative expression and problem-solving are included.

The role of the teacher in fine arts development is to observe and encourage children's active experimentation with media. Informal, unobtrusive intervention in children's artistic efforts can facilitate development. Teachers can talk with children about their art, encourage the use of new media or novel experimentation with standard materials, and facilitate collaboration on projects. Showing respect for children's work will give them confidence as artists.

The same kinds of encouragements can be provided as children sing or move to music. When encouraged to invent their own songs or solve problems with voices, bodies, or instruments, children will come to enjoy music as an important mode of personal expression. Even whole-group, teacher-guided musical experiences are more meaningful if they contain elements of spontaneity and creativity.

Suggested Activities

1. On a visit to an early-childhood classroom (or while observing in your own classroom), watch children in the art center or those who are engaged in artistic activities in other areas. Listen also for times during your visit when music or movement are encouraged. Write an analysis of your observations guided by the following questions:

    a. Describe those activities that you consider to be "true art," as defined in this chapter. What elements of these activities make them so?

    b. Describe activities that did not involve genuine artistic expression, as defined by this author. What elements of these activities lead you to believe these are not true art? What adaptations, if any, could be made to make them so?

    c. How has children's artwork been displayed throughout the classroom? To what degree do these displays reflect respect for children's work and diversity in creative expression? To what degree do children appear to have some control over how artwork is exhibited?

    d. To what degree are music and movement incorporated in all activities of the classroom?

    e. How are children encouraged to express themselves in music or movement activities in an open-ended way (e.g., making up lyrics to a song, making up the steps to a dance, playing instruments to music in any way they choose)?

2. Observe a teacher interacting with children as they engage in art activities (or observe a videotape of your own interactions with children in your classroom). Write an analysis of these interactions guided by the following questions:

    a. Which style of interaction (correcting, judging, question-asking, child-initiated discussion) was most common in these interactions?

    b. In what ways did the teacher facilitate creative expression (e.g., providing materials, encouraging new projects, asking questions, posing challenges)?

    c. What recommendations would you give the teacher in regard to these interactions?

3. Observe a teacher engaging children in musical or movement experiences. Write an analysis of your observations guided by the following questions:

    a. In what ways did the teacher encourage creative musical expression?

    b. Which music or movement activities were most successful in regard to participation and creative expression? Why do you think they were successful?

    c. What recommendations would you give the teacher in regard to these interactions?

4. Interact with a group of children engaged in art activities. Write an analysis of your interactions guided by the following questions:

    a. In what ways did you discuss children's art with them? Which interactions were most effective? least obtrusive? most obtrusive?

    b. Describe interactions, if any, where you judged children's work. How did children react?

    c. Describe interactions, if any, where you prompted greater creativity or problem solving. How did children react to these interactions?

    d. What signs of self-doubt (e.g., "I can't draw," or "Will you draw for me?"), if any, did you see? How did you react?

5. Conduct a creative musical or movement experience with a small group of children during free play or outdoor time. Write an analysis of your experiences guided by the following questions:

   a. To what degree did children engage in open-ended musical or movement expression? What elements of your interactions with them encouraged this?

   b. In what ways did you feel uncomfortable singing or moving with children? Where do these feelings come from?

Further Reading

Andress, B. (1991). From research to practice: Preschool children and their movement responses to music. *Young Children, 47*(1), 22–29.

Clemens, S. G. (1991). Art in the classroom: Making every day special. *Young Children, 46* (2), 4–11.

Hitz, R. (1987). Creative problem solving through music activities. *Young Children, 42*(2), 12–19.

Lasky, L., & Mukerji, R. (1982). *Art: Basic for young children.* Washington, D.C.: National Association for the Education of Young Children.

Schirrmacher, R. (1986). Talking with children about their art. *Young Children, 41*(5), 3–10.

Seefeldt, C. (1987). The visual arts. In C. Seefeldt (Ed.), *The early childhood curriculum: A review of current research* (pp. 183–210). New York: Teachers College Press.

Wolf, J. (1992). Let's sing it again: Creating music with young children. *Young Children, 47*(2), 4–11.

CHAPTER

9

FOSTERING MOTOR DEVELOPMENT

Four children sit quietly under a climber during outdoor time in a child-care center. They chat with one another as they watch more active peers playing around them. They do not notice a teacher who creeps up behind them with a parachute under his arm.

The teacher quickly but gently flings the parachute up over the climber; it covers the surprised children underneath. They begin to giggle.

"Ah, ha!" The teacher shouts in a make-believe voice. "I have you now. You are prisoners in my cave. You may not escape. And if you try, I will catch you!"

One child pokes her head out from under the parachute. "What are you?" she inquires of her captor.

"I am a guggly-wump. Ever heard of me?"

The child giggles and shakes her head, "no."

"You may not escape," the teacher says again, clearly inviting the children to try. Finally one makes a break for it, running out from under the back of the climber. The teacher chases her, making spooky cackling noises. He catches up with the escapee, hugs and tickles her. He then carries her back to the "cave." While the creature is off capturing this child, however, two others have taken the opportunity to escape. They stand now on the opposite side of the playground, taunting their captor: "We escaped! Ha, ha!" The teacher charges after them. And so the game begins in earnest—the children escape, the teacher captures them and carries them back to the climber. Three of the children will play until outdoor time has ended; one decides to quit after a time to join other peers on a tire swing.   ❖

This vignette raises many issues about children's motor play and the role of teachers in promoting physical development. This play appears quite wild and silly, maybe even a little frightening; is it appropriate for a teacher to get children so "wound up"? (Certainly, helping these children regain a quieter, calmer manner when outdoor play is over will be a challenge!) Is this kind of rough-and-tumble play unbecoming or unprofessional for a teacher? Will children continue to respect him as a teacher after these interactions? These children seemed content to sit quietly; must children always be encouraged to run, chase, or climb on the playground? Can they benefit equally from quiet outdoor play? Doesn't this open-ended "free-for-all" leave motor skills learning to chance? Wouldn't more organized group games or gymnastics lessons lead to more systematic large muscle development?

These issues will be addressed in this chapter. Guidelines for teacher-child interactions that facilitate gross and fine motor development will be presented; the value of open-ended play activities for physical growth will be emphasized.

❖ ❖ ❖

Motor Development in Early Childhood

During the early years, children experience rapid growth in motor development. They acquire gross motor skills (large muscle abilities like running, jumping, throwing, or kicking), fine motor skills (abilities in small muscle coordination required for drawing, making puzzles, handling books, or molding clay), and perceptual motor skills (abilities to coordinate movements with perception). Examples of specific motor skills that develop in the early years are presented in Table 9-1.

Often, advancement in these areas appears to be so rapid that adults come to believe these abilities are acquired "overnight." One teacher describes the high speed, death-defying tricycle-riding prowess of a four-year-old child who only several days before was unable to get this riding toy moving at all. Another teacher reports that a three-year-old child who seemed to struggle with fine motor tasks announced one morning that she could now tie her own shoes. The teacher watched in amazement as she successfully demonstrated her new-found skill.

Actually, motor development is characterized by a gradual refinement in abilities; steps towards mastery of a particular skill are many, although each step is often imperceptible. Although a child might demonstrate sudden accuracy in throwing, for example, acquisition of this skill likely took place in small steps beginning with primitive swiping and grasping in infancy. The child may have begun throwing underhand, then overhand but with awkward body movements (e.g., stepping forward with the same foot as the throwing arm). The child may have practiced timing the release of objects from the earliest days of life. In infancy, overcoming reflexive grasping was needed; in toddlerhood, control of timing release of an object to be thrown had to be refined (Cratty, 1970). It was only after many of these small and unnoticed advancements, however, that throwing competence may have become suddenly apparent to adults.

Small motor development progresses in much the same way. Although adults might marvel at how quickly a child has gained control over a crayon or marker, this may have been an equally gradual and complex process. Reaching and grasping objects in infancy may have been the first step in acquiring this control. Developing a "pincer grasp," in which tiny objects are picked up with the thumb and forefinger, may also have been critical to these writing and drawing movements. Gradual refinement in holding the drawing or writing implement likely took place with the child first gripping a crayon or marker in a fist, arm raised up off the drawing surface. Gradually the child may have come to rest the drawing arm on the table, noticing that this adjustment led to greater control. Experimentation with writing or drawing grip may have taken place as the child sought to gain additional control (Schickedanz, Schickedanz, & Forsyth, 1982). By the time adults noticed this remarkable mastery over the crayon, the child may have been in the process of acquiring drawing competence for many years.

Table 9-1
Motor Skills Acquired in Early Childhood

Skills	Description of Development
Large motor skills:	
Balance	As children's center of gravity lowers during the preschool and early elementary years, greater balance in motor activities is achieved. Young preschoolers are able to walk in a straight line; older preschoolers can walk in a circle (e. g., around a tire). Balance beams are difficult for children before the primary years; children will often step off on the way across.
Walking	Children can walk rapidly and more surely in the early preschool years; they no longer toddle as they did several years before. Adapting their walking to different surfaces—up and down hill or through sand or snow—is still challenging.
Climbing stairs	In the early preschool years, children display "marked time climbing," where one foot and then the other is brought to the same step before another step is attempted. Later, alternate-foot climbing on stairs, then ladders, appears. Going down steps is more difficult than going up. Even at age four or five, children use "bottom-thumping" or other cautious approaches when descending steep stairs.
Running	Young preschoolers engage in the first "real running," in which both feet leave the ground at once. As children get older, they are better able to change direction quickly and control starting and stopping. Coordinating running direction with the movements of peers—as in a game of tag—is not perfected until the early elementary years.
Jumping/hopping	Two-footed jumping appears early in the preschool years, although initially children will not display body movements (leaning forward or swinging arms) that help in achieving height or distance. Younger children often land with one foot striking the ground first. Older children refine body movement and land squarely with two feet. Four- and five-year-olds can hop for several steps on one foot. Complex one-footed hopping games are not mastered until the primary grades.
Skipping	When children before age six are encouraged to skip, they usually gallop—moving forward rhythmically with a lead foot. Only in the primary grades can many children perform true, alternate leg skipping.
Throwing	Early throwing is inaccurate as children have difficulty controlling the moment when objects are to be released by the hand. In the later preschool years more accurate over-handed throwing is common, although children may step with the wrong foot or lack other body movements to enhance a throw. In the elementary years, throws become longer, more accurate, and faster.

Table 9-1
continued

Skills	Description of Development
Catching	As toddlers and young preschool children attempt to catch objects, they look like passive, rigid targets. Balls often bounce off their bodies, since they do not bend elbows or sway backwards to absorb the impact of a throw. Children are significantly more competent catchers in the elementary years.
Riding	Toddlers are often seen straddling riding toys and "walk-riding" rather than using pedals. By age three many children can ride tricycles or big wheels; some may need assistance from block extenders to reach the pedals. By five, children can be extremely proficient at steering, stopping, and starting their riding toys. Some children do not ride a two-wheeler until well into the elementary years.
Small motor skills: Dressing/self-help skills	Children can manipulate velcro straps or snaps in toddlerhood. They are better able to undress than dress. Other self-help skills such as washing or toileting may be mastered by two. By the end of the preschool years, children can zip or button; some can even tie. Some may still need assistance with troublesome coat zippers or tangled shoe laces. Elementary school children can take responsibility for most aspects of their personal care.
Drawing/writing	Drawing and writing develop in stages. Composition becomes more complex with cognitive development. Greater control is acquired as children change from a fist grip to a finger grip and begin to rest their arms on the drawing or writing surface.
Scissors	Younger preschoolers enjoy working with scissors but have difficulty manipulating them. It is not unusual for a child to hold a pair of scissors stationary and simply tear the paper. During the preschool years, children learn to manipulate the scissors, though cutting is not completely accurate until the elementary years.
Constructing	Block building and construction-toy play can be quite complex even in the early preschool years. Three-year-olds may be observed creating rather elaborate block structures or "Lego" towers. In the later preschool and elementary years, block structures become more representative; often real buildings or neighborhoods are accurately replicated.
Handling moveable objects	Although large toys predominate most preschool play environments, very young children can benefit from manipulating tiny objects. Once children are no longer in an oral stage, tiny objects can be incorporated into math and science areas; children appear to delight in handling very small objects.
Eye-hand coordination	The above skills could not be mastered without eye-hand coordination which becomes increasingly sophisticated during the preschool years. Children show a growing capacity to coordinate perceptions and movement: Their burgeoning skill in puzzle-making, cutting, and pasting demonstrates this.

Adapted from Cratty (1970), Elkind & Weiner (1978), Schickedanz, Schickedanz, & Forsyth (1982), Williams (1983).

Rich play environments enhance motor development (Poest, Williams, Witt, & Atwood, 1992). When children are given opportunities to run, climb, swing, ride, throw, and kick, large muscle abilities are enhanced. Puzzles, art materials, writing utensils, dressing dolls, and sand and water play equipment will lead to small muscle competence. Indoor classroom environments should be equipped with areas for large muscle activities as well as small. Bean bag games, balance beams, scooter boards, even low climbers and riding toys can be provided indoors if space allows (Weinstein & David, 1987). Outdoor play areas must be designed and equipped to enhance social interaction and play (see Frost & Klein, 1979; Kelly & Kelly, 1985; Miller, 1989; and Weinstein & David, 1987 for ideas).

Is the design of an enriching play environment sufficient to ensure motor development? The following vignette suggests that merely providing equipment is not enough.

The director of an inner-city day-care center was truly excited about the creation of a new playscape on a small parcel of green space that was the playground. He had grown concerned about the lack of large motor activity among children at his center; during outdoor time they would often sit around, "hang on to" the teachers, and fight a good deal. The problem was caused by inadequate space, he concluded—there was nowhere to run or ride, nothing to climb on. Now a community group was to build a beautiful climber on their playground. Surely there would be an immediate, positive change in children's outdoor activities.

The day after the playscape was built, the director was dismayed to observe that children's play behaviors had changed very little. Certainly some students engaged in active climbing and make-believe—the sorts of behaviors such equipment was designed to elicit. But many others did not use the climber; they continued with previous behavior patterns, sitting passively, clinging to teachers, arguing with peers.

It wasn't until a very energetic substitute teacher visited the center that the director came to understand the real problem. The sub climbed with children, modeling activities and suggesting games. She invited less active children to play. She posed challenges, asked questions, and prompted make-believe. The impact of these interchanges was remarkable. Children were at last displaying the organized, involved play that the director had hoped for. At the next staff meeting, strategies were formulated for engaging children in active motor play. Although some teachers were reluctant—outdoor time had always been a period for teachers to sit back and rest—eventually all staff came to enjoy active involvement on the playground. The benefits to children were enormous.   ❖

This director has discovered the power of teacher intervention in promoting motor activity. Equipment alone does not prompt all children to climb, jump, or run; modeling, question-asking, problem-posing, and encouragement are needed. Issues concerning the degree and nature of adult involvement on the playground are addressed in the next few sections.

The Nature-Nurture Debate: New Perspectives

One issue raised in the introductory vignette, as well as in the story of the day-care director above, is whether adult intervention in children's motor activities is needed at all. Some believe that motor development is primarily the result of maturation. From this perspective, motor abilities simply "unfold" as children get older. Why should teachers engage children in more vigorous physical activities on the playground, some might ask? Both active and quiet children will eventually acquire the motor abilities that have been pre-determined by genetics. If it is "nature" that explains motor development, from this way of thinking, the role of adults in the process is merely to observe children grow (Ames, 1937; Shirley, 1933).

Early movement education specialists have argued that motor development can be "nurtured" through systematic adult intervention. Influenced by the behaviorist tradition of their time, in which direct instruction and isolated skills learning were emphasized, these authors developed perceptual-motor training programs in which children were taught motor abilities directly (Chaney & Kephart, 1968; Delacato, 1966; Frostig, 1969). From their perspective, the teacher in the introductory vignette may have been correct in attempting to enhance physical growth through environmental intervention. They would disagree with his seemingly chaotic and haphazard approach, however. An activity in which individual children were systematically taught to catch a ball or climb stairs, or one in which they were asked to copy shapes, would more directly lead to motor learning.

Modern perspectives on motor development acknowledge the influence of both maturation and experience on children's large and small muscle abilities (Frost & Klein, 1979; Hendrick, 1992; Kaplan-Sanoff, Brewster, Stillwell, & Bergen, 1988). Recent authors would find both the nature and nurture approaches described above to be extreme. They would argue that adults do have an important role to play in enhancing motor growth; enriching children's activities, they contend, is crucial for the acquisition of skills. They have cited research showing that in many schools, adults take a laissez-faire approach to outdoor activities, sending children out to play on their own and expecting development to occur (Poest, Williams, Witt, & Atwood, 1992). These authors would also oppose a training approach in which skills are taught in isolation from meaningful social experience. They have pointed to studies showing the ineffectiveness of perceptual-motor instruction (Shick & Plack, 1967).

What modern theorists propose, instead, is a play-based approach to motor skills acquisition in which meaningful activities are provided, and where teachers intervene to encourage creative movement (Coleman & Skeen, 1985; Gallahue, 1982). By playing with children, teachers can create challenges, encourage creative problem solving, elicit activity levels that are sufficient to ensure cardiovascular fitness, or enhance social interaction (Stillwell, 1987; Myers, 1985).

Contemporary play theory and research, then, support the kinds of interventions illustrated by the teacher with the parachute described at the beginning of this chapter. This teacher's playful interchanges are authentic, play-based, and social. The inclusion of make-believe, complete with scary characters and silly voices, relates to the play interests of children of this age. Although the teacher initiates the play theme, children are not coerced into playing along. They may play any character they wish, or choose not to play at all. These interventions prompt more global and creative movements than do adult-directed motor lessons. Children can run, wrestle, climb, crawl; they may use their bodies to portray make-believe characters related to the chasing-and-catching play theme.

Although the teacher's interventions appear frivolous and anarchistic, they are actually quite serious in purpose. This kind of playful intervention may be more powerful in supporting motor growth than planned whole group activities.

The Rough and Tumble Play Debate

Another issue in motor education is whether wild, silly play should be allowed or, as in the introductory vignette, encouraged in the classroom or on the playground. Many teachers would argue that such behavior is unprofessional, that to encourage "rough" activities may even be unethical (Johnson, Christie, & Yawkey, 1987). A growing body of research suggests that "rough and tumble play"—a form of play that involves wrestling, play-fighting, rolling about, or chasing, accompanied by screams, laughter, and noise-making—is useful for motor development and social learning (Pellegrini & Perlmutter, 1988). Such play likely relieves tension, exercises many different muscles simultaneously, leads to close physical contact with peers and teachers, and is generally great fun. Rough and tumble play with nurturing adults may contribute to greater competence in peer interactions (MacDonald & Parke, 1984). Contrary to what might be expected, this form of play does not lead to aggression, nor does it result in unruly or uncontrollable behavior (Pellegrini & Perlmutter, 1986). It has been this author's experience that playing in this way actually enhances rather than diminishes a teacher's status among students.

Rough and tumble play may be the ideal context for promoting movement for some children. Those who are less active might be enticed into activity by such open-ended, humor-filled interchanges. Children who do not care for organized games or who prefer make-believe activities might be attracted to the competition-free, highly symbolic features of rough and tumble play. It is argued here that running and shouting with children on the playground is an appropriate and powerful motor development intervention.

The teacher in the introductory vignette models one form of rough and tumble play intervention. Another example is provided below.

❖ ❖

Six-year-olds are playing with a parachute on the playground. They had begun by playing a conventional ball game in which each player would wiggle a part of the parachute in order to keep a ball rolling at its center. This activity has quickly broken down into a spontaneous rough and tumble activity in which children raise up the parachute, then all run underneath as it begins to float down. The children bump into one another, fall to the ground, giggle, and wrestle under the parachute. Once it has settled they lie still a moment. One or the other of the children will eventually make the pronouncement, "Let's do it again." All children climb out and repeat the action. A teacher watches this child-invented game with some interest. Concerned that someone might be hurt, she moves into the area.

Teacher:	I am going to play this game. Are there any rules?
Child A:	(To her peers) Oh! The teacher's going to play!
Child B:	(Speaking at the same time as Child A) Nope. No rules. You just run under.
Teacher:	How do you keep from running into each other? Don't you bump one another?
Child C:	Yeah. It's fun.
Teacher:	Do you get hurt?
Child D:	No. I don't think so.
Child B:	(To Child D) You bumped my knee, Jennifer.
Teacher:	Oh, dear. We could say you can't bump anyone. That could be a rule.
Child A:	Okay. Are you going to play?
Teacher:	Sure.

The teacher and children raise the parachute and run under. All fall to the ground wrestling with each other.

Child C:	Marsha bumped me.
Teacher:	Oops. Remember: We can't bump each other when we run under.
Child C:	Let's say we have to *crawl* under now. When we count three you have to crawl.

Child D: No. I want running.

Teacher: We could take turns picking how we go under. We'll crawl this time. Next time you can pick, Jennifer.

The children continue with the game, taking turns calling out "ways to go under." Although the activity becomes quite silly and loud, no one is hurt. The children are in constant motion for over a half hour.   ❖

Teachers often respond to a rough game by ending it ("Someone could get hurt. Let's go back to the game with the ball we were playing before."). This teacher has recognized the value of this child-created game; very few activities an adult could invent would lead to the same levels of exercise (Myers, 1985). She chooses to facilitate rough and tumble play, rather than inhibit it. She plays along, suggesting a rule to insure safety. She encourages an adaptation of the game that leads to more creative movement. Her interventions may have led to greater large muscle activity—not to mention social interaction and verbalization—than would occur in a more organized adult-initiated group game.

Teachers can engage in rough-and-tumble play with children to foster social and physical development.

Structured Games or Open-Ended Movement?

Not all motor interventions should be of the rough and tumble variety. Many times, teachers will wish to initiate more organized activities—games with rules, movement and music experiences, or problem-solving tasks. There is much debate about how much teacher guidance and structure are appropriate in these activities (Kaplan-Sanoff et al., 1988). It is common for some teachers to organize group games on the playground that include all students and consume the entire outdoor play period. Do children benefit from such adult-guided activities or are they deprived of open-ended play experiences?

Hendrick (1992) recommends a balanced approach in which both child-centered and teacher-guided activities are provided. She argues that children should spend much time in open-ended free play on the playground or in motor areas within the classroom. Mainly, teachers should observe and keep children safe; too much direct interference can inhibit free play. She suggests that unobtrusive interventions can be made to pose challenges, help children resolve social problems, and encourage creative use of materials. Teachers might also enhance children's make-believe or even rough and tumble play, as the teacher in the last vignette has done. These interventions should be minimal and reflect children's ongoing play interests, as the vignette below illustrates.

Two children have stacked rubber inner tubes together on end on the playground; they have leaned them against one another so that they stand alone and create a tunnel. The children, each standing at an opposite end of the "tunnel," gaze through at each other. They wave at and call to each other. A teacher who has been observing approaches.

Teacher:	Will you try to crawl through?
Child A:	(In an excited tone) Can we?
Child B:	Would we get stuck?
Teacher:	I don't think so. This is soft rubber and you can squeeze through. I'll be right here if you need help.
Child A:	Will we suffocate?
Teacher:	No. You wouldn't suffocate.
Child A:	What is suffocate anyway?
Teacher:	Oh, that's where you have no air to breathe. You would have lots of air crawling through there.

With this assurance the children climb into the tunnel they have created. For more than twenty minutes they crawl in and out.   ❖

Here the children have invented a creative use for playground materials. With minimal encouragement and reassurance from the teacher they embark on a new enactment that is motorically challenging, increases activity level, and involves problem solving.

Hendrick (1992) suggests that at times adults can initiate more organized problem-solving activities that fall under the category of "movement education." These might be presented in a group time or introduced less formally on the playground where children are running, climbing, or throwing. The following vignette illustrates one of these less formal interchanges.

❖ ❖

Five kindergarten children are jumping off a low platform. Their movements are quite repetitive; a teacher intervenes to add variety to the activity.

Teacher:	I see you are playing a jumping game.
Child A:	Yeah. Watch this! (Jumps)
Teacher:	Yes. I wonder how many different ways you can think of to land.
Child B:	(Stops jumping, looks at the teacher) Huh?
Teacher:	Can you think of lots of different ways to land?
Child C:	Oh. Watch this. (Jumps and collapses into a heap as she lands)
Child D:	Yeah. Look! (Lands on one foot)

All five children begin to experiment with ways to land. After a few minutes of watching, the teacher withdraws; the children continue to experiment with their jumping until outdoor time is over.   ❖

This activity could be initiated with positive results during group time. This teacher chooses instead to introduce it informally, thus tying movement education directly to children's natural self-selected play interests. Teachers can make movement activities more authentic by watching for moments when they can be incorporated into spontaneous free play.

Another type of adult-initiated movement experience involves music and dance. Hendrick (1992) argues that "dancing can be the freest and most joyful of all large motor activities" (p. 101). She warns against over-reliance on adult-invented dances in which all movements or steps are worked out in advance. Activities in which children are encouraged to move freely to music lead to the most creative body motion. Children might be provided with all kinds of props to use as they dance (e.g., scarves, Hula Hoops, ribbons, streamers, bean bags, clothing and hats of various kinds) (Myre, 1991). Finger plays, action songs, and rhythm instrument activities also provide open-ended experimentation with movement (Hitz, 1987). Such group-oriented musical experiences are extremely valuable; teachers can also informally introduce movement and music during free play time as the following vignette reveals.

A large group of four-year-olds is blowing bubbles on the playground. A teacher produces a "boom box" and plays a tape of bluegrass music as the children play. They react immediately to the music: Their movements quicken; some begin to dance along, waving their bubble "wands" to and fro in time to the banjo and fiddle. A small group begins to dance in a circle, surrounding themselves with a wreath of floating bubbles. ❖

In this vignette the teacher has chosen to integrate movement experiences within children's spontaneous play activities. Children can choose to respond to the music or not; some invent their own dances.

The Competition Debate

Group games are another type of motor activity that are common on school playgrounds. They may be distinguished from other forms of play in that they have group-accepted rules and usually end with one or more players winning, others losing. The effects of such competition on young children have been debated. Kamii and DeVries (1980) have argued that games are ideal not only for motor growth but also for sociomoral and logico-mathematical development as well (see Chapter 6 for a full discussion). Children will often organize themselves into games, particularly in the primary grades. Teachers can introduce games themselves, although this should be done sparingly; much time should be provided for children to plan their own activities. One approach in initiating a game is to ask a small group of children whether they wish to play. Once the game has begun, others may join; but children have the freedom to decline as well.

Two four-year-olds sit unoccupied on the grass on the playground. A teacher chooses to initiate a game.

Teacher:	Would you like to learn a new game? What you do is run around and then you stop very suddenly.
Child A:	How do you play?
Teacher:	Well, you just move around—I might tell you to walk, run, wiggle—until I yell "stop!" Then what do you suppose you do?
Child B:	(Laughs) You stop!
Teacher:	Right! Are you ready to play? I think we'll start with running. Run around, but when I say "stop" you need to freeze. You can't even wiggle.
Child B:	(Laughs) No wiggles?
Teacher:	Right. Okay, ready? Run!

The two children run wildly about. After a time the teacher yells "stop;" the children freeze. All this giggling and running about have caught the attention of several other children who join the group.

Child C:	Can I play?
Child A:	(Stands frozen. Just barely moves her mouth in reply) Yeah. We're frozen.
Teacher:	Come join us. I tell you how to move. But when I yell "stop," you freeze. Lets try wriggling like snakes this time. Ready?
Child A:	Wriggling?
Child D:	Yeah. Look. (Lies on the ground, demonstrates)

By the end of outdoor time, over half the class has joined the game. Some children have chosen not to play, however, and continue with other activities. ❖

Had the teacher called all children together and organized this game, those with completely different play interests would have been obligated to join in. Here they may choose whether to play or not. They may watch for a time to decide, then enter the game gradually when they are ready. Children who are in a stage in which they watch more than they participate (see Chapter 4) are able to look at activities from the periphery without being drawn into interaction.

Several concerns must be raised about games. Competition may be difficult for some children to handle (see Chapter 6 for a full discussion). Preschoolers have a particularly troublesome time understanding rules; they may become confused and upset when they lose or have to be "out" (Ramsey & Reid, 1988). Teachers might wish to adapt games so that competition is minimized or eliminated altogether. In the vignette below a teacher has altered a game of musical chairs so that no one is excluded from the play.

❖ ❖

A group of six-year-olds is playing musical chairs. The music has stopped; one child cannot grab a seat and, so, is eliminated. He shows signs of upset; a teacher moves over to the group.

Teacher:	It isn't a lot of fun when you are "out," is it?
Child A:	No. I don't want that.
Child B:	But that's how you play. You're out if you can't get a chair.
Teacher:	Is there a way we can play so that everyone stays in the game?
Child A:	Let's add another chair.
Child C:	No. That's not how it goes.
Teacher:	That's a different way to play, isn't it? But if we add another chair then everyone gets to play.
Child D:	But that's not so fun.

Child B: It would be fun, 'cause you still have to quick grab a chair. You still rush around and around, you know?

Finally all children agree to the new rule; an additional chair is added. Although the competition is reduced, children scramble and scream as intensely as before when the music stops.   ❖

This teacher has altered a game so that children cannot lose. Such adaptations are important to those who have overly intense reactions to competition. Teachers can be on the lookout on the playground for times when altering rules will assure that all get to play and that no one suffers overwhelming feelings of defeat.

Another concern about some games is that they involve an inordinate amount of waiting (Kaplan-Sanoff et al., 1988). Research has indicated that a high percentage of time at recess or in physical education class is spent waiting for a turn to play (Hovell, Bursick, Sharkey, & McClure, 1978; Myers, 1985). The traditional circle game, "Duck, Duck, Goose," provides a good illustration. While the child who is "it" endlessly rounds the group of children, they must wait patiently. They may fidget, scold their peer to "come on and touch someone," and even sit down. When someone is finally tapped it is only that child and the one who is "it" who get a chance to run. An individual could play for many minutes without getting any cardiovascular exercise at all. Teachers can adapt such games to increase the amount of movement or even enhance creative play.

❖ ❖

Six-year-olds have organized themselves into a game of Duck, Duck, Goose. Only a few are running; those who are "it" continually tap their friends, so that most stand and wait. A teacher suggests an adaptation.

Teacher: I have an interesting new way to play that game.

Children: (Many speaking at once) How?

Teacher: When the person who is "it" taps somebody, everyone has to run around the circle.

Child A: What? How do you catch the person?

Teacher: In this version you just run around. You don't have to catch the person you touch.

Child B: Okay!

Child C: But who is "it" next?

Teacher: The child who gets tapped is "it" next.

Child A: Even if he doesn't get caught?

Teacher: This isn't really a catching game. You don't try to catch the person you tap. You just run. Everybody runs.

Child C: Yeah.

Teacher:	But there's another part to tell you.
Children:	(Many together) What?
Teacher:	When you are it and you tap someone you don't say "goose." You say "run!" or "walk!" or "skate!" or "skip!" Then everyone has to go around the circle that way.

The teacher demonstrates the new rules. After several chaotic first attempts to play by them, the children eventually get the hang of it. They may be observed running, crawling, or jumping around the circle together until outdoor time is over.   ❖

Here the teacher has changed the rules to increase both the quantity and quality of movement significantly.

Enhancing Specific Motor Skills

As teachers intervene in both informal and organized movement activities, they can encourage development of specific motor skills. Although an exhaustive treatment of all important large and small motor abilities is beyond the scope of this book, examples of strategies to promote game-related skills are provided. These skills—jumping, walking/running, ball handling, climbing, riding, balancing, and reacting—are discussed here because they are the abilities that are most often used in the group games of children within Western society; in non-Western cultures other skills may be more relevant (Kaplan-Sanoff et al., 1988). Competence in these areas will lead to enjoyment of active play and greater peer acceptance in the later elementary years.

As teachers encourage practice of specific skills, they should keep in mind more general goals for motor development. Children should be assisted in acquiring both "movement consistency" and "movement constancy" (Keogh, 1977). The former refers to acquisition of basic movement skills such as running or catching; the latter to an ability to adapt these movements to meet varying environmental challenges (e.g., being able to catch balls of different sizes or being able to run up hill and down as well as on flat surfaces).

Not only must children learn to coordinate the movements of their own bodies, but they must adapt movements in relation to other persons (Keogh, 1977). A child may be able to change directions quickly while running, for example, but may not be able to coordinate this behavior in anticipation of another child's movements in a game of tag. Interventions that not only encourage practice at basic movements but that challenge children to adapt these in relation to the environment and other persons are necessary.

Catching and Throwing

Balls predominate children's play in Western societies (Kaplan-Sanoff et al., 1988). Children acquire throwing and catching activities gradually; only in the elementary years will they display highly coordinated ball-handling abilities (Williams, 1983). Children practice throwing without great coaxing from adults; spontaneous throwing games predominate free play. (Without warning, very young children may invent indoor throwing games with inappropriate objects that threaten life and limb!) Simply providing enticing materials (e.g., balls of different sizes, balled paper, bean bags—all soft, of course, to ensure safety) is often enough to stimulate throwing and catching behaviors. The teacher might occasionally intervene to enhance skill development or the ability to adapt movements to changes in the environment. Two examples are provided below.

❖ ❖

Two children are throwing balls at objects—riding toys, the climber, and eventually their peers. Children are complaining about this game; the teacher moves over to redirect the activity.

Teacher:	You seem to enjoy throwing at things. But I can't let you throw the ball at other children. I know a throwing game you might want to try.
Child:	We want to throw at things.
Teacher:	Yes. This is a game where you have to hit objects and make them move. (Places a huge rubber ball a few feet away from the children) Now what you do is try to hit the big ball with your little ones. You can make it move if you hit it just right.

The children begin throwing at the large ball. As they do, the teacher poses challenges: "Can you make it move past this line?" or "Can you make the big ball roll toward the climber?" One child now complains about one aspect of the game.

Child:	These balls keep rolling away. You have to keep running to get them when you throw. I get tired of all this running and running.
Teacher:	We could throw bean bags instead. Would that help?
Child:	Um . . . yeah. They won't roll off.

The children try the bean bags. The task is quite different now, though. The bean bags must be thrown harder than the balls in order to start the large ball rolling.

Teacher:	How are the bean bags different?
Child:	Oh, they're hard. You have to really throw 'em.

The teacher leaves the children for a while. Later he returns with some new targets—some cardboard blocks, a plastic milk bottle, an empty box and one filled with wooden blocks. The children eagerly try knocking these down or moving them with their bean bags.   ❖

Rather than discouraging these children from throwing after they have inappropriately aimed balls at their peers, this teacher redirects their behavior into a useful ball-handling experience. By altering the objects thrown and the targets they aim at, the teacher has enhanced movement constancy—the ability to adapt movement in response to new stimuli.

Another teacher engages several children in a catching activity.

A child stands on the playscape and rolls several rubber balls down the slide that extends from one side. A teacher sees an opportunity to initiate a useful motor experience. She begins to catch the balls that the child rolls down. Others observe this and join her. She encourages them to catch; the balls are small—an ideal size for hands-only catching practice

As the rolling and catching game continues, the teacher initiates modifications.

Teacher:	Henry, try rolling the balls down in different ways. We'll have to guess how you'll roll it. You could roll it fast, bounce it, make it zig-zag. (Gestures to show what this means)
Child A:	Okay. Here it comes. (Bounces the ball down the slide; it takes a funny hop at the end of the slide and goes over the children's heads)
Teacher:	Oh, what happened?
Child B:	We should back way up, I think. (Backs away. Misses the next catch because Child A rolled it down more slowly and it has dropped off the end of the slide) Oh.

The teacher suggests several other changes in the game. She encourages children to take turns rolling; later in the activity she suggests dropping the ball straight down from the other side of the climber.   ❖

In this interchange, coordinating movements of self with those of others is facilitated. Children must not just catch, but adapt their catching strategies in anticipation of what another child will do.

Climbing

Climbing competence requires large motor development, but also a positive disposition toward taking risks (Gallahue, 1982). Not only must children have strength and coordination when climbing a net ladder, for example, but they must overcome the anxiety of being up so high. Teachers can reassure children who are fearful (e.g., "I'm right here if you need help," or "This climber is very safe; you're very safe climbing up there."). Acknowledging children's risk-taking instills confidence and a desire for more adventurous play (e.g., "Oh, my! Look how high up you are! You are way over my head! How did you climb so far up?"). Avoiding overprotection out of a concern for children's safety is critical. One must ask how comments like "be careful" or "that's very dangerous" will in any way protect children from accidents. In fact, continual warnings such as these may inspire fear and doubt; children's climbing may actually become less sure.

Teachers can introduce problems to children while they climb, as the following vignette illustrates.

Five-year-olds are engaged in a traditional game of "look at me" on a climber on the playground. Experienced teachers are familiar with the routine: Children perform daring feats—hanging by one arm or upside down—then shout out, "Look at me!" The teacher at this point in the game emits an expression of shock or amazement.

This teacher decides to enhance problem solving and adaptability by introducing a new element to the game.

Teacher: Let's say you have to climb up with only two parts of your body touching the climber.

Child: Just two? (Tries this and finds that it is a challenging task. Speaks to herself) Just one arm and one leg, I guess.

Children climb to the top; the teacher then poses another challenge: "Can you climb down the exact same way you climbed up?" Children struggle with this task; it requires both motor and cognitive skill. Once the children are down, the teacher offers another problem.

Teacher: How about this time you have to have four parts of your body touching the climber—always. Four parts of your body must touch.

Child: Wait. You mean you *have* to touch?

Teacher: Right. You have to have four parts of your body touching the wood.

Child: What if it's like your belly. Is that a part?

Teacher: Yes. Your belly is part of your body. But you have to have four parts always touching the climber.

This is the most difficult task of all and children spend many minutes developing systems to accomplish it. They give one another suggestions, point out when they have violated the rule. Eventually all succeed. ❖

These interactions not only prompt children to exercise large muscles but engage them in problem solving experiences with their bodies. They must adapt climbing skills to varying challenges; these interactions promote motor constancy, then, as well as consistency.

Running/Walking

Running and walking are behaviors that are also regularly exercised as children engage in free play (Ridenour, 1978). Everyday classroom life, both indoors and out, affords opportunities for varied walking experiences—tip-toeing quietly to the bathrooms, climbing up and down steps, keeping up with the older children on a field trip—all require adaptation in walking behaviors. It is impossible to keep children from running; even teachers in "sit quiet and listen" classrooms learn this quickly. Simply letting children move uninhibited about the classroom or on the playground will result in much running practice.

"Look what I can do!": Teachers can encourage creative problem solving on the climber.

Teachers can intervene to encourage adaptability in these skills. Coordination of walking or running behaviors with those of others can also be promoted.

❖ ❖

A teacher and three children are playing a make-believe game in which a giant chases and captures people.

Teacher: (In a gruff, make-believe voice) Oh, I am a very tired giant. I am going to sleep now. But I sure hope no one throws leaves on me during my nap.

Child A: (Takes a handful of leaves that have been raked up on the playground, throws them on the sleeping "giant")

The teacher doesn't stir here, but continues snoring loudly.

Child B: (With eager anticipation is her voice) Oh, oh. Throw some more leaves on.

Child C: (Giggling) I'll do it. (Throws more leaves)

Suddenly the teacher raises up and emits a roar. She darts after one child, then quickly shifts direction and chases another. At first, the children run quickly; they then slow, eager to be captured. The teacher snatches up one child and carries him back to the leaf pile.

Teacher: (To the captured child) Now you stay there while I take my nap. And I hope no one throws leaves on me while I sleep.

The game continues for many minutes. Slight variations occur—children come to the rescue of peers who are captured, the giant keeps sleeping for many minutes while the children throw leaves, the giant runs in slow motion during the chase.   ❖

In this rough and tumble episode, children have been encouraged to run. They must anticipate the direction and speed with which the giant pursues them. This running activity contrasts sharply with a relay race or organized running game. Here there are no winners or losers (in fact, it may be preferable to be caught by the giant now and then; the hugging and tickling that results is irresistible).

Walking and running constancy can be promoted with interventions like the following.

❖ ❖

A child approaches a teacher on the playground with the complaint, "There's nothing to do." The teacher suggests a kind of follow-the-leader game in which the child must follow directly behind him and do whatever he does. As the game begins, others fall in line behind the two; soon nearly half the children on the playground are following in a long human chain behind the teacher.

As they move along, the teacher alters his movements. He jogs, skips, runs, then walks again. At one point he turns and walks backwards. With each alteration, children laugh and scramble to change their own movements to match his. He travels over different surfaces as he walks—up a steep grass hill and down, over tires, up the climber steps, and down a slide. He walks in a zig-zagging pattern, now on the sidewalk, now on the grass. Children struggle to adapt their movements to the texture of the walking surface.   ❖

In this interchange, children are encouraged to adapt movement to both environmental elements (changes in walking surface) as well as the movements of another. The game is offered as an option to children; many choose to participate, others do not.

Jumping

Jumping competence also develops in stages (Cratty, 1970). Girls and boys differ in their abilities; girls are more precise in their jumps, boys can leap higher (Cratty & Martin, 1969). Hopping and jumping are often incorporated into music and movement activities; creative problem solving to promote jumping abilities can be facilitated during free play as well.

A seven-year-old lies on the highest platform of a climber, dangling his hand down through a space between its protective slats. "You can't touch me," he calls to several children below. The children attempt to jump up and touch his hand. A teacher, sensing an opportunity to engage children in creative movement, enters the play area.

Teacher:	Can you touch his hand when you jump?
Child A:	Yep. (Jumps up and gives the child on the climber a "high five" hand slap to demonstrate)
Child B:	Just barely. Watch. (Jumps, but misses the child's hand; he has drawn it up so that it is out of reach) No! Don't pull it up, Sean! (He drops his hand back down; Child B jumps and touches him)
Teacher:	What would happen if you only used one foot?
Child B:	I could still do it. (Jumps on one foot, does not touch the child's hand)
Teacher:	What happened?
Child A:	You can't jump as high with only one foot. See? (Demonstrates)
Child C:	(From up in the climber) Let me stretch. See if you can touch it now. (Stretches arm downward)
Child A:	With only one foot?

Child C:	Yeah. Try it.
Child B:	I'll do it. (Jumps, just misses the child's hand)
Child A:	Wait. How about if I run and do it? (Backs away a few paces, gets a good running start, leaves the ground with just one foot. Touches the child's hand) I got it!
Child B:	No, but you didn't do it with one foot.
Child A:	Yes, I did. I ran with two feet, then I jumped with one feet.
Child B:	Let me try. (Successfully touches the child in the climber)

After the children experiment a while longer, the teacher suggests that they take turns up on the climber. She also poses new challenges: "Can you jump up with your eyes closed?" "Can you touch his hand when you're facing away from the climber?" ❖

This intervention has created a collaborative problem-solving experience. The children debate and discuss new approaches to the one-foot problem; even the child in the climber contributes by extending his hand further down.

Balance

As children grow taller, their center of gravity becomes lower, providing them with greater balance in motor activities (Lowrey, 1978). Balance is required for many games; children often engage in play in which their "vestibular balance systems" are tested, by deliberately causing themselves to be out of balance (Aldis, 1975). Examples are spinning around and around and then trying to walk, or sliding down a particularly slippery slide and then trying to regain balance at the bottom. Low balance beams and other equipment are useful for balance play. Many common playground materials lend themselves to balancing games.

Two children stand and bounce on one of several old tires that lie horizontally on the playground. A teacher approaches.

Teacher:	Here's a trick: Try to walk around the tire.
Child A:	Oh. Easy. (Begins to walk around the tire rim, stops when he gets to his peer who has not moved) Hazel! Move!
Child B:	All right. (Begins to move in the same direction as her peer)
Teacher:	Oh. And let's say there are sharks down there. (Points to the ground) If you step off the tire they might gobble you up. (Laughs)
Child B:	I see a shark. (Points between the tires, keeps walking in a circle)

Teacher: Do you think you could switch directions?

Child B: Sure. (Switches before her peer does; they bump into each other and almost fall off) Whoa! Close one!

As the children walk round and round, the teacher continues to pose challenges: "Can you walk in opposite directions?" "Can you walk from one tire to another?" "Can you walk once around each tire without ever touching the ground?" "If you stand on this tire and Hazel stands on that one, can you touch one another without falling off?"   ❖

Here once again children solve motor-related problems posed by the teacher. Social interaction and collaboration are emphasized in these interchanges.

Riding Toys

"Big Wheels" and other riding toys are prevalent in day-care centers and preschools. By five years of age, children become proficient at riding them (Elkind & Weiner, 1978). Most children learn riding skills through self-directed practice; no amount of adult instruction will be successful if children are not motorically ready. Teachers can give pointers to children who are having difficulty getting started on a riding toy. Very young children may be encouraged to straddle a riding toy and simply walk along with it, ignoring the pedals altogether for a time. This will help children to learn to manipulate handlebars and give feelings of confidence. Children who cannot reach the pedals may be given block extenders to allow them to reach. Once children are riding, providing large and interesting riding spaces are most important for ensuring development of riding abilities.

Teachers can encourage experimentation on riding toys, as the following vignette illustrates.

❖ ❖

Two children are riding round and round a small concrete patio on the playground. A teacher decides to challenge their riding skills.

Teacher: Would you like an obstacle course to ride through?

Child A: What?

Teacher: I could put these milk cartons down. You'd have to ride around them. Want to try?

Children: (In unison) Yeah.

The teacher places the cartons on the riding surface and shows the children the "course." Once they understand how to weave in and out of the cartons, the teacher makes the course more challenging. After many minutes she offers another suggestion.

Teacher:	You can change the course any way you like. Move the cartons around so that the course is really hard.
Child A:	We can put 'em any way?
Child B:	Yeah, look. Let's put these real close together. We'll never get through there. (Laughs)

Together the children design a new course. After riding on it for several minutes they collaborate on another design. The teacher withdraws; then returns to suggest a new element—she provides cardboard and markers for the children to make signs. The children incorporate road signs—"Stop," "Danger," and "One Way"—into their next course. ❖

The teacher has initiated a new riding game that promotes motor play, social interaction, and experimentation with spatial design. She eventually integrates writing into the activity; many motor games can be adapted to include literacy experiences.

Reacting

Reaction time is important in many childhood pastimes. Traditional games such as musical chairs, "red light, green light," even "slapjack," require quick motoric reactions to stimuli. Reaction time is composed of two components—movement time, which is the time between the beginning and end of a movement; and decision time, which is the time between the presentation of a stimulus and the start of the movement (Surwillo, 1971). Practice at quick movement is not all that is required for developing reaction time; children must have experiences in which they see or hear a stimulus and then quickly judge how to react. In musical chairs, for example, not only do children need to be quick sitters; they must notice that the music has stopped and decide instantly where they will sit. As children develop from toddlerhood into the early elementary years, reaction time diminishes significantly (Connolly, 1970).

Opportunities abound for challenging children's reaction time—and particularly thinking time—in spontaneous classroom activities. In the following vignette, the teacher guides open-ended free play into a reaction-time game.

❖ ❖

Four six-year-old children are "running races" on the playground. One child says "Go!" and all race off across the grass. There is very little concern about winners and losers; the experience of running and giggling together seems to be all that is important. Several children now announce they are tired of running; it appears that this play theme will soon dissolve. A teacher steps in to revive it.

| Teacher: | Let's play that stop and go game. Remember? You run as fast as you can when I yell "go." But when I yell "stop" you freeze in your tracks. |

Child A:	Like "red light, green light." I been playing this.
Teacher:	Yes. But you don't have to go back if you accidentally move after I've said "stop."
Child B:	What happens if you move?
Teacher:	Well, what do you think should happen?
Child C:	I know. If you are still moving when you yell "stop" then you have to go backwards next time. Like if you yell "stop" and Meredith keeps going, you know? Then she has to turn around and run like this (demonstrates running backwards) next turn.
Child D:	Yeah. And after *that* if you don't stop you need to kind of crawl. (Laughs)
Child B:	(Laughs) And after *that* you like roll around in the grass.
Teacher:	All right, guys. I get the idea. Let's play. Ready? (The teacher waits a full minute as the children giggle and fidget in anticipation) Go! (Then immediately) Stop!
Child A:	Ah! I moved! That's too fast. You have to say it slower.
Child B:	Yeah. Like say, "Go!" (Waits a few seconds) "Stop!" Like that.
Teacher:	I tricked you, didn't I? But you need to run backwards now.

The teacher continues the game, varying the intervals between "gos" and "stops"—sometimes starting and stopping the group immediately, other times leaving long intervals for running. Now and then she will follow a "stop" with another "stop" to throw players off. Giggling and friendly, half-hearted protesting abound.   ❖

The game the teacher has initiated here requires quite different abilities than simple racing. Not only must children move quickly in order to play well; they must hear and interpret the signal, deciding in an instant whether to move their bodies or hold still. Such "freeze" games can be played throughout the school day inside and out and have been used by more than one teacher as an enjoyable quieting technique at group time.

A Word About Safety

Many of the interventions described here encourage children to be active, spontaneous, even "rough" in their play. It has been argued that such open-ended, free experimentation with one's body is most useful for motor development. Such play can also lead to injury if not carefully supervised. As teachers reduce their direct guidance of children's activities on the playground, as has been recommended here, they must be careful not to reduce supervision as well. Teachers must position themselves close to children engaged in active play and must be watchful for the presence of unsafe conditions (e.g., throwing hard objects, using sticks or other sharp materials, playing too near to unprotected areas, crashing riding toys together at high speeds). Regular teacher interventions to remove potential hazards is very appropriate; independent play is actually enhanced when the environment is kept safe.

Fine Motor Development

Most discussions and examples in this chapter have centered on large muscle development. This is not to minimize the importance of developing fine motor skills; however, the reader may have come to realize that these skills have already been addressed often in earlier chapters. Children refine small muscle coordination when they handle books, turn the pages, or point to print and pictures as suggested in Chapter 5. When children handle small movable objects or build with blocks, as described in Chapter 6, they coordinate fine muscle movements with visual perception. Science experiences recommended in Chapter 7 often require the manipulation of small objects. Playing rhythm instruments or performing finger plays can also provide fine motor practice. Of course, there is no more useful fine motor activity than drawing, sculpting, or painting in the art area, as highlighted in Chapter 8. Adult interventions that encourage these activities are most important in fine motor development.

One fine motor experience that requires special consideration is dressing. When children zip, tie, take off, tuck in, pull on, roll up, snap, clasp, buckle, or button their clothing, they are engaged in a truly authentic fine motor task. Crayons and puzzle pieces provide playful practice at small object manipulation; clothing poses a real life challenge. Dressing is one of the first self-care responsibilities children are given. Dressing is serious business.

Frequently, children love to dress themselves. Undressing is also enjoyable, if not inconvenient for teachers who must find discarded clothing after nap time or during outdoor play. Conflict arises when children wish to tackle dressing tasks they are not yet able to perform. Teachers will frequently encounter children who insist on zipping a jacket or tying shoes independently, even though these tasks are beyond their abilities. One child was observed sitting in a cubbie room during the entire outdoor play at a child-care center because he refused to let others help zip his coat, but couldn't do it himself.

Vygotsky's (1962, 1978) framework for giving children assistance is especially useful when deciding how to intervene in such difficulties. He suggests that children be encouraged to do as much as they can do on their own. Some tasks may be performed independently; to give responsibility to children for snapping, buttoning, or fastening, when they can do these things, is important for self-image and also for fine motor development. When children run into difficulties completing dressing tasks, he suggests scaffolding strategies. In some cases a "Let me get you started" response may be in order; other times an "I'll do this part, you do that part" approach is more appropriate. Each will be described here.

"Let Me Get You Started."

Vygotsky has said that hints, prompts, and subtle guidance will help children who are confronted with some challenging tasks. The vignette below demonstrates this kind of interaction.

A child cannot get his coat zipped. Others in the child-care center have dressed themselves and are leaving for the playground. The child is clearly upset that he cannot manage his own zipper. A teacher assists.

Child:	I just can't get this. I need to zip. But it's kinda not working quite right.
Teacher:	Do you need help?
Child:	No. I can zip. It's just not working.
Teacher:	I know. I'll just start it for you. You can zip most of it.
Child:	All right. You do just a little.
Teacher:	(Connects the two sides of the zipper) There. I just got you started.
Child:	(Zips his coat up) There. Got it. ❖

Many four- and five-year-olds have difficulty with zippers that separate completely (Schickedanz, Schickedanz, & Forsyth, 1982). Even older children with special needs may need assistance zipping clothing (Fallen & Umansky, 1985). The teacher in this vignette gives just a little assistance, while helping the child maintain feelings of competence.

"I'll Do This Part; You Do That Part."

Sometimes dressing tasks are insurmountable. Long, frustrating, unsuccessful attempts will not lead to fine motor development and could inhibit positive self-concept. In these cases, teachers should complete these for children. This can be done in ways that help children maintain views of self-competence, as the following vignette shows.

A child attempts to tie laces on her snow boots. She becomes angry when she can't succeed. A teacher moves over to help.

Child:	I don't see how mom and daddy can make those bows.
Teacher:	In their shoes?
Child:	Yeah. They just wiggle and wiggle their hands like this. (Twists the laces together) Then they have a bow. But I don't have a bow. (Continues twisting the laces)

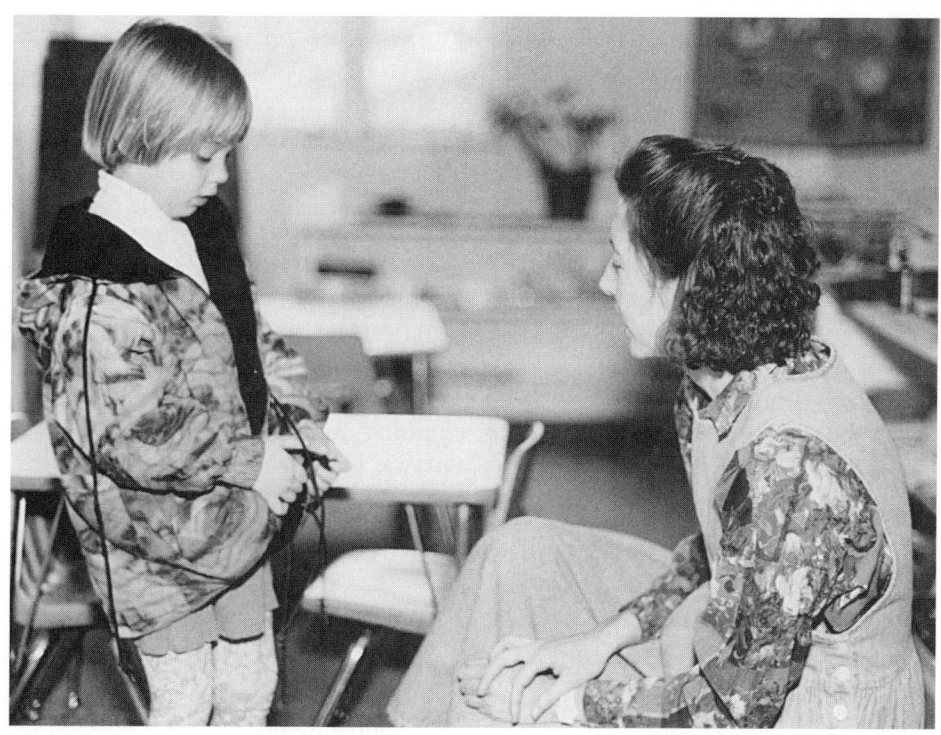

"I'll get it started for you, then you can zip it up." Encouraging children to do as much as they can for themselves will foster fine motor development and autonomy.

Teacher:	Yes, it's very hard to tie your shoes so that you get a bow. It took me many years to learn. I was much older than you before I could do it. You can snap your coat, though. I've seen how well you can do that. Why don't I tie your shoes; you snap your coat.
Child:	(Reflects a moment) Together?
Teacher:	What?
Child:	We do it together? I snap my coat and you tie my shoes? We do it at the same time?
Teacher:	Yes. (Ties her shoes quickly while the child snaps her coat)
Child:	All done, I guess. But I still don't know how they get that bow. ❖

Here the teacher has directly completed a needed task but has taken great care to preserve feelings of competence.

Other self-help tasks besides dressing afford fine muscle experiences—washing hands, scrubbing tables, brushing teeth, pouring juice, and brushing hair are examples. Encouraging independent action in these activities may be the most authentic way to enhance small motor development.

Summary

There is much debate about the role of the teacher in motor development. Some authors have argued that children simply mature physically and that adults have little impact on the development of motor abilities. Others have suggested that teachers can directly train children in motor skills. Modern approaches to motor education recognize the influence of both environment and maturation. Recent research suggests that motor development is enhanced when adults intervene in spontaneous free play activities and pose problems, ask questions, or increase activity level. These interventions may be initiated within organized, adult-guided activities, although informal guidance may also be as useful. When teachers join children's rough and tumble play; suggest new elements to chasing, climbing, or throwing games; or assist in real-life self-help tasks; they may be more effective in promoting motor growth than when planning organized teacher-directed games.

Suggested Activities

1. Observe teachers and children on a playground. Write an analysis of your observations guided by the following questions:

   a. Describe the games and activities of children. What motor areas were exercised as they played? What portion of these activities were adult directed? What portion involved informal adult intervention? What portion were purely child-initiated without any adult involvement?

   b. Describe adults' interventions in children's play. To what degree did they pose challenges, ask questions, or in other ways enrich children's activities? Was the level of adult intervention optimal? Was there too much or not enough? Was adult intervention only reserved for trouble-shooting or "correcting" misbehavior?

   c. What recommendations would you give to teachers you observed in regard to motor intervention?

2. Play with children on a playground. As you do, practice one or more intervention strategies described in the chapter. Write an analysis of your experiences guided by the following questions:

   a. Describe the intervention strategies you used. To what degree did you pose challenges or motor problems? To what degree did you initiate make-believe or rough and tumble play elements? To what degree did you suggest adaptations of games to promote motor skills learning?

   b. How did children react to your interventions? To what degree did their activity levels increase? To what degree were more complex or imaginative movements encouraged? To what degree did your interactions lead to less play or activity level?

c. Which were your most successful interventions? your least successful? What were features that made these more or less successful?

3. Spend a significant amount of time in a "cubbie" or coat room helping children get ready for outdoor play (helping children get ready for nap or lunch are alternatives). Practice assisting children in performing fine motor self-help skills. Practice "scaffolding"—encouraging independence when appropriate, giving hints or even performing tasks for children when needed. Reflect upon your experience, or better yet videotape these interactions. Write an analysis of this experience guided by the following questions:

a. Which self-help tasks could children perform on their own? Which were difficult for them? What specific motor skills were practiced as children performed these?

b. How would you characterize your role during this experience? To what degree were you an uninvolved observer? To what degree did you give pointers, hints, or minor assistance? To what degree did you need to complete tasks for children?

c. What were children's responses to your interventions? To what degree did they accept or even invite your assistance? To what degree did they resist? Were you successful in helping all children to feel competent? How did you accomplish this?

Further Reading

Coleman, M., & Skeen, P. (1985). Play, games, and sport: Their use and misuse. *Childhood Education, 61*, 192–198.

Frost, J. L., & Klein, B. L. (1979). *Children's play and playgrounds*. Boston: Allyn and Bacon.

Frost, J. L., & Sunderlin, S. (1985). (Eds.). *When children play*. Wheaton, MD: Association for Childhood Education.

Gallahue, D. L. (1982). *Understanding motor development*. New York: Wiley.

Kelly, N. T., & Kelly, B. J. (1985). *Physical education for preschool and primary grades*. Springfield, IL: Charles C. Thomas.

Miller, K. (1989). *The outside play and learning book: Activities for young children*. Mount Ranier, MD: Gryphon House.

Poest, C. A., Williams, J. R., Witt, D. D., & Atwood, M. E. (1992). Challenge me to move: Large muscle development in young children. *Young Children, 45*(5), 4–10.

Stillwell, J.L. (1987). *Making and using creative play equipment*. Champaign, IL: Human Kinetics.

10

SUPPORTING EMOTIONAL DEVELOPMENT THROUGH POSITIVE CLASSROOM MANAGEMENT

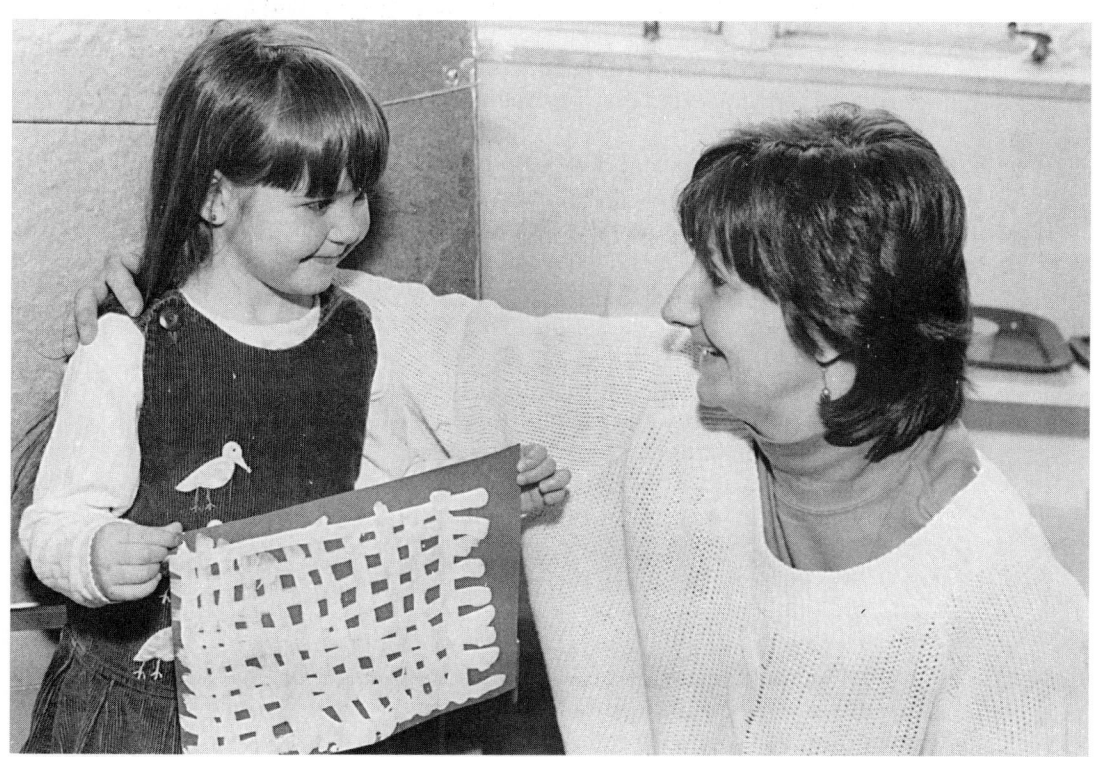

Five-year-old Jonathan announces at group time that tomorrow he will be going to the doctor "to get shots." Probing further, the teacher learns that he will be receiving a number of immunizations in preparation for his enrollment in public school. During free-play time, the teacher places a variety of medical props in the dramatic play area. She invites this child and several others to play with her there. The children immediately organize a medical play theme; Jonathan insists upon being the doctor.

"We'll give some shots to these guys, all right?" he suggests, pointing to two dolls. "They need to get some shots so they will stay well." He says this in an adult tone suggesting that he is repeating an explanation his parents have given him.

Jonathan begins to give injections to the dolls. He produces make-believe crying noises indicating that his patients are upset. The teacher moves over to him now and asks, "Why are they crying so loudly?"

"They got shots. They have sore arms. See?" He holds up one of the dolls, rubs its arm. "They are very, very sore."

"Yes, shots hurt for a little while. Then the hurting stops."

Jonathan now says to the dolls, "We have to give some more shots. There are lots and lots. And a blood test."

"Are your patients children? Are they getting immunizations for school?" the teacher asks.

"Yep. Now, let's do this blood test." He uses a syringe to pretend to draw blood from the doll.

"How do you think these children are feeling about all of these injections?"

"They're very sore. And they're afraid because all their blood might come out."

"Is that what they think?"

"Yeah. All the blood just goes out in the shot."

"May I be the nurse? I'd like to talk to your patients and help them not be so afraid." The teacher now speaks to the dolls in a gentle tone: "I know you are afraid to get shots. They hurt for a little while but they stop hurting. And in a blood test they only take a little bit of your blood; not all of it."

Jonathan now addresses the dolls in an adult tone as well: "Yeah. They can't really take all the blood. Don't worry. Don't cry."

"It's okay to cry, though, if you want. Shots do hurt," the teacher adds.

"Yeah. You can cry too. Okay, now I have to give you the next shot." Jonathan gives another make-believe injection.

The teacher plays with Jonathan for several more minutes, then withdraws. Jonathan spends most of his morning with the medical props and even brings one of the plastic syringes to lunch with him.   ❖

It is evident from the above vignette that play allows children to explore emotions and to gain mastery over anxieties and feelings of powerlessness. Playing the role of doctor, for example, allows Jonathan to "act out" an upcoming troublesome event, and explore feelings associated with it. As the doctor, he is the one in control; he is no longer the powerless recipient of painful medical procedures as in real life. Play often restores feelings of self-control and competence in this way.

The teacher plays an important role in this play episode. Through carefully phrased questions, she has elicited verbalization of fears and concerns about medical encounters. She has unearthed Jonathan's misconceptions about blood tests and, through make-believe, dispelled them. Generally, the teacher both encourages open-ended expression of feelings and provides more accurate information about worrisome events. Such interchanges can be initiated across the curriculum; skillful teacher intervention can contribute to healthy emotional growth.

The purpose of this chapter is to describe specific ways that teachers can intervene in children's classroom activities to enhance emotional development and mental health. In the first section, strategies for promoting general feelings of security, autonomy, and competence will be examined. In the final section, strategies for helping children cope with stress and anxiety are presented.

Promoting Healthy Emotional Growth

Early childhood is a formative period for the development of positive feelings towards self, others, and the larger world. Children who are nurtured, encouraged, and accepted by adults and peers will be well-adjusted emotionally; those who are neglected or rejected can suffer social and mental health difficulties.

The work of Erik Erikson (1963, 1982) has long guided teachers, mental health professionals, and parents in understanding how to promote emotional well-being in children and adults. He has proposed eight "ages" through which humans must pass from birth to adulthood if they are to feel competent and self-fulfilled. These stages are presented in Table 10-1.

This chapter provides an in-depth discussion of each of Erikson's first four stages—those of early childhood. The emotional struggles between Trust versus Mistrust in infancy, Autonomy versus Shame and Doubt in toddlerhood, Initiative versus Guilt in the preschool years, and Competence versus Inferiority during school age will be considered. Interventions that guide children through each stage are suggested.

Trust

According to Erikson, each stage of emotional development is characterized by a conflict or struggle between two opposing emotional states—one positive, the other negative (see Table 10-1). These polar states push and pull at the individual, creating tension and posing unique interpersonal problems.

Table 10-1

Erikson's Eight "Ages" of Emotional Development

Stage	Approximate Age	Description
Trust vs. Mistrust	Birth to eighteen months	Children must come to trust that basic needs will be met by caregivers and that the world is a predictable and safe place. If not, feelings of mistrust in others and in the world will predominate.
Autonomy vs. Shame/Doubt	Eighteen months to three and one-half years	Children must acquire a sense of independence from parents and a belief that they can do things on their own. If children are overly restricted when asserting this independence, feelings of shame and doubts about their individuality will pervade.
Initiative vs. Guilt	Three and one-half to six years	Children must feel free to act, to create, to express themselves creatively, and to take risks. Children who are inhibited in these pursuits can become overwhelmed with guilt.
Industry vs. Inferiority	Six to twelve years	Children must come to feel competent in skills valued by society. They need to feel successful in relation to peers and in the eyes of significant adults. If they experience failure too often, they will come to feel inferior.

Source: Adapted from Erikson (1963)

In adolescence, for example, an internal struggle ensues between identity—that is, having a clear sense of being and purpose, and role confusion—a feeling of disorientation over one's own roles, values, and place in society. For Erikson, the primary psychological work of a particular stage is to resolve this emotional conflict in a mainly positive direction. Although humans never fully resolve the identity struggle and will always experience some role confusion, for example, healthy adolescents are those who are mainly successful in discovering their identities. The role of teachers, parents, and mental health professionals in this process is to assist children in striving toward positive emotional states that are critical to their particular stage of psychosocial development.

The first struggle of young children—the conflict of infancy—is between Trust and Mistrust. Emotionally healthy babies come to understand that they have nurturing, responsive caregivers who meet their basic needs. They come

Table 10-1
continued

Stage	Approximate Age	Description
Identity vs. Role Confusion	Adolescence	Adolescents must develop a clear sense of self. They must acquire their own unique roles, values, and place in society. If they are unable to piece together these elements into a coherent view of self, role confusion results.
Intimacy vs. Isolation	Young adulthood	Young adults must be willing to risk offering themselves to others. An inability to give to another can lead to feelings of isolation.
Generativity vs. Stagnation	Mature adult	Adults must gain a sense that they have contributed to the world in some lasting fashion. Through child-rearing, civic deeds, or paid work, they must come to feel they have in some way given to others. Those who do not achieve this sense may suffer stagnation—a sense that there is no direction or purpose to one's life.
Integrity vs. Despair	Older adult	Older adults must come to feel great satisfaction with the events and accomplishments of their lives. They must look back on their experiences with pride and acceptance. Those who cannot feel this satisfaction as life draws to an end suffer great despair.

to view the world as safe and predictable. They enter into trusting relationships with caregivers, and later with other human beings. "Security" is another word to describe this emotional state. Although humans always experience feelings of mistrust in which doubts about their relationships or the security of the world emerge, the emotionally healthy baby becomes mainly trusting of the world and the people within it.

Children who are abused or neglected, who do not have caregivers who respond to their needs, or in other ways have come to doubt the trustworthiness of the world, will not resolve this emotional conflict in a positive way. Their ability to enter into relationships may be impaired, and they may be wary of new situations or people. They may be unable to advance to later stages of psychosocial development, and so are more likely to suffer mental health problems later in life.

Concern about trust should not be limited to parents or caregivers of infants. Many children who enter day care, preschool, or school programs have not formed secure attachments to their parents and display signs of mistrust in interactions with peers (Thompson, 1988). This absence of trusting relationships has been linked to a variety of social and mental health difficulties (Erikson, Sroufe, & Egeland, 1985). Teachers must create classroom environments that foster feelings of trust among all children—particularly those who were deprived of secure relationships early in life. As a first step, teachers should strive to nurture strong bonds between themselves and their students (Balaban, 1985).

Nurturance

Several specific teacher behaviors can assist children in acquiring feelings of trust. Warm and friendly teachers provide children with a sense of comfort; when teachers smile, touch, even hug their students, a bond may form (Lay-Dopyera & Dopyera, 1987). Cautions about too much warmth are provided in Chapter 2. Teachers must be sensitive to the children's unique preferences in regard to touch and personal space (Irujo, 1988). Cultural differences in responses to warmth and touching, discussed in the next chapter, must be considered. Overall, however, research supports an optimal amount of warmth as a vehicle for fostering trust (Lay-Dopyera & Dopyera, 1987). The following vignette demonstrates the effects of nurturing behaviors with a child who avoids adult contact.

❖ ❖

Robert is a loner who rejects invitations to play from both peers and teachers. He engages in solitary activities; when other students get too close he can be aggressive. The teachers have been struggling for months to create bonds with Robert. Their strategy has been to have one teacher, to whom he responds most positively, maintain close though not imposing contact with him. On this day Robert is playing alone with Legos.

Teacher:	(Sits down near Robert; smiles. Begins to work with the Legos; says nothing)
Robert:	(Looks up. Returns to his work; says nothing)
Teacher:	(After many minutes. Using a gentle, quiet voice) You've been working for such a long time on that.
Robert:	(In a very quiet mumble) Yeah. It's . . . something.
Teacher:	Hmm . . . Let me take a look. (Moves close to Robert, gently puts a hand on his shoulder, studies his work)
Robert:	(Looks up and gives a half-smile) It's a kind of gun where you shoot light beams.
Teacher:	Oh? Tell me about it.

Robert:	(Reclines so that his back is resting against the teacher) Well, you know those spaceship kind of guns?
Teacher:	(Puts an arm around his shoulder, holds him lightly so that he does not feel confined) Oh. I think I know. I saw a movie, "Star Wars," where the characters would shoot these things.
Robert:	Yeah. That's what it's like.

The teacher remains in this position with Robert for many minutes, conversing with him for longer than she ever has before. Eventually he squirms away and returns to his work. ❖

This teacher has made a major breakthrough. By being physically present but unobtrusive, using a gentle, friendly manner and light touch, the teacher elicits the first physical warmth Robert has shown since he enrolled at the center. Later, Robert will come to trust other teachers in the center. Though he is never a "social butterfly," he will eventually form trusting relationships with staff and a few peers.

Responsiveness

In Chapter 2, responding was identified as one of the key play-intervention tools. Besides encouraging children to learn, this teacher behavior also enhances trust. If teachers respond with enthusiasm when students complete tasks, make verbal initiatives, or seek assistance, they strengthen bonds with them. Just as infants are more likely to become attached to adults who respond in interesting ways to their smiles, coos, or wiggles, so older children will come to recognize responsive teachers as those who genuinely care about them and their accomplishments (Ainsworth, 1973). In the vignette below, the connection between responsive teaching and attachment may be seen.

 ❖ ❖

Early one morning, a seven-year-old child who rarely speaks completes a drawing and holds it up without comment to show a teacher. The teacher recognizes an opportunity to make a contact and moves over to the area quickly.

Teacher:	(Smiles) There is certainly a lot of color in your drawing. You've used several different markers.
Child:	(Nods, says nothing)
Teacher:	I'd love to hear about your drawing if you'd like to tell me about it.
Child:	It's Ninja Turtles fighting. There's Michelangelo.
Teacher:	Why are they fighting?
Child:	(Smiles, establishes eye contact) They fight the evil Shredder.

They discuss the drawing several more minutes before the teacher moves on. Later in the day, this same child makes another contact, bringing his journal to show the teacher in the math center. The teacher excuses herself from an activity there in order to respond to the child's initiative. She is amazed that within one day the child has approached her twice.   ❖

This teacher's prompt and enthusiastic response has shown the child that she has a genuine interest in and respect for his accomplishments. The first encounter is reaffirming; the child chooses to make a similar contact after writing in his journal. Children become attached to adults who not only are warm, but also respond in interesting and authentic ways to their activities (Ainsworth, 1973).

Positive, Supportive Classroom Management

Another way teachers can create a secure environment and foster emotional bonds with their students is through positive and supportive classroom management techniques. A number of highly controlling and punitive discipline systems have been advocated in recent years (Canter, 1988). Research has shown that not only are these methods ineffective in managing classroom behavior but they may impair the process by which students become attached to their teachers (Hitz, 1988; Honig, 1985a, 1985b). More positive and supportive approaches to handling aggression and the violation of classroom rules have been recommended (DeVries, Haney, & Zan, 1991; Honig, 1985a, 1985b; Hendrick, 1992). Key elements of these strategies are presented in Table 10-2.

Inductive strategies involve teaching children about the purposes for rules and assisting them in reflecting about alternative classroom behaviors. An example is the following response to a block-throwing incident in a four-year-old class: "You can't throw the blocks because someone might get hurt. Feel how hard they are. What else could you do if you are angry, besides throwing the blocks?" Not only do such approaches increase the likelihood that rules will be internalized, but they also are less likely to lead to anger, hostility, and mistrust among children (Hoffman, 1975; Honig, 1985a, 1985b).

Proactive management strategies entail redirecting behavior in order to avoid difficulties before they arise. When a teacher sees a child about to misuse art materials, for example, a comment such as the following may settle the problem: "Let me show you how to use the playdough. Can you help me knead it? It's so hard." Before two angry toddlers break into a fight over a toy a teacher might say: "Jamie, there's a truck over here that would roll very well down your ramp. Let me show you." Such strategies help children construct an understanding of appropriate patterns of behavior and avert the need for punitive or negative reactions after misbehavior has occurred.

Positive, supportive discipline strategies include both inductive and proactive techniques, as described above, as well as other approaches where adults avoid physically (or even psychologically) controlling children's behavior. In Table 10-3, examples of controlling interventions and noncontrolling alternatives are presented.

Table 10-2
Elements of Positive Classroom Management

Element	Description	Example
Inductive classroom management	Management strategies that attempt to teach social understandings or support moral reasoning.	A child hits another on the playground. The teacher guides the child in thinking about the consequences of these actions: "What happened when you hit him? Do you see how he is crying? Hitting hurts; we can't let you hit because that hurts people. What would be another way to let him know you are angry?"
Proactive classroom management	Management strategies in which "trouble spots" are anticipated and addressed proactively. The teacher intervenes to head off classroom misbehavior before it occurs.	A particular child always becomes more aggressive late in the afternoon. Anticipating this, a teacher is always assigned to engage her in art or construction play activities—her greatest play interests—right after nap time before any aggression can occur.
Non-controlling management	Management strategies in which behavior is not controlled externally. The teacher gives the child responsibility for resolving a problem.	A child is being very disruptive at group time. A teacher calmly gives the child a choice: "You can stay here with us in group, but you will need to stop being so silly. Or you can do something else in the classroom. It may be you just don't feel like sitting in the group today. You can choose."

In each example, coercion is replaced with reasoning, gentle guidance, and choice-giving. These are kinder, quieter, less public techniques that help children to feel safe and cared for even though teachers may disapprove of their behavior. Generally, calm, rational, and gentle reactions to misbehavior will contribute to feelings of trust; shouting and scolding will not.

Consistent, Predictable Classroom Environments

Feelings of trust stem not just from warm relationships with adults, but from a knowledge that the world is predictable and constant. When children are unsure from day to day who will care for them, where they will spend their time, or even when their caregivers will return, feelings of trust are threatened. Teachers can provide a classroom that is a constant and predictable place—a place children can count on—by adhering to a predictable routine, setting consistent limits, and minimizing sudden and dramatic classroom changes. When children are new to a classroom, for example, teachers might reassure them of the events of the day that lead up to their parents' return to pick them up. In the vignette below, a child is soothed by such reassurance.

Table 10-3
Alternatives to Coercive/Controlling Management Strategies

Coercive/Controlling Strategy	Alternative
Giving a child "time out" for riding the "big wheel" too fast after she was asked not to.	Engaging the child in a conversation about the dangers of "big wheel" riding. Asking: "What can we do to help children remember that going too fast is dangerous?" Based on the child's suggestion, having the child construct a warning sign in the art center.
Separating two children who are fighting over a car in the block area.	Sitting with the two children for a short while and facilitating a conversation about the conflict. Asking for their suggestions for resolution: "You both want to use the car. What can we do about that?" Leaving them alone in the block area so that they can attempt to resolve the difficulty themselves.
Making a child leave the art area immediately after she has thrown clay.	Giving a child a choice: "You're making quite a mess here. The clay is all over the floor now. I will give you a choice: You can play with the clay without throwing it, or you can leave this area and do something else. It would be nice for you to make something here with the clay. But it's your choice."

A four-year-old child who is spending his first day at the day-care center has just asked a teacher for the third time when his mother will return. His mother will pick him up at 4:30; it is now just 10:30 in the morning.

Teacher: Let me tell you about all the things we will do today before your mother comes. First we will play. Then we'll have a story. You can sit right on my lap while I read. After the story we eat a snack.

Child: Snack?

Teacher: Yes. We're having celery and peanut butter, I think. Have you had that at home?

Child: Yeah.

Teacher: After snack we'll play some more until lunch. After lunch we'll take a rest—remember I showed you the cots we use?

Child: Yeah. And then is Mommy coming?

Teacher: Well, first, when you wake up from your nap we'll have another snack.

Child: Will it be celery?

Teacher: Crackers and cheese, I think.

Child: I have that at home.

Teacher: Then we'll play just a little more. And then your mother will come.

The child seems satisfied with this explanation and leaves the teacher at last to play in the blocks. Regularly, the child returns to the teacher to review the day's events again.   ❖

This teacher is very patient in reviewing and re-reviewing daily events, recognizing that the child needs to come to trust that classroom routines—particularly pick-up time—will be followed as planned.

Facilitating Separation

The above vignette shows that trust is often threatened when children are first separated from their parents for extended periods. Teachers can do much to ease separation by providing the warm and nurturing interactions described above. Although one approach to first days at school has been to encourage parents to say a quick goodbye and depart without fanfare, some writers question whether this is the best approach for long-range emotional well-being (Balaban, 1985; Bloom-Feshbach, Bloom-Feshbach, & Gaughran, 1980; Hock, McKenry, Hock, Triolo, & Stewart, 1980).

The goal during periods of separation should be to help both parents and children to come to trust caregivers and this new environment. From this perspective, separation should not be a rushed affair. It takes time for bonds to form. Parents can be invited to visit for long portions of several days (perhaps even a week, if this is possible) at the beginning of school. They can get to know their children's teachers and classroom routines in this way. This trust will lead them to be less anxious and ambivalent themselves when eventually separating from their children. Transitions to new classrooms are always smoother when children are accompanied by people familiar to them for a significant period of time (Bronfenbrenner, 1979).

Once separation has occurred, a gentle and nurturing response is required so that a firm bond forms between the child and the teacher (Balaban, 1985). Crying should be treated with patience and warmth; upset children should not be discouraged from expressing emotion or be asked to sit away from the group because they are "disturbing others." Discussing objects and events that remind them of home (rather than trying to distract them from thinking about their families—a common practice in some schools and centers) will help soothe the child and lead to attachment. One teacher, for example, was observed spending many minutes with a child talking about her lunch; it contained familiar objects reminiscent of home and was "made by mommy."

Autonomy

Once children are trustful of adults and know that their basic needs will be met, they are willing to venture out away from the safety of parents and family. They now wish to become individuals apart from those to whom they have bonded. With this striving for individuality, children often assert themselves, rebel against rules, and assume a negative affect when confronted with adult control. These challenging, though necessary, characteristics are explained, according to Erikson (1963; 1982), by the next emotional conflict that humans encounter—that between autonomy versus shame and doubt. The emotionally healthy toddler gradually acquires a sense of autonomy—a feeling of individuality and uniqueness apart from parents. It has been argued that autonomy in both thought and action is the most important disposition for later learning and development (Kamii, 1982).

Children who are overly restricted or harshly punished for attempts at becoming individuals (e.g., toddlers who explore forbidden objects around the home and are subjected to incessant hand-slapping) will come to doubt their individuality, and suffer shame for their efforts. Gradually, such children can become timid, lack confidence in their abilities, and assume identities as mere extensions of their parents. Kamii (1982) argues that many preschool and elementary children are consumed by feelings of doubt, as they experience harsh and controlling adult authority both at home and in school.

Creating classroom environments in which children can become independent in thought and action contribute to feelings of autonomy; rigid, adult-directed classrooms where conformity is stressed can lead to shame and doubt (Kamii, 1982).

Encouraging Choice and Decision-Making

When children are encouraged to choose what they will do and when they will do it within a school day, they become more independent and show long-lasting intellectual advantages over peers in teacher-directed classrooms (Miller & Bizzell, 1983). Teachers can facilitate decision-making by structuring classrooms so that children make choices and regulate their own behavior and learning. Through carefully designed interventions, teachers can encourage doubtful children to assume greater independence. The following is an example of such an interchange.

A five-year-old has never been in an environment where choice was allowed. It is her first day in a child-centered kindergarten. Looking bewildered, she stands among the rich array of activity choices. A teacher chooses to guide her choice making.

Teacher:	Sheila, why don't we play together for a while.
Child:	Okay.
Teacher:	Why don't you decide which center we'll play in? Let me show you the choices. There's dramatic play, blocks, books . . .
Child:	(Interrupts) Books.
Teacher:	Okay. Let's read a little. (Leads the child over to the library center) What would you like to read?

Child:	Um . . . (Stands silently scanning the books)
Teacher:	Let me show you some of my favorites. You can pick. There's "Where the Wild Things Are." This is one of my favorites . . . (The teacher now removes four additional books from the shelf, enthusiastically introducing each to the child in this same manner)
Child:	Oh. I'll take this one. (Selects a book, sits on the teacher's lap to read) ❖

The teacher assists this child in decision-making by encouraging independent choices but also by limiting the overwhelming selection to a more manageable size.

Some children regularly will need this kind of support in choice making. They may be observed spending large amounts of time considering alternative activities or "flitting" from one area of the classroom to another, unable to make a decision about what to do. In one study it was found that children who have difficulty making decisions about activities often end up doing nothing at all (Trawick-Smith, 1992).

Such children may not have been provided experience in making decisions either at home or in previous school settings. Adults may have made all choices for them; they may have become dependent on parents or teachers to guide their decisions. With the kind of support illustrated in the vignette above such children eventually may be able to select from a larger array of activities; the need for teacher assistance will gradually diminish.

Occasionally, teachers are confronted with children whose strong feelings of autonomy create a challenge. It is difficult, when dealing with such children, not to resort to the controlling adult behaviors with which most of us grew up. Nurturing, rather that stifling individuality, however, is important for all children. In the vignette below, a teacher encourages a particularly autonomous child to regulate her own behavior.

❖ ❖

A young five-year-old has announced loudly that she does not wish to attend group time on a given morning. This has never happened before in this classroom; until now all children have been excited about this whole class meeting.

Teacher:	Why have you decided not to join us, Samantha?
Child A:	Well, I just can't today. I want to do some other things.
Teacher:	Oh? What do you have planned?
Child A:	Oh. Just gonna draw a little over here. (Points to the art center)
Teacher:	We would miss you if you didn't join us. But if you choose to work on art instead, that will be fine.
Child A:	Yep. (Moves to the writing center)

Some children need guidance in deciding what activities to pursue.

As the teacher calls the group together, several other children notice that Child A is not joining them.

Child B: Why isn't Samantha coming? (To Child A) Samantha, it's group time.

Child A: (Shakes her head, says nothing, continues with her drawing)

Teacher: Samantha has decided she will not attend our group today.

Child B: Oh. I'm not coming either. Can I go over with Samantha?

Teacher: Are you sure you don't want to join us? I'll be reading an interesting story today.

Child B: No. Can I go? (Points to where Child A is working)

Teacher: All right. If you wish. Maybe you could listen to the story from over there while you draw.

Eventually, two other children also decide not to attend group time. The teacher proceeds with her group activities; the four absentees play quietly, stopping now and then to listen in from a distance. On the next day all four children choose to join the group meeting again. ❖

Many teachers would have insisted on Samantha's attendance at group time. After all, a lot of hard work has gone into planning creative and meaningful experiences. Shouldn't all children enjoy the benefit of these? Also, what would happen if all students en masse boycotted group meetings?

This teacher, however, recognizes this child's need to be alone and respects her decision not to attend. Even when several other children follow suit, the teacher continues to support this autonomy. She has given a powerful message in doing so: Children have control over their lives in this classroom; their personal decisions are trusted and respected. No group time activity could provide such a valuable lesson.

Encouraging Autonomy in Personal Care

Throughout the school day, there are opportunities to encourage autonomy in personal care. When children are eating, toileting, dressing for outdoor play, getting ready for nap, or cleaning up their classroom, teachers can encourage autonomy. Although children should not be pressured to perform tasks for which they are not ready, the adage, "never do anything for a child that she/he could do independently," is a good maxim for teachers to live by. A careful analysis of classroom life reveals many instances where teachers, due to tradition or convenience, perform personal care tasks for children that could be accomplished independently. Teachers should take care to respect children's accomplishments; re-doing cleaning jobs (e.g., wiping up a table in the presence of children who have just wiped it) or re-doing personal care tasks (e.g., retucking in a shirt after a child has just tucked it in) gives the message that ultimately adults must perform these tasks; children cannot care for themselves.

Encouraging children to take responsibility for their own care will give them feelings of power and control—components of the sense of autonomy that Erikson describes.

Encouraging Autonomy in Thought

Allowing children to move about the classroom, make choices, and care for themselves can go a long way toward enhancing autonomy. Kamii (1982) has argued, however, that it is autonomy in thought—that is, trusting one's own reasoning and problem solving—that is most useful for later development. When children are encouraged to choose among math activities but may use them only in one "right" way, when they are provided opportunities to manipulate science materials but must come to one "correct" conclusion following an experiment, when they may write anything they wish in journals but their handwriting is then corrected, autonomy is addressed in only a superficial way.

True autonomy involves thinking as well as acting on one's own. The antithesis of autonomous thought is a "right answers" curriculum in which work is continually corrected so that accurate knowledge is imparted.

Teacher interventions for encouraging autonomous thought are presented throughout this book, particularly in Chapters 5 and 6. An additional illustration is provided below.

❖ ❖

A doubtful five-year-old is composing a story at the writing center. Periodically she stops, carries her paper over to a teacher in the science area and asks, "Is this how you write it?" or "Did I spell this right?" The teacher finally moves over to her at the writing table.

Teacher:	You can write your story any way you wish, Jamie. Just write an interesting story.
Child:	But I can't write so good.
Teacher:	Jamie, your stories are exciting and funny. I love reading them.
Child:	But my brother says I can't spell good.
Teacher:	You know I can read anything you write. You write your own way. Your brother writes differently because he's much older than you. Just keep writing how you wish. You're a creative author.
Child:	All right. But I still can't write good. ❖

This child has come to doubt her writing competence because of criticism from a family member. She is reluctant to trust her own writing abilities and to take risks. The teacher does his best to nurture a sense of autonomy; he is imparting in his interactions the message that you do not always need an adult standing over you, correcting or accepting your work, in order to accomplish things. Many more such interchanges are needed, however, before this doubtful child is convinced.

Autonomy and Classroom Management

One way to promote autonomy is to establish a classroom management system that gives children control and choice. This is not to say that children should be allowed to behave in any way they wish. Rules must be established in order to protect the rights of students in the classroom. A minimum number of rules—those truly necessary for physical and emotional safety—should be created; teachers should avoid setting petty limits that have no true purpose. Within these limits, children must be free to explore, express themselves, and resolve their own problems. They should have input into governance of the classroom.

Children can be involved in making classroom rules. DeVries and Kohlberg (1990) have suggested that democratic classroom meetings be held in which rules are written and regularly reviewed by children themselves. Teachers take a turn in such discussions and may add rules to the list or raise questions about unreasonable rules suggested by children. Devries and Kohlberg recommend that children also assist in establishing consequences for violations of rules. Research shows that not only are children more likely to adhere to student-generated rules, but they gain feelings of autonomy as they participate in such decision-making (Devries & Kohlberg, 1990; DeVries, Reese-Learned, & Morgan, 1991).

The following vignette highlights benefits as well as challenges in implementing such a system.

❖ ❖

A group of four-year-olds will be taking a bus trip to the library. At group time, the teacher presents a large sheet of paper and suggests that children dictate rules for behavior on the trip. The following rules are generated:

1. Be quiet.
2. Be nice to your friends.
3. Be nice to people.
4. Listen when the teacher's talking about something.
5. Look at books.

Many of these rules reflect children's many years of experience living under the unquestioned authority of adults (e.g., "Listen when the teacher's talking"). There is much debate in creating the rules; but eventually everyone is satisfied with the list. A child now offers a suggestion for consequences should a rule be violated.

Child A:	(In an adult tone) Now if you break one of these rules then . . . (thinks) you can't go home on the bus.
Teacher:	Let's think about that one. Do you all agree with Simon's idea?
Child B:	(Laughs) Then how would you get home?
Child A:	Well, your mother has to come.
Teacher:	That would be very hard, Simon. Your mother works at the bank. Lots of parents aren't at home during the day.
Child A:	Well, my mom can get out of work.
Teacher:	How would it feel not to be able to come back to school on the bus? What if you were too loud—that's rule number two—and so you couldn't come back with us?
Child A:	Maybe that won't be what happens.
Child C:	You'd be scared if you got left behind.
Child D:	What it should be is if you break one of these rules then someone tells you to stop.

Teacher: That's a thought. We could say, "You're being too loud. That breaks one of our rules. Please talk more quietly."

The children all agree on this less harsh consequence. The teacher notices that the field trip goes more smoothly than most. Children are quite conscientious in reminding one another of rules.   ❖

Another aspect of classroom management that facilitates autonomy is choice-giving, in which children are given opportunities to control their own behavior before adults impose sanctions. The teacher of this vignette demonstrates this approach.

A six-year-old is creating quite a disturbance in the block area. She is running wildly about shouting in a silly voice. She has knocked down a peer's building. The others in the block area are clearly annoyed by her behavior. A teacher moves into the area.

Teacher: (Quietly, calmly) Janette, you are being very loud and bothering other children. I'm going to give you a choice. You can choose to play with blocks without being loud and knocking others' blocks down or you can choose to play in another part of the room. You can choose.

Child: All right. I'll play blocks.

Although the child continues to be silly as she builds, she is less loud and is now careful to avoid bumping into peers' work. The teacher does not intervene further.   ❖

Here the teacher sees the need to intervene firmly in order to maintain a positive classroom environment and to ensure safety. Rather than imposing a heavy-handed consequence, however, she gives the child a choice, allowing her to regulate her own behavior. If the child had continued to behave in inappropriate ways the teacher would simply remind the child that she had now made a choice: "I see you have chosen not to play without being loud and wild. You've chosen to leave the block area and play somewhere else."

Autonomy and Conflict Resolution

Teachers sometimes settle negative social interactions quickly by separating children, giving "time outs", or taking away toys that are at the center of disagreements. One of the least meaningful strategies for resolving disputes is insisting that one or both children say, "I'm sorry." DeVries and Kohlberg (1990) argue that when teachers use such strategies they may be depriving children of opportunities to solve social problems on their own. They suggest that teachers hold back when conflicts arise and observe to see whether these can be settled independently. When children successfully resolve peer disputes on their own, they gain a sense of autonomy as Erikson describes it.

If arguments become very heated or violence appears imminent, a teacher might choose to facilitate the interactions. DeVries, Reese-Learned, & Morgan (1991) argue that this is far different from separating or isolating the children involved; the teacher encourages them to continue interacting with one another in this approach. An illustration of such an intervention is presented below.

❖ ❖

Two five-year-old children have begun pushing each other in the sandbox on the playground. A teacher determines that the violence will escalate and moves over quickly.

Teacher:	(In a calm voice) My. What is going on over here?
Child A:	(Begins to cry) He wrecked my sand thing. (Now screaming at his peer) I hate you!
Child B:	(Tries to attack Child A; the teacher steps between) You stupid thing! You're stupid!
Child A:	(Begins to sob loudly; says nothing)
Teacher:	Let's just calm down here. Let's just sit here together a minute. (Sits down on the sandbox, helps the two children sit next to each other)
Child A:	Well, you didn't have to wreck my castle. I was working on it, ya know!
Child B:	I didn't wreck it, you stupid!
Teacher:	Tell Mark what you mean, Lawrence. He thinks you wrecked his castle. What do you mean, you didn't wreck it?
Child B:	Well, I just stepped back and then he started pushing me.
Teacher:	You stepped on his castle?
Child B:	I don't know.
Child A:	(Begins to cry again) You did. You wrecked it.
Teacher:	I can see you are very upset. But I don't think Lawrence even knew he stepped on your work.
Child A:	Well, he wrecked it.
Child B:	I didn't even see it.
Teacher:	(After a long pause) Well, what should we do here?
Child A:	(Gets up, moves back into the sandbox. Speaks angrily to Child B) Don't step on my things. Watch where you're going.
Child B:	(Watches a moment as Child A begins to dig in the sand. Finally moves back into the sandbox near him)

Within minutes the two children are playing together, talking and sharing sand toys as though nothing has happened. ❖

If the teacher above had just separated the two children, they would never have had an opportunity to express their anger or reflect on the events leading up to the dispute. Too, they would not have been able to resume their play together and re-establish their friendship. By giving them some control over settling the problem, the teacher has contributed to their feelings of autonomy.

Sometimes whole-class difficulties arise. DeVries argues that these can be resolved by children, as well, in whole class meetings. An example of this is provided below.

❖ ❖

A kindergarten teacher has chosen not to limit the number of children who may play in the block area. Her feeling is that rigid limits on numbers could inhibit social play. Too, she believes that when the area gets too crowded, children will have a useful social problem to solve. Such an opportunity has, indeed, arisen; children are complaining that they are knocking one another's buildings down. A group time discussion is held.

Teacher:	Well, I understand your concern about the blocks. What could we do about that?
Child A:	We should be careful not to knock down someone's building. Like you knocked mine down, Cheryl.
Child B:	But I didn't mean to. It was too crowded.
Teacher:	Would you want to make a limit on how many can play there? Would that help?
Child C:	No. Then everyone can't play. Let's make the block area a whole, whole lot bigger.
Teacher:	Well, that's one way.
Child D:	Yeah. That way we can play without knocking down blocks.
Teacher:	Well, I wonder if we have enough room to make it bigger.
Child E:	Sure. You can just push that shelf over. (Gestures toward the block area)
Child B:	Yep. Just move it over.
Teacher:	(Laughs) Well, at free play let's try to move things around.

Later, the teacher and some children enlarge the block area at the expense of the math center. The teacher is pleasantly surprised at the results. The change leads to higher quality play in the blocks without reducing children's involvement with math activities.   ❖

Here the teacher empowers the children to solve a classroom problem. Her expectation was that they would decide to limit the number of children at the block center. Although she has reservations about the solution they have come up with, she implements their plan and so has given a powerful boost to their feelings of autonomy.

A caution must be given about facilitating child-directed conflict resolution with highly aggressive children. Careful guidance and close supervision are needed when facilitating arguments among children who are violent. In some cases, the above strategies should not be attempted at all until a particular child has been provided individual or family therapy to address underlying sources of hostility.

Initiative

During the preschool years, children who have previously developed a strong sense of autonomy desire to take action and assert themselves. They want to create, to invent, to pretend, to take risks, and to engage in lively and imaginative activities with peers. This urge to make creative efforts has been called "initiative" by Erikson (1963). When adults encourage these divergent activities and avoid criticism or excessive restriction, the sense of initiative will grow; guilt arises when children are led to believe their efforts are wrong. This struggle between initiative and guilt explains why preschool and kindergarten children are so energetic in pursuit of imaginative play activities. It also explains how some children come to view themselves as "bad" or "naughty." Although feelings of guilt have a positive role in development in that they lead children to assume responsibility for their own behaviors, overwhelming guilt can inhibit emotional growth. Children who are punished or criticized for their efforts will gradually stop pursuing them and will construct understandings of themselves as bad people. Erikson suggests that adults can promote a sense of initiative by creating noncritical environments in which children may take risks. Encouragement of creative processes with less emphasis on finished products will also facilitate initiative.

Modeling and Encouraging Creative Attempts

Teachers can encourage creative efforts in a variety of ways. Providing and enriching divergent activities such as dramatic play, art, block building, or writing, which have been described in other chapters, can lead to initiative. As children engage in these activities, teachers can both model and encourage highly creative behavior. In the following vignette a teacher uses humor to demonstrate creative thinking.

❖ ❖

A teacher sits in the book area reading to a small group of three-year-olds. The children have heard three books now; they are showing signs of losing interest. The teacher begins to adapt the book as he reads. The children gradually notice that he is not reading the original text.

Teacher: (In a book-reading voice) On Wednesday the caterpillar ate some avocado pizza from Papa Gino's. But he was still hungry.

Child A:	Wait. Where does it say that?
Teacher:	(Laughs. Keeps reading) On Thursday the caterpillar ate some green noodle stew with just a little applesauce and chocolate sprinkles.
Child B:	No. That's not how it goes.
Child C:	No, wait. Let me read. (Takes the book from the teacher) On Thursday he ate . . . he ate some bug sauce. (Giggles)
Child A:	(Laughing at his peer's joke) No. No, Kyle. He ate stinky spaghetti. (Laughs even harder)
Child B:	No. He ate some ice cream and peanut butter. (Laughs)
Teacher:	Now let me read the rest. (Takes the book back) And after a while the caterpillar decided to play with his toys. But he didn't. Do you know why?
Children:	(Together, with looks of anticipation) Why?
Teacher:	(In a dramatic voice) Because caterpillars don't have toys. (Laughs)

The teacher and children continue to invent silly words to the story for several more minutes. When the teacher leaves, the children continue to joke and giggle until snack time. ❖

At first glance, this might appear to be a particularly absurd way for a teacher to act. These interactions, however, are purposeful. They give children the message that wide-open, even silly initiatives are appropriate in the classroom; that even adults sometimes engage in purely divergent behaviors.

By responding with enthusiasm to children's divergent ideas, a sense of initiative is fostered. Too often children are encouraged to get the right answer or perform tasks in just one way; they may come to feel guilty about diverging from norms or expectations. When teachers accept and even celebrate nonconformity they help build a sense of initiative, as the vignette below reveals.

A seven-year-old child asks a teacher to read a book she has written in invented spelling. The teacher reads it aloud to the author and several other children.

Teacher:	I love reading your books, Julia. Let me read it to all of you. (Opens the book) "Once there was a princess who hated dragons so badly . . ." (Reads many pages of the book)
Child:	(Giggles as the teacher comes to a particular place in her story) This is a really funny part.
Teacher:	(Continues reading) " . . . and the dragon chased her around and around . . ." (Turns the page) "And the princess said, 'Oh no. I have to go back and get my cigarettes.'"

Child: (Giggling loudly) She has cigarettes!

All the children who are listening roll on the floor laughing. The teacher laughs along. Eventually the laughter subsides.

Teacher: You know what I love about this book? You read along and it's a very serious adventure. Then you turn the page and there's a very funny part.

Child: It's a surprise kind of book.

Had the teacher shown some dismay that the child's book took a peculiar turn or had he engaged in a serious discussion about the harmful effects of cigarettes, the child could have come to feel guilty about this creative attempt. Instead, the teacher encourages creative thought; these interactions will inspire the child to take further risks in the future.   ❖

Emphasizing Attempts, Not Finished Products

Hendrick (1992) has noted that young children are "better planners and starters than they are finishers" (p.114). Children striving toward a sense of initiative are centered on what they will do and how they will act, not on how things turn out in the end. Cautions about product-oriented art or right-answer-oriented tasks, presented in previous chapters, should be carefully heeded particularly at this stage of emotional development. Teachers should respond to actions, not outcomes; they should encourage open-ended experimentation, not "correct" adult-selected responses. Being accepting of pure process in children's activities can be extremely challenging as the two vignettes below indicate.

Vignette 1

A primary teacher has been collecting art work from his students to display in the classroom for a parent open house. He tries to find colorful paintings that will make the environment look bright and alive. He notices that a child is now at the easel creating just the sort of richly textured work he is looking for. He approaches the child to ask if she will contribute her painting to the classroom display.

Teacher: Would you like me to hang your painting in the room when you are finished?

Child: Yes. Fine.

Teacher: Great. Let me know when you're finished. We'll hang it to dry, then put it up. You can pick a spot.

Child: (Nods. Continues painting)

The teacher leaves the area for a while. When he returns, he is startled to discover that the once-bright painting is now becoming slightly grey in color.

Child: I am going to use every color. See? (Dips her brush now into the black paint)

Teacher: Yes. Interesting.

Child: Here goes the black. (Adds black streaks to her painting)

The teacher shamefacedly admits to himself that he is disappointed that the bright painting that would have added such color to the classroom has now been transformed. He watches as she finishes her work, holding his tongue.

Child: All right. Done. Now where should we hang it?

Vignette 2

A four-year-old approaches a teacher who is playing with other children in the dramatic play area. He asks for more paper at the art center; there are no more sheets, he informs her.

Teacher: Oh, Peter, that can't be. I put so many sheets out just this morning.

Child: It's gone. Come on. (Leads the teacher over to the art area)

There on the table the teacher sees at least thirty sheets of paper lying about; each has a single tiny scribble on it.

Child: See? I'm drawing. I used it all.

Teacher: Yes. You've been busy here.

The teacher places another stack of paper on a shelf in the art center and silently estimates the cost of the paper that will be used by the end of the morning. On the next day she brings many sheets of computer paper donated to the center to replace the more expensive brand.   ❖

These teachers feel the temptation to guide children toward more adult-pleasing end products. The first teacher desires a more aesthetic decoration for the classroom; the second is tempted to insist that a child "fill up" one sheet of paper before starting another drawing. In both instances the teachers resist the temptation; they appreciate the initiative reflected in each creative work. They allow the children to pursue their imaginative pursuits without restriction; in so doing they have enhanced a healthy sense of initiative.

Promoting Social Initiative

One way that initiative manifests itself in the developing child is through energetic interactions with peers. Once a child has a clear sense of autonomy, she feels a growing interest in reaching out to others, making social contacts, trying out social behaviors (Erikson, 1963). The healthy preschool child displays an eagerness to engage others; one who is burdened by guilt is more hesitant in social interactions and is more likely to be neglected by peers (Erikson, 1963). In Chapter 4 specific strategies for enhancing social participation and interpersonal skills are reviewed. The vignette below shows directly how such interventions can contribute to feelings of initiative.

❖ ❖

A five-year-old has appeared quite tentative in trying new materials, engaging in creative activities in the classroom, and interacting with peers. He is very hesitant on the playground, for example, avoiding loud and active games, taking risks on the climber, or chasing around with other children. He frequently stands near the teacher watching. When he does try activities he looks to the teacher regularly for assurance or approval.

On this warm summer afternoon on the playground, the teacher has just given children materials to blow bubbles. Most of the children are engaged in the activity, chasing after their bubbles, laughing, and talking. This particular child stands and watches. A teacher approaches.

Teacher:	(Presenting two bubble "wands") Chris, there's a great game you can play with these bubbles. Do you want to play?
Child A:	(Looks at the teacher with interest, says nothing)
Child B:	(Blowing bubbles) What is it? I'll play.
Teacher:	Chris and I can try to catch the bubbles you blow.
Child C:	(Moving over from another part of the playground) I'll do it too. Chris, you catch my bubble. (Blows a bubble and sails it in his direction)
Child A:	(Watches the bubble sail by, does not move. Looks to the teacher for encouragement)
Child C:	No, Chris. You catch them. See? (Blows a bubble and demonstrates catching it on his wand)
Teacher:	(To Child A) Isn't that amazing how it sticks without popping? (To Child C) Send us another one.

Child C blows another bubble; Child A very cautiously approaches and catches it. He now turns toward the teacher for a reaction.

Child A:	Look.
Teacher:	You caught it.
Child B:	Try and catch a whole lot of bubbles, Chris. (To Child C) Let's give Chris lots of bubbles. (Along with Child C, begins blowing many bubbles in Child A's direction, laughs as they land all around him) It's raining bubbles, Chris! (Laughs)
Child A:	(Laughs, tries catching bubbles as they pass by) Raining!

Early in the game, Child A is hesitant. As he comes to feel more comfortable with his peers and with this loud and active behavior, he becomes more animated. He laughs aloud, talks occasionally with his classmates, and runs full speed to catch bubbles. By the end of outdoor time his initial reluctance seems to have disappeared altogether.   ❖

This vignette demonstrates the power of peer encouragement in fostering initiative in play. Once the teacher has engaged the child in interactions with classmates, they do the rest. They entice him into action with requests, enthusiastic pronouncements, and much humor. They have prompted him to a level of involvement that he would never have achieved by himself or with a teacher alone. An important way that teachers can enhance a sense of initiative, then, is by promoting social competence and facilitating friendships (Hartup & Moore, 1990).

Competence

In the preschool years, children are perfectly happy making many creative attempts regardless of their outcomes. In the early elementary years, children wish to master real skills—the skills of older children and adults. They want to read and write like grownups, to excel at sports and other games, or to be strong and smart (Stipek & MacIver, 1989). Those who feel they are capable in these areas are said to have a sense of "industry." A more commonly used term for this feeling is "competence." Erikson (1963) has said that children who have genuine successes in the early years and whose accomplishments are

Through play intervention, teachers can facilitate positive interactions among children.

accepted and appreciated by adults and peers will develop a sense of competence; the opposite state, inferiority, results from significant experience with failure. The main psychological work of primary children is to come to view themselves as competent persons.

Preschool-age children tend to see themselves as competent (Blumenfeld, Pintrich, & Hamilton, 1986). In one study it was found, for example, that even when four-year-olds had just failed several times to complete a difficult task they reported that they would be successful on their next try (Stipek, 1984). Preschool children have been described as "exceedingly optimistic in self-ratings of their abilities and expectations for academic success" (Curry & Johnson, 1990, p. 69). Only preschoolers who have been overly restricted or criticized for their creative initiatives or who attend rigid, academic preschool or kindergarten programs will not enjoy this positive view of self (Stipek & MacIver, 1989).

As children approach school age, however, their perspectives about their own competence change dramatically. Many who felt good about themselves in earlier years now come to question their abilities (Stipek & MacIver, 1989). There are several reasons that a sense of competence is threatened as children enter the primary grades. First, children of this age can now understand better what it means to be "smart" or "good at something." Whereas younger children associate competence with peer acceptance, appropriate behavior in school, and hard work, early elementary children come to understand that abilities in performing school tasks determine whether one is considered "smart" (Stipek & MacIver, 1989).

In the early elementary years, children increasingly compare themselves to peers (Aboud, 1985; Morris & Nemcek, 1982). This leads them to base judgments about their competence on where they stand within their peer group. As early as age six, children may express that they cannot run as fast, read as well, or learn math as quickly as peers. Elementary-age children are also more likely to consider adult rewards and feedback (both positive and negative) in their self-assessments (Barker & Graham, 1987; Pintrich & Blumenfeld, 1985). When a teacher criticizes a child's written work, gives a low grade or score on a test, or in other ways provides negative feedback on school performance, the elementary child is likely to internalize these adult judgments. Overall, the early elementary years are sensitive ones for the formation of self-concept.

Unfortunately, elementary schools can contribute to feelings of inferiority. The following practices have been found to threaten positive views of self (Stipek & MacIver, 1989):

1. *Rewards, stickers, grades, and other evaluative symbols.* Evaluative symbols predominate American education. Increasingly children incorporate this symbolic feedback into their assessments of their own competence. When asked, "How do you know when someone's smart?" elementary children regularly name grades as the primary indicator (Blumenfeld et al., 1986) Poor grades or failure to earn stars, stickers, or happy faces can have a lasting negative impact on self-concept (Curry & Johnson, 1990).

2. *Public comparison.* Teachers compare their students with one another both formally and informally in many schools (Stipek & MacIver, 1989). When charts are posted indicating how many books one has read, who hasn't completed homework, or which children have not been behaving appropriately, feelings of competence can be threatened (Higgins & Parsons, 1983). More subtle forms of comparison including ability grouping (Hallinan & Sorensen, 1983) and inequitable teacher treatment of competent and less competent children (Stipek & MacIver, 1989) also lead to negative judgments about self.

3. *Academic, whole group instruction.* In many elementary schools, children spend much time being instructed as a whole group in a "right answer" mode. Since all are engaged in the same tasks at the same time, comparison with peers is more likely in such a classroom; since only right answers are acceptable, failure for some is inevitable (Stipek & MacIver, 1989).

4. *Formal, impersonal relationships with the teacher.* Preschool and daycare teachers have been found to be remarkably positive and accepting. They tend to respond to processes rather than end products and to accept any effort as satisfactory (Potter, 1982). In the elementary years, private, personal interactions with teachers are replaced by more public, impersonal encounters that revolve around learning and teaching (Brophy & Evertson, 1976). This reduction in warmth and encouragement may threaten children's feelings of self-worth.

By eliminating some of these classroom practices, teachers can enhance feelings of competence. Through positive and encouraging interventions in children's play they can also promote positive feelings about self.

Guiding Children Toward Success

Children must experience success in order to feel competent; empty praise is not sufficient. The best way to assure that children will succeed is to provide open-ended, process-oriented activities from which they may choose; in this way they can pursue those activities that they enjoy and are good at (an interesting practice in some schools is to insist that children spend most of their time on things they are not good at—e.g., poor readers are inundated with phonics drill). A comparison of two types of activities—block building versus a math worksheet—illustrates the differences between success-oriented and failure-oriented experiences. In the latter activity, performance is judged by a letter grade or "how many I got wrong." Children readily discover whether they have given the correct answers and how they measure up with peers. The opportunities are great to experience failure.

How can one fail when building with blocks, however? In this activity, performance at any level can be genuinely considered successful. A stack, a row, a tower, a sophisticated enclosure, and a highly representational airport all represent significant accomplishments; no one structure is "correct" or deemed better than another.

On occasion, children encounter challenges even in a developmentally appropriate classroom environment. At these times teachers can "scaffold" children's learning, following Vygotsky's (1962, 1978) guidelines (see Chapter 2). For example, a teacher may directly help a child get beyond an insurmountable step in a task or give hints or encouragement to assist in solving a problem independently. By giving just the right amount of help, a teacher assures that a child will have some degree of success no matter how difficult the problem. The following teacher-child interaction during group time illustrates this point.

❖ ❖

A teacher is guiding four-year-old children in a discussion of a science experiment. They are making predictions about what will happen over the course of the morning to snow that has been brought into the classroom and placed in the water table.

Teacher:	What will happen to all that snow? Sara, can you guess?
Child:	Um . . . (Pauses for many seconds) I don't know.
Teacher:	How does our classroom feel different from outside on this wintery day?
Child:	Oh. It's hot. You don't have to wear coats.
Teacher:	So what will happen to snow in the classroom, do you think?
Child:	(Pauses) Oh! The snow will freeze!
Teacher:	Tell me more about that.
Child:	Well, 'cause it will get hotter and hotter. And then . . . Oh! It will melt, I mean.
Teacher:	Okay. Sara's prediction is that the snow will melt. Does everyone agree?

The teacher records various guesses about how the snow will look after it has melted. Later in the day they examine the mess in the water table and draw conclusions about what has occurred. ❖

A common response when a child gives a "wrong" answer or hesitates during a group time discussion is to encourage another child to talk (e.g., "Can anyone help Sara?" or "You think about it for a while, Sara; we'll come back to you later."). Sometimes a teacher should do this so that a child will not feel uncomfortable or under pressure to answer; however, research suggests that adults are often too quick in moving on when a child can't solve a problem (Dillon, 1988). If the teacher in the above vignette had simply told this child that she was wrong or even asked a peer to help, the message would be given that she was unable to solve the problem herself. By continuing to give hints, the teacher has supported this child in solving the problem independently; such success can lead to feelings of competence.

When young children encounter failure, they can generalize this negative feeling to all aspects of their lives (Curry & Johnson, 1990). Children who have difficulty learning to read, for example, may construct a view of themselves as generally poor students; those who are not effective with peers may come to see themselves as unlikable. Teachers should watch for signs that children are feeling inferior; guiding them toward activities in which they will be very successful may help restore a sense of competence. A child who becomes frustrated because her drawing does not come out as she would like might be guided toward the dramatic play area where success is assured. A child who is not accepted by a group playing in the blocks might be guided to a smaller or more pro-social group of children who are more likely to accept him. Helping children to select activities that will give them feelings of success is a critical teaching responsibility.

Attending to Processes, Not Products

Throughout this book, the value of process-oriented materials is described. Even within the most open-ended activities, however, children can come to feel they have failed, particularly if adults or peers make too much fuss over finished products. Teachers can encourage children to reflect on their creative processes, rather than end products, as illustrated below.

❖ ❖

Two children are building with blocks. A teacher overhears a conversation in which one child is comparing her building to a peer's. She enters the play area.

Child A:	(To the teacher) Look! See how tall mine is. It's taller than Cheryl's.
Teacher:	I see. Tell me about how you built that.
Child A:	Well, I put these huge blocks down, then smaller and smaller, and smaller. (Gestures toward her block structure)
Teacher:	So the very smallest blocks are at the very top, I see. (Now to Child B) Cheryl, you built yours quite differently. Tell me about how you made this.
Child B:	It's just a house for these guys. (Points to plastic figures)
Teacher:	Do they live in the house?
Child B:	Oh, yes. This is a family. See? Here's the mom. (Holds up one figure) And these are the rest of the children. (Points to the pile of figures on the ground)
Teacher:	This part is very interesting. (Points to an enclosure Child B has constructed) Was this difficult to make?
Child B:	Oh, no. You just put these together and make corners for the house. (Demonstrates how she created her structure)
Teacher:	Well. You've both been working here for quite a while now. How long would you say you've been working on your buildings?

Child A: At least . . . oh . . . lots of minutes.

Child B: Maybe like nineteen minutes.

Child A: Maybe more minutes.

Teacher: That's a long time. You must be enjoying your work here.   ❖

     The teacher in this vignette has chosen to redirect the discussion away from comparisons of finished products (which building is tallest) toward reflection on each child's building process. The children are able to express their unique approaches to block building; feelings of competence come from pride in their efforts rather than end products. This focus on process is important; in Curry and Johnson's (1990) words: "The value of people should be measured in terms of *how* they use their talents, not in terms of *what* their talents are" (p. 131).

Helping Children Monitor Their Own Successes

In classrooms in which praise and rewards are used excessively, children come to rely on external feedback in order to determine if they have been successful. Children will construct more realistic and positive views of themselves if encouraged to assess their own competence (Curry & Johnson, 1990). Teachers can assist children in monitoring their own successes through question-asking or other intervention strategies that encourage self-analysis. The following interaction demonstrates this approach.

❖ ❖

     A seven-year-old child has just finished reading a book he has written to a teacher. The teacher asks him to reflect on his accomplishment.

Teacher: Which is your favorite part of your story?

Child: I think when the boys go down in the cave. (Pages through his book) Here. See? Where they go in the cave.

Teacher: Yes. That was kind of scary. Why do you like that part so much?

Child: I like this drawing. The guys are looking pretty scared. I just like the scary parts.   ❖

     Here the teacher refrains from evaluating a child's book and instead encourages self-analysis. By prompting children to reflect on works that they like best, that they worked hardest on, or that were most enjoyable to complete, teachers can guide them in discovering their own strengths and abilities.

Avoiding Comparisons

Since social comparison is a common source of tension in the early primary grades, teachers should be cautious not to compare students' efforts. The focus of teacher interventions should be on encouraging children to reflect on their own individual work without reference to external norms. In previous chapters, warnings were issued about behaviors that elicit comparisons with peers—hanging all the same kind of painting or project together on the bulletin board, praising just one student's drawing or book, placing children in ability groups, or asking more questions of highly competent children. Even during group games teachers can reduce the intensity of ability comparisons and help children focus on individual performance and on issues of fairness, cooperation, and personal development (Curry & Johnson, 1990). At the end of a card game, for example, a teacher might ask an individual child who was not the winner, "Did you win more cards in this game than you did in the last?" After a game of "Concentration" a teacher might say, "It must be very difficult to remember where all those cards are. How do you do that? Do you have a special way of remembering?" Such interactions redirect the discussion from winning and losing to a focus on personal performance.

Genuine Acceptance

A sense of competence is not something that merely can be given to children by their parents or teachers; children must construct an understanding of self-worth through genuine experience with success and acceptance by others. No amount of empty praise from a teacher, then, will assure positive feelings of self, particularly if that teacher shows nonacceptance through body language, subtle verbal cues, or peer-comparative classroom practices. Feelings of inferiority arise, for example, when a teacher bestows lavish but unauthentic praise on a child who is painting, then chooses to display only other children's work in the classroom. When a teacher compliments children but indicates by aloofness or unenthusiastic intonation that their work is not truly appreciated, feelings of competence are threatened.

When adults and peers truly accept children's unique abilities, temperaments, and interpersonal styles a sense of competence will be enhanced (Harter, 1990). Teachers must analyze their own biases toward children in their classrooms and struggle to abandon these. They must come to value all students and articulate their acceptance, not just with words, but through respectful, equitable, and caring classroom interaction (Curry & Johnson, 1990).

A Word about Parents

It has been argued here that teachers can promote emotional growth. They are not the only adults who influence children's mental health, however; there are limitations to what teachers alone can accomplish in the classroom. If teachers provide warmth, security, encouragement, and feelings of competence, but parents do not, children may continue to suffer mistrust, doubt, and low self-esteem. Parent education and support are imperative. Research has shown the positive effects of parenting programs on children's social and emotional development (Johnson & Breckenridge, 1982; Lally, Mangione, & Honig, 1988). Only when parents and teachers work together toward positive emotional growth will mental health be assured.

Helping Children Cope with Crisis

When adults experience depression or anxiety they frequently talk to other trusted adults about their problems; sharing feelings with family members or mental health specialists helps reduce stress. Young children often lack the willingness or ability to verbalize their feelings clearly; they cannot "talk out" their anxieties as adults do. What children can do is play. Playful activities that are common in developmentally appropriate classrooms provide outlets for worry. Through play, children regain a sense of power, mastery, and autonomy; they bring anxieties to the surface, confront them, and often abandon them (Axeline, 1969).

Play therapy has been utilized for many decades as a way to assist children in coping with crisis (Curry & Bergen, 1988). Through a variety of clinical interventions in children's play, mental health specialists have assisted young clients in coping with child abuse and neglect (Mann & McDermott, 1983), divorce (Mendell, 1983), hospitalization (Golden, 1983), and poor peer relations (Willock, 1983).

Play intervention has been less widely used as a technique for helping children in crisis within classroom settings (Yawkey & Pellegrini, 1984). In recent years the major purpose of play intervention in classrooms has been to foster cognitive growth or teach school-related skills (Sutton-Smith, 1983); under pressure to "teach children something," teachers can miss opportunities to help children play out stress and anxiety.

All children will benefit from self-expressive play activities. Teachers can ask children questions about their play that guide the resolution of everyday stresses or bring fears and anxieties to the surface. These interventions are especially helpful for children undergoing personal or family crises; guidelines for helping such children to cope are presented in this section. It is important to note that some children suffer such severe emotional impairment that regular classroom interventions are ineffective. In some cases, in-depth individual and family therapy and placement in special classroom settings are required.

Nondirective Play Therapy

There are many different approaches to play therapy (Curry & Bergen, 1988). The most useful form for teachers is "nondirective therapy" (Axline, 1969) in which children engage in open-ended expressive activities to which adults informally respond. By giving support, asking an occasional question, or providing special play materials, teachers help children bring underlying concerns to the surface. For example, a teacher who knows that a student is suffering through a painful family crisis might provide dramatic play props (e.g., "I see you are the mother. Would you like these dolls to be your children?"), then later ask questions that guide self-expression (e.g., "You sound very angry at your baby. Tell me about that.").

Unlike in other play therapies, the child maintains full control of all aspects of the play in this approach. The teacher follows the child's lead in regard to what, when, and where to play; the role that the teacher will play is determined by the child. In the case of the child described above, for example, the teacher does not initiate family-related play, but responds to the child's angry-parent play theme after it has arisen in a spontaneous, self-directed activity. This unobtrusive form of therapy has been found to reduce stress and promote long-range mental health even when it is provided by nontrained professionals (Sensue, 1981).

Creating Special Environments

A first step in assisting a child who is confronted with crisis is to provide an environment that affords ample opportunities for self-expressive activity. Many of the play experiences described in this book allow open-ended expression—art, block building, writing, dramatic play, outdoor play (Elkind, 1981). If a teacher is aware that a particular child is going through a stressful time, she might make an effort to guide that child toward these activities (e.g., "Would you like to come with me and use the new markers in the art center?"). Of course, children's wishes not to engage in these experiences should be respected.

Special props or materials that relate directly to a child's circumstances can be provided (Guerney, 1983). If a child is facing an upcoming hospitalization, for example, medical equipment can be introduced into the dramatic play area or syringes can be provided for "squirt painting" in the art center. A child whose parents have just divorced might be provided standard home-related play props, such as dolls, toy dishes, and housekeeping furniture. Great care should be taken not to force these toys on children; play props can be so realistic as to frighten children, and thus exacerbate the stress.

Observing and Listening

Carlsson-Paige and Levin (1985) have argued that teachers must listen carefully to children's concerns before discussing troubling issues with them. It is quite common, they contend, for adults to prejudge children's anxieties and respond inappropriately. An example is a comment made by a teacher to a child whose mother had just been sent overseas during the Gulf War: "You must be very worried about your mother going to war. You can talk with me about it any time you wish." It may have been that the child was quite worried; but it was also possible that she was not. As it turns out, the child's family had not fully explained potential dangers. By making such a comment, the teacher suddenly increased the child's stress. Through careful observation, a teacher can assess the level of anxiety and the child's understanding of a situation.

Sometimes worries are revealed in subtle or symbolic ways in play. A child whose grandmother recently died, for example, was observed repeatedly playing war and gun play on the playground. A ritual of being "shot," falling dead, then getting up and "not being dead any more" was carried out. Children whose families are in crisis may scribble nothing in particular on paper, but in harsh, violent strokes. Before teachers can decide how to intervene, they must watch for and interpret these signs of upset. Simply positioning oneself close to a child in crisis is the first intervention in play therapy (Guerney, 1983).

Empathic Responding

As teachers intervene in play, their main role is to respond to what children are doing. "Empathic responding" involves simple acknowledgment of children's feelings (Guerney, 1983). The following is an example.

A child who has just suffered the death of a pet is playing in the block area. She is knocking down a building and pretending that plastic people are getting crushed under the blocks as they fall. She makes screaming noises to pretend the people are frightened and in pain.

Teacher:	The people must be very afraid about being injured.
Child:	They could die. So they're scared.
Teacher:	It is scary thinking about dying, isn't it?
Child:	Yeah. Because if you die you never wake up again.
Teacher:	Yes, that's right.
Child:	These people are very sad.
Teacher:	Oh?
Child:	Yes. They're going to die.
Teacher:	Death is sad. It's sad for people who don't die, too. It's sad for people who have a pet or family member who dies.
Child:	Yeah. You have to cry. ❖

The purpose of this intervention is to show empathy for the child's situation and to encourage her to continue expressing her feelings about death. The teacher is careful not to pressure the child to speak of her own personal crisis; he lets the child take the lead.

Giving Emotional Support

A related response to stress-related play is giving warmth and reassurance to children. Carlsson-Paige and Levin (1985) suggest that in play, children bring fears to the surface. Although this is a purpose of play therapy, the experience can be frightening. Children often need reassurance that they are safe. In the following vignette, a teacher notices that anxiety about hospital play has grown very high. He moves in to reassure the child.

A child who will soon be hospitalized is watching two peers give injections to a doll in a rather violent manner. He has an anxious expression on his face. A teacher moves over to him and puts his arm around the child.

Teacher: They're playing a silly game here. Doctors and nurses would never give shots like that.

Child: They're pretending that that guy is bleeding.

Teacher: Yes. But when you really get an injection you don't bleed like that. A shot hurts but it stops hurting and you don't bleed like that.

Child: I don't like shots.

Teacher: (Hugging the child) They do hurt. But they stop hurting pretty soon.   ❖

Here the teacher has provided much warmth and given the message: "You are safe with me right now." Warm touching and hugging are very therapeutic for children under stress.

Giving Factual Information

Highly imaginative play activities are useful in coping with anxiety; adults should generally not serve as "spokesmen-for-reality," continually challenging children's make-believe (Johnson, Christie, & Yawkey, 1987). The vignette presented above demonstrates, however, that there are times when children's play reveals potentially harmful misconceptions. Now and then teachers can intervene in children's play to clear these up. The following is an illustration.

A child has just written a book about hospitals. He reads his work to a teacher.

Child: (Reads his book) A hospital can be very sad. You die in hospitals.

Teacher: Most people go to the hospital and then go home again when they are well.

Child: Yeah, but my aunt went to the hospital and she died.

Teacher: Some people who are very old or very sick might die in the hospital. But most people get well and go home again.   ❖

In most cases it would be inappropriate to correct the information in a child's story in this way. Now and then such an intervention is necessary to assist children in understanding troublesome life events.

Probing

Sometimes it is appropriate to probe children gently regarding their beliefs or feelings. Carlsson-Paige and Levin (1985) suggest that as children raise issues of stress or anxiety, teachers can use open-ended questions to learn what they are thinking or worrying about. They cite the example of a teacher who observed a child drawing an airplane dropping bombs on a house. The teacher asked, "What do you know about airplanes?" The child's response indicated that she believed all airplanes carried bombs. Since they regularly flew over her house, she was certain that a bomb would be dropped on her one day. The teacher was able to clear up this misconception and reassure the child of her safety. In this case a single question got to the root of the child's anxiety.

Asking about feelings is important; unobtrusive queries about the emotional states of various characters within a dramatic play theme, for example, can lead to revelations about worrisome life events. The follow vignette illustrates this.

❖ ❖

A child is playing alone in the dramatic play area. She is screaming at a doll—telling the doll she is bad and lazy. A teacher watches for a time, then intervenes.

Open-ended activities allow children to express feelings and relieve stress.

Teacher:	Oh, my. What did your child do?
Child:	She's a bad girl. She just makes too much noise in the house. (Now to the doll) I try to tell you to stop it!
Teacher:	(To the doll) What did you do that was bad?
Child:	(Pretends the doll is talking. Uses a make-believe voice) I just can't be loud in the house.
Teacher:	How do you feel when your mother yells at you?
Child:	(Still in a make-believe voice) I'm really angry at her. She just yells and yells.
Teacher:	You are angry. I can tell.
Child:	(In her own voice now) But why does she have to always yell? ❖

Through question-asking this teacher has brought feelings to the surface and helped the child explore them. This interchange has led into a real-life discussion about the problem of being yelled at.

The reader is cautioned against attempting highly invasive therapy techniques with children in crisis. To deal with many of modern society's family stressors, intervention by trained mental health professionals is required. Teachers can serve a useful role as part of a social services team, providing meaningful play experiences and gently encouraging self-expression in the classroom. The importance of communicating with other professionals serving children and their families cannot be overemphasized.

Summary

Many of the chapters in this book focus on promoting cognitive development or social skills. An important purpose of play intervention is to foster emotional development as well. Teachers can help children to resolve key emotional conflicts identified by Erik Erikson. Trust can be strengthened through warmth and responsiveness. Autonomy and Initiative can be enhanced by encouraging independent thought and action and by celebrating nonconformity. Reducing a focus on finished products will also help children to acquire these emotional states. In the early elementary years, children's feelings of competence may be promoted by helping them to experience genuine success and acceptance. Simple praise is not enough to ensure positive self-concept; helping children to recognize their own authentic accomplishments is most helpful.

Play is a vehicle for expressing anxieties and stress. Teachers can intervene to encourage children to play out worrisome events; by supplying warmth, emotional support and empathy, teachers can encourage self-expression in play. Asking questions that encourage the exploration of feelings is also important.

Suggested Activities

1. Observe three young children of different ages as they interact within the classroom. Write descriptions in your own words of their emotional states (e.g., anger, frustration, determination, excitement). Later, write an analysis of your observations guided by the following questions:

   a. Describe the key emotional states you observed. Did they differ among children? What were the behavioral indicators of each state that you observed?

   b. What behaviors did you observe that indicated that children were in one or another of Erikson's stages (e.g., Trust vs. Mistrust, Autonomy vs. Shame and Doubt, Initiative vs. Guilt, Competence vs. Inferiority)?

   c. In what ways, if any, did you observe subjects expressing excitement, stress or anxiety?

2. Observe children and teachers interacting in a classroom. Write an analysis of the emotional climate of this classroom and the nature of teacher-child relationships, guided by the following questions:

   a. What trusting relationship was established between children and teachers? Which children appeared securely attached to teachers? Which did not? What behavioral indicators did you rely on to determine this?

   b. Which behaviors did teachers display that indicated a positive, supportive classroom management system?

   c. In what ways were teachers responsive to children's initiatives, verbalizations, or accomplishments?

   d. In what ways was the overall environment consistent and predictable? In what ways was it not?

   e. In what ways did the classroom or the teacher promote autonomy? In what ways, if at all, was autonomous action or thought inhibited?

   f. How was open-ended initiative encouraged? Describe interactions in which teachers promoted this.

   g. How successful were teachers in avoiding public evaluation or comparison? In what ways did they help children to value their own accomplishments and monitor their own successes?

   h. What was the ratio of successes to failures in the classroom? In which activities did children experience success? In which did they feel failure?

3. Review the section in this chapter on one of the following teaching behaviors:

   ❑ Giving Warmth/Nurturance

   ❑ Responding

   ❑ Providing Positive/Noncontrolling Classroom Management

   ❑ Prompting Creative, Process-oriented Initiatives

   ❑ Encouraging Autonomy (in both thought and action)

❏   Guiding Children Toward Success

❏   Helping Children Monitor Their Own Success

Now focus on just this behavior as you interact with children for several hours in a classroom. Write an analysis of your experience guided by the following questions.

a.   What were your successes in performing your selected behavior in the classroom?

b.   What were the challenges you encountered in practicing this behavior? In what ways did this behavior seem awkward or difficult to perform? How often did opportunities arise to practice it?

c.   How did children respond when you performed this behavior? Were reactions similar to those predicted in the chapter? Did you observe interesting or puzzling reactions to your interventions?

4. Observe a group of typically developing, emotionally healthy children in a dramatic play center. Write an analysis of your observations guided by the following questions:

a.   What roles did children play? In what ways were their roles influenced by television? family life? school?

b.   In what ways did children reveal their emotions in their play? How did they "play out" events that they were excited or anxious about?

c.   In what ways, if any, did highly emotional issues regarding school or family life emerge in play?

d.   In what ways did play give children feelings of power and control?

Further Reading

Balaban, N. (1985). *Starting school: From separation to independence.* New York: Teachers College Press.

McCracken, J.B. (1987). *Reducing stress in young children's lives.* Washington, DC: National Association for the Education of Young Children.

Carlsson-Paige, N., & Levin, D. E. (1985). *Helping young children understand peace, war, and the nuclear threat.* Washington, DC: National Association for the Education of Young Children.

Curry, N. E., & Johnson, C. N. (1990). *Beyond self-esteem: Developing a genuine sense of human value.* Washington, DC: National Association for the Education of Young Children.

Erikson, E.H. (1963). *Childhood and society* (2nd ed.). New York: Norton.

Honig, A. S. (1985a). Compliance, control, and discipline (Part 1). *Young Children, 40*(2), 50–58.

Honig, A. S. (1985b). Compliance, control, and discipline (Part 2). *Young Children, 40*(3), 49–51.

Trawick-Smith, J. W., & Thompson, R. H. (1986). Preparing young children for hospitalization. In J.B. McCracken (Ed.), *Reducing stress in young children's lives* (pp. 20–24). Washington, DC: National Association for the Education of Young Children.

CHAPTER

11

DIVERSITY AND PLAY INTERVENTION

A kindergarten teacher has been practicing effective one-on-one interactions with children that have been described in Chapter 2 and elsewhere in this book. When he speaks with students he gets down on their level, establishes eye contact, uses a language-rich conversational style, and responds with enthusiasm to comments and questions. All the children in the class seem to appreciate this mode of interaction. The teacher marvels at how much students have grown in their communicative and social abilities since he has begun implementing this one-on-one approach.

Midway through the year, a new child is enrolled. Although his name is "José," an unenlightened assistant principal has introduced him as "Joe." José is Mexican-American. The teacher admits to himself that he is anxious about meeting José's needs. He has always worked in monocultural classrooms; most of his students are Anglo, as is he. He wonders if José will have unique communication or learning-style differences, or if his students will come to accept a child of another culture. He recognizes at this moment how poorly his teacher education program has prepared him for teaching culturally diverse groups.

Over the next few months, the kindergarten teacher learns much from José. By carefully studying his interactions with others in the class, the teacher recognizes communicative differences that he has come to understand and appreciate. (He is clearly a sensitive and accepting teacher; some professionals would consider these communication deficits, not differences!) He gradually adapts his style of one-on-one interaction to meet José's needs. He uses less language than he does when approaching other children in the class, for he notices that José appears overwhelmed when he is "bombarded" with questions or conversation. When initiating contact, the teacher positions himself near José, but often does not immediately initiate conversation. He waits for José to speak first. He uses touch and other physical cues more often to guide José. He makes no attempt to establish direct eye contact, noticing that José will often avert his gaze. He accepts José's native language, and encourages him to write and converse in Spanish. Although the teacher is not fluent in Spanish, he learns key words and phrases in that language that will help him to communicate with his new student.

After several months the kindergarten teacher has a conference with José's parents in which he shares his insights regarding their child's interactions in the classroom. He is pleased to learn that the ways he has adapted his one-on-one interactions with José match how José's family interacts at home. José's parents explain that establishing eye contact with an adult, for example, can be interpreted as a sign of disrespect; physical touch rather than language, they explain, is a primary mode of communication within their family. Spanish is spoken almost exclusively at home; José's parents wish him to become proficient in his native language.

The kindergarten teacher takes pride in having been sensitive to José's needs. He wonders how José will fare in other classrooms with other teachers during his school career. Will others be as observant and respectful of José's unique style of interaction?   ❖

T his book has focused on beneficial teacher-child interactions, based on research on "average children." "Average children" do not really exist, however; there is such diversity within classrooms today that it can no longer be expected that all students will conform to profiles provided in the literature. Much of the research has been done with "typically developing" children of white, middle-class background (McLoyd & Randolph, 1984). There has been far less study of children with unique social and cognitive styles, and those of diverse ethnic and social class groups.

The intervention strategies described in this book must be regularly adapted to meet the unique needs of individual children. If a child comes from a family where interaction is less verbal and more physical, as does José, teachers should modify the language interventions described in Chapter 5. If a student is deaf, very different forms of question-asking or problem-posing are required. Even boys and girls differ in their social interactions and learning styles; gender-sensitive interventions are required. The purpose of this chapter is to illustrate how play intervention might be adapted to meet diverse needs.

Several sources of diversity in play and learning are considered here—cultural, gender, and developmental diversity. Teachers must be extremely cautious not to confuse each source. They should not assume that children of color, for example, are automatically at risk of developmental delay. References to children of color as "culturally disadvantaged" are so frequent in professional literature and the press that it is easy to understand why this erroneous assumption is prevalent in our society.

In order to clarify distinctions among different sources of diversity, definitions of key phrases used in this chapter are presented below.

Unique/Diverse Needs. These phrases refer to the social, emotional and learning needs of all individuals regardless of gender, ethnicity, or cognitive ability. This wording is used to indicate that each individual within a classroom has unique ways of learning or interacting with others and that no group of students will be all alike.

Special Needs. This phrase refers to the needs of children with social, emotional, cognitive, or physical delays or disabilities. The term "special" is borrowed from the field of Special Education. This terminology should not be confused with "cultural needs"; it is an inaccurate assumption that children of some ethnic groups necessarily have special needs.

Cultural/Ethnic Diversity. These phrases refer to variations in the needs or play and learning styles of children of various cultural groups. Children of different cultures, for example, have different styles of communicating. "Diversity" must not be confused with "deficit"; differences across cultures are viewed in this chapter as just that—differences to be celebrated, not deficits to be remediated.

Socioeconomic Status. This phrase refers to variations in children's needs due to family economic and educational levels. Children of poverty, for example, have unique needs, as do those of extremely wealthy families. "Socioeconomic status" must not be confused with "cultural or ethnic diversity"; children of color, for example, are not necessarily of low socioeconomic status. Nor should these phrases be equated to "special needs"; children of poverty do not automatically have developmental delays.

Teacher-Child Interaction and Cultural Diversity

By the year 2000, children of color—often called "minorities"—will comprise a new majority within the United States (Spencer, 1990). Early childhood classrooms, then, are becoming increasingly diverse; teachers must be prepared to meet the unique needs of young children of varying backgrounds. Even teachers of monocultural classrooms must assist their students in understanding and appreciating other cultures. A primary goal of teachers today is to provide skills and understandings that allow children to live in a pluralistic society.

Children of different cultures vary in the ways they communicate and interact with adults and peers, in how they play and learn, and in how they view teachers and school (Ramsey, 1987). Parental socialization practices and beliefs vary markedly across cultures (Garcia Coll, 1990). Teachers must come to understand, appreciate, and show sensitivity to these differences as they interact with children in the classroom. They must devise ways to provide their students with knowledge of and positive and significant experiences with those of other cultures.

One approach has been to develop multicultural curricula in which topics and issues of diversity are directly presented to children through meaningful, developmentally appropriate experiences (Derman-Sparks, 1989; Ramsey, 1987; Williams & De Gaetano, 1985). Ramsey, for example, recommends that diversity be addressed through multicultural experiences with holidays (e.g., focusing on the harvest festivals of many different cultures, rather than solely on Thanksgiving). She recommends that the physical environment be structured to reflect diversity (e.g., providing dolls representing different racial groups, or cooking utensils used by various cultures within the dramatic play area). She suggests that physical knowledge activities, such as those described in Chapter 5, be adapted to teach about varying cultures. For example, children could be encouraged to experiment with different kinds of clothing; they could be guided in reflection about why people in different regions of the world dress as they do. Derman-Sparks (1989) suggests that teachers plan specific activities that help children to reflect upon the histories, language, and holidays of families represented in the class. She urges the use of children's literature and other culturally sensitive materials to promote appreciation of diversity.

Ramsey (1987) has argued, however, that multiculturalism is not a unit of instruction, but a perspective. It is a way of looking at the world that must be woven through all aspects of classroom life. Adults teach as much about diversity through their informal interactions with children as through carefully planned activities (Derman-Sparks, 1989). When teachers reflect cultural sensitivity in their interchanges with students, tolerance and appreciation of diversity are enhanced. Less sensitive interventions can contribute to bias and xenophobia—a fear of those who are different. The focus of this section is on culturally sensitive play intervention.

Communication Differences and Play Intervention

People of various cultures communicate in different ways. When children of varying backgrounds interact within the classroom, rich experience with different conversational styles is provided. Teachers can support and encourage children to use their own styles within the classroom; great care must be taken not to give the message that only Euro-American modes of interaction are appropriate.

Amount of Language Used

Some cultures are less verbal than others. Mexican-American families such as José's (portrayed in the last vignette) are more likely to use physical cues and touch in interactions. Western Apache families have also been found to be quieter; this style has led unenlightened Euro-Americans to conclude that Native Americans are "strange or rude" (Menyuk & Menyuk, 1988, p. 155). Euro-Americans, in contrast, are in general quite talkative. Care must be taken not to assume that because this style is that of the dominant culture, it is the norm or the only "correct" way for all children to communicate.

When children show signs of being overwhelmed by teacher comments or questions, reducing verbal interaction may be appropriate. In such cases teachers might place themselves close by children physically, give warm touches or smiles, but refrain from "verbal bombardment." Although research cited in this book has suggested that highly conversational forms of teacher-child discourse are beneficial, teachers need to be more moderate in their verbalization with children of quieter cultures.

Uses of Silence

Silence in conversation means different things in different cultures, as the vignette below illustrates.

Two children, a Euro-American and a Chinese-American, have just gotten into a disagreement over a toy car in the block area. A teacher intervenes.

Teacher:	What is going on over here? It seems like you two are having an argument.
C-A child:	(Looks down, says nothing)
E-A child:	(In an angry tone) She took my car. (Now shouting at her peer) I was playing with that, you know!
C-A child:	(Says nothing, does not establish eye contact)
Teacher:	Is that right, Ding Fang? Did you take Maura's toy car?
C-A child:	(Remains silent)
Teacher:	Ding Fang? Can you tell me what happened?
C-A child:	(Still silent)
Teacher:	Well, you don't seem to want to talk about it. Why don't we come out of the blocks now and do something else. We'll let Maura play here alone. (Leads the Chinese-American child out of the block area) ❖

In this vignette, the teacher has misread the meaning of silence. She appears to assume that the Chinese-American child either is unwilling to cooperate in solving the conflict or does not care how the matter is settled. The teacher does not understand that in Chinese-American culture silence is used to avoid threatening situations or severe conflict; this child may in fact be very troubled about the incident. She may be communicating upset in a manner unique to her culture. The teacher has missed the message.

In many families, silence is a response to situations "which, within the context of other cultures, would call for a good deal of verbal interaction" (Menyuk & Menyuk, 1988, p. 155). Brazilians and Peruvians, for example, often use silence as a means of greeting guests; such a welcome might be construed as impolite within Euro-American culture. Arabs use silence to achieve privacy; an Arab child in a day-care center might stop talking as a way of saying: "I need to be alone now." In many cultures, disputes are not settled through verbal argument as they often are in Euro-American society. Overall, Euro-Americans, unlike some other ethnic groups, feel the need to "fill in the gaps" in conversation and are uncomfortable with silence (Irujo, 1988).

Teachers must come to recognize and respect the uses of silence in their classrooms. They must learn from individual children what silence means and respond appropriately, not always insisting on verbalization. The teacher in the vignette, for example, might sit in silence with the two children in conflict, waiting for the anger to pass and the threatening nature of the situation to diminish, before attempting to help them resolve the disagreement.

Turntaking Versus Collective Conversation

Some Euro-American families engage in very orderly conversations in which one speaker takes a turn, then another (Condon & Yousef, 1975). For decades this turntaking style of communication has been considered the norm; children who could not wait until their turn to speak were considered "deficient" in their abilities to communicate. Such children were often chastised in school as being self-centered or immature in impulse control. Studies of cross-cultural communication patterns reveal that in some families it is the norm for all persons to speak at once. In many African-American, Puerto Rican, and Jewish families, for example, much discourse involves spontaneous and simultaneous talk. Waiting for a turn, in fact, might result in exclusion altogether from the discussion (Condon & Yousef, 1975). It is no wonder that some children can have trouble adapting to the typical hand-raising or turn-taking routines of classroom discussions or lessons.

Teachers can be sensitive to variation in turn-taking style; avoiding harsh criticism of those who have trouble taking turns is a first step. Providing experience of both types of discourse—collective as well as one-at-a-time discussion—will benefit all children. The vignette below illustrates how this can be done within a single discussion.

❖ ❖

A teacher is in the science area discussing with three four-year-olds their observations of a snake that recently has been brought into the classroom for observation.

Teacher:	Tell me what you've observed.
Child A:	It just sleeps there.
Child B:	(Speaking at the same time) Nothing . . . nothing.
Child C:	(Also at the same time as Child A and B) You can see his tongue wiggle sometimes . . .
Child A:	(Cuts off Child C) Look at his tongue!
Child D:	(Tries to speak) Well . . .
Child B:	He just wiggles it, you know? Like it's just quick sticks out there.
Teacher:	Why do you think it sticks out?
Child A:	He's like tasting the air, I think.
Child B:	(Speaking at the same time as Child A) They just do it. I don't know.
Teacher:	Those are interesting ideas. (Turns to Child D) Let's hear what Hanna was going to say about the snake's tongue.
Child A:	(Speaks before Child D can) I think it eats things when it sticks it out.
Teacher:	Yes. Why don't we wait a moment, though, until Hanna has a chance to talk. Hanna, what do you think?
Child D:	Well, it sticks out its tongue to tell what's out there. It's like how he sees and hears.
Teacher:	It's a way he can check out what's in his cage?

Child D: Yeah. Like he can check for danger.

Child A: Yeah.

Child B: And he can check for food.   ❖

Here the teacher has accepted two different styles of communication. She listens intently to children who all talk at once, showing interest and responding where possible. She observes that one child is not participating in this collective conversation and creates an opportunity for her to take a turn without interruption. After this brief one-to-one dialogue, children are again able to contribute whenever they wish. During group times teachers can structure periods where students take turns and other times when spontaneous verbalization is encouraged.

Body Language

Body language is an important component of communication; misreading the gestures, expressions, or postures of those of other cultures can lead to irritation and discomfort (Ramsey, 1987). Avoiding eye contact is a good example. In some cultures, looking a speaker straight in the eye shows interest and attention. In other cultures, eye contact with those in positions of authority may be interpreted as a sign of disrespect (Irujo, 1988). In some African-American, Puerto-Rican, and Mexican-American families, for example, children do not look adults directly in the eyes, particularly when they are being reprimanded. This is in sharp contrast to some Euro-American families where eye contact is viewed as evidence that one is listening. More than one Anglo teacher has been heard getting a child's attention with the imperative, "Look right at me so I can tell you are listening."

In some cultures, a "peripheral gaze" is used in conversation; in others, interaction is simply not possible without direct and continuous eye contact (Irujo, 1988). Teachers must be sensitive to cultural differences in the meaning of gazing. Although getting on a child's level and establishing eye contact have been recommended in previous chapters as a feature of positive teacher-child interaction, teachers must be cautious not to expect eye contact of all children. When a student is clearly uncomfortable with direct gazing, teachers can deliver the same positive interventions while looking away to another part of the room.

Another physical cue that varies in social meaning across cultures is smiling. Although smiling appears a universal expression of positive affect (Eibl-Eibesfeldt, 1979), subtle differences exist across cultures in some of the additional meanings of a smile (Irujo, 1988). In the following vignette a teacher discovers one meaning of a smile for a Japanese-American child.

❖ ❖

A five-year-old Japanese-American child has just been pushed off a tire swing. After discussing the event with the aggressor a teacher now comforts the victim.

Teacher:	Are you all right, Misaka?
Child:	(Smiles broadly, says nothing)
Teacher:	It looks like you are okay. Did you get hurt?
Child:	(Continues to smile, still does not speak)
Teacher:	Something doesn't seem quite right here. Why don't we sit together for a few minutes and relax. (Pulls the child onto his lap)

After several minutes of sitting with the teacher, the child begins to speak to the teacher.

Child:	(Tears form in his eyes) He pushed me off.
Teacher:	Yes. I'll bet that hurt.
Child:	(In an angry tone) I don't like him! ❖

Initially this teacher misreads a smile as a sign that this child is happy and unaffected by the aggression. He senses that something is wrong, however, and wisely stays with and nurtures the child until he is ready to express his anger. This teacher has learned through real experience that some Japanese-Americans may use a smile to conceal embarrassment, sorrow, or anger (Eckman, 1972).

Cultures vary in regard to the amount of touching that is comfortable or appropriate. In Euro-American and British families there is less touching than in many other cultures. Japanese-Americans may be particularly unlikely to touch one another, particularly when interacting with members of the opposite sex. Although warmth is important when interacting with children of these cultures, teachers should be sensitive to these less tactile styles of interaction. Warm smiles or close physical presence may be more appropriate than hugs and stroking for some children. In contrast, Puerto Ricans and African-Americans are generally more likely to touch one another in their interactions. Teachers with children of such cultures might expect to be regularly hugged or patted by them and should feel comfortable reciprocating this physical warmth.

A final component of body language that varies across cultures is use of personal space—the distance one speaker stands from another while conversing. Euro-Americans tend to keep a greater distance between themselves and others in interactions, especially when speaking to those with whom they are not well acquainted. African-Americans and Puerto Ricans are more likely to stand close to conversation partners; often the standard conversing distance of these groups is equivalent to the distance between Euro-Americans in intimate conversation among themselves. These differences in use of space have led some Euro-Americans to describe those of other cultures as "too close, too pushy" (Irujo, 1988, p. 144).

Teachers must honor these differences in space needs. For some children, very close, personal contact may be expected; for others, a respectful distance should be maintained. Generally, teachers should attend to individual differences in children's preferred proximity to others and adapt their interactions accordingly.

Multilingual Education and Play Intervention

Multilingual classrooms provide challenges but also many language learning opportunities for children. High-quality multilingual programs lead to positive gains in language competence as well as self-esteem (Egan & Goldsmith, 1981). Children who speak Spanish, Laotian, Black English or other "nonstandard" languages were at one time considered to be "deficient" or "linguistically disadvantaged"; compensatory programs were developed to intensively train these students in "correct" English (Bereiter & Englemann, 1966). It is now believed that these language differences are just that—differences (Ramsey, 1987). Each language or dialect has its own syntax, semantics, and phonology. Each is rule-governed and holds as much communicative power as any other. Although some still cling to a biased view that English (and some European languages) are more "sophisticated" than others (Menyuk & Menyuk, 1988), no one language—not even that of the dominant culture—is superior. Most educators now believe that one goal of early childhood programs should be to enhance children's abilities to communicate with those of all cultures represented in society (Ramsey, 1987). That means that children should come to value and grow proficient in their own native languages while learning those of other cultures. Latinos should learn English as well as Spanish, for example; Euro-Americans should learn Spanish as well as English.

Several bilingual education models in which children learn both their native language and that of the dominant culture have been found to be effective in enhancing language development (Egan & Goldsmith, 1981). The ideal program is one in which all languages represented in a classroom are spoken for a portion of the day; children of all cultures learn their own, as well as other languages. In such programs the emphasis is on maintaining competence in one's home language; parents are encouraged to speak to children in the language of their own culture. Ramsey (1987) provides an example of a bilingual preschool classroom in which monolingual teachers, one of whom is fluent in Chinese and the other in English, each converse with children in their own language. When speaking with one teacher, a child would learn Chinese; English would be learned when speaking with the other. In another program, Vietnamese-speaking primary grade children spend their morning in a classroom where their home language is exclusively spoken. In the afternoon they are integrated into an English-only classroom. In each case there is recognition that all languages are equally important and that learning occurs best, initially, in one's native language.

Many teachers are monolingual, yet find themselves in multilingual settings. It is quite common for children speaking several different languages to be integrated into preschool or day care programs, for example (Ramsey, 1987). Teaching in a multilingual classroom requires special skill. Specific interventions for promoting language acquisition and valuing the diversity of native languages represented in a classroom are provided in this section.

Showing Appreciation for All Languages

When all native languages represented within a classroom group are regularly spoken during the school day, the message is given that these are equally respected. When only English is spoken (or when children are actually discouraged from speaking their native language—a practice that is still prevalent in some schools) children are given the impression that there is only one correct language. Much tension is created when children are made to believe that the language spoken by their families is inferior to and unworthy of use in school.

Ramsey (1987) suggests several approaches to showing appreciation for all languages in the classroom. An ideal arrangement, she contends, is one in which teachers learn the languages of all children. She argues that in many countries fluency in several languages is common; Euro-Americans may be unique in their monolingualism. Teacher preparation programs would do well to emphasize second language learning; when a teacher speaks Spanish and English fluently, for example, the cultural pride and self esteem of Spanish-speaking children is greatly enhanced.

It is unreasonable to assume, however, that teachers can become fluent in all languages; our society is becoming increasingly multilingual. There may simply be too many languages represented in the classroom to learn. Monolingual teachers can make the effort to learn key phrases or words of other languages. Starting with important messages (e.g., "It's time for lunch." "Do you have to go to the bathroom?" "Your father will be back soon.") teachers can begin to build a repertoire of statements. They might seek assistance from children in learning a new language (e.g., "How do you say 'blocks' in Spanish, Jorge?"). Presenting signs, labels, bulletin board displays and other environmental print in two languages is also important. Overall, presenting information, naming objects, or guiding learning in two languages reaffirms the importance of both.

Avoiding Criticism

In Chapter 5, cautions about correcting or criticizing children's language were given. Avoiding criticism is especially important when working with children of diverse cultures. Not only will harsh correction impede language acquisition (Nelson, 1973), it will also threaten children's sense of ethnic pride and self-esteem. Ramsey (1987) has argued that teachers very often are accepting of European children who display a "charming French accent," or Euro-

American children who make attempts to speak in Spanish; yet will be more critical of Latino children in their early stages of English speaking. Teachers should be encouraging and positive with all children who are learning a second language, whether they are Vietnamese, Spanish, or Chinese speaking children learning English or Euro-Americans learning a "foreign" language. Constructing the rules of a second language is exceedingly difficult (it is a myth that young children can learn another language more quickly). Teachers should not expect or even encourage all children to speak English perfectly (Krashen, 1981).

Teachers also must be cautious not to give subtle messages that English is the most important language. Ramsey (1987) suggests that describing a child as "not speaking English," rather than "speaking Thai," suggests that English-speaking is the norm by which language competence is judged. Although subtle, comments like these can imply that language differences are deficits.

Encouraging Cross-Linguistic Conversation

Children may learn one another's languages by interacting in highly engaging and collaborative classroom activities. They will often interact across languages, using physical cues, facial expressions, and intonation when language barriers prohibit verbal communication. Occasionally teachers can help children to converse in different languages. A teacher might serve as interpreter, for example, translating one child's utterance into the language of the listener (e.g., "Maria is saying she wants you to come with her."). Now and then a teacher might take advantage of cross-linguistic conversations to teach words or phrases of a second language (e.g., "Sonia is saying *escaparse*. That means she wants to run away. She wants to *escaparse*, to run away from Noah and Sean."). Teachers can intervene to help children learn gestures and other nonverbal modes of communication (e.g., "How can you show Ding Fang how to play this game?") Ramsey (1987) suggests occasionally holding a "silent circle" in which an entire group time is conducted with gestures, facial expressions, miming, and no verbalization. Such an experience enhances competence in nonverbal communication and shows children a way to interact with peers who speak other languages.

Facilitating Second-Language Acquisition

Strategies for enhancing language learning presented in Chapter 5 can also be useful in promoting second language acquisition. These interventions should be tailored to a particular child's level of competence in the second language, however. Asking open-ended questions in English of a child who does not yet produce statements in that language would be inappropriate, for example. Ramsey (1987) describes stages of second language learning and the types of interventions appropriate at each stage. In the "preproduction stage," children are quite silent; they focus on understanding the second language rather than trying to speak it. Rich auditory experiences with the new language can be pro-

Teachers can facilitate verbal and nonverbal communication among children who speak different languages.

vided. Reading books with which children are familiar in the second language is useful. Naming objects (e.g., "Look, Joshua has an animal puzzle"), describing events that occur in the classroom (e.g., "Amanda is laughing"), or holding informal conversations at snack time (e.g., "M-m-m. This soup is good") are recommended (Derman-Sparks, 1989). At this stage, no effort should be made to encourage children to talk. Listening without speaking is an important beginning to second-language learning; pressured attempts to get children to imitate words or phrases will inhibit acquisition (Ramsey, 1987).

In the "transition to production stage," children demonstrate a readiness to make brief verbalizations in the second language (Ramsey, 1987). During this period, teachers might ask yes/no questions, accepting verbal answers or nods. They might also try questions requiring gestures or one-word responses (e.g., "Where should we hang your painting?" or "What is this?"). Although it was suggested in Chapter 5 that these "low level" questions are less useful, at this stage in second-language learning they actually facilitate development. Teachers must be very sensitive to children's comfort levels and should avoid any pressure to answer.

In the "early production stage," Ramsey (1987) suggests, questions eliciting short-phrase responses are appropriate. As children build with blocks a teacher might say: "Tell me about what you are building." In the dramatic play area a teacher might ask: "What are you making for dinner?" Only in the "expansion of production stage" are children able to respond to open-ended, cognitively-challenging questions (e.g., "Why did your block building fall?"). At this stage, guidelines for good question-asking, presented in previous chapters, should be followed. Teachers should not expect perfectly fluent verbal responses at this stage; semantic, syntactical, and phonological features of one's native language may pervade second-language speech even into adulthood.

Ramsey (1987) proposes a final stage—"introduction to written forms"—in which children show an interest in reading and writing in the second language. Until this point, children should be encouraged to read and write in their home language; literacy emerges first in the language of one's own culture. Only when children are competent in their primary language and comfortable and fluent in the second should formal second-language literacy experiences be encouraged.

Overall, the task of the teacher working with children of diverse linguistic backgrounds is to observe children's second-language competence and to adapt linguistic interventions accordingly. Careful reflection on the needs of individual children is extremely important; there is no single formula for effective language teaching.

Diversity in Play and Social Interactions

Early play research indicated that children of certain ethnic groups are deficient in play and social skills (Lovinger, 1974; Rosen, 1974; Smilansky, 1968). More recently, authors have argued that these studies have confused ethnicity with social class; that is, it is the experience of poverty, not being African-American, Mexican-American, or Native-American, that explains these play differences (Johnson, Christie, & Yawkey, 1987). Moreover, some researchers argue that conclusions about play deficits among poor children of diverse cultural backgrounds are the result of ethnocentric interpretations about what high-quality play is (Bloch & Walsh, 1983; McLoyd, 1982). Play differences exist, these authors contend, but these should not be considered deficiencies; children's play reflects what is important in their particular cultures. Teachers should be sensitive to and appreciative of cultural variations in children's play, then, and cautious not to try to change play behavior to conform to the play styles of the dominant culture.

One way that children's play differs from one culture to another is in the sociodramatic play themes selected. Whereas middle-class Euro-American children may play out home-related play themes in which mothers care for children and fathers go off to work; some Navajo children might be observed pretending to hunt or cook a meal over an open fire (Curry, 1971). Johnson, Yawkey, and Christie (1987) argue that "the typical day care or preschool environment is designed for white middle-class children; we should be ready to add to or to modify that environment to accommodate the diverse backgrounds of other children" (p. 144).

Two interventions will encourage children to engage in culturally relevant play: providing new play props and encouraging themes that reflect cultural diversity. These strategies are illustrated in the vignette below.

❖ ❖

An African-American four-year-old is playing with two Euro-American children in the dramatic play area. A dispute has arisen over the roles that each will play. The African-American child wishes to play the grandmother who lives with the family and watches the children. Her peers argue with her.

Child A: No, Robin, grandmas don't live with the family. They have their own houses. You be the mother.

Child B: Grandmothers do live with the family and take care of the babies. My grandmother takes care of me after day care.

Child C: No. My grandmother's dead.

Teacher: Grandmothers do sometimes live with the mother and father and children. Grandmothers are very important. In some families they take care of the children so the parents can go to work.

Child A: Okay. This can be a family like that. You be the grandmother, then. These will be the babies. (Holds up a Caucasian doll)

Teacher: There's another doll here. (Produces an African-American doll) This could be one of your children.

Child B: (Eagerly accepting the new doll) Yeah. This is our baby. I'll take care of her.

The teacher observes for a few minutes as the children begin their play theme; then he withdraws.   ❖

The teacher recognizes that this African-American child lives in an extended family—grandmothers play a more direct caregiving role in some African-American families (Hale-Benson, 1986). Further, he is sensitive to the child's need to "care for" a baby of her own ethnic group. His interventions have not only reaffirmed the African-American child's family and culture, but have helped the two Euro-American children to understand diverse family configurations and cultural variations.

Children's activity level and the amount of "rough and tumble play"—play in which children wrestle or engage in friendly physical contests—vary as a function of culture. African-American children, for example, can be more active and engage in "rougher" play (Hale-Benson, 1986); Euro-American children report that they are sometimes threatened by this play style (Ramsey, 1987).

Teachers might now and then assist some children in modulating their physicality and activity level in so that less physical children feel more comfortable (e.g., "Don't push too hard, James. Henry doesn't like it when you are so rough."). On the other hand, teachers might help more passive children understand rough and tumble play and distinguish it from true aggression (e.g., "James is just playing a wrestling game with you. He isn't really angry. It's fun to wrestle around sometimes."). Since there is evidence that rough and tumble play is valuable for children (Pellegrini & Perlmutter, 1988), teachers can even facilitate this form of play where appropriate (e.g., "I know something fun you could try. You could both roll down the hill in the box together. Let's get your shoes off first so you don't hurt each other while you wiggle around."). Actually encouraging moderate amounts of such "wild" activity meet a variety of developmental needs and provide outlets for children with more active play styles.

Children's peer relations are influenced by culture. Ramsey (1987) cites a study conducted in New Zealand in which European and Polynesian children were compared in regard to how "inclusive" or "exclusive" they were. European children were more likely to exclude peers from their play groups (e.g., "You can't play, Michael!"); Polynesian children were more likely to invite peers to join in play in progress. The needs of children from both exclusive and inclusive cultures must be considered. Teachers should be sensitive to the desires of exclusive children to select their own playmates and play without disruption. Requiring that children accept another into a group or in other ways forcing children to play together should be avoided. Providing small, isolated "get away" space might allow exclusive children to play in small groups uninterrupted. Children of inclusive cultures may need assistance in peer group entry strategies as described in Chapter 4. Since they may have had very little experience within their own culture in group rejection, much support may be needed to help them acquire entry skills.

Independence and individual initiative are highly valued by many Euro-American families. Competitiveness and individuality are traits that are nurtured at a young age in these families; play that involves individual effort and competitive games with rules are emphasized. In some cultures, collective thought and action is more highly valued. Collaborating, relying on others, and checking with others before acting are more common among children of these families. Children of African-American, Puerto Rican, Mexican-American, Native American, and Japanese-American families, to name a few, are more likely to display a cooperative/collective orientation in their play (Harrison, Wilson, Pine, Chan, & Buriel, 1990; Ramirez, 1988). Teachers must intervene in ways that reflect these individual differences. Encouraging individual initiative (e.g., "What part of your work today are you most proud of?") and providing for optimally competitive games are ways that individual/competitive children's needs may be met. Creating many opportunities for cooperation and minimizing or eliminating competition in some activities (see the section on competition in Chapter 5 for ideas) will be helpful for cooperative/collective children. This latter group may need special assistance in understanding individual ownership; they are more likely to use others' toys or materials without permission. On the other hand, they are more likely to share their materials with peers, providing excellent models of cooperative behavior (Harrison et al., 1990).

Overall, teachers should be sensitive to individual variation of some of these interpersonal dimensions. Adapting activities and interventions so that children feel comfortable in the classroom, but are also exposed to different social and play styles, is required.

Cultural Diversity and Teacher-Parent Interactions

Although the focus of this book is on teacher-child interactions, it is important to note that teachers must develop skills to work effectively with adults as well—other teachers, administrators, and most notably parents. Teacher-parent relationships are extremely important. Every successful early childhood education model has a significant parent involvement component; it may be that changes in parental practices and attitudes explain in part the long term success of early education (Lazar, 1988).

Working with parents can be both challenging and extremely rewarding. Parents and teachers are often highly supportive of one another. When both groups collaborate in setting goals, resolving problems, or enhancing learning, children reap huge benefits. Such collaboration is possible when parents and teachers hold mutual respect for one another. As they come to understand and appreciate one another's unique perspectives about education and the socialization of children, teachers and parents can enter into true partnerships in support of positive development.

Teachers and parents will naturally disagree on some issues, since they play very different roles in a child's life (Katz, 1980). Whereas parents should be "optimally irrational," for example, in their assessments of their own children—that is, they should think mostly positive things about and serve as unquestioning advocates for their own children—teachers should be "optimally rational"—holding slightly more objective perspectives on students in the classroom (Katz, 1980). These differences can create for children some discontinuity between home and school life.

Children can benefit from moderate parent-teacher discontinuity. By experiencing different styles of interaction at home and school they may acquire skills of copability and adaptability.

Mild home-school discontinuity can also be a source of positive interaction when both parents and teachers come to feel comfortable discussing their unique positions and attitudes towards children. One child care director, for example, recently brought teachers and parents together to view and discuss videotapes portraying incidents of child misbehavior. Wonderful dialogue, including a good deal of playful interchange and laughter, resulted; participants came away with greater insight into one another's perspectives.

Problems can arise when home-school discontinuities become too great (Powell, 1989). If the socialization practices and beliefs of home and school clash significantly, for example, a child may have difficultly adjusting to classroom life (Hess, Price, Dickson, & Conroy, 1981). Home-school discontinuity can be severe in instances where children have teachers who do not understand their culture. In this section, guidelines for interacting with parents of diverse cultural backgrounds are considered.

Sources of Discontinuity

Cultural differences may be observed in parenting practices and beliefs (Garcia Coll, 1990). Parents vary in beliefs about adult-child relationships, for example. In some cultures, children are expected to exhibit absolute compliance and respect for adults (Mizio, 1983; Norton, 1983). In others, adult-child relationships are less formal; children are encouraged to assert their desires and feelings in interactions with teachers and parents.

Parenting styles vary across cultures. In a classic study by Baumrind (1972), cultural differences were noted in the degree to which parents assume authoritarian, authoritative, or permissive parenting styles. She found that children whose parents are authoritarian—that is, more controlling and less democratic—were less competent than others. Her finding that African-American parents tended to be more authoritarian led many to the misinterpretation that parents of this culture were deficient in parenting skills. In fact, what she found was that African-American children, particularly girls, were more competent if they had parents of this more directive style. This makes sense given the experience of oppression (Hale-Benson, 1986); a better name for this parenting style would be "high control/high concern." Parenting differences, then, are just that: differences, not deficits. Care should be taken not to judge parenting based on one's own cultural norms.

Differences between parenting and teaching styles can create discontinuity, however. Hale-Benson (1986) describes a situation in which an African-American child, from a community where much adult control is necessary for safety, enters a classroom with a permissive teacher. For a long time this child has difficulty adjusting to an environment with few rules and little adult guidance. She suggests that teachers adapt classroom routines to the socialization experiences of children. Ramsey (1987) recommends, for example, that it may be appropriate to increase external guidance for a time until a child adjusts.

Teachers should never, of course, act in conflict with their own values and beliefs. It is important, however, to be sensitive to individual differences in the need for adult direction and to adapt teaching practice accordingly. Research suggests that improvements in achievement and problem-solving occur when learning environments are made to resemble home environments more closely (Hare, 1985; Slaughter, 1988).

Another source of discontinuity arises from cultural differences in attitudes about school. Parents of all cultures view schooling as important (Garcia Coll, 1990). Differences exist in how school is valued relative to other aspects of life, including family obligations. In some cultures, for example, no duty is more important than meeting family needs (e.g., caring for a sick grandparent or a baby brother or sister) (Ogbu, 1988). There are variations across cultures in beliefs about who is responsible for teaching children. In one study (Steward & Steward, 1974), for example, Chinese mothers reported that parents should play a primary and formal teaching role when interacting with children; Euro-American mothers felt that teaching was only one small part of parenting; and Mexican-American mothers responded that they were parents, not teachers. All mothers in the study expressed concern for their children's education; the differences lay in perceptions of who was responsible for teaching.

Parents also differ across cultures in how comfortable they feel in schools. People of color are more likely than middle-class Euro-Americans to report that schools are hostile, unfriendly places (Tharp, 1989).

These, and parenting family-life differences, can lead to misunderstandings and conflict. When a parent declines a conference in order to help a cousin move into a new apartment; when another expresses a lack of desire to do informal math tutoring with a child; when another does not attend P.T.O meetings at the school, teachers can interpret these behaviors as a lack of caring. Each could merely be a result of cultural beliefs and values; understanding and appreciation of these is critical to positive parent-teacher relationships.

Smoothing Home-School Discontinuities

What can teachers do when discontinuities exist? First, they must come to fully understand the cultures of children in their classrooms. Reading about other cultures is important; engaging parents in discussions about cultural norms and practices is also useful. Ramsey (1987) suggests holding a parent-teacher meeting at which vignettes of various behavior management dilemmas are read and discussed. As participants describe how they would respond to these dilemmas, both teachers and parents gain an understanding of socialization beliefs and practices.

Interacting with parents in culturally sensitive ways is important. Taking care not to judge parenting and family life through ethnocentric perspective is critical to positive relationships with parents. An example illustrates this point.

❖ ❖

A primary grade teacher has just received word from a Puerto Rican mother that she will be unable to attend a scheduled parent conference; a close friend of the family will attend instead. The teacher is initially disturbed by this response. Does the parent care so little about her child's education that she will send a neighbor to attend the conference for her?

She consults a Puerto Rican colleague who helps her to understand the situation. "Fictive kin are quite common in Puerto Rican families," she explains. "'Padres de crianza,' informally selected co-parents, may share parenting responsibilities in times of family hardship. Although these relationships are not recognized by American legal institutions, in Puerto Rican culture they are considered true family bonds. Generally, caring for children is a collective, community affair, more so than in Anglo culture."

The teacher resolves the conflict by calling the parent and rescheduling the conference at a time when both she and the family friend can attend together. She marvels at how involved and concerned the friend is during the conference.   ❖

Bronfenbrenner (1979) offers other recommendations for smoothing home-school discontinuities. These are presented in Table 11-1.

Planning transitions to school is critical; having children visit a new classroom for a significant period of time accompanied by family members or familiar peers will help establish trust. Providing regular face-to-face dialogue is also important. Bronfenbrenner (1979) argues that one-way communication through newsletters or notes from the teacher are not enough; genuine dia-

Table 11-1
Strategies to Address Home-School Discontinuity

Establishing goal consensus	Teachers and parents resolve conflicts or set developmental goals through negotiation and compromise. For example, a teacher and parent agree to facilitate a child's native language as well as English both at home and in school.
Planning transitions	Teachers invite parents and siblings to accompany the child as often as possible during the first week of school. They facilitate pre-enrollment, out-of-school play experiences among children who will be classmates there and will be familiar peers at school on the first day.
Providing supportive linkages	Teachers organize parent support groups to explore child rearing issues and school-related topics. These include open-ended, culturally sensitive sessions that do not focus on imparting "correct" parenting skills.
Engaging in two-way, face-to-face dialogue	Teachers and parents meet regularly before and after school or converse on the phone. Problems are resolved as they arise, not just at parent conference time.

Source: Adapted from Bronfenbrenner (1979) and Powell (1989)

logue around issues and concerns is necessary. Providing "supportive link-ages" through parenting programs will smooth discontinuities. A distinction is made here between ethnocentric parent education programs in which "cor-rect" parenting behaviors are presented, and support programs in which par-ents share issues from their own cultural perspectives (Powell, 1989). The lat-ter programs are likely to be more culturally sensitive and articulate acceptance of variations in parenting.

Bronfenbrenner's recommendation of establishing goal consensus is per-haps most difficult to achieve. He argues that when teacher-parent conflicts arise, consensus can be reached through negotiation about what is best for children. Compromise and adaptation are required of both teachers and par-ents to accomplish this. The challenge is to reach consensus without compro-mising the beliefs or practices of either parents or teachers.

An example of this parent-teacher negotiation process is presented below.

An African-American child has been enrolled in a predominantly white kinder-garten classroom. Her mother is quite worried about how being "different" from other children will affect her daughter's self-esteem and achievement in school. Several weeks after start of the school year she notices changes in her daugh-ter's behavior. She is less respectful and compliant; she seems particularly "wound up" after getting off the school bus in the afternoons. Her mother begins to suspect that the teacher is not providing enough guidance in the classroom. She wonders if the teacher holds the same expectations for her daughter in regard to classroom behavior and learning that she does for other children in the class. Her response to the problem is to establish firm discipline at home; she requires her daughter to sit on the couch whenever she is "out of hand."

The teacher of this classroom is very much concerned about meeting the needs of her new African-American student. She worries about acceptance by peers; she has noticed "adjustment problems" during the first few weeks of school. This child appears to be anxious about the new school experience; this anxiety is sometimes expressed in loud and "wild" behavior. The teacher has also noted at a meeting with parents before school that this child's mother is quite firm and expects high academic achievement from her daughter. The teacher wonders if this parenting style is also creating stress. The teacher's response to these circumstances is to provide the child with as many open-ended, expressive activities as possible. She sets few limits on the child's play and avoids restricting her sometimes loud expressive activities. The solutions of parent and teacher to this problem are clearly at odds.

The parent requests a conference with the teacher to discuss her concerns. In an hour-long conversation they each candidly express opinions. It becomes clear after a short time that a clash in beliefs has arisen. The teacher explains her commitment to open-ended play and self-expression and defends her strategy of giving the child some freedom during this adjustment period. She suggests that play activities are ideal for nurturing friendships and assuring peer acceptance. She argues that administering harsh discipline at home might exacerbate the problem. The parent asserts that it is the lack of limits and adult guidance that is causing the problem. She shares that in her community children are always under the watchful eye of adults—parents, relatives, even neighbors. The freedom is simply too much for her child.

After all opinions have been expressed, the teacher suggests that they try to come to consensus on the best way to assist the child. She identifies areas of agreement and suggests ways each might compromise. The following is a portion of this discussion that illustrates consensus-building.

Teacher:	So let me review here. I will give more guidance to your daughter, since you believe this would help her to feel more secure. We'll remind her of the rules when she breaks them.
Parent:	Right. And you said you'd have her stop playing if she didn't mind.
Teacher:	Right. If she breaks a rule in the blocks, for instance, she would need to play somewhere else. But I'll encourage her to play and interact with her classmates and to be as active as she wishes when it's appropriate.
Parent:	Now, what I'll do is try letting her play more at home. I'll try to handle the noise a little better (laughs). It's just that some days she and her sisters really drive me crazy with the noise.
Teacher:	(Laughs) Listen—you don't have to tell me about noise! I have fifteen children in this classroom. ❖

This teacher has come to goal consensus with a parent. She acknowledges differences in beliefs about child socialization and agrees to provide more guidance until the child becomes comfortable in this new environment. She insists, however, that the child continue to play in open-ended and even loud, active ways; the parent agrees to allow more of this at home. Ultimately the child adjusts to school; such collaboration is critical for the success of early childhood programs.

Gender Differences and Play Intervention

The play of girls and boys is very similar during the early years (Johnson, Christie, & Yawkey, 1987). Although differences have been found "on the average" between the sexes, individual variation in play behaviors and styles is so great that it is hard to make conclusions about what is "boy-play" and what is "girl-play." The teacher must make decisions about play intervention based on individual needs, then, rather than on gender expectations; one cannot assume that boys must always be guided toward more housekeeping play, girls to the block area.

Boys tend to be as "person-oriented" and as sociable as girls (Jennings, 1975; Johnson & Roopnarine, 1983). Counter to expectations, girls and boys tend to explore, pretend, and build with objects in much the same ways (Johnson, Christie, & Yawkey, 1987). Both sexes perform the same amount of make-believe, although differences have been found in the nature of pretend episodes (Johnson & Roopnarine, 1983; McLoyd, 1980). Only a few play differences can be identified from research; implications of these findings for play intervention will be considered in this section.

Rough and Tumble Play and Activity Level

Boys tend to be more active in their play both indoors and out; they also engage in more rough and tumble play. Girls' play, in contrast, tends to be quieter and more reflective (Johnson, Christie, & Yawkey, 1987). To some degree these differences in play preference should be respected; they may be as much a result of maturational differences and play interests as sex-role stereotyping. However, both quiet and active play are useful. To the degree that children feel these activities are gender inappropriate, teachers should intervene to broaden their activity repertoire. Since there is evidence that rough and tumble play is developmentally useful and that girls refrain from such activities unless give explicit permission to do so (Pellegrini & Perlmutter, 1988), teachers might unobtrusively suggest or model this more active play form for girls. Statements such as: "Would you like to help us chase the wolves away?" or "Can you think of some silly ways to slide down the slide?" may draw girls into useful activities that they would not have otherwise considered.

Boys sometimes might be guided to quieter, more reflective activities. After a morning of wild play in the block area, a child might be invited to the writing center: "You've been playing race-car driver. You could write about what you've been playing in your journal. I'm writing an entry in mine. Will you join me?" Teachers can also create less open-ended, more organized motor play for boys now and then: "You are all playing wild animals. Are you in a zoo? Is there a zoo keeper who feeds you?" Such interactions may lead to greater coordination of roles, symbolization, and interpersonal negotiation. The focus of these interventions is not to inhibit either rough and tumble or quiet/passive play, but to broaden children's play repertoires. A balance of quiet and active experience is optimal for all young children.

Play Themes

Girls and boys have different play interests. Boys choose to play outside more often than girls (Harper & Sanders, 1975) and when indoors choose more active and adventuresome activities such as block building or pretending with toy vehicles. Girls select art activities and dramatic play more frequently (Sutton-Smith, 1979). When in the dramatic play area, girls more often select home and family themes; boys are more inclined to choose superhero or adventure roles (Grief, 1976). Although girls and boys both show clear play preferences, boys are more "asymmetric" in their play choices; that is, they are far less likely to engage in stereotypically "girl" activities than girls are in "male" ones. Girls seem interested in using "boy toys" as well as "girl toys" (Johnson, Christie, & Yawkey, 1987).

Interventions to broaden children's play repertoires are in order. Teachers can gently guide children toward activities that they rarely try, particularly those activities that are stereotypically considered gender-inappropriate. Boys can be guided into nurturant family-related themes in the dramatic play area: "It's almost supper time. Would you like to help me cook some dinner for our family?" Girls might be encouraged to build with blocks or to go outdoors: "Why don't you come out with me to the climber? I'm putting a parachute over the top of it to make a cave."

Children as young as three are resistent to engage in activities that they consider gender-inappropriate (Derman-Sparks, 1989); it may take persistence to break down stereotypes. Teachers should entice, but never pressure children to try new activities. Since peer pressure often promotes stereotypical play, particularly among boys, individual children might be encouraged to try new activities on their own. One study found that sex-typed behavior was far less prevalent when children played by themselves (Serbin, Conner, Burchardt, & Citron, 1979).

Symbolization in Play

Boys and girls tend to perform the same amount of make-believe in their play. Several studies have found, however, that girls' pretend play is more symbolic and abstract (McLoyd, 1980; Trawick-Smith, 1990). Girls are more likely to use nonrealistic props, such as boxes or wooden rods, to stand for things that are completely different (e.g., using a block as if it were a broom to sweep a pretend kitchen). This may be due to maturation; boys may simply be less ready cognitively to symbolize in this abstract way. Since these highly symbolic enactments may be developmentally useful (Trawick-Smith, 1990; Vygotsky, 1976), teachers might make a special effort to introduce nonrealistic materials to boys and encourage them to transform these into imaginary play objects. A teacher might suggest: "Matthew, you could use this box to be your airplane" or "Michael, you can stir the soup with this spoon" (handing the child a wooden rod). Many other examples of such interventions are provided in Chapter 3.

Mixed-Gender Play Groups

A number of studies have shown that children prefer same-sex play groups. Girls show this preference by age two; boys slightly later in development

(LaFreniere, Strayer, & Gauthier, 1984). Although this phenomenon has been explained by pointing to similarities in maturation and play interests of same-sex children (Johnson, Christie, & Yawkey, 1987), learned bias toward those of the opposite gender may also play a part.

Same-sex play preferences create a dilemma for teachers. On the one hand, it is important for children to select their own playmates; friendships must emerge from genuine mutual liking. To tamper too vigorously with gender divisions in play may threaten naturally emerging peer relations. On the other hand, negative gender attitudes can form early; positive experiences with those of the opposite sex may counter these. A teacher might choose a hands-off policy on some occasions, then, allowing children to pair up with same-sex playmates. At other times they can facilitate mixed-gender play groups by guiding both boys and girls to activities of mutual interest (e.g., "Phil and Janet, you should come see the new materials I have put in the math center."). In some cases they might even structure special projects to which both boys and girls are included (e.g., "We're making stone soup in the kitchen. Rachel and Timothy, would you like to come help us?"). Thus, a balance can be struck in classroom social interactions between self-selected play groups and more heterogeneous groupings that break down stereotyping and bias.

Stereotyped Pretend Play

Within dramatic play and other creative activities young children often demonstrate stereotyped behavior (Matthews, 1981). Boys often take on stereotypically masculine roles in the dramatic play area, for example. What is more worrisome, they often treat female characters (e.g., wives and mothers) as if they were inept, helpless, and responsible only for housekeeping and child-care duties. Girls are more likely to take on nurturing roles such as mother and wife, often acquiescing to the leadership initiatives of boys (Grief, 1976). These play patterns give a "snapshot" of emerging sex role stereotypes at this young age.

Although vigorously altering play roles or directing children to adopt less stereotyped behaviors constitute inappropriate intrusions into children's activities, teachers can subtly challenge gender bias as they play with children. By taking on make-believe characters and modeling or prompting less stereotypic behaviors, they may raise questions for children about the roles and responsibilities of males and females in society. The two vignettes below illustrate this approach.

❖ ❖

A five-year-old boy joins two girls of the same age in the dramatic play area. He quickly assumes the role of firefighter and rescues his two peers from a burning building. A teacher takes a role in the theme—that of another firefighter.

Teacher: (Gesturing) Let me help you handle this fire hose. It is pretty heavy.

Child A:	Wait. You be one of the mothers. I'm saving you from the fire.
Teacher:	I'd like to be one of the firefighters.
Child A:	But you're a girl.
Teacher:	Both men and women can be firefighters. Come on! Let's put out that blaze!
Child B:	(Making a gesture as if working with another fire hose) I'm going to squirt some water over here. There's more fire over here.
Child A:	No! You're the mom.
Child B:	I'm going to be a firefighter.
Child A:	Who can we rescue then?
Teacher:	Come on! We need to put this fire out. The whole building could burn to the ground. (To Child B) Can you call in to the fire station and ask for more help? We need more firefighters for this blaze! ❖

Without altering the play theme or issuing harsh challenges to this young boy's stereotyped images of firefighters, the teacher dispels myths about male and female responsibilities and draws a girl into a nonstereotypic role. As she plays with the children she demonstrates attributes of courage, strength, and leadership—showing children that females may possess these traits.

❖ ❖

A four-year-old boy watches two four-year-old girls play a home-related theme. They dress dolls, pretend to cook and serve a meal. One of the girls invites the boy to play. A teacher joins them as well.

Through modeling, teachers can reduce sex role stereotyping in play.

Child A:	Alonzo, you could be the dad, all right? You come eat our dinner we made for you.
Child B:	(Moves over to the table where the make-believe feast is served) What are we eating?
Child C:	Oh. We've made you some delicious scrambled eggs and bacon.
Child B:	We don't eat eggs for dinner. That's breakfast!
Child A:	Let's say it's breakfast, 'cause it's morning and you are going to work.
Teacher:	(Moves into the play area) I'll join you for breakfast if that's all right.
Child A:	Sure. You eat too. It's scrambled eggs.
Teacher:	(To Child B) And after breakfast we'll wash the dishes, all right, Alonzo? They cooked, so we clean. That's how we do it at my house.
Child B:	No, 'cause I have to go to work. They're the mothers.
Teacher:	But the mothers might need to go to work too. (To Children A and C) Do you go to work outside the home?
Child A:	I think we do, right, Lawanda?
Child C:	Yeah, we have to go work at the grocery.

They finish their pretend breakfast; then the teacher and Child B wash the dishes. ❖

Here the teacher prompts children to assume less stereotyped roles. He encourages a boy to assume housekeeping responsibilities; he assists girls in broadening their mother roles to include outside-the-home work responsibilities. Overall, dramatic play is an excellent context for modelling and suggesting nonstereotypic behaviors in nonjudgmental and unobtrusive ways.

Play Intervention and Children with Special Needs

Several pieces of landmark federal legislation have made the integration of young children with special needs into regular classrooms more prevalent. Public Law 94-142 provides for a free and appropriate education for all preschool and school-age children—including those with special needs. This education must occur in the "least restrictive alternative" according to the law; children whose special needs are best served in a regular classroom must be integrated into "the mainstream." Public Law 99-457 extends rights and supports programs specifically for infants, toddlers, and preschoolers with special needs. The net effect of this legislation has been to blur the once-clear division between the roles and responsibilities of regular and special educators. Teachers in regular classrooms must now acquire skills and knowledge to work with exceptional children. Play-intervention strategies presented in this book must be adapted in some ways in order to meet some children's special needs.

Children with varying exceptionalities may be successfully integrated into the regular classroom; several exceptionalities that teachers might encounter are listed in Table 11-2.

Table 11-2
Categories of Exceptionalities of Young Children

Category	Description
Mentally retarded	Children of significantly limited intellectual functioning.
Deaf/hearing impaired	Children with complete hearing loss or with impairments that cause them to miss considerable spoken information.
Speech or language impaired	Children with atypical functional or structural communicative impairments that inhibit communication. Speech and language disorders frequently accompany other disabilities.
Visually impaired	Children who can not see better than 20/200 after correction or those whose field of vision is limited to an angle of less than 20 degrees. Many visually impaired children are unable to benefit from print material; pre-braille and braille literacy experiences are required.
Socially/emotionally maladjusted	Children who display intense negative affect and are unable to function effectively in social contexts. The sources of social/emotional maladjustment are diverse and under great debate—environmental, neurological, and chemical causes are cited.
Orthopedically impaired	Children who have any disorder interfering with the health or normal functioning of bones, joints, or muscles. This category includes a broad range of conditions, including cerebral palsy, muscular dystrophy, and spina bifida.
Learning disabled	Children with various specific learning impairments, including perceptual-motor difficulties, word-retrieval and other communication problems, and attention deficits.
Multiply impaired	Children who display various combinations of above-described exceptionalities. These often interact with one another to compound learning and teaching challenges.

Source: Adapted from Fallen and Umansky (1985)

Special needs are often addressed following a transdisciplinary team approach in which professionals from various fields—psychologists, social workers, teachers, speech and language pathologists, physical therapists, pediatricians, and classroom teachers—work with parents to plan and deliver an appropriate educational program (Fallen & Umansky, 1985). One goal of the team is to adapt the curriculum and the classroom environment to meet special needs. Children with delayed motor development, for example, can be provided with adapted large muscle equipment—e.g., scooter boards, special supportive chairs, pencil holders that fasten around the hand to facilitate writing or drawing—that will help develop coordination and allow greater movement and independence. Important large motor activities (e.g., aiming games or climbers) might be provided within a special large-motor center right in the classroom (Fallen & Umansky, 1985).

Children with cognitive impairments might be challenged with special problem-solving activities within the classroom that meet unique learning needs. Children with learning disabilities, for example, might be provided with materials that are especially stimulating—bright, loud, textured materials, and those that relate to individual interests—in order to capture and maintain attention (Fallen & Umansky, 1985). The book center might be enhanced, for instance, with dramatic taped readings of available books to heighten children's involvement in book-looking.

Children who are mentally retarded would benefit from classroom activities that reflect a range of learning modalities—auditory, visual, and tactile/kinesthetic (Fallen & Umansky, 1985). Although this is important for typically developing students as well (all learners show preference for one modality or another), children with mental retardation need special opportunities to learn through several channels—particularly kinesthetic. Multimodal classrooms, generally, assure that all children will have opportunities to construct information through a preferred input channel and also to refine secondary learning modes (Fallen & Umansky, 1985).

A child who is socially/emotionally maladjusted might be provided special adult-guided play experiences with small groups of children (see Chapter 4 for guidelines). Opportunities for symbolic/expressive activities such as open-ended drawing, sculpting, or sand play will provide healthy outlets for aggressive impulses (Fallen & Umansky, 1985).

In-depth examination of curricular adaptations to meet special needs is beyond the scope of this book. These classroom adaptations are essential to ensure that young children with special needs will thrive—but they are not sufficient. The theme of this book has been that teacher-child interactions are most important in fostering positive development. This is nowhere more true than in classrooms where children with special needs are served. Many of the teacher interactions described in this book are extremely useful in meeting special needs; modeling, question-asking, prompting, hint-giving, encouraging, and nurturing are all recommended tools for engaging children with exceptionalities (Fallen & Umansky, 1985). Several special interventions are particularly useful when working with young children with exceptionalities; these will be examined in this section.

Activation

Some children with special needs have a more difficult time with activation—the process of initiating interactions with the environment. Although all children will display unengaged behavior now and then in the classroom, some may need regular assistance in noticing and getting started on available activities (Musselwhite, 1986). Commenting on and guiding children's attention to attractive materials is helpful (e.g., "I'd like to show you the great shells I added to our science center."). Orienting children to what peers are doing is also important (e.g., "Oh look, Sean. Patricia and Mark are fingerpainting."). Sometimes sensory stimulation will activate a child; placing a textured object from the science center in a child's hand, creating a visually captivating design with blocks, or reading a book in a particularly dramatic voice at the library center may grab a child's attention. Generally, teachers should monitor children with activation difficulties; assistance in getting started might be needed throughout the school day, especially during transition times.

Exploring, Constructing, and Symbolizing with Objects

Once children have been activated—their attention has been successfully directed toward classroom materials or activities—teachers can continue to lend support to those whose knowledge of toy or object use is limited (Musselwhite, 1986). Some children with special needs may not know what to do with available materials; some will perform simple, repetitive, motoric enactments that are less useful for development. Teachers can guide such children in more organized and stimulating toy use.

A first step may be to help children explore classroom materials. Children often explore the properties of objects before playing with them (Hutt, 1971); those with special needs might benefit from adult interventions to facilitate exploration. Teachers might give children with special needs regular "tours" of the classroom to show materials and how they work—e.g., "Look at this puzzle. See how tiny the pieces are? Would you like to feel some of the pieces?" (handing several puzzle pieces to the child). Simply making children aware of classroom materials may be the only goal of these interventions; these students may not be expected to play with toys in conventional ways until they have become fully familiar with the environment.

When children show interest, teachers can help them learn how to use materials in the ways that they are intended. Using guidelines from previous chapters on modeling, hint-giving, and prompting, teachers might encourage "conventional object use" (Musselwhite, 1986, p. 98). Children with special needs might first be guided to simple, less symbolic activities; push toys, water play, and large motor games are good places to begin. Eventually, teachers can prompt construction play, assisting children in block building or encouraging spontaneous construction activities in other parts of the classroom (e.g., "I see you're stacking all the dishes into a tall tower.").

Children with cognitive, language, or motor impairments will have more difficulty pretending. They may need special support from adults in learning to make object or other make-believe transformations as described in Chapter 3. Almost all children can perform some dramatic-play enactments, even if these are simple pretenses. The vignette below demonstrates how a teacher engages a child with Down's Syndrome in simple make-believe.

❖ ❖

A child plays alone in the dramatic play area, repetitively placing dishes out on a table then collecting them all and returning them to the cupboard. A teacher approaches.

Teacher:	Looks like it is almost dinner time.
Child:	(Looks at the teacher, says nothing)
Teacher:	I am quite hungry. Think I'll sit down and eat. (Sits at the table)
Child:	(Says nothing, places dishes in front of the teacher)
Teacher:	Ah, thanks. Dinner. (Pretends to eat with play utensils)
Child:	(Watches, says nothing)
Teacher:	Would you like to eat? There's plenty of broccoli left. (Continues to model make-believe eating)
Child:	(Picks up a fork and pretends to eat)
Teacher:	It's very good, don't you think?
Child:	(Smiles) Yeah. ❖

Here the teacher has used modeling to prompt simple make-believe with objects. Musselwhite (1986) argues that even this most basic form of symbolization is useful for children with special needs; there is a link between this type of activity and children's language and cognitive development.

The guidelines presented here for initiating and enhancing classroom activities are not unlike those proposed in earlier sections of the book to facilitate the play of typically developing children. Children with special needs may need more frequent or more extensive guidance, however; effective teachers are particularly energetic in monitoring and engaging those with exceptionalities.

Visual Tracking

Many types of exceptionalities involve problems of visual tracking—the ability to smoothly follow moving objects visually. Children with cerebral palsy, for example, may be restricted in head control and range of vision, making it difficult for them to watch objects as they move across their field of vision. An inability to track may be related to numerous school-related and communication difficulties (Fieber, 1983); tracking may be even more important for children with special needs who may have limited body movement and must rely more heavily on eye motion. Play contexts are ideal for enhancing tracking abilities. When teachers play with children in the blocks, they might move plastic people or toy cars across a child's field of vision and encourage watching. While reading a book, teachers can ask children to scan and find a particular illustration or page in the book. During outdoor play, teachers can invite children to blow, follow, and pop bubbles (Musselwhite, 1986). Overall, engaging children in active play experiences is an enjoyable and natural way to enhance perceptual competence.

Adapting Toys

Typical early childhood activities may be inaccessible to children with special needs; slight adaptations could lead to greater accessibility. Although teachers can often anticipate and address these problems before they arise, sometimes spontaneous adaptation of an activity during play-in-progress is required (Musselwhite, 1986). The teacher below demonstrates such an adaptation.

A child with large motor delays is attempting to join another child in making drawings in cornmeal poured into a tray. As he tries to join in, he knocks the tray to the floor; the corn meal spills out. His peer expresses upset.

Child A:	Look! He spilled it all out!
Child B:	(Looks down, says nothing)
Teacher:	Oops! That tray slides off the table so easily.
Child A:	He knocked it!
Teacher:	It was an accident. I have that problem sometimes. I have knocked things off a slippery table. What could we do to attach the tray so it doesn't slide?
Child B:	Glue it, I think.
Teacher:	Well, then the tray would stay stuck forever. How about if I clamped it? (Retrieves a metal clamp from the woodworking area; clamps the tray to the table and adds more cornmeal) There. Try that.

The children draw in the cornmeal for many minutes without further spills.   ❖

Here the teacher has quickly assessed that a motor limitation has made a useful activity inaccessible. By adapting the materials the teacher has remedied the situation. Teachers must monitor activities throughout the classroom and be ready to make such adaptations to meet special needs.

Decision Making

Some children with special needs have a hard time making decisions (Musselwhite, 1986). This may stem from an impairment, but also may be the result of overly protective teachers, parents, or peers who have not encouraged them to make choices in their lives. Teachers should be vigilant throughout the school day for opportunities to give choices to children. When students with special needs first enter a new learning environment, a teacher might initially limit choices to a manageable few (e.g., "Would you like to use this car or that one?"). As they show an ability to make decisions, more open-ended strategies can be employed (e.g., "What would you like to do on the playground today?"). Eventually, all children, even those with special needs, will be able to make most decisions about what, where, when, and with whom they will play without a great deal of adult guidance. It is especially important for teachers not to make all choices for children, nor to allow peers to do this. It is a common misconception that children with special needs must have others always to make decisions for them.

Self-Help Skill Development

Children with special needs sometimes require greater assistance in personal care. Often such needs can be addressed through adaptation of the environment (e.g., special toileting facilities or velcro snaps on clothing). Sometimes children will seek assistance from adults in completing a self-help task (e.g., zipping a zipper or pouring juice). On occasion children with more significant needs are integrated into regular classrooms; teachers will have added responsibilities in fostering independent personal-care skills.

Basic eating skills such as drinking from a cup or using utensils, which are often mastered by typically developing children in the preschool years, may pose a great challenge to some. Through modeling and giving suggestions, teachers can help most children learn to feed themselves. However, in many early-childhood classrooms—even those serving a significant number of exceptional children—teachers spend no time guiding children in eating skills (Bailey, Harms, & Clifford, 1983).

A single lunchtime experience may not provide enough opportunities for teachers to assist in eating skill development. One suggestion has been to break meals down into hourly "mini-meals" for some children. During these eating periods teachers can facilitate skills development. Using the Montessori approach of having children eat a snack individually or in pairs whenever they wish might be useful in some cases. When a child with special needs eats with only one other child at the "snack center," teachers can devote individualized attention to promoting eating abilities.

Toileting and grooming skills are usually fostered in any program that enrolls very young children; those with special needs may require extra support in these self-help areas. There is much evidence to suggest that a casual, nonpressured approach to toileting is best; harsh correction or even tangible rewards for success may create stress and be counterproductive (Fallen & Umansky, 1985). Teachers may need to help children with special needs learn specific steps in some procedures. It is recommended that these be taught through demonstration coupled with verbalization. For some toileting or grooming activities teachers might provide a mirror so that children can observe themselves and come to conceptualize the tasks they are engaged in (Finnie, 1975). Tips for more easily accomplishing self-care routines should be provided (e.g., children might be encouraged to lie on the floor while dressing or lean against a wall with knees bent to put on shoes). Environments can be adapted to accommodate special needs (e.g., a basin can be provided on the floor for those unable to stand up in front of a sink).

Overall, children should be encouraged to perform self-help tasks to the degree that they are able, but should not be pressured to attempt activities for which they are not ready.

Facilitating Social Interaction

The most important responsibility of teachers of children with special needs is to facilitate their social interaction with peers. Children with mental retardation, learning disabilities, social/emotional maladjustment, or other exceptionalities are at risk of peer neglect or rejection (Strain & Kohler, 1988). Strategies for fostering social skills have been described in detail in Chapter 4; enhancing abilities such as entering and exiting peer groups, responding positively to peer initiatives, making play suggestions, or using language effectively and appropriately are even more important for children with special needs. Pairing children with socially competent peers may be effective (Musselwhite, 1986).

When adults play with children they can encourage social participation (e.g., "Jeremy, Sherrie and I are looking at a funny book. Would you like to join us?"), positive interaction (e.g., "Maybe you and Martin could be pilots. You can fly the plane; Martin can work the radio. What do you think?"), and verbalization (e.g., "That is a very funny story. You ought to tell Sharon about it.") among children with exceptionalities and typically developing peers. Such interventions are most effective when delivered in authentic child-directed play settings, rather than contrived adult-guided group lessons.

A story told by a teacher who recently integrated several children with communicative disorders into her regular kindergarten classroom raises cautions about social skills facilitation. This teacher made a number of disturbing observations in watching the reactions of her typically developing students. First, a number of children were observed interacting with these new classmates in a very patronizing fashion. They would talk to them in simple baby talk and perform tasks for them; in one case a student washed a child's hands for her! In an effort to foster caring and empathy among typically developing children, this teacher had unconsciously portrayed these language delayed children as helpless. It took her much of a year to undue this image; she had to intervene directly at times to extinguish this indulgent behavior (e.g., "No, Rachel, Nicky can wash his own hands. Why don't you each wash your own hands together? You could share the soap.").

This teacher reports another equally troubling observation: Children of this classroom would often imply or even state directly that they were expected to play with their new classmates whether they wished to do this or not. The following vignette illustrates this pattern of interaction.

❖ ❖

Two children are playing together. A language-delayed peer approaches.

Child A: We have to let Nicky get on the climber.

Child B: No, Andy! This is our cave! He can't play.

Child A: I know, but the teacher makes us play with him.

Child B: Why?

Child A: 'Cause he can't do anything by himself.

Child B: All right, but he can't be one of the hunters.   ❖

There are several disturbing elements in this vignette. The children clearly believe that they are required to play with this peer; such a mandate, whether imagined or real, will inhibit formation of true friendships. The children speak to one another, ignoring the child with special needs. Although they allow him on the climber, they do not interact with him in any genuine way. The messages of the vignette are clear: Teachers must be cautious not to portray some children as helpless; they should refrain from heavy-handedness in facilitating peer interaction.

More authentic, less directive interventions will facilitate true friendships, as the following vignette reveals.

❖ ❖

A child with Down's Syndrome watches a peer play at the water table. The peer continues to play and ignores him. A teacher enters the area.

Teacher: (To Child A) Look, Patrick. I have some new water play containers. Let's give them a try.

Child A: (Says nothing. Moves with the teacher over to the water table)

At this point the teacher and Child A begin to pour water down clear plastic tubes and fill containers. The teacher comments on their activities; his animated manner quickly captures the attention of the other child playing there.

Child B: Let me try those.

Teacher: Patrick, show Samantha what we're doing. Show her how these tubes work.

Child A: See? (Demonstrates pouring water)

Child B: (Laughs) Let's try to pour more water. Let's use a bigger cup.

The two children begin to experiment with the water play toys; the teacher withdraws.   ❖

Here the teacher has facilitated genuine interaction. He assists the child with special needs in inventing an enticing game; a peer joins him without any prompting. The teacher enhances feelings of confidence by encouraging the child with Down's Syndrome to demonstrate how the toys are used; such interventions promote acceptance and respect among non-handicapped peers.

Augmentative Communication

Language intervention strategies are particularly important for children with special needs. Approaches outlined in Chapter 5 can be implemented for children with a wide range of exceptionalities. It must be noted that examples given in that chapter involve verbal communication. Some children will communicate through augmentative systems—for example, American Sign Language or physical communication boards. Teachers must adapt language interventions to meet the needs of children communicating in these ways. A first step is for the teacher to learn the augmentative system—this is not an easy task but an important one if teachers wish to be effective language facilitators.

Once the system is learned, challenges still exist; research suggests that there are significant barriers to rich communication between children using augmentative communication and their teachers or typically developing peers (Musselwhite, 1986). Nonspeakers often are not provided with as many opportunities to communicate; when they are given a turn in a conversation, they are frequently not allowed enough time to get their ideas across (Harris, 1982; Yoder & Kraat, 1983). Nonspeakers often produce only short, one-word utterances; also, they rarely hear rich and varied language from either adults or peers (Shane, Lipschultz, & Shane, 1982). Teachers must make a concerted effort, then, to use rich, complex language even when signing or using aided communication systems. Giving extra "wait time," as described in previous chapters, is critical. Teachers can assist typically developing peers in learning an augmentative system and encourage them to take turns and wait longer for responses when interacting with children with communication disorders (e.g., "Wait a moment, Sharon. Max isn't quite finished with what he was saying. See? He's still signing.").

Musselwhite (1986) suggests the use of open-ended, nonpressured communication games to be played between typically developing and language-impaired children. An example she provides is a game in which children sit on opposite sides of a board; neither can see the other's side. The nonspeaker (perhaps with assistance from a teacher) makes a design with stickers that the other player cannot see. Then with the use of a communication board or through signing, that player describes the design; the other player must attempt to reproduce it. In such a game both children are encouraged to use rich descriptive language and to take turns.

The Anti-Bias Curriculum

The focus of this chapter has been on adapting teacher-child interactions to meet the unique needs of children of diverse cultural and developmental backgrounds. Louise Derman-Sparks and the Anti-Bias Curriculum Task Force (1989) have argued that teachers' obligations go beyond such adaptations; proactive strategies to counteract bias are also required. Initiatives that target attitudinal change in children are necessary. They have designed an "Anti-Bias Curriculum"; a brief description of key components is provided here.

Creating an Anti-Bias Environment

The task force has documented that even very young children recognize when the environment does not reflect their own culture, gender, or developmental background. When an African-American child finds only Caucasian dolls in the dramatic play area, when a child with cerebral palsy finds no books that depict persons with disabilities, when girls see only pictures of male scientists in the science area, they can be deeply affected (Derman-Sparks, 1989). A first step in counteracting bias, then, is to assess and adapt the classroom environment to better reflect diversity.

Activities That Raise Consciousness and Challenge Bias

The task force also recommends planned activities that challenge children's stereotypes and misconceptions about culture, gender, and exceptionality. Conducting conversations that openly acknowledge and celebrate differences rather than denying them are suggested. An example is cited of a teacher leading a group time discussion on "where people get their color" (Derman-Sparks, 1989, p. 33). The teacher listens with respect to one child's theory that darker skin is the result of being colored with pens. Finally she clears up the misconception by describing how skin color comes from "mommies and daddies." She gives examples of children of various races in the classroom: "Denise's skin is lighter brown because she is a mixture of her mommy's white skin and her daddy's black skin" (p. 33). This openness is rare; many teachers feel uncomfortable addressing differences so directly.

In another example, a teacher brings a wheelchair to the class and children take turns riding in it. One child refuses to sit on it, saying that if he gets in, he "won't walk" (Derman-Sparks, 1989, p. 43). This fear of "catching" disability is common; activities such as this help break down such misconceptions.

Anti-Bias Teacher-Child Interaction

The most powerful way to counteract bias, however, is to engage in respectful and equitable interactions with children in the classroom (Hendrick, 1992). Without thinking, teachers will treat subgroups of students differently. They ask questions of, respond to, and discuss learning tasks with children of color less often (Leacock, 1982; Mejia, 1983). They respond to boys' questions and comments more quickly than to girls' and give boys more explicit freedom (Derman-Sparks, 1989). They allow boys to interrupt more, and are more likely, themselves, to interrupt girls (Hendrick & Stange, 1990). Children notice this differential treatment at a young age (Stipek & MacIver, 1989). The task force recommends that teachers videotape their interactions with children and analyze the tapes for evidence of bias. Serbin, Connor, and Citron (1978) have shown that teachers become more equitable in their distribution of questions or attention after these videotaping sessions.

Another kind of teacher-child interaction that is important in the anti-bias classroom is responding to discriminatory behaviors. A common teacher reaction to statements of prejudice is discomfort; the resulting response is often silence. Teachers may ignore some biased comments or actions because they are at a loss for what to say or do. Derman-Sparks and colleagues (1989) argue that teachers should respond immediately to such behaviors, expressing concern and discussing directly why a particular act or comment is hurtful or inappropriate. They should help children explore sources of discomfort with people who are different and give alternative strategies for dealing with these feelings. The following vignette illustrates their approach.

❖ ❖

A Euro-American five-year-old runs his hand over the skin of an African-American peer.

Child A: Ick. You're all dirty.

Child B: No!

Child A: (To peers sitting nearby) Anton's got icky, dirty skin. (Laughs)

Child B: I do not!

Teacher: Oh, when you say that, Raymond, you make Anton feel so badly. His skin is not dirty. He has pretty brown skin. That's its color. I can't let you say things that hurt people's feelings.

Teachers must be equitable in giving encouragement, warmth, and guidance to all children—boys and girls and those of all cultures.

Child B:	It looks dirty.
Teacher:	You might think it looks funny because you haven't seen brown skin very much before. It is just like your skin except for its color.
Child A:	Let me see. (Takes Child B's arm and rubs it; then rubs his own)
Teacher:	What do you think?
Child A:	Hm . . . I think . . .
Child B:	I'll try. (Takes Child A's hand, feels his skin) No, there's a bump. (Points to a bone in his wrist) See? He's got this.
Child A:	You have that bump, too, Anton. See? (Points to Child B's wrist)
Teacher:	So you both have that bump in your wrist?
Child B:	Yep. We got these bumps.
Child A:	(Laughs) These are our big mosquito bites.

The two children begin to play together; the teacher withdraws. ❖

Here the teacher has expressed clearly a classroom rule that hateful statements or actions are not allowed. Beyond this, she has tried to demonstrate how the victim of a discriminatory act feels. She has helped the other child to understand where his bias comes from—discomfort and unfamiliarity. Finally, she facilitates interaction and an open discussion about body differences and similarities.

In sum, teachers must be sensitive to differences in communication, social, and play styles, but also to intervene directly when peers do not accept these differences. A clear expression of concern about prejudice may be the best way to alter negative racial or gender attitudes or the mistreatment of the disabled.

Summary

Teachers must be sensitive to individual variation in children's modes of communicating, playing, and learning. Children of diverse cultures or exceptionalities may use a wide range of discourse patterns or physical cues in their interactions with adults and peers. Unfamiliarity with these can lead to frustration, annoyance, even prejudice. When teachers model acceptance of these variations in classroom interactions and adapt their interventions to reflect these attitudes, they enhance ethnic or gender pride and self-esteem.

Besides adapting interactions to individual needs, teachers must proactively counteract prejudice among children. The "Anti-Bias Curriculum" provides a framework for celebrating diversity. A fundamental component of the curriculum is the open discussion of racial, gender, or developmental differences. Clear expressions of concern about discriminatory acts or statements as they arise in the classroom will assist all children in understanding and appreciating diversity.

Suggested Activities

1. Observe in a classroom in which diverse cultural and developmental backgrounds are represented. Focus your observations on four children—two boys and two girls—who appear to have very different patterns of communication and interaction. Write an analysis of this experience guided by the following questions:

   a. How did these four children differ in language? To what degree did children speak different dialects? Were augmentative communication systems used? How successful were children of different dialects or communicative methods in clearly expressing ideas or understanding one another?

b. How did these four children differ in the body language that they displayed? How did they differ in regard to amount of touch or their uses of gestures or physical cues? What differences in quietness or the uses of silence were observed? What variations in the use of physical space were evident? What problems or misunderstandings, if any, were the result of these body language differences?

c. In what ways did children differ in regard to play style? In what ways did play interests, activity level, or level of social interaction vary according to gender or culture?

2. Observe a teacher interacting within a classroom that reflects diversity. Write an analysis of teacher-child interactions, guided by the following questions:

a. Did the teacher demonstrate equity in attention and question-asking? In what ways, if any, did the teacher interact differently with boys and girls, children of color, or those with special needs? In what ways did these differences reflect sensitivity; in what ways did they reflect bias?

b. In what ways did the teacher adapt interactions to meet the special needs of children? How was acceptance and an appreciation of diversity communicated in the classroom? What signs of teacher intolerance or bias were evident?

c. To what degree did the classroom environment and teacher-child interactions reflect an anti-bias curriculum? How did the teacher respond to students' biased statements or behaviors?

d. What recommendations would you give this teacher regarding sensitive teacher-child interactions?

3. Play with a small group composed of children of diverse cultural backgrounds, gender, and developmental needs. Reflect upon and write an analysis of your interactions with these children guided by the following questions.

a. To what degree were you successful at "reading" the unique social, communication, and play needs of individual children in this group? What specific, individual needs were you able to pick up on?

b. In what ways did your interactions differ with children of varying cultures? How did your treatment of boys and girls differ? What adaptations were required to meet children's special needs? To what degree did these differences reflect sensitivity to unique needs? To what degree did they reflect bias?

c. What special challenges did you experience working with such a diverse group? What special learning opportunities arose?

Further Reading

Derman-Sparks, L. D. (1989). *Anti-bias curriculum: Tools for empowering young children.* Washington, DC: National Association for the Education of Young Children.

Fallen, N. H., & Umansky, W. (1985). *Young children with special needs* (2nd ed.). New York: Merrill/Macmillan.

Hale-Benson, J. E. (1986). *Black children: Their roots, culture, and learning styles.* Baltimore: Johns Hopkins University Press.

Kendall, F. E. (1983). *Diversity in the classroom: A multicultural approach to the education of young children.* New York: Teachers College Press.

Klein, S. S. (Ed.). (1985). *Handbook for achieving sex equality through education.* Baltimore: Johns Hopkins University Press.

Musselwhite, C. R. (1986). *Adaptive play for special needs children: Strategies to enhance communication and learning.* London: Taylor and Francis.

Powell, D. R. (1989). *Families and early childhood programs.* Washington, DC: National Association for the Education of Young Children.

Ramsey, P. G. (1987). *Teaching and learning in a diverse world: Multicultural education for young children.* New York: Teachers College Press.

Williams, L. R., & De Gaetano, Y. (1985). *Alerta: A multicultural, bilingual approach to teaching young children.* Menlo Park, CA: Addison-Wesley.

REFERENCES

Aboud, F. (1985). The development of a social comparison process in children. *Child Development, 56*, 682–688.

Ainsworth, M. A. (1973). The development of infant-mother attachment. In B. Caldwell & H. Ricciuti (Eds.), *Review of child development research* (Vol. 3). Chicago: University of Chicago Press.

Aldis, O. (1975). *Play fighting*. New York: Academic Press.

Allen, R. V., & Allen, C. (1968). *Language experience in reading*. Chicago: Encyclopedia Britannica.

Ames, L. B. (1937). The sequential patterning of prone progression in the human infant. *Genetic Psychology, 19*, 409–460.

Andress, B. (1991). From research to practice: Preschool children and their movement responses to music. *Young Children, 47*(1), 22–29.

Asher, S. R., & Dodge, K. A. (1985). Identifying children who are rejected by their peers. *Developmental Psychology, 22*, 444–449.

Asher, S. G., & Renshaw, P. D. (1981). Social knowledge and social skills training. In S. R. Asher & J. M. Gottman (Eds.), *The development of children's friendships*. New York: Cambridge University Press.

Ashton-Warner, S. (1963). *Teacher*. New York: Simon and Schuster.

Athey, I. (1988). The relationship of play to cognitive, language, and moral development. In D. Bergen (Ed.), *Play as a medium for learning and development*. London: Heinemann.

Axeline, V. M. (1969). *Play therapy*. New York: Ballantine Books.

Bailey, D. B., Harms, T., & Clifford, R. M. (1983). Social and educational aspects of mealtimes for handicapped and nonhandicapped preschoolers. *Topics In Early Childhood Special Education, 3*(2), 19–32.

Balaban, N. (1985). *Starting school: From separation to independence*. New York: Teachers College Press.

Bandura, A. (1969). Social learning of identificatory processes. In D. A. Goslin (Ed.), *Handbook of socialization theory and research*. Chicago: Rand McNally.

Bandura, A. (1986). *Social foundations of thought and action*. Englewood, NJ: Prentice-Hall.

Barker, G., & Graham, S. (1987). Developmental study of praise and blame as attributional cues. *Journal of Educational Psychology, 79*, 62–66.

Barnett, L. A., & Storm, B. (1981). Play, pleasure, and pain: The reduction of anxiety through play. *Leisure Sciences, 4*, 161–175.

Barron, L. (1979). *Mathematics experiences for the early childhood years*. Columbus, OH: Merrill.

Baumrind, D. (1972). An exploratory study of socialization effects on Black children: Some Black-White comparisons. *Child Development, 43*, 261–267.

Berbner, G., & Signorielli, N. (1990). *Violence profiles 1967 through 1988–89: Enduring trends*. Philadelphia: University of Pennsylvania.

Bereiter, C., & Engelmann, S. (1966). *Teaching the culturally disadvantaged child in preschool*. Englewood Cliffs, NJ: Prentice-Hall.

Bergen, D. (Ed.). (1988). *Play as a medium for learning and development*. Portsmouth, NH: Heinemann.

Bloch, M. N., & Walsh, D. J. (April, 1983). *Young children's activities at home: Age and sex differences in activity, location, and social context*. Paper presented at the biennial meeting of the Society for Research in Child Development, Detroit.

Bloom, L., Hood, L., & Lightbown, P. (1974). Imitation in language development. *Cognitive Psychology*, 6, 380–420.

Bloom, M. (1983). Of continuity and discontinuity and the magic of language development. In R. M. Golinkoff (Ed.), *The transition from prelinguistic to linguistic communication*. Hillside, NJ: Erlbaum.

Bloom-Feshbach, S., Bloom-Feshbach, J., & Gaughran, J. (1980). The child's tie to both parents: Separation and nursery school adjustment. *American Journal of Orthopsychiatry*, 50, 291–311.

Blumenfeld, P., Pintrich, P., & Hamilton, V. (1986). Children's concepts of ability, effort, and conduct. *American Educational Research Journal*, 23, 95–104.

Boivin, M., & Begin, G. (1989). Peer status and self-perception among early elementary school children: The case of the rejected children. *Child Development*, 60, 591–596.

Bradbard, M. R., & Endsley, R. C. (1983). How can teachers develop young children's curiosity? In J. F. Brown (Ed.), *Curriculum planning for young children*. Washington, DC: National Association for the Education of Young Children.

Bredderman, T. (1982). Activity science: The evidence shows it matters. *Science and Children*, 20(1), 39–41.

Bretherton, I. (Ed.). (1984). *Symbolic play: The development of social understanding*. New York: Academic Press.

Bronfenbrenner, U. (1979). *The ecology of human development: Experiments by nature and design*. Cambridge, MA: Harvard University Press.

Brophy, J. E. (1981). Teacher praise: A functional analysis. *Review of Educational Research*, 51, 5–32.

Brophy, J. E., & Evertson, C. M. (1976). *Learning from teaching: A developmental perspective*. Boston: Allyn and Bacon.

Brophy, J., & Evertson, C. (1987). Context variables in teaching. *Educational Psychologist*, 12, 310–316.

Brophy, J. E., & Goode, T. (1974). *Teacher-student relationships: Causes and consequences*. New York: Holt, Rhinehart, and Winston.

Brown, R., & Bellugi, U. (1964). Three processes in the child's acquisition of syntax. *Harvard Educational Review*, 34, 133–151.

Brown, R., Cazden, C., & Bellugi, U. (1969). The child's grammar from I to III. In P. J. Hill (Ed.), *Minnesota symposium on child psychology* (Vol. 2). Minneapolis, MN: University of Minnesota Press.

Bruner, J. (1980). *Under five in Britain*. Ypsilanti, MI: High/Scope Press.

Cain, S., & Evans, J. (1990). *Sciencing* (3rd ed.). New York: Merrill/Macmillan.

Caldwell, B. N. (1977). Aggression and hostility in young children. *Young Children*, 32(2), 4–13.

Calkins, L. M. (1986). *The art of teaching writing*. Portsmouth, NH: Heinemann.

Canter, L. (1988). Assertive discipline and the search for the perfect classroom. *Young Children*, 43(2), 24.

Carlsson-Paige, N., & Levin, D. E. (1985). *Helping young children understand peace, war, and the nuclear threat*. Washington, DC: National Association for the Education of Young Children.

Carlsson-Paige, N., & Levin, D. (1987). *The war play dilemma: Balancing needs and values in the early childhood classroom*. New York: Teachers College Press.

Castaneda, A. M. (1987). Early mathematics education. In C. Seefeldt (Ed.), *The early childhood curriculum: A review of current research*. New York: Teachers College Press.

Cazden, C. (1972). *Child language and education*. New York: Holt, Rinehart, and Winston.

Cazden, C. B. (1976). Play with language and metalinguistic awareness. In J. S. Bruner, A. Jolly, & K. Sylva (Eds.), *Play: Its role in development and evolution*. New York: Basic Books.

Chandler, T. A. (1981). What's wrong with success and praise? *Arithmetic Teacher*, 29(4), 10–12.

Chaney, C. M., & Kephart, N. C. (1968). *Motoric aids to perceptual training*. Columbus, OH: Merrill.

Chomsky, N. (1965). *Aspects of the theory of syntax*. Cambridge, MA: MIT Press.

Christie, J. F. (1983). The effects of play tutoring on young children's cognitive performance. *Journal of Educational Research, 76,* 326–330.

Christie, J. F. (Ed.). (1991). *Play and early literacy development.* Albany, NY: SUNY Press.

Clemens, S. G. (1991). Art in the classroom: Making every day special. *Young Children, 46*(2), 4–11.

Cobb, P. (1985). A reaction to three early number papers. *Journal for Research in Mathematics Education, 16,* 141–145.

Coleman, M., & Skeen, P. (1985). Play, games, and sport: Their use and misuse. *Childhood Education, 61,* 192–198.

Condon, J. C., & Yousef, F. S. (1975). *An introduction to intercultural communication.* Indianapolis: The Bobbs-Merrill Co.

Connolly, J. A., & Doyle, A. B. (1984). Relation of social fantasy play to social competence in preschoolers. *Developmental Psychology, 20,* 797–806.

Connolly, K. (1970). Response speed, temporal sequencing, and information processing in children. In K. Connolly (Ed.), *Mechanisms of motor skill development.* New York: Academic Press.

Cratty, B. J. (1970). *Perception and motor development in infants and young children.* New York: Macmillan.

Cratty, B. J., & Martin, M. M. (1969). *Perceptual motor efficiency in children.* Philadelphia: Lea and Febiger.

Crick, N. R., & Ladd, G. W. (1987). *Children's perceptions of the consequences of aggressive behavior: Do the ends justify the means?* Paper presented at the biennial meeting of the Society for Research in Child Development, Baltimore, MD, April, 1987.

Cross, T. G., & Morris, J. E. (1980). Linguistic feedback and maternal speech. *First language, 1,* 98–121.

Curry, N. E. (1971). Consideration of current basic issues on play. In N. Curry & S. Arnaud (Eds.), *Play: The child strives toward self-realization* (pp. 51–61). Washington, DC: National Association for the Education of Young Children.

Curry, N. E., & Bergen, D. (1988). The relationship of play to emotional, social, and gender/sex role development. In D. Bergen (Ed.), *Play as a medium for learning and development* (pp. 107–133). Portsmouth, NH: Heinemann.

Curry, N. E., & Johnson, C. N. (1990). *Beyond self-esteem: Developing a genuine sense of human value.* Washington, DC: National Association for the Education of Young Children.

Dale, P. S. (1976). *Language development: Structure and function.* New York: Holt, Rinehart, and Winston.

Dansky, J. L. (1980). Make-believe: A mediator of the relationship between play and creativity. *Child Development, 51,* 576–579.

Delacato, C. H. (1966). *Neurological organization and reading.* Springfield, IL: Charles C. Thomas.

Derman-Sparks, L. D. (1989). *Anti-bias curriculum: Tools for empowering young children.* Washington, DC: National Association for the Education of Young Children.

DeVries, R. A., Haney, J. P., & Zan, B. (1991). Sociomoral atmosphere in direct-instruction, eclectic, and constructivist kindergartens: A study of teachers' enacted interpersonal understanding. *Early Childhood Research Quarterly, 6,* 449–472.

DeVries, R. A., & Kohlberg, L. (1990). *Constructivist early education: Overview and comparison with other programs.* Washington, DC: National Association for the Education of Young Children.

DeVries, R. A., Reese-Learned, H., & Morgan, P. (1991). Sociomoral development in direct-instruction, constructivist, and eclectic kindergarten programs: A study of children's enacted interpersonal understanding. *Early Childhood Research Quarterly, 6,* 473–517.

Di Leo, J. H. (1982). Graphic activity of young children: Development and creativity. In L. Lasky & R. Mukerji (Eds.), *Art: Basic for young children.* Washington, DC: National Association for the Education of Young Children.

Dillon, J. T. (1988). *Questioning and discussion: A multidisciplinary study.* Norwood, NJ: Ablex.

Dodge, K. A. (1980). Social cognition and children's aggressive behavior. *Child Development, 51*, 162–170.

Dodge, K. A. (1983). Behavioral antecedents of peer social status. *Child Development, 54*, 1386–1399.

Dodge, K. A., McClaskey, C. L., & Feldman, E. (1985). A situational approach to the assessment of social competence in children. *Journal of Consulting and Clinical Psychology, 53*, 344–353.

Dunn, J., & Wooding, C. (1977). Play in the home and its implications for learning. In B. Tizard & D. Harvey (Eds.), *Biology of Play* (pp. 45–58). London: Heinemann.

Dunn, L., & Smith, J. (1965). *Peabody language development kits, Level 1*. Circle Pines, MN: American Guidance Service.

Durkin, D. (1966). *Children who read early*. New York: Teachers College Press.

Dyson, A. H. (1988). Appreciate the drawing and dictating of young children. *Young Children, 43*(3), 25–32.

Eckman, P. (1972). Universals and cultural differences in facial expressions of emotion. In J. K. Cole (Ed.), *Nebraska symposium on motivation* (pp. 46–52). Lincoln: University of Nebraska Press.

Egan, L. A., & Goldsmith, R. (1981). Bilingual bicultural education: The Colorado success story. *Monographs of the Center For Bilingual Education Research and Service, 2*(1).

Eibl-Eibesfeldt, I. (1979). Universals in human expressive behavior. In A. Wolfgang (Ed.), *Nonverbal behavior: Applications and cultural implications* (pp. 124–129). New York: Academic Press.

Elder, J. L., & Pederson, D. R. (1978). Preschool children's use of objects in symbolic play. *Child Development, 49*, 500–504.

Elkind, D. (1981). *The hurried child*. Reading, MA: Addison-Wesley.

Elkind, D. (1987). *Miseducation: Preschoolers at Risk*. New York: Alfred A. Knopf.

Elkind, D., & Weiner, I. R. (1978). *Development of the child*. New York: John Wiley and Sons.

Endsley, R. C., & Clarey, S. (1975). Answering young children's questions as a determinant of their subsequent question-asking behavior. *Developmental Psychology, 11*, 863.

Erikson, E. H. (1963). *Childhood and society* (2nd ed.). New York: Norton.

Erikson, E. H. (1982). *The life cycle completed: A review*. New York: Norton.

Erikson, E. H., Sroufe, L. A., & Egeland, B. (1985). The relationship between quality of attachment and behavior problems in preschool in a high-risk sample. In I. Bretherton & E. Waters (Eds.), Growing points in attachment theory and research. *Monographs for the Society for Research in Child Development, 50* (1–2, Serial No. 209).

Eron, L., & Heusmann, L. (1987). Television as a source of maltreatment of children. *School Psychology Review, 16*, 195–202.

Ervin, S. (1964). Imitation and structural change in children's language. In E. H. Lenneberg (Ed.), *New directions in the study of language*. Cambridge, MA: MIT Press.

Evans, E. E. (1975). *Contemporary influences in early childhood education*. New York: Holt, Rinehart, and Winston.

Fallen, N. H., & Umansky, W. (1985). *Young children with special needs* (2nd ed.). New York: Merrill/Macmillan.

Farrar, J. (1987). *Immediate effects of discourse on grammatical morpheme acquisition*. Paper presented at the biennial meeting of the Society for Research in Child Development, Baltimore, MD, April, 1987.

Feeney, S., Christensen, D., & Moravcik, E. (1991). *Who am I in the lives of children?* (4th ed.). New York: Merrill/Macmillan.

Fein, G. (1984). The self-building potential of preschool play or "I got a fish all by myself." In T. D. Yawkey & A. D. Pellegrini (Eds.), *Child's play: Developmental and applied*. Hillsdale, NJ: Erlbaum.

Fein, G., & Rivkin, M. (1986). *The young child at play. Reviews of research* (Vol. 4). Washington, DC: National Association for the Education of Young Children.

Feitelson, D., & Ross, G. S. (1973). The neglected factor—play. *Human Development, 16*, 202–223.

Fieber, N. (1983). Informal assessment of visual skills needed for non-speech development. In *Working with pre-readers: Practical approaches*. Omaha: University of Nebraska Medical Center.

Finnie, N. R. (1975). *Handling the young cerebral palsied child at home* (2nd ed.). New York: Dutton.

Forman, G., & Kaden, M. (1987). In C. Seefeldt (Ed.), *The early childhood curriculum: A review of current research*. New York: Teachers College Press.

Forman, G., & Kuschner, D. S. (1984). *The child's construction of knowledge: Piaget for teaching children*. Washington, DC: National Association for the Education of Young Children.

Freud, S. (1961). *Beyond the pleasure principle*. New York: Norton.

Freund, L. S. (1990). Maternal regulation of children's problem solving behavior and its impact on children's performance. *Child Development, 61*, 113–126.

Friedlander, B. (1970). Receptive language development in infancy. *Merrill-Palmer Quarterly, 16*, 7–51.

Frost, J. L., & Klein, B. L. (1979). *Children's play and playgrounds*. Boston: Allyn and Bacon.

Frost, J. L., & Sunderlin, S. (1985). (Eds.). *When children play*. Wheaton, MD: Association for Childhood Education.

Frostig, M. (1969). *Move—grow—learn*. Chicago: Follett.

Fuson, K. C., Richards, J., & Briars, D. J. (1982). The acquisition and elaboration of number word sequence. In C. S. Brainard (Ed.), *Children's logical and mathematical cognition*. New York: Springer-Verlag.

Gallahue, D. L. (1982). *Understanding motor development*. New York: Wiley.

Garcia Coll, C. T. (1990). Developmental outcome of minority infants: A process-oriented look into our beginnings. *Child Development, 61*, 270–289.

Gardner, H. (1980). *Artful scribbles*. New York: Basic.

Gardner, H., Wolf, D., & Smith, A. (1982). Max and Mollie: Individual differences in early artistic symbolization. In H. Gardner (Ed.), *Art, mind, and brain: A cognitive approach to creativity*. New York: Basic Books.

Garvey, C. (1977). *Play*. Cambridge, MA: Harvard University Press.

Garvey, C., & Baldwin, T. (1970). *Studies in convergent communications: Analysis of verbal interactions*. Johns Hopkins Center for the Study of Social Organization of Schools (ERIC document No. ED 045 647).

Gelman, R., & Gallistel, C. R. (1978). *The child's understanding of number*. Cambridge, MA: Harvard University Press.

Gleason, J. (1975). Fathers and other strangers: Their speech to children. In D. P. Dato (Ed.), *Developmental psycholinguistics: Theory and applications*. Washington, DC: Georgetown University Press.

Gleitman, L., Newport, E. L., & Gleitman, H. (1984). The current status of the motherese hypothesis. *Journal of Child Language, 11*, 43–80.

Golden, D. B. (1983). Play therapy for hospitalized children. In C. E. Schaefer & K. J. O'Conner (Eds.), *Handbook of Play Therapy*. New York: John Wiley and Sons.

Goodman, Y. (1986). Children coming to know literacy. In W. H. Teale & E. Sulzby (Eds.), *Emergent literacy: Writing and reading*. Norwood, NJ: Albex.

Gottman, J. M. (1983). How children become friends. *Monographs of the Society for Research in Child Development, 48*(3, Serial No. 201).

Gowen, J. W. (1987). Facilitating play skills: Efficacy of a staff development program. *Early Childhood Research Quarterly, 2*, 55–66.

Graves, D. (1983). *Writing: Teachers and children at work*. Portsmouth, NH: Heinemann.

Graves, D., & Hansen, J. (1983). The author's chair. *Language Arts, 60*, 176–183.

Green, D., & Lepper, M. R. (1974). How to turn play into work. *Psychology Today, 8*(4), 49–54.

Greenberg, P. (1992). Positive peer relations. *Young Children, 47*(4), 51-59.

Grief, E. B. (1976). Sex role playing in preschool children. In J. Bruner, A. Jolly, & K. Sylva (Eds.), *Play: Its role in development and evolution*. New York: Basic Books.

Guerney, L. F. (1983). Client-centered (nondirective) play therapy. In C. E. Schaefer & K. J. O'Conner (Eds.), *Handbook of Play Therapy*. New York: John Wiley and Sons.

Hale-Benson, J. E. (1986). *Black children: Their roots, culture, and learning style*. Baltimore, MD: Johns Hopkins University Press.

Hallinan, M., & Sorensen, A. (1983). The formation and stability of instructional groups. *American Sociological Review*, *48*, 838–851.

Hare, B. R. (1985). Reexamining the achievement central tendency: Sex differences within race and race differences within sex. In H. P. McAdoo & J. L. McAdoo (Eds.), *Black children: Social, educational, and parental environments*. Newbury Park, CA: Sage.

Harper, L. V., & Sanders, K. (1975). Preschool children's use of space: Sex differences in outdoor play. *Developmental Psychology*, *11*, 119.

Harris, D. (1982). Communication interaction processes involving non-vocal physically handicapped children. *Topics In Language Disorders*, *2*, 21–37.

Harris, S. (1986). Evaluation of a curriculum to support literacy growth in young children. *Early Childhood Research Quarterly*, *1*, 333–348.

Harrison, A. O., Wilson, M. N., Pine, C. J., Chan, S. Q., & Buriel, R. (1990). *Child Development*, *61*, 347–362.

Harste, J., Woodward, V., & Burke, C. (1984). *Language stories and literacy lessons*. Portsmouth, NH: Heinemann.

Harter, S. (1990). Causes, correlates, and the functional role of global self-worth: A life span perspective. In R. J. Sternberg & J. Kolligan (Eds.), *Competence considered*. New Haven: Yale University Press.

Hartup, W. W., Laursen, B., Stewart, M. I., & Eastenson, A. (1988). Conflict and the friendship relations of young children. *Child Development*, *59*, 1590–1600.

Hartup, W. W., & Moore, S. G. (1990). Early peer relations: Developmental significance and prognostic implications. *Early Childhood Research Quarterly*, *5*, 1–17.

Hartup, W. W., & Sancilio, M. F. (1986). Children's friendships. In E. Schopler & G. B. Mesibov (Eds.), *Social behavior in autism*. New York: Plenum.

Hatch, J. A., & Freeman, E. B. (1988). Kindergarten philosophies and practices: Perspectives of teachers, principals, and supervisors. *Early Childhood Research Quarterly*, *3*, 151–166.

Hazen, N., Black, B., & Fleming-Johnson, F. (1984). Social acceptance: Strategies children use and how teachers can help learn them. *Young Children*, *39*(3), 26–36.

Hendrick, J. (1992). *The whole child* (5th ed.). New York: Merrill/Macmillan.

Hendrick, J., & Stange, T. (1990). *Do actions speak louder than words? An effect of the functional use of language on dominant sex role behavior of boys and girls*. (ERIC Document No. ED 323 039).

Hess, R. D., Price, G. G., Dickson, W. P., & Conroy, M. (1981). Different roles for mothers and teachers: Contrasting styles of child care. In S. Kilmer (Ed.), *Advances in early education and day care* (Vol. 2). Greenwich, CT: JAI.

Higgins, E. T., & Parsons, J. (1983). Social cognition and the social field of the child: Stages as subcultures. In E. T. Higgins, D. N. Ruble, & W. W. Hartup (Eds.), *Social cognition and social development: A sociocultural perspective*. New York: Cambridge University Press.

Hinitz, B. F. (1987). Social studies in early childhood education. In C. Seefeldt (Ed.), *The early childhood curriculum: A review of current research*. New York: Teachers College Press.

Hipple, M. L. (1985). Journal writing in kindergarten. *Language Arts*, *62*, 255–261.

Hirsch, E. S. (Ed.). (1984). *The block book* (rev. ed.). Washington, DC: National Association for the Education of Young Children.

Hitz, R. (1987). Creative problem solving through music activities. *Young Children*, *42*(2), 12–19.

Hitz, R. (1988). Assertive discipline: A response to Lee Canter. *Young Children*, *43*(2), 25.

Hitz, R., & Driscoll, A. (1988). Praise or encouragement. New insights into praise: Implications for early childhood teachers. *Young Children*, *43*(5), 6–13.

Hock, E., McHenry, P. C., Hock, M. D., Triolo, S., & Stewart, L. (1980). Child's school entry: A stressful event in the lives of fathers. *Family Relations*, *29*, 467–472.

Hoffman, M. L. (1975). Moral internalization, parental power, and the nature of parent-child interaction. *Developmental Psychology, 11*, 228–239.

Holdaway, D. (1979). *The foundations of literacy*. New York: Ashton Scholastic.

Honig, A. S. (1985a). Compliance, control, and discipline (Part 1). *Young Children, 40*(2), 50–58.

Honig, A. S. (1985b). Compliance, control, and discipline (Part 2). *Young Children, 40*(3), 49–51.

Honig, A. S. (1987). The shy child. *Young Children, 42*(4), 54–64.

Honig, A. S. (1989). Quality infant/toddler caregiving: Are there magic recipes? *Young Children, 44*(4), 4–10.

Hovell, M. F., Bursick, J. H., Sharkey, R., & McClure. J. (1978). An evaluation of elementary students' voluntary physical activity during recess. *Research Quarterly, 49*, 460–474.

Howes, C. (1983). Patterns of friendship. *Child Development, 54*, 1041–1053.

Howes, C. (1987). Peer interaction of young children. *Monographs of the Society for Research in Child Development, 53*(1, Serial No. 217).

Howes, C., Unger, O., & Beizer-Seidner, L. (1989). Social pretend play in toddlers: Parallels with social play and solitary pretend play. *Child Development, 60*, 77–84.

Hutt, C. (1971). Exploration and play in children. In R. E. Herron & B. Sutton-Smith (Eds.), *Child's play*. New York: Wiley.

Hyson, M. C. (1986). Lobster on the sidewalk: Understanding and helping children with fears. In J. B. McCracken (Ed.), *Reducing stress in young children's lives*. Washington, DC: National Association for the Education of Young Children.

Inhelder, B., & Piaget, J. (1958). *The growth of logical thinking from childhood to adolescence*. New York: Basic Books.

Irujo, S. (1988). An introduction to intercultural differences and similarities in nonverbal communication. In J. S. Wurzel (Ed.), *Toward multiculturalism: A reader in multicultural education*. Yarmouth, ME: Intercultural Press.

Jacobson, J. J., Boersma, D. C., Fields, R. B., & Olson, K. L. (1983). Paralinguistic features of adult speech to infants and small children. *Child Development, 54*, 436–442.

Jennings, K. D. (1975). People versus object orientation, social behavior, and intellectual abilities in preschool children. *Developmental Psychology, 112*, 511–519.

Johnson, D. L., & Breckenridge, J. N. (1982). The Houston Parent-Child Development Center and the primary prevention of behavior problems in young children. *American Journal of Community Psychology, 10*, 305–316.

Johnson, D. W., Skon, L., & Johnson, R. T. (1980). Effects of cooperative, competitive, and individualistic conditions on problem solving performance. *American Educational Research Journal, 17*, 89–93.

Johnson, H. M. (1984). The art of block building. In E. S. Hirsch (Ed.), *The block book* (rev. ed.). Washington, DC: National Association for the Education of Young Children.

Johnson, J. E., Christie, J. F., & Yawkey, T. D. (1987). *Play and early childhood development*. Glenview, IL: Scott, Foresman and Company.

Johnson, J. E., Ersler, J., & Lawton, J. T. (1982). Intellective correlates of preschoolers' spontaneous play. *Journal of General Psychology, 106*, 115–122.

Johnson, J. E., & Roopnarine, J. L. (1983). The preschool classroom and sex differences in children's play. In M. Liss (Ed.), *Social and cognitive skills: Sex roles and children's play*. New York: Academic Press.

Kamii, C. (1982). *Number in preschool and kindergarten: Implications of Piaget's theory*. Washington, DC: National Association for the Education of Young Children.

Kamii, C., & DeVries, R. (1978). *Physical knowledge in preschool education*. Englewood Cliffs, NJ: Prentice-Hall.

Kamii, C., & DeVries, R. (1980). *Group games in early education*. Washington, DC.:

National Association for the Education of Young Children.

Kamii, C., & Lee-Katz, L. (1983). In J. F. Brown (Ed.), *Curriculum planning for young children*. Washington, DC: National Association for the Education of Young Children.

Kaplan-Sanoff, M., Brewster, A., Stillwell, J., & Bergen, D. (1988). The relationship of play to physical/motor development and to children with special needs. In D. Bergen (Ed.), *Play as a medium for learning and development*. Portsmouth, NH: Heinemann.

Katz, L. G. (1980). Mothering and teaching: Some significant distinctions. In L. G. Katz (Ed.), *Current topics in early childhood education* (Vol. 3). Norwood, NJ: Ablex.

Kelly, N. T., & Kelly, B. J. (1985). *Physical education for preschool and primary grades*. Springfield, IL: Charles C. Thomas.

Kemp, J. C., & Dale, P. S. (1973). Spontaneous imitation and free speech. Paper presented to the Society for Research in Child Development. Philadelphia, 1973.

Kendall, F. E. (1983). *Diversity in the classroom: A multicultural approach to the education of young children*. New York: Teachers College Press.

Keogh, J. (1977). The study of movement skill development. *Quest* (Monograph No. 28), 76–80.

Klein, S. S. (Ed.). (1985). *Handbook for achieving sex equality through education*. Baltimore, MD: Johns Hopkins University Press.

Kostelnik, M. J., Whiren, A. P., & Stein, L. C. (1986). Living with He-Man: Managing superhero fantasy play. *Young Children*, *41*(4), 3–9.

Krashen, S. D. (1981). Bilingual education and second language acquisition theory. In *Schooling and minority students: A theoretical framework*. Los Angeles: Evaluation, Dissemination, and Assessment Center.

Kuhn, D. (1974). Inducing development experimentally: Comments on a research paradigm. *Developmental Psychology*, *10*, 590–600.

Ladd, G. (1981). Effectiveness of a social learning method for enhancing children's social interaction and peer acceptance. *Child Development*, *52*, 171–178.

Ladd, G., & Mize, J. (1983). A cognitive-social learning model of social skill training. *Psychological Review*, *90*, 127–157.

LaFreniere, P., Strayer, F., & Gauthier, R. (1984). The emergence of same-sex affiliative preferences among preschool peers: A developmental ethological perspective. *Child Development*, *55*, 1958–1965.

Lally, J. R., Mangione, P. L., & Honig, A. S. (1988). The Syracuse University Family Development Research Program: Long-range impact of an early intervention with low income children and their families. In D. R. Powell (Ed.), *Parent education as early childhood intervention*. Norwood, NJ: Ablex.

Lasky, L., & Mukerji, R. (1982). *Art: Basic for young children*. Washington, DC: National Association for the Education of Young Children.

Lay-Dopyera, M. & Dopyera, J. E. (1987). Strategies for teaching. In C. Seefeldt (Ed.), *The early childhood curriculum: A review of current research*. New York: Teachers College Press.

Lazar, I. (1988). Measuring the effects of early childhood programs. *Community Education Journal*, *15*, 8–11.

Leacock, E. (1982). The influence of teacher attitudes on children's classroom performance: Case studies. In K. M. Borman (Ed.), *The social life of children in a changing society*. Hillsdale, NJ: Erlbaum.

Leeb-Lundberg, K. (1984). The block builder mathematician. In E. S. Hirsch (Ed.), *The block book* (rev. ed.). Washington, DC: National Association for the Education of Young Children.

Lindfors, J. W. (1980). *Children's language and learning*. Englewood Cliffs, NJ: Prentice-Hall.

Lindfors, J. W. (1987). *Children's language and learning* (2nd ed.). Englewood Cliffs, NJ: Prentice-Hall.

Lovinger, S. (1974). Sociodramatic play and the language development in preschool disadvantaged children. *Psychology in the Schools*, *11*, 313–320.

Lowrey, G. H. (1978). *Growth and development of children*. Chicago: Year Book Medical Publishers.

MacDonald, K., & Parke, R. (1984). Bridging the gap: Parent-child play interaction and peer interactive competence. *Child Development, 55*, 1265–1277.

Mann, E., & McDermott, J. F. (1983). Play therapy for victims of child abuse and neglect. In C. E. Schaefer & K. J. O'Conner (Eds.), *Handbook of Play Therapy*. New York: John Wiley and Sons.

Manning, K., & Sharp, A. (1977). *Structuring play in the early years at school*. London: Ward Lock Educational.

Martin, D. L. (1977). Your praise can smother learning. *Learning, 5*(6), 43–51.

Matheson, C., & Wu, F. (April, 1991). *Friendship and social pretend play*. Paper presented at the biennial meeting of the Society for Research in Child Development, Seattle.

Matthews, W. S. (1981). Sex-role perception, portrayal, and preferences in the fantasy play of young children. *Sex Roles, 1*, 979–987.

McCracken, J. B. (1986). *Reducing stress in young children's lives*. Washington, DC: National Association for the Education of Young Children.

McCune-Nicholich, L., & Fenson, L. (1984). Methodological issues in studying early pretend play. In T. Yawkey and A. D. Pellegrini (Eds.), *Child's play: Developmental and applied*. Hillsdale, NJ: Erlbaum.

McGee, L. M., & Richgels, D. J. (1990). *Literacy's beginnings: Supporting young readers and writers*. Boston: Allyn and Bacon.

McLoyd, V. C. (1980). Verbally expressed modes of transformation in the fantasy play of black preschool children. *Child Development, 51*, 1133–1139.

McLoyd, V. (1982). Social class differences in sociodramatic play: A critical review. *Developmental Review, 2*, 1–30.

McLoyd, V. C., & Randolph, S. (1984). The conduct and publication of research on Afro-American children: A content analysis. *Human Development, 27*, 65–75.

Mejia, D. (1983). The development of Mexican-American children. In G. J. Powell (Ed.), *The psychosocial development of minority children*. New York: Brunner/Mazel.

Melson, G. G., & Fogel, A. (1988). The development of nurturance in young children. *Young Children, 43*(3), 57-65.

Mendell, A. E. (1983). Play therapy with children of divorced parents. In C. E. Schaefer & K. J. O'Conner (Eds.), *Handbook of Play Therapy*. New York: John Wiley and Sons.

Menyuk, P., & Menyuk, D. (1988). Communicative competence: A historical and cultural perspective. In J. S. Wurzel (Ed.), *Toward multiculturalism: A reader in multicultural education*. Yarmouth, ME: Intercultural Press.

Miller, K. (1989). *The outside play and learning book: Activities for young children*. Mount Ranier, MD: Gryphon House.

Miller, L. B., & Bizzell, R. P. (1983). Long-term effects of four preschool programs: Sixth, seventh, and eighth grades. *Child Development, 54*, 727–741.

Miller, L. B., Bugbee, M. R., & Hybertson, D. W. (1985). Dimensions of preschool: The effects of individual experience. In I. E. Sigel (Ed.), *Advances in applied developmental psychology* (Vol. 1). Norwood, NJ: Ablex.

Mize, J., & Ladd, G. W. (1990). A cognitive-social learning approach to social skills training with low-status preschool children. *Developmental Psychology, 26*, 388–397.

Mize, J., Ladd, G. W., & Price, J. M. (1985). Promoting positive peer relations with young children: Rationales and strategies. *Child Care Quarterly, 14*, 221–237.

Mizio, E. (1983). The impact of macro systems on Puerto Rican families. In G. J. Powell (Ed.), *The psychosocial development of minority children*. New York: Brunner/Mazel.

Montessori, M. (1964). *The Montessori method*. New York: Schocken Books.

Moore, G. T. (1986). Effects of the spatial definition of behavior settings on children's behavior: A quasi-experimental field study. *Journal of Environmental Psychology, 6*, 205–231.

Moore, S. G., & Bulbulian, K. N. (1976). The effect of contrasting adult-child interaction on children's curiosity. *Developmental Psychology, 12,* 171–172.

Morris, W., & Nemcek, D. (1982). The development of social comparison motivation among preschoolers: Evidence of a stepwise progression. *Merrill-Palmer Quarterly, 28,* 413–425.

Morrow, L. M. (April, 1991). *Relationships among physical design of play centers, teachers' emphasis on literacy play, and children's literacy behaviors during play.* Paper presented at the annual meeting of the American Educational Research Association, Chicago, IL.

Musselwhite, C. R. (1986). *Adaptive play for special needs children: Strategies to enhance communication and learning.* London: Taylor and Francis.

Myers, G. D. (1985). Motor behavior of kindergartners during physical education and free play. In J. Frost & S. Sunderlin (Eds.), *When children play.* Wheaton, MD: Association for Childhood Education International.

Myre, S. (1991). Creative movement ideas. *Young Children, 46*(2), 29.

National Association for the Education of Young Children. (1986). Position paper on developmentally appropriate practice in programs for 4- and 5-year-olds. *Young Children, 41,* 20–29.

National Association for the Education of Young Children. (1990). NAEYC position statement on media violence in children's lives. *Young Children, 45*(5), 18–21.

Nelson, K. (1973). *Structure and strategy in learning to talk.* Chicago: University of Chicago Press.

Neuman, S., & Roskos, K. (April, 1991). *Literacy objects as cultural tools: Effects on children's literacy behaviors.* Paper presented at the annual meeting of the American Educational Research Association, Chicago, IL.

New, R. (1990). Excellent early education: A city in Italy has it. *Young children, 45*(6), 4-10.

Newport, E., Gleitman, L., & Gleitman, H. (1977). Mother I'd rather do it myself: Some effects and noneffects of motherese. In C. Snow & C. Ferguson (Eds.), *Talking to children: Input and acquisition.* Cambridge: Cambridge University Press.

Newport, E. L. (1976). Motherese: The speech of mothers to young children. In N. J. Castellan, D. B. Pisoni, & J. R. Potts (Eds.), *Cognitive Theory,* Vol. II. Hillsdale, NJ: Erlbaum.

Nickerson, E. T. (1983). Art as a play therapeutic medium. In C. E. Schaefer & K. J. O'Conner, *Handbook of play therapy.* New York: John Wiley.

Norton, D. G. (1983). Black family life patterns, the development of self, and cognitive development of Black children. In G. J. Powell (Ed.), *The psychosocial development of minority children.* New York: Brunner/Mazel.

Oden, S. (1986). Developing social skills instruction for peer interaction. In G. Carledge & J. F. Milburn (Eds.), *Teaching social skills to children.* New York: Pergamon Press.

Ogbu, J. U. (1988). Cultural diversity and human development. In D. T. Slaughter (Ed.), *Black children and poverty: A developmental perspective.* San Francisco: Jossey-Bass.

Ohanian, S. (1982). There's only one true technique for good discipline. *Learning, 11*(1), 16–19.

Parker, J. B., & Asher, S. R. (1987). Peer relations and later adjustment: Are low-accepted children "at risk"? *Psychological Bulletin, 102,* 357–389.

Parten, M. B. (1932). Social participation among preschool children. *Journal of Abnormal and Social Psychology, 27,* 243–269.

Pellegrini, A. D. (1980). The relationship between kindergartners' play and achievement in pre-reading, language, and writing. *Psychology in the Schools, 17,* 530–535.

Pellegrini, A. D. (1984). The effects of exploration and play on young children's associative fluency: A review and extension of training studies. In T. Yawkey and A. D. Pellegrini (Eds.), *Child's play: Developmental and applied.* Hillsdale, NJ: Erlbaum.

Pellegrini, A. D. (1986). Communicating in and about play: The effect of play centers on preschoolers' explicit language. In G. Fein & M. Rivkin (Eds.), *The young child at play: Reviews of research*, Vol. 4 (pp. 79–92). Washington, DC: National Association for the Education of Young Children.

Pellegrini, A. D., & Galda, L. (1982). The effects of thematic fantasy play training on the development of children's story comprehension. *American Educational Research Journal, 19*, 443–452.

Pellegrini, A. D., & Perlmutter, J. C. (1988). Rough-and-tumble play on the elementary school yard. *Young Children, 43*(2), 14–17.

Peppler, D. J., & Ross, H. S. (1981). The effects of play on convergent and divergent problem solving. *Child Development, 52*, 1202–1210.

Pflaum, S. W. (1986). *The development of language and literacy in young children* (3rd ed.). New York: Merrill//Macmillan.

Piaget, J. (1965). *The child's conception of number*. New York: W. W. Norton.

Piaget, J. (1986). *The construction of reality in the child*. New York, Ballantine.

Piaget, J., & Inhelder, B. (1963). *The child's conception of space*. London: Routledge & Kegan Paul.

Pintrich, P., & Blumenfeld, P. (1985). Classroom experience and children's self-perceptions of ability, effort, and conduct. *Journal of Educational Psychology, 77*, 646–657.

Pitcher, E. G., Feinburg, S. G., & Alexander, D. A. (1989). *Helping young children learn* (5th ed.). New York: Merrill/Macmillan.

Poest, C. A., Williams, J. R., Witt, D. D., & Atwood, M. E. (1992). Challenge me to move: Large muscle development in young children. *Young Children, 45*(5), 4–10.

Potter, E. (March, 1982). *Demands upon children regarding quality of achievement: Standard setting in preschool classrooms*. Paper presented at the annual meeting of the American Educational Research Association, New York.

Powell, D. R. (1989). *Families and early childhood programs*. Washington, DC: National Association for the Education of Young Children.

Putallaz, M., & Wasserman, A. (1989). Children's naturalistic entry behavior and sociometric status: A developmental perspective. *Developmental Psychology, 25*, 297–305.

Ramirez, M. (1988). Cognitive styles and cultural democracy in action. In J. S. Wurzel (Ed.), *Toward multiculturalism: A reader in multicultural education*. Yarmouth, ME: Intercultural Press.

Ramsey, P. G. (1987). *Teaching and learning in a diverse world: Multicultural education for young children*. New York: Teachers College Press.

Ramsey, P. G. (April, 1989a). *Successful and unsuccessful entry attempts: An analysis of behavioral and contextual factors*. Paper presented at the biennial meeting of the Society for Research in Child Development, Kansas City, KS.

Ramsey, P. G. (April, 1989b). *Friendships, groups, and entries: Changing social dynamics in early childhood classrooms*. Paper presented at the biennial meeting of the Society for Research in Child Development, Kansas City.

Ramsey, P. G. (April, 1991). *Initiating and maintaining social contact: The relation between entries and level of social participation*. Paper presented at the biennial meeting of the Society for Research in Child Development, Seattle, WA.

Ramsey, P., & Reid, R. (1988). Designing play environments for preschool and kindergarten children. In D. Bergen (Ed.), *Play as a medium for learning and development*. London: Heinemann.

Reifel, S. (1984). Block construction: Children's developmental landmarks in representation of space. *Young Children, 40*(2), 61–67.

Ridenour, M. V. (1978). Program to optimize infant motor development. In M. V. Ridenour (Ed.), *Motor development: Issues and applications*. Princeton, NJ: Princeton Books Co.

Rogers, C. S., & Sawyers, J. K. (1988). *Play in the lives of children*. Washington, DC: National Association for the Education of Young Children.

Rogers, D. L., & Ross, D. D. (1986). Encouraging positive social interaction among young children. *Young Children, 41*(3), 12-36.

Roopnarine, J. L., & Honig, A. S. (1985). The unpopular child. *Young Children, 40*(6), 59-64.

Rosen, C. (1974). Effects of problem solving behavior among disadvantaged children. *Child Development, 45*, 920–927.

Rosenblatt, D. (1977). Developmental trends in infant play. In B. Tizard & O. Harvey (Eds.), *The biology of play*. Philadelphia: Lippincott.

Rosenthal, B. A. (1974). *An ecological study of free play in the nursery school*. Unpublished doctoral dissertation, Wayne State University, Detroit, MI.

Rowe, M. B. (1974). Wait-time and rewards as instructional variables, their influences on language, logic, and fate control. Part I: Wait time. *Journal of Research in Science Teaching, 11*, 81–94.

Rubin, K. H. (1980). Fantasy play: Its role in the development of social skills and social cognition. In K. H. Rubin (Ed.), *Children's play*. San Francisco: Jossey-Bass.

Rubin, K. H. (1982a). Nonsocial play in preschoolers: Necessary evil? *Child Development, 53*, 651-657.

Rubin, K. H. (1982b). Early play theories: Contributions to contemporary research and theory. In D. J. Peppler & K. N. Rubin (Eds.), *The play of children: Current research and theory*. Basel, Switzerland: Karger AG.

Rubin, K. H. (1985). Play, peer interaction, and social development. In C. C. Brown & A. W. Gottfried (Eds.), *Play interactions: The role of toys and parental involvement in children's development*. Skillman, NJ: Johnson and Johnson.

Rubin, K. H. (1988). Some "good news" and some "not so good news" about dramatic play. In D. Bergen (Ed.), *Play as a medium for learning and development*. London: Heinemann.

Rubin, K. H., Fein, G. G., & Vandenberg, B. (1983). Play. In E. M. Hetherington (Ed.) & P. H. Mussen (Series Ed.), *Handbook of child psychology: Vol. 4. Socialization, personality, and social development*. New York: Wiley.

Rubin, K. H., Hymel, S., LeMare, L. J., & Rowden, L. (1989). Children experiencing social difficulties: Sociometric neglect reconsidered. *Canadian Journal of Behavioral Science, 21*, 94–111.

Rubin, K. H., Maioni, T. L., & Hornung, M. (1976). Free play behaviors in middle and lower class preschoolers: Parten and Piaget revisited. *Child Development, 47*, 414–419.

Sachs, J. (1980). The role of adult-child play in language development. In K. H. Rubin (Ed.), *New directions in child development: Children's play*. San Francisco: Jossey-Bass.

Sachs, J., Brown, R., & Salerno, R. A. (1976). Adults' speech to children. In W. von Raffler-Engel & Y. Lebrun (Eds.), *Baby talk and infant speech*. Amsterdam: Swets and Zeitlinger.

Salz, E., & Brodie, J. (1982). Pretend-play training in childhood: A review and critique. In D. J. Peppler & K. H. Rubin (Eds.), *The play of children: Current theory and research*. Basel, Switzerland: Karger AG.

Salz, E., & Johnson, J. (1974). Training for thematic fantasy play for culturally disadvantaged children: Preliminary results. *Journal of Educational Psychology, 66*, 623–630.

Scarlett, W. G. (1983). Social isolation from age-mates among nursery school children. In M. Donaldson, R. Grieve, & C. Pratt (Eds.), *Early childhood development and education*. New York: Guilford.

Schaefer, C. E., & O'Conner, K. J. (1983). *Handbook of play therapy*. New York: John Wiley.

Schickedanz, J. A. (1978). "Please read that story again!": Exploring relationships between story reading and learning to read. *Young Children, 33*(5), 43–55.

Schickedanz, J. A. (1982). "Hey! This book's not working right!" In J. F. Brown (Ed.), *Curriculum planning for young children*. Washington, DC: National Association for the Education of Young Children.

Schickedanz, J. A. (1986). *More than ABCs: The early stages of reading and writing*. Washington, DC: National Association for the Education of Young Children.

Schickedanz, J. S., Schickedanz, D. I., & Forsyth, P. D. (1982). *Toward understanding children*. Boston: Little, Brown.

Schirrmacher, R. (1986). Talking with children about their art. *Young Children, 41*(5), 3–10.

Schneiderman, J., & Sousa, C. (1986). Superheroes in the preschool classroom. *Child Care News, 12*(9), 1–5.

Schweinhart, L. J., Weikart, D. P., & Larner, M. B. (1986). Consequences of three preschool curriculum models through age 15. *Early Childhood Research Quarterly, 1*, 15–45.

Seefeldt, C. (1987). The visual arts. In C. Seefeldt (Ed.), *The early childhood curriculum: A review of current research*. New York: Teachers College Press.

Selman, R. L., & Demorest, A. P. (1984). Observing troubled children's interpersonal negotiation strategies: Implications of and for a developmental model. *Child Development, 55*, 288–305.

Sensue, M. (1981). *Filial therapy follow-up study: Effects on parental acceptance and child adjustment*. Unpublished doctoral dissertation, The Pennsylvania State University.

Serbin, L. A., Connor, J. M., & Citron, C. C. (1978). Environmental control of independent and dependent behaviors in preschool boys and girls: A model for early independence training. *Sex Roles, 4*, 867–875.

Serbin, L. A., Conner, J. A., Burchardt, C. J., & Citron, C. C. (1979). Effects of peer presence on sex-typing of children's play behavior. *Journal of Experimental Psychology, 27*, 303–309.

Shade, D. D., & Watson, J. A. (1990). Computers in early education: Issues put to rest, theoretical links to sound practice, and the potential contribution of microworlds. *Journal of Educational Computing Research, 6*, 375–392.

Shane, H. C., Lipschultz, R. W., & Shane, C. L. (1982). Facilitating the communicative interaction of nonspeaking persons in large residential settings. *Topics in Language Disorders, 2*, 73–84.

Shick, J., & Plack, J. (1967). Kephart's motor development training program. *Journal of Physical Education and Recreation, 47*, 58–59.

Shipley, E. F., Smith, C. S., & Gleitman, L. R,. (1969). A study of the acquisition of language: Free responses to commands. *Language, 45*, 322–342.

Shipman, V. (1976). *Notable early characteristics of high and low achieving black low-SES children*. Princeton, NJ: Educ. Testing Service.

Shirley, M. M. (1933). *The first two years: A study of twenty-five babies*. Minneapolis, MN: University of Minnesota Press.

Shymansky, J. A., Kyle, W. C., & Alport, J. M. (1982). How effective were hands-on science programs of yesterday? *Science and Children, 20*(1),14–15.

Siegel, I. E., & Saunders, R. (1979). An inquiry into inquiry: Question asking as an instructional model. In L. G. Katz (Ed.), *Current topics in early childhood education* (Vol. 2). Norwood, NJ: Ablex.

Simon, T., & Smith, P. K. (1985). A role for play in children's problem-solving: Time to think again. In J. L. Frost & S. Sunderlin (Eds.), *When children play*. Wheaton, MD: Association for Childhood Education International.

Slaughter, D. T. (1988). Black children, schooling, and educational interventions. In D. T. Slaughter (Ed.), *Black children and poverty: A developmental perspective*. San Francisco: Jossey-Bass.

Smale, S. (1985). *Music-basic for the young child*. Edina, MN: LEA/DECE.

Smilansky, S., & Shefatya, L. (1990). *Facilitating play: A medium for promoting cognitive, socioemotional, and academic development in young children*. Gaithersburg, MD: Psychosocial & Educational Publications.

Smilansky, S. (1968). *The effects of sociodramatic play on disadvantaged preschool children*. New York: Wiley.

Smith, F. (1983). *Essays into literacy*. Portsmouth, NH: Heinemann.

Smith, N. R. (1983). *Experience and art: Teaching children to paint*. New York: Teachers College Press.

Smith, P. K., Dagleish, M., & Herzmark, G. (1981). A comparison of the effects of fantasy play tutoring and skills tutoring in nursery school. *International Journal of Behavioral Development, 4*, 421–444.

Smith, P. K., & Dodsworth, C. (1978). Social class differences in the fantasy play of preschool children. *The Journal of Genetic Psychology, 133*, 183–190.

Smith, R. F. (1983). Early childhood science education. In J. F. Brown (Ed.), *Curriculum planning for young children* (pp. 143–150). Washington, DC: National Association for the Education of Young Children.

Smith, R. F. (1987). Theoretical framework for preschool science experiences. *Young Children, 42*(2), 34–40.

Smothergill, N. L., Olson, F., & Moore, S. G. (1971). The effects of manipulation of teacher communication style in the preschool. *Child Development, 42,* 1229–1239.

Snow, C. E. (1972). Mothers' speech to children learning language. *Child Development, 43,* 549–565.

Spencer, H. (1954). *Principles of Psychology* (Vol. 2). New York: Appleton.

Spencer, M. B. (1990). Development of minority children: An introduction. *Child Development, 61,* 267–269.

Sroufe, L. A., & Fleeson, J. (1986). Attachment and the construction of relationships. In W. W. Hartup & Z. Rubin (Eds.), *Relationships and development*. Hillsdale, NJ: Erlbaum.

Stallings, J. (1975). Implementation and child effects of teaching practices in Follow Through classrooms. *Monographs of the Society for Research in Child Development, 40,* Serial No. 163.

Steward, M. S., & Steward, D. S. (1974). Effect of social distance on teaching strategies of Anglo-American and Mexican-American mothers. *Developmental Psychology, 10,* 797–807.

Stillwell, J. L. (1987). *Making and using creative play equipment*. Champaign, IL: Human Kinetics.

Stipek, D., & MacIver, D. (1989). Developmental change in children's assessment of intellectual competence. *Child Development, 60,* 521-538.

Stipek, D. (1984). Young children's performance expectations: Logical analysis or wishful thinking? In J. Nicholls (Ed.), *The development of achievement motivation*. Greenwich, CT: JAI.

Strain, P. S., & Kohler, F. W. (1988). Social skills intervention with young children with handicaps: Some new conceptualizations and directions. In S. L. Odom & M. B. Karnes (Eds.), *Early intervention for infants and children with handicaps: An empirical base*. Baltimore, MD: Paul H. Brooks.

Stringer, B. R., & Hurt, H. T. (April, 1981). *To praise or not to praise: Factors to consider before utilizing praise as a reinforcing device in the classroom communication process*. Paper presented at the annual meeting of the Southern Speech Communications Association, Austin, TX.

Sulzby, E. (1986). Children's elicitation and use of metalinguistic knowledge about word during literacy interactions. In D. B. Yaden & S. Templeton (Eds.), *Metalinguistic awareness and beginning literacy*. Portsmouth, NH: Heinemann.

Surwillo, W. W. (1971). Human reaction time and period of the EEG in relation to development. *Psychophysiology, 8,* 468–482.

Sutton-Smith, B. (1979). The play of girls. In C. G. Kopp & M. Kirkpatrick (Eds.), *Becoming female: Perspectives on development*. New York: Plenum.

Sutton-Smith, B. (1983). One hundred years of change in play research. *Association for the Anthropological Study of Play Newsletter, 9*(2), 13–17.

Sutton-Smith, B. (1986). The spirit of play. In G. Fein & M. Rivkin (Eds.), *The young child at play: Reviews of research*, (Vol. 4). Washington, DC: National Association for the Education of Young Children.

Sylva, K., Roy, C., & Painter, M. (1980). *Childwatching at playgroup and nursery school*. Ypsilanti, MI: High/Scope Press.

Tharp, R. G. (1989). Psychocultural variables and constants: Effects on teaching and learning in schools. *American Psychologist, 44,* 349–359.

Thompson, R. A. (1988). The effects of infant day care through the prism of attachment theory: A critical appraisal. *Early Childhood Research Quarterly, 3,* 273–282.

Tizard, B. (1977). Play: The child's way of learning? In B. Tizard & D. Harvey (Eds.), *Biology of play*. London: Heinemann.

Tobin, K. G. (1987). The role of wait time in higher cognitive level learning. *Review of Educational Research, 57,* 69–95.

Trawick-Smith, J. W. (1990). The effects of realistic versus nonrealistic play materials on young children's symbolic transformation of objects. *Journal of Research in Childhood Education, 5,* 27–36.

Trawick-Smith, J. W. (1988). Let's say you're the baby, OK?: Play leadership and following behavior in young children. *Young Children, 43*(5), 51–59.

Trawick-Smith, J. W. (1987). The validity and reliability of an instrument to measure the dramatic play behavior of young children. ERIC document No. 286 654.

Trawick-Smith, J. W. (1992). A descriptive study of persuasive preschool children: How they get others to do what they want. *Early Childhood Research Quarterly, 7,* 95–115.

Trawick-Smith, J. W. (1985). Developing the dramatic play enrichment program. *Dimensions, 13*(4), 7–11.

Trawick-Smith, J. W. (1989). Play is not learning: A critical review of the literature. *Child and Youth Care Quarterly, 18,* 161–170.

Trawick-Smith, J. W., & Thompson, R. H. (1986). Preparing young children for hospitalization. In J. B. McCracken (Ed.), *Reducing stress in young children's lives.* Washington, DC: National Association for the Education of Young Children.

Tzelepis, A., Giblin, P. T., & Agronow, S. J. (1983). Effects of adult caregivers' behaviors on the activities, social interactions, and investments of nascent preschool day-care groups. *Journal of Applied Developmental Psychology, 4,* 201–216.

Vukelich, C. (April, 1991). *Adult participation and literacy-enriched playsettings: A description of young children's writing-related interactions in play.* Paper presented at the annual meeting of the American Educational Research Association, Chicago, IL.

Vygotsky, L. (1978). In M. Cole, V. John-Steiner, S. Scribner, & E. Souberman (Eds.), *Mind in society.* Cambridge, MA: Harvard University Press.

Vygotsky, L. (1962). *Thought and language.* Cambridge, MA: MIT Press.

Vygotsky, L. (1976). Play and its role in the mental development of the child. In J. Bruner, A.

Jolly, & K. Sylva (Eds.), *Play: Its role in development and evolution.* New York: Basic Books.

Watson, M. M., & Jackowitz, E. R. (1984). Agents and recipient objects in the development of early symbolic play. *Child Development, 55,* 1091–1097.

Weinstein, C. S., & David, G. T. (1987). *Spaces for children: The built environment and child development.* New York: Plenum.

Weist, R. M., & Stebbins, P. (1972). Adult perception of children's speech, *Psychonomic Science, 27,* 359–360.

Wells, G. (1981). *Learning through interaction: The study of language development.* Cambridge: Cambridge University Press.

Williams, C. K., & Kamii, C. (1986). How do children learn by handling objects? *Young Children, 42*(1), 23–26.

Williams, H. G. (1983). *Perceptual and motor development.* Englewood Cliffs, NJ: Prentice-Hall.

Williams, L. R., & De Gaetano, Y. (1985). *Alerta: A multicultural, bilingual approach to teaching young children.* Menlo Park, CA: Addison-Wesley.

Willock, B. (1983). Play therapy and the aggressive, acting-out child. In C. E. Schaefer & K. J. O'Conner (Eds.), *Handbook of Play Therapy.* New York: John Wiley and Sons.

Winsor, C. B. (1984). Blocks as a material for learning through play—The contribution of Carolyn Pratt. In E. S. Hirsch (Ed.), *The block book* (rev. ed.). Washington, DC: National Association for the Education of Young Children.

Wolf, D. P. (1984). Superheroes: Yes or no?: An interview with Carolee Fucigna and Michelle Heist. *Beginnings, 1*(1), 29–32.

Wolf, J. (1992). Let's sing it again: Creating music with young children. *Young Children, 47*(2), 4–11.

Woodill, G. (1987). Critical issues in the use of microcomputers by young children. *International Journal of Early Childhood Education, 19,* 50–57.

Wright, J. L., & Samaras, A. S. (1986). Play worlds and microworlds. In P. F. Campbell & G. G. Fein (Eds.), *Young children and microcomputers.* Reston, VA: Reston Publishing.

Yarrow, M. R., Scott, P. M., & Waxler, C. Z. (1973). Learning concern for others. *Developmental Psychology, 8,* 240–260.

Yawkey, T. D., & Pellegrini, A. D. (Eds.). (1984). *Child's play: Developmental and applied.* Hillsdale, NJ: Erlbaum.

Yeats, K. O., Schultz, L. H., & Selman, R. L. (April, 1991). *The development of interpersonal negotiation strategies in thought and action: Predictions of behavioral adjustment and social status.* Paper presented at the biennial meeting of the Society for Research in Child Development, Seattle.

Yoder, D., & Kraat, A. (1983). Intervention issues in nonspeech communication. In J. Miller, D. Yoder, & R. Schiefelbusch (Eds.), *Contemporary issues in language intervention.* Rockville, MD: The American Speech-Language-Hearing Association.

INDEX

ABOUT THE AUTHOR

Jeffrey Trawick-Smith is a professor of Education and Chair of the Education Department at Eastern Connecticut State University. He holds a doctorate in Early Childhood Education from Indiana University. He currently conducts research on children's play and social development; his work appears in numerous professional and research journals. He has been a teacher and administrator in preschool, child-care, kindergarten, and primary grade programs.